Biomechanics of Human Movement

First Edition

Robert E. Schleihauf Ed.D.
Department of Kinesiology
San Francisco State University

authorHOUSE

1663 LIBERTY DRIVE, SUITE 200
BLOOMINGTON, INDIANA 47403
(800) 839-8640
WWW.AUTHORHOUSE.COM

First published by AuthorHouse 09/10/04

ISBN: 1-4184-6958-0 (sc)

Library of Congress Control Number: 2004095144

Printed in the United States of America
Bloomington, Indiana

This book is printed on acid-free paper.

Preface to the First Edition

The study of biomechanics presents numerous challenges to teachers and students alike. Certainly, a good biomechanics textbook must present the basic biomechanical theories that govern human motion. However, a good textbook should also bridge the gap between theory and practice and encourage students to apply their knowledge to real world problems. Biomechanics is a particularly interesting subject matter because all students have movement experiences that will reinforce their understanding of mechanical principles. The challenge for the textbook author is to draw these everyday movement experiences into the course activities. Unfortunately, forming connections between practical experiences and traditional "textbook" materials is often difficult. In particular, the printed page provides a very poor mechanism for the communication of *movement*. The use of video-clips and graphical animations can greatly improve the communication of critical concepts, particularly in a biomechanics course. Further, mechanical concepts are best communicated to students through illustrations that allow easy *visualization* of the relationships that exist between human movement and biomechanical variables. Thus, the ideal textbook for a course in biomechanics should, in fact, be a part of an integrated suite of educational tools that blend textbook theories with multimedia content.

This Biomechanics of Human Movement textbook is the "hard copy" portion of a multimedia-based courseware application program suite. This courseware package includes three components: 1) this traditional print textbook, 2) the BHMViewer CD-Rom textbook viewer software, and 3) the KAVideo biomechanical analysis software program suite.

This printed version of the courseware is where learning will "begin" for most students. However, the learning experience provided by this textbook is designed to extend well beyond the printed page. The BHMViewer software provides assess to animated color illustrations, slow motion and stop action video-clips, and interactive questions. The Kinematic Analysis software clarifies the relationships between mechanical variables and video data for a wide variety of human movement examples. This scientific visualization software is tied to the BHMViewer program through dozens of "KA Example Exercises". These computer based laboratory experiences reinforce critical theoretical concepts and guide you through "mini" research data analysis exercises. These introductory research experiences prepare you for your own, original, video analysis term paper project. The research skills needed for your term paper project are developed through every chapter in the text. In particular, most of the movement examples used throughout the textbook have been drawn from San Francisco State University student research projects. These projects, coupled with other term paper projects from your fellow classmates will help you to integrate "textbook theory" with your own "real life" movement experiences.

Laboratory-Support Software Distribution

A multimedia based textbook is an obvious choice for use with a course in biomechanics. The combination of digital video, PC software and interactive instructional materials is perfectly suited to the study of human movement. However, the choice of a delivery mechanism for a multimedia based text is difficult. Traditional publishing companies often bundle CD-Rom disks with print textbooks but this strategy only causes already expensive textbooks to become still more expensive. I am hopeful that the Laboratory-Support distribution mechanism used by this textbook / courseware project will provide an inexpensive way to deliver quality educational materials to students in a way that serves to further improve their educational opportunities.

Laboratory-Support software distribution relies upon a direct agreement between college departments and textbook authors. (For details on purchasing the BHM / KA software, visit the KAVideo software web site at www.kavideo.sfsu.edu). By eliminating numerous "middle men" it is possible to make the cost of a CD-Rom based textbook very economical. Not only does the Laboratory-Support distribution concept keep textbook costs low, it also provides a mechanism for upgrading college laboratory equipment. In particular, the Laboratory-Support distribution contract allows college departments to sell the BHMViewer / KAPro CD-ROM very economically to every student in their program. The contract further requires that all funds raised through the sale of CDs must be used to purchase instructional equipment and materials that will be used by students.

As a result, I am hopeful that this textbook and the BHMViewer software package will benefit students and college departments alike. The Laboratory-Support software distribution plan can be used to break the vicious cycle of more and more expensive textbooks. Under this plan, students can work in better equipped laboratories while they simultaneously take advantage of educational materials that are both more economical and more up to date.

Acknowledgements

The task of creating this textbook and the associated software was made possible through the help of numerous of people. I am indebted to Joe Higgins for showing me, by example, that work in academics is more rewarding (at least intellectually) than work in engineering. I was also extremely fortunate to have had the opportunity to work with Susan Higgins, first at Hunter College and then at San Francisco State University. Susan's quest for academic excellence in our programs helped to shape the design of my courses and my educational philosophy.

Perhaps the most important support for the book has come from the students in my classes over the past 20 years. Many of the book's best illustrations have been generated from student research projects. Finally, I am thankful for the feedback from the readers of the book's original manuscript: Peter Francis, Wanda Boda and Jill Crussemeyer.

Contents in Brief

Table of Contents

Part 1 – Introduction

Chapter 1: Basic Concepts
Chapter 2: Issues in Biomechanical Analysis
Chapter 3: Kinematic Analysis Software

Chapter 1: Basic Concepts

Introduction

In recent years, the discipline of biomechanics has undergone significant growth. Technological advancements in microcomputers, video analysis and laboratory data acquisition hardware have provided tools for improved biomechanical research and instructional programs (Figure 1-1). These tools can be applied to the study of human movement in a wide range of settings – from the detailed analysis of Olympic athletes to the qualitative inspection of a child's gait. The high tech tools themselves allow biomechanists to make better and better measurements of human motion. In the end however, the meaning of the data must be interpreted and evaluated. Thus, while tools for analysis are improving, they do not, by themselves, answer our questions. Skilled practitioners must perform the last and most critical step in the analysis. The ability to interpret data and create improved programs for instruction, training and rehabilitation hinges upon our ability to apply theoretical positions in the solution of practical problems.

We will see in this course that the mechanical constraints that influence human movement can sometimes be reduced to discrete mathematical relationships. Under these circumstances, it will be possible to generate specific answers to clear-cut questions. In other instances, we will see that the biomechanical analysis of movement leads us to only partial answers for movement problems. We will find that most movement problems do not lend themselves to a complete mathematical solution. Instead, we will need to understand how a broad variety of biomechanical principles can be integrated with information from other fields of study to produce a better understanding of realistic movement problems.

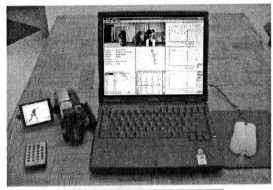

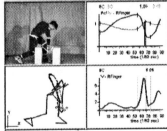

Figure 1-1. A digital video camcorder, video capture notebook PC and analysis software.

Definitions of Biomechanics

Our work in Biomechanics will focus upon the application of mechanical principles to the analysis of human motion. At a more general level, biomechanics can be defined as "the science involving the study of biological systems from a mechanical perspective." (Nelson, 1980). Under this definition, the mechanical principles that influence motion are seen to apply to any organism or the systems within an organism, such as the fluid mechanics of blood flow. Hay (1993) provides a more human-centric definition of biomechanics:

"Biomechanics is the science concerned with the internal and external forces acting on the human body and the effects produced by these forces."

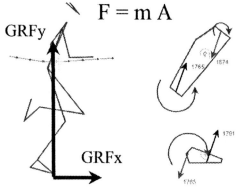

$$F = m A$$

GRFy

GRFx

Figure 1-2. Biomechanical measures for a skillful runner. The ground reaction forces (external forces) are labeled as GRFx and GRFy. The joint reaction forces (internal forces) are shown acting at the proximal and distal ends of the shank and foot segments.

This definition reflects the organization of materials in this book. The forces acting on the human body will be studied in our chapters on kinetics (Chapters 10-13, Linear Kinetics, Chapters 20-23, Angular Kinetics and Chapters 24-25 Fluid Mechanics), and the *effects* produced by forces applied to the body will be studied in our chapters on kinematics (Chapters 4-9, Linear Kinematics and Chapters 14-19, Angular Kinematics).

While we will focus on mechanical principles in this course, it will be very important for us to see the role of biomechanics within the larger area of study in kinesiology. In particular, we should understand the interrelationships between biomechanics and other areas in kinesiology, such as exercise physiology and motor learning.

Disciplines in Kinesiology

The following simplified definitions define the key roles of three important courses that you will take in the kinesiology major:

Biomechanics - the science underlying skilled or efficient techniques.
Motor Learning - the science underlying the acquisition of skills.

Exercise Physiology - the science underlying training.

Kinesiology

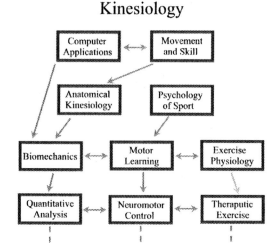

Figure 1-3. The interrelationships between courses in a typical kinesiology curriculum

It will be interesting to investigate the interrelationships between these three areas. As a "not very serious" exercise, let's try to answer the following oversimplified question: Which of the three core courses (biomechanics, exercise physiology or motor learning) is most important? The question has three possible answers; let's consider each one in turn and use an example from sport instruction as a test case:

Biomechanics – It could be argued that biomechanics is clearly more important than exercise physiology or motor learning. Study in biomechanics will tell us the model techniques that we will use to guide our work with students and clients. In short, biomechanics will tell us *what* to teach. Without a detailed knowledge of what to teach, our skills from motor learning or exercise physiology will be useless. For example, if we are very effective in the use of motor learning principles, but we do not know the technical details that must be taught, we may only be successful in effectively teaching our students the wrong way to move. Similarly, we can use our knowledge of exercise physiology to design training programs. However, if we are very effective in the use of physiological principles, but we do not know the muscle groups that must be trained, we may only be successful in training our students for the wrong motions.

Motor Learning – Of course, an expert in motor learning will argue (and rightly so) that our knowledge of what to teach will not actually help our students to perform better unless we have the skill to communicate our recommendations for improvements in technique. Thus, unless we can design effective instructional programs, our knowledge of model technique is of no practical value. Similarly, if our students are well trained in performing incorrect movements their chances for success will be minimal. As a result, it would appear that motor learning principles are more important than those from biomechanics or exercise physiology.

Exercise Physiology – Finally, an exercise physiologist can argue (and rightly so) that our knowledge of optimal techniques will be of no use to our students unless we can actually train them to perform the movements to meet the demands of the performance environment. Further, our skill in teaching modifications in technique will have no practical value unless our students can develop the strength and endurance to meet the actual demands of the task. As a result, exercise physiology would have to be seen as more important than either biomechanics or motor learning.

The Real Answer - Of course the true answer to the question is that all three areas are equally important and a deficit in knowledge for any one of the areas could result in very poor results for our students or clients. Thus, we see that biomechanics will provide an important component in our overall program of study in kinesiology. This component, when combined with those of other courses, such as exercise physiology and motor learning, will provide you with the foundation skills that will be necessary for success in your chosen field.

Athletics and Biomechanics

The discussion of biomechanical principles sometimes involves abstract concepts. To simplify these difficult discussions, we will look for clear, sometimes even exaggerated examples to illustrate our points. For example, in our discussions of force, we will see that a discussion of the very large forces involved in a dance leap will lead to a simpler discussion than the more subtle forces involved in a child's gait. As a result, we will often use large, forceful, athletic motions as examples to illustrate our discussions of biomechanical principles in this

course. Once we have begun to understand the principles behind larger than life examples, we will be able to apply our knowledge to the subtleties of more involved problems.

When we make use of athletic examples, we will be careful to avoid the oversimplification that skill is only possible for those who are the biggest, the fastest, or the strongest. We will not approach the analysis of movement problems as gold medal hungry Olympic coaches. Instead, we will identify more with the gifted teacher who strives to help each student to do their very best. Given this mental set, our evaluation of movement techniques will be individualized. We will acknowledge that technique is independent of strength. For example, given two athletes with equal strength and endurance, the athlete with the best *technique* will win. Further, strength alone can be a very poor indicator of skill level. Many performers can find ways to "muscle" their way through a movement to achieve a given result. A better, more coordinated movement could be used to produce the same performance with less effort. Thus, when we evaluate movement skill and efficiency, we must be careful to separate the movement *process* from the movement *product*.

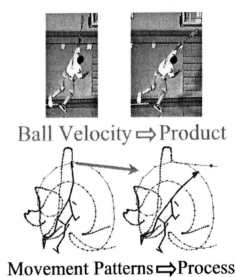

Ball Velocity ⇨ Product

Movement Patterns ⇨ Process

Figure 1-4. A comparison of the product (ball velocity), and the process (measures of the movement expressed over time) for a tennis serve motion.

The *process* of the movement reflects the techniques or movement strategies that are used to solve the movement problem. The *product* of the movement is often a simple measure of the movement outcome that provides no information at all about the movement itself. We will use biomechanical analysis techniques to quantify crucial aspects of the movement process. This information will lead to a better understanding of the mechanical factors associated with skillful and efficient performance.

Problem Solving and Biomechanics

It will be interesting to discuss the place of biomechanics within the range of the "hard" and "soft" sciences you may encounter in your studies.

Question 1:
Which of the following areas might you expect to be most similar to biomechanics in the way that data is collected and analyzed?

O A. Psychology
O B. Physics
O C. Tarot card reading

Note: the answers to chapter questions are included at the end of every chapter.

Psychology is known as a "soft" science because concepts like motivation cannot be directly measured, even with sophisticated equipment. In psychology, an instrument for measuring motivation would be a well-designed questionnaire. This questionnaire will enable a psychologist to *indirectly* acquire information about the thought processes of a patient. Our inability to directly measure psychological concepts "softens" our ability to make cut and dry decisions about motivation levels.

Physics, on the other hand, is an "exact" science, where discrete measurements can be made and entered into explicitly defined equations to solve specific problems. Sometimes the solutions to physical problems can be astonishing, as they can lead to landing a man on the moon. However, it should be noted that an enormous amount of information must be available in order to solve the system of equations that lead to a successful moon landing.

Many aspects of problem solving in biomechanics are identical to those employed in mechanical engineering. Consider, for example, a softball throw for distance. In this movement, the optimal angle of projection can be determined almost entirely from an analysis of purely physical variables. These variables may include the height of release, the velocity of release and the wind conditions.

It is interesting to note that a typical mechanical analysis of projectile motion does not consider the actual throwing technique employed by the performer. At this level of analysis, the "thrower" could be replaced by a catapult without any influence on the eventual projection angle calculation.

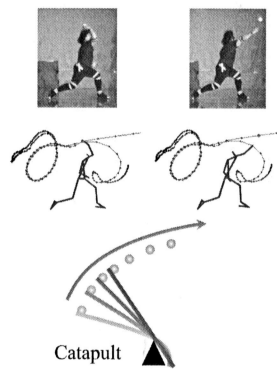

Figure 1-5. A comparison of a throwing motion and the action of a catapult

A *bio*mechanical study of a throwing motion, unlike a purely mechanical study, would be incomplete without an analysis of the movement of the throwing arm and the various body parts of the performer. This biological component of the analysis adds a layer of variability to the analysis. If the goal of the throwing motion is maximal distance, and if we can assume that our research is aimed at performers with similar anatomical characteristics, we can still expect to find a clear-cut "solution" to the throwing problem. For example, a comparison of throwing techniques for samplings of skilled softball players would be expected to find many similar movement characteristics across all performers. The range of motion and timing of the shoulder, elbow and wrist joint actions would be similar enough that we could define a model technique for use with the instruction of softball throwing technique for novice performers.

The similarity in movement characteristics across skilled throwers is a result of the constraints placed upon the movement performance. For a general throwing motion, a performer could elect to use any style of motion at all, including underhand, sidearm or overhand. However, because, for this example, we are interested in maximal force production, any successful movement strategy would need to converge upon the single solutions to the problem that results in maximal throwing velocity for the given angle of projection. This confines the range of effective solutions to the problem, and the result of this constraint is that most skilled throwers use very similar technique.

If the constraints that are placed upon a movement change, the optimal movement must change as well. Consider the example of dart throwing. From a purely mechanical standpoint, this is simply another projectile motion problem. If we consider only the flight of the dart in the air, we may conclude that, as with a softball throw, an angle of projection of about 45 degrees will result in a maximal throwing distance for a given application of force. However, with dart throwing, the challenge of the movement is not to maximize distance. It is instead to be very accurate over a relatively short range. This new constraint will dramatically influence the performer's throwing motion, and we may expect that the ranges of motion and timing of the movements of the arm joints would be very different from those of a softball throw. In particular, we may expect that a very limited range of motion at the elbow and wrist will be employed, and a nearly simultaneous wrist / elbow joint extension motion will be used to maximize movement accuracy. Again, an analysis of a sample of skilled dart throwers will likely find a fairly concise movement style for most performers. This biomechanical analysis can then be used to define a model technique that could be used in the instruction of novice dart throwers.

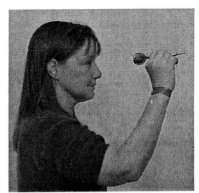

Figure 1-6. Dart throwing technique.

Interestingly, the factors that constrain the movement characteristics of skilled dart throwing will be partially mechanical and partially biological. The movement organization has been altered to assure that maximal control of the movement results. Thus, the neurophysiological make-up of the performer influences the outwardly observable movement characteristics even more than the mechanical constraint. In this instance we see that biomechanical problems can be considerably more involved than purely mechanical problems.

Finally, let's consider the case of a tennis serve. This movement involves both maximal force output and maximal accuracy. If you have had occasion to watch a number of different professional tennis players, you will know that their movements do not all look alike. The variability in serving technique reflects the variability in body type, flexibility and innate strengths of the various performers. The range of movement techniques complicates our biomechanical analysis of the serve. We cannot define a single model movement style for use by all players. Further, we may even find that the optimal technique of a given individual way change as the person grows, becomes fatigued or adapts to a chronic injury. Thus, we see that with some movements, a biomechanical analysis will not result in a clear-cut solution that defines a model technique for use by all performers.

Figure 1-7. An illustration of the differences in serving technique between John McEnroe and Jimmy Conners. Photos courtesy John Yandel, www.tennisplayer.net.

Biological Factors

Looking back over our three examples of a softball throw, a dart throw and a tennis serve, we see that mechanical principles will always be a factor, but depending upon the movement circumstances, the biological factors will tend to complicate the solution of the problem. At first glance, we may think that the uncertainty of our tennis serve analysis could be solved if only we had a more powerful computer or better analysis software. We often long for the security and mathematical certainty of a purely mechanical solution to movement problems. On the other hand, such a situation trivializes the differences between individuals and ignores the *bio* in the word biomechanics. Is it our goal, as teachers, therapists or trainers to solve problems by forcing all of our clients into the same pre-determined mold?

*Bio*mechanics ≠ Mechanics

A purely deterministic approach to biomechanics would be relevant if one "small" change were made to our work environment:

> If our athletes, students and patients could all be replaced with *robots*, then, our work as biomechanists would become greatly simplified. So simplified, that all teachers, coaches and therapists could be replaced by *computers*.

Luckily for us, we will all be working with human beings in our chosen fields of endeavor. These people will all be unique and it will be our challenge to use theories from multiple disciplines to solve their problems. As we work, we can occasionally pause for a moment to admire the work of mechanical engineers. Then we can return to reality and be thankful that we get to solve problems that extend beyond the reach of computer analysis.

Limits of Computer Analysis

The above arguments note that our work in biomechanics will be built upon a solid base of mechanical principles. Further, part of our work will rely upon reductionism. We will break down human movements into their component parts to gain increased insight into the organization of skillful and efficient movement. This portion of our work will benefit enormously from computer based data collection and analysis techniques.

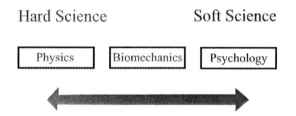

Figure 1-8. An illustration of the "hard science" - "soft science" continuum

At the same time we will acknowledge that a purely mechanical analysis may oversimplify our analysis and limit our appreciation of the field of kinesiology. Let's consider an example to evaluate the relative importance of computer analysis. In medical practice, there are many evaluation procedures that can be performed by computerized data collection equipment to assist in a medical diagnosis. If you have an MRI (magnetic resonance imaging), EKG (electrocardiogram) or sonogram test performed by a trained medical technician, you can expect that the data collected on your medical condition is exactly correct. However, when the time comes for an analysis of the data and a recommendation for a course of treatment, you will rely upon the expert judgment of an experienced physician. The computerized equipment plays an important role in your treatment, but it is nevertheless simply a tool to be used by a qualified professional.

Research, Data Analysis and Education

I am hopeful that the previous discussion has convinced you that it is very unlikely that you will be replaced by a computer. We must now turn our attention to a *really* important matter.

As you follow along with the materials in the CD-Rom version of this textbook, do you think that perhaps, *I* will be replaced by a computer program?

Figure 1-9. The textbook as an educational tool

In reality, our courseware software is simply an educational tool that can be used to replace or supplement a printed textbook for your course. A printed textbook will never take the place of a faculty member. Neither will the software based components of this textbook.

The value of your educational experience is derived from many factors. The quality of your interactions with your course professor and the other members of your class will be crucially important. The various class activities that will be organized and managed by your professor will also be very important.

A video analysis project is an important class activity that is planned for this course. This project will allow you to select a movement for analysis and, under the guidance of your instructor, conduct a detailed analysis of the movement. This project will provide an opportunity for you to extend your studies further than would be possible with a "textbook only" learning experience. You will see that your involvement in a research project will actually be an extension of the educational challenge of this course.

Figure 1-10. An example of a video analysis project on a box jump movement

Cognitive Domain

Cognitive psychologists have identified a number of stages that are commonly associated with educational experiences. The cognitive domain can be broken into a number of levels, with each level associated with a key term:

Knowledge – *Knowledge* identifies an aspect of relatively low-level learning. An example from biomechanics would be the knowledge that Newton's second law is identified by the equation $F = mA$. Note that this stage of learning can be accomplished with memorization.

Newton's Second Law:
$F = m A$

The following five terms represent successive stages associated with higher-level learning:

Comprehension – The knowledge of facts is important. The *comprehension* of the meanings and implications of these facts is still more important. For Newton's second law, the understanding that for a given mass, force and acceleration are proportional goes a step beyond memorization (see figure 1-11).

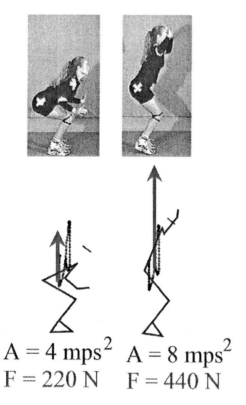

$$A = 4 \text{ mps}^2 \quad A = 8 \text{ mps}^2$$
$$F = 220 \text{ N} \quad F = 440 \text{ N}$$

Figure 1-11. An illustration of the relationship between the net force and center of gravity acceleration measures that occur during the performance of a vertical jumping motion

Application – The ability to *apply* knowledge to a practical problem represents an important step in education. In biomechanics, we can apply Newton's second law to the analysis of video data on a jumping motion. Given the body weight and body center of gravity acceleration, we can compute the ground reaction force produced during a jump.

Analysis – Given an interest in jumping ground reaction forces, we can perform an *analysis* of jumping technique under different conditions. For example, we can analyze jumping ground reaction forces for conditions with and without a knee brace.

Synthesis – Our analysis of jumping technique with and without a knee brace may well find differences in the ground reaction forces produced by our research participants. Our next step will be to *synthesize* the information from various measurements in our analysis and reach a better understanding of the overall meaning of the data.

Evaluation – The end result of our jumping research project may result in an evaluation of the influence of the knee brace on jumping performance. Our findings may lead us to ideas for a new knee brace design that could be studied in further research experiments.

The above review indicates that research can be used as a vehicle to provide access to more advanced levels of learning. In this course we will not embark upon a large-scale research project and wrestle with the challenge of a statistical analysis of extensive quantities of data. We will instead perform a small, pilot study research report. This project will allow us to extend our textbook level knowledge to the cognitive levels of analysis, synthesis and evaluation.

Conclusions

Our introduction to biomechanics is now complete. We have covered the basic definitions of biomechanics and discussed the role of biomechanics within the kinesiology curriculum. We have also seen the important role that research will play in our mastery of biomechanical concepts. The next chapter will discuss biomechanical research issues in more detail.

References

Nelson, R. C., 1980. Biomechanics: Past and Present. In Cooper, J. M., and Haven B., Eds: Proceedings of the Biomechanics Symposium. Bloomington, Indiana.

Hay, James G., 1993. The Biomechanics of Sports Techniques. Prentice-Hall Inc., Englewood Cliffs, New Jersey.

Answers to Chapter Question

Question 1:
Which of the following areas might you expect to be most similar to biomechanics in the way that data is collected and analyzed?

O A. Psychology   O B. Physics   O C. Tarot card reading

The correct answer is B. Physics often makes use of direct measurements and mathematical equations to solve problems.

Chapter 2: Issues in Biomechanical Analysis

The video analysis project for this course will require careful planning. Our first concern will be to select a movement that will be both interesting to study and also "well-suited" to biomechanical analysis. At the onset, we must acknowledge that some movements are not appropriate for a video based analysis. For example, a study of isometric exercise, while a great idea for an EMG (electromyographic) based study, would be a very poor choice for a video analysis. (Note: EMG equipment is used to study the electrical activity produced during a muscular contraction). In this course, we are interested in the study of motion, not the lack of motion.

Video Project Ideas

We will discuss many of the issues related to the biomechanical analysis of movement in the remaining sections of this chapter. To get you thinking about possible topics for a video analysis project, we will now take a quick look at some of the research ideas that have been used by other students in this course.

Skilled / Novice Research Design

Some students in biomechanics have experience participating in athletics or are particularly interested in a given athletic movement. Projects of this type can often take advantage of a "skilled / novice" research design. This approach allows you to look for differences between two performers and make suggestions for improvement in the technique of the novice. This type of research project can be used to evaluate virtually any athletic movement. Tennis serves, golf swings, throwing motions, kicking motions, track and field events, dance and swimming motions are all very good movement topics for this type of project. This approach can also be used in developmental projects, where the movement technique of an adult is compared to that of a child.

Figure 2-1. A comparison of the movements of a skilled (right side) and novice (left side) performer in a tennis serve. The tennis serve is one of many movements that can be studied with a skilled / novice research design.

One of the challenges of a Skilled / Novice design is that you must find participants that will provide for an interesting data analysis. Your analysis will be much easier if your skilled participant is very proficient in the chosen movement.

Condition A / Condition B Design

It is often very interesting to study how the movement of a given performer will change under different circumstances. For example, you could study the effect of fatigue on a vertical jumping motion. Other interesting manipulations include: laterality studies (i.e., throwing or kicking with the preferred and non-preferred limb), changes in technique (i.e., fastball pitching versus curve ball pitching) and changes in implements (normal walking versus walking with a backpack).

Figure 2-2. Walking with and without a backpack is one example of a Condition A / Condition B research design.

It is best to use a single performer in this type of project. This allows us to control for differences in variables like size, strength and gender. We can then focus upon the differences in the movement that are caused by the different movement conditions.

As a general guideline, try to select a project topic and design that will produce video trials that show clear differences in the performance of the movement. We can expect that any topic that involves no movement (an isometric exercise) or very little movement (a golf putt) will be very difficult to analyze with video. Further, movements that are not free to vary across subjects or conditions, for example, pedaling on a stationary bike, will be poor choices for analysis.

Issues in Biomechanical Analysis

We will use our video project as both a mechanism for conducting research and as a mechanism to spur discussion of important issues in biomechanical analysis. Our discussion in this section is intended to sharpen your understanding of how a movement analysis can be conducted on *any* movement. Given this broad background, you should be able to design a very good video analysis project.

Ideal Form Models

Before you decide upon the movement that you would like to study this semester, we should take time to discuss some basic issues in biomechanical analysis. First, we should step back and ask how far we might expect our computer-based analysis can take us. For example, if we were to use the skilled / novice research design, should we expect that there will be a single ideal form model that can be used as a template to evaluate the technique of the novice, and for that matter, all other people?

This concept is often referred to as the *ideal form myth*. As we have mentioned in the last chapter, biomechanics considers not only the role of mechanical principles but also the influence of biological variables in human movement. Thus, if we were to determine the dimensions of a golf drive motion from a skillful performer, it would be foolhardy to expect that we could use these exact measures to guide the instruction of a novice performer (see Figure 2-3 below).

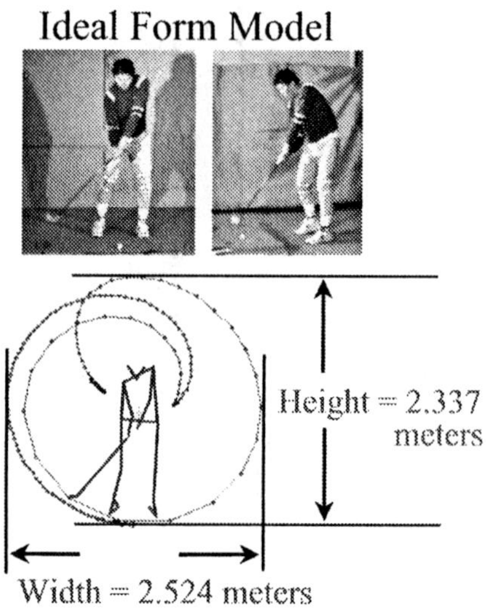

Ideal Form Model

Figure 2-3. Measurements for a model performer in golf.

The optimal movement technique for a given person will vary as a function of numerous factors including body size and structure, flexibility and training background. A tennis backhand is a good example of a skill that can be performed in very different ways (with one hand and with two hands) without changing the effectiveness of the movement outcome (see Figure 2-4 below).

Variations in Style

Figure 2-4. One handed and two handed backhand techniques. Photos courtesy of John Yandell, www.tennisplayer.net

Thus, we should expect our analysis of movement to provide insight into the principles of skillful movement, but it should not be expected to provide us with cut and dry simplistic answers.

If you think about a variety of movements you will realize that while the ideal form models will never provide perfect answers to movement problems, there will be some movements where such models have some value. For example, in springboard diving, exceptional performance is defined by a performer's ability to match an explicitly defined movement sequence. For diving, gymnastics, ice-skating and dance, the goal of the performance is the movement itself. Under these circumstances, narrowly defined models of "skilled" performance are imposed upon all athletes by the authors of scoring books. Most other athletic movements have *performance* goals where the form of motion is not rigidly specified. For these movements, the goal of the athlete is to find a movement technique that allows for a maximal performance (i.e., a higher jump, a faster swim, a longer throw, etc.).

Thus, we see that our approach to the analysis of movement must take into account different types of movement challenges. It will be interesting to consider the ways that various authorities in kinesiology have categorized different skills. Researchers in motor learning have defined two broad categories of skilled movements: *open skills* and *closed skills* (Poulton, 1957).

Open and Closed Skills

An open skill takes place in an unpredictable environment and therefore requires the performer to be able to adapt his/her movements to match a wide variety of circumstances. A football pass interception is a good example of an open skill. Successful performers of open skills develop a broad repertoire of movements to enable them to react quickly to changing conditions. John McEnroe at the net (see Figure 2-5) or Michael Jordan driving toward the basket bring to mind images of open skill performances taken to the highest level.

Forehand Volley

Figure 2-5. The technique used on an effective tennis forehand volley will change as a function of the circumstances of the point and the strategy of the performer. Photos courtesy of John Yandell, www.tennisplayer.net.

A closed skill takes place in a stationary environment (the environmental factors that regulate the movement do not change over time). A golf drive is a closed skill. Because the golf ball does not move, the golfer will produce a very consistent motion on every swing in an effort to maximize force and accuracy. Tiger Woods in golf and Janet Evans in swimming bring to mind examples of closed skill performances taken to the highest level.

Figure 2-6. A butterfly swimming pull is a good example of a closed skill movement.

Question 1:
Which type of skill would you expect to be the easiest to analyze for your project this semester?

O A. Closed Skill   O B. Open Skill

Closed Skills

Closed skills are easy to analyze simply because a single movement trial can be taken to be representative of a given performer's technique. In contrast, an open skill is expected to vary from trial to trial. If we were to videotape Michael Jordan driving toward the basket a dozen times, we would likely see a dozen different variations of the movement. Skill in basketball involves being unpredictable (Jordan would be much easier to guard if he moved the same way every time). Thus, we cannot evaluate Jordan's skill unless we collect data on the many ways that he can solve the movement problem.

When you collect data for our video project this semester, you will be required to manually digitize all of the points on the body for each trial of video in your project. This digitizing work will enable you to view stick figures of the movement and inspect velocity curves for each point on the body. It will take about one hour of work to accomplish the manual digitizing for a trial, and it will take many more hours to evaluate the meaning of the data.

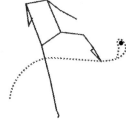

Figure 2-7. Video data is typically collected by manually positioning the mouse cross-hair over a landmark point and clicking the mouse. When all points on the body are digitized for all frames in the image set, a stick figure can be drawn.

A single trial of video data for a closed skill can be assumed to be representative of a given performer's technique. As a result, it is clear that the study of a closed skill will be far less time consuming than that of an open skill. Further, the evaluation of the data will be simpler. The illustration below graphically represents the process of skill acquisition for a closed skill. The left side, broad part of the arrow shows the range in movement strategies that are used as the learner first begins to learn the

movement (i.e., a golf drive). As the performer becomes more and more proficient in the golf drive, his movement becomes more and more consistent. By the end of the skill acquisition process, the performer will have arrived at a very specific solution to the movement problem. This skill acquisition process for closed skills is termed *fixation* (Higgins, 1977).

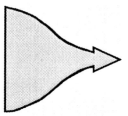

Figure 2-8. The closed skill fixation process. As a closed skill is learned, the performer's movements become more and more consistent. (Higgins, 1977).

Note that the fixation process does not imply that an ideal form model is appropriate for closed skills. We can be certain that the fixation process for quarterback Joe Montana resulted in a virtually perfect movement pattern for him. Similarly, the technique of Dan Marino is also the result of a extended optimization process. However, these two football quarterbacks should not be expected to have identical techniques, because they have different morphologies and, as a result, the movement optimization process would have to lead to different end results.

Question 2:
Can we characterize Arnold Palmer's drive technique as near perfect if he does not hold the world record for the longest drive ever hit?

O A. Yes.   O B. No.

Many athletes develop a "perfectionist" personality that drives them to never accept their given level of performance as good enough. This is an interesting motivational tactic but an inaccurate approach to performance evaluation. Finding fault with the best performers in the world is an unproductive approach that trivializes the unique contributions of individuals. There is not one perfect way to move for all people. Further, some people will have biomechanically optimal movement patterns and not achieve the world record as a result of other factors in their development.

Open Skills

The process of skill acquisition for an open skill is shown in the figure below. The successful mastery of an open skill involves the development of a movement repertoire, where a variety of movement solutions are developed. As a result, the right side of the figure shows multiple arrowheads, with each arrow representing an optimal solution to a given movement circumstance.

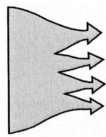

Figure 2-9. The open skill diversification process. As an open skill is learned, the performer develops a flexible movement repertoire. (Higgins, 1977).

While it will not be possible, due to limited computer resources and time, to completely study an open skill for our project this semester, it will be possible to do a partial analysis of an open skill. Let's say that we are interested in a softball batting motion, and we are planning to use the Skilled / Novice research design to study two college-aged students. We will need to think carefully about the best way to collect our video data.

Question 3:
How should we deliver the ball to the novice and skilled performer? After you make your first choice, select the other two possibilities and read their comments.

O A. We should recruit a skilled softball pitcher and pitch the ball exactly as it is done in a game.
O B. We should get a pitching machine and adjust the pitch location to the middle of the strike zone for both participants.
O C. We should put the ball on a tee and set the tee height and position to the middle of the strike zone for both participants.

An open skill like softball batting can be studied with two trials of video data, as long as the variables in the data collection session are well controlled. Because we want to study the influence of experience level (skilled / novice) on the movement performance, we need to hold all other variables fixed. Thus, we need to control the pitch location

and speed by using a pitching machine (or, in a pinch, a very consistent pitcher). When we study the movement data, differences in the movement trials can be attributed to different swing techniques and not different pitch conditions.

Our resulting analysis will provide information on a sub-set of skilled batting technique. We will not know how the batter modifies her swing technique to adjust to a curve ball or change up, but we will have a basic idea of some of the factors associated with skill in softball batting. It is interesting to note that the strategy for analyzing an open skill is to break it down to a less variable movement that more closely approximates a closed skill.

Closed Skill Analysis Details

Let's now investigate closed skill movements more carefully. We will see that some types of closed skill movements are better suited to biomechanical analysis than others.

The figure below shows information for three different closed skill movements.

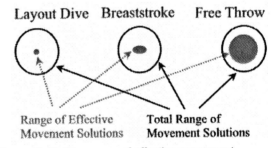

Figure 2-10. The range of effective movement solutions for the layout dive, breaststroke swimming and the basketball free throw.

The outer circle for each movement represents the *total range of movement solutions.* For example, in breaststroke swimming, any movement that can be recognized as breaststroke would fall within the limits of the large circle.

The central area for each circle represents the *range of effective movement solutions* for each movement. The small dot in the middle of the springboard diving figure indicates that there is a very limited number of ways to score a 10 on a front layout dive. Because the form of motion for a springboard dive is determined, at least in part, by an outside source, we will call it a *prescribed form* movement.

In contrast, the range of effective movement solutions for a free throw is extensive. Any movement that allows a given performer to consistently make the basket must be considered skilled. Because almost all adult performers have more than enough strength to throw the ball as far as the basket, lots of different movement variations can be used to make the throw. The throw can be made with one hand or two hands, overhand or underhand, with a high arc or a flat trajectory, with a bank off the backboard or as a "swish shot". Interestingly, a middle-aged college professor held the Guiness book world record for the highest number of consecutive free throws in the early 1990's. This professor set the record by throwing the ball with an underhand motion. If we acknowledge that being the best in the world indicates a high level of skill, then we must admit that an underhand technique may be a good choice for many people. As a result, because of the variability among individuals, and because of the nature of the free throw movement challenge, there will be a wide range of effective movement solutions for the free throw. We will call movements like the free throw *accuracy movements* because the precise outcome of the movement is more important than any other factor.

The center figure on breaststroke swimming presents us with an interesting middle ground. While there are lots of ways to perform a movement that appears to be a breaststroke arm pull, there is a relatively limited number of ways to effectively solve this movement problem. In order to be a successful competitor in breaststroke, the pattern of motion of your hand and even the angle of your hand as it moves through the water will need to be carefully adjusted to generate a maximal propulsive force. If you were to change the angle of your hand by as little as 5 degrees, the result of your movement will be far less effective. Similarly, if the angle on a boat propeller blade is increased above its optimal position, the speed of the boat will decrease and the wear and tear on the motor will increase.

We see that for some movements, the *biomechanical constraint* has a strong influence on the successful solution to the movement problem. Purely mechanical factors, such as the relationship between a swimmer's hand angle of pitch and the resulting propulsive force, will regulate how the breaststroke pull is generated. In the same way that wind tunnel studies can be used to design better airplane wings and boat propeller blades, so too,

studies of human hand models can be used in the "biomechanical design" of optimal swimming motions. Because the goal in breaststroke is to generate a maximal propulsive force, there are a limited number of ways to perform an effective arm pull. We will identify breaststroke, and other movements like it, as *maximal force output movements*.

Figure 2-11. Breaststroke – front view.

The breaststroke pull motion is almost entirely regulated by mechanical factors, and it is therefore very different from a springboard dive. Swimming rulebooks do not specify the hand angle of pitch or pulling pattern for the breaststroke event. If you were to observe a group of nationally ranked breaststroke competitors, you would see that they do not all swim alike. The morphological differences that exist across performers will cause differences in the solution of the movement problem even among a group of very highly skilled competitors. As a result, the shaded range of effective movement solutions is larger for breaststroke than it is for a springboard dive.

Natural Adjustment & Closed Skills

There are those who argue that all people have an innate ability to solve movement problems, and given enough practice, everyone will find an optimal way to move. The concept of *natural individual adjustment* has merit, but it can easily be taken to an extreme. It is true that all people will find individualized solutions to movement problems, but it is not true that every trial and error learning experience ends in perfection. We should always remember:

Practice *does not* make perfect.
***Perfect* practice makes perfect.**

When you practice a closed skill, your movement will evolve over time to result in a consistent technique that may well feel very natural to you. However, the mere fact that you have done thousands of repetitions of a movement does not assure you that your resulting technique will be optimal. If you go to a swimming pool and observe "old-timers" doing laps for exercise, you will see the end result of perhaps, a million-repetition trial and error learning experience. Nevertheless, a biomechanical analysis of many of these performers will identify numerous errors in technique. The figure below shows three possible outcomes of the closed skill fixation process.

Closed Skill Fixation

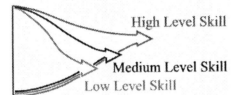

Figure 2-12. The closed skill fixation process. As a learner practices a closed skill more and more, his / her movements will become more and more consistent. With poor instruction, the movements may become consistent but relatively ineffective. With good instruction the movements may become consistent and highly effective.

Given a determined learner and little or no instructional guidance, the result of the learning experience will often be a very consistent, low-level skill. If the same performer is given a moderate level of instruction, we can expect that a medium-level of skill will result. Finally, if the performer is given high quality instruction, it is quite possible that a high-level of skill will be developed. We would like to think that anyone could achieve skillful technique if quality instruction is provided, but unfortunately, a given level of talent is often needed on the part of the performer. However, we can expect that quality instruction will allow anyone to perform "their best" on any given skill.

Let's now consider the role of the natural individual adjustment concept to the three closed skills of diving, swimming and the free throw. As we have noted above, natural adjustment has limited application to maximal force output skills like swimming.

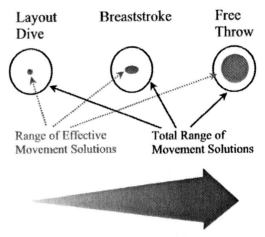

Natural Individual Adjustment

Figure 2-13. Different movements will involve differences in the range of effective movement solutions and in the influence of the natural individual adjustment theory.

For springboard diving, natural adjustment has virtually no application at all. Imagine for a moment a diver who prefers to hop to the end of the diving board and then waves to the crowd while she is in the air. It seems unlikely that this diver will score a "10" in the Olympics.

On the other hand, the natural adjustment concept has extensive value in the instruction of a free throw. If a given individual finds a way to move that consistently scores a goal and at the same time feels natural, we should forget about making adjustments in technique and leave well enough alone.

Figure 2-14. A basketball free throw.

Implications for Teaching

The natural adjustment concept has important implications for those of us who teach skills. If we are teaching accuracy movements, we should provide a very general idea of the movement to our students and then let them adopt any movement style that feels natural.

For maximal force output movements, it would seem that fairly detailed instruction in technique should be given, especially for middle school students and above. Some will argue that only minimal instructional guidelines should be given and many students will find the right way to move naturally. While this may be true for motor geniuses like Christy Yamaguchi or Mark Spitz, it will not be true for the remaining 99.9% of the population.

Figure 2-15. The discus throwing event is an example of a maximal force output skill.

Finally, prescribed form movements are obvious candidates for the detailed instruction of movement techniques. If we know the rulebook requirements for a high score and we also know the biomechanical factors associated with skill, we will have the information needed for very effective teaching.

Figure 2-16. The tour jete in dance is an example of a prescribed form skill.

Implications for Analysis

The above discussions show that our analysis of movement technique must vary for different movements. For prescribed form movements like a springboard dive, the movement will be organized to address two constraints. First, the performer will need to address the biomechanical challenges associated with the movement. For example, the force generated between the feet and the board will need to be maximized. A second, but equally important concern for the diver will be to pick an angle of projection for his body that causes a diving trajectory that is more up and down than outward. If the dive is done properly, the diver will enter the water fairly close to the end of the board. This second constraint has nothing to do with mechanics and everything to do with the aesthetic requirements of the diving scorebook. As a result, prescribed form movements require us to analyze the movement at two levels: the biomechanical level and the aesthetic level.

Figure 2-17. A back one and one half somersault dive in tuck position.

For example, the performance of a dance leap can be judged for both aesthetic value and for biomechanical proficiency. The biomechanics behind the generation of force for the leap and the absorption of force on the landing can be very interesting. Detailed study of these biomechanical aspects will allow us to distinguish the mechanical factors associated with skill and perhaps identify areas where the scorebooks or footwear of the dancer should be changed to minimize the chance of injury.

Dance:
Aesthetics & Biomechanics

Figure 2-18. A dance leap is a good example of a movement that is regulated by both mechanical and aesthetic influences.

Maximal force output movements like swimming should provide us with a very clear analysis challenge. The form of the movement will certainly be influenced by mechanical principles. Further, we will be able to use reductionism to break the movement down and evaluate every component of the movement in detail. We can then make attempts to isolate the flaws in the movement and make suggestions for improvement in technique.

Stroke
Mechanics

Figure 2-19. Stroke mechanics is crucially important aspect of success in competitive swimming.

Accuracy movements like the free throw present us with a more difficult analysis challenge. For these types of movements, the biomechanical constraint may play only a minor role in the solution of the movement problem. Under these circumstances, we can still perform a standard biomechanical analysis to quantify the movement characteristics used by various performers. However, our expectations for

the results of our analysis will be very different from that of a maximal force output skill.

For an accuracy movement, we will need to study multiple trials of movement data for each research participant. We will then use statistical analysis techniques to help use to evaluate the *consistency* of the performer's movement. The specific movement style used for an accuracy movement may vary considerably across individuals. However, the consistency of movement within the trials of a given individual will be closely associated with skill level.

Figure 2-20. The skillful performance of a basketball free throw is more dependent upon the accuracy of the movement than upon the development of maximal force.

Movement Style

Maximal force output movements will often present us with interesting problems in the interpretation of research data. Suppose we are evaluating the data for three members on the Olympic team (Joe, Mike and Bill) in the long jump event. The figure below shows the "locations" of these individuals within the range of effective movement solutions.

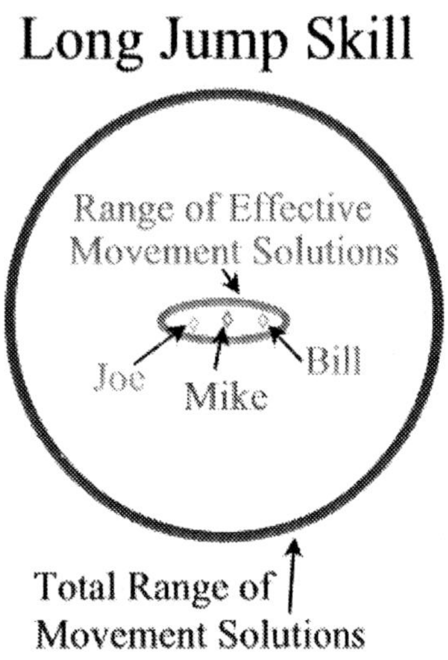

Long Jump Skill

Range of Effective
Movement Solutions

Joe   Mike   Bill

Total Range of
Movement Solutions

Figure 2-21. While the mechanical constraint in the long jump largely determines the characteristics of model performance, there will still be individual differences among different performers.

We can imagine that a large sample of skilled long jumpers have been analyzed on a number of important biomechanical variables. Let's say that one of the analysis variables is the range of motion of the knee joint on the take off stride. When we compare the scores for our three long jumpers to the larger sample, we see that Mike's score falls close to that of the average score for the large sample. Joe, on the other hand, uses a slightly different movement style and his score on knee range of motion is different. It could be misleading to think of Joe's score as higher or lower than Mike's because many people will jump to the conclusion that higher scores must be better. When we study skill and we look for biomechanical characteristics that are held in common among skilled performers, we are not looking for extreme measures, we are looking for representative measures. The average score will normally be the most representative measure for a normally distributed sample. Scores that are "above this average" should not be expected to be better.

Question 3:
Your challenge is to do a vertical jump and jump as high as possible. You will start in a standing position, bend down to a crouch and then jump straight up. How much should you bend your knees when you crouch down to assure the highest possible jump?

O A. You should bend your knees as much as possible to assure a maximal range of motion at the knee.

O B. You should bend the knees about 90 degrees at the bottom of the crouch.
O C. You should bend your knees very little, about 10 degrees will be ideal.

Upward Jump Knee Bend Angles

A   B   C

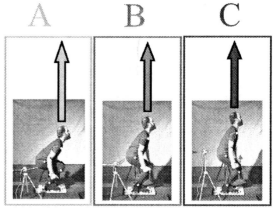

Figure 2-22. A study of 3 different knee bend angles on vertical jump performance.

The vertical jump example indicates that it is possible to have too little or too much knee range of motion in a long jump movement. A middle, or average, value of knee range of motion will clearly be better than more extreme values. This implies that videos of Mike's long jump performance may be the best *model technique* for use with the instruction of novice long jump competitors. However, Joe is also an outstanding long jumper, and his technique may be considered to be the best for him and for others who have similar morphological attributes. Thus, we see that the "right" technique for a given movement must be selected from a *range* of effective movement solutions to account for the differences between individuals. For the long jump, it will be fairly easy to evaluate the movement techniques of novice performers because there is a relatively limited range of values associated with skilled performers.

Tennis Backhand Technique

Let's now imagine that we are interested in evaluating the skill of tennis players for the backhand ground stroke. This particular movement presents us with two models of skillful performance.

Backhand Ground Stroke

Total Range of Movement Solutions

Figure 2-23. The backhand ground stroke in tennis provides an interesting example of a movement with two distinctly different movement solutions.

If you are a fan of tennis, you will know that Chris Evert popularized the two handed backhand ground stroke. Other players, like Jimmy Connors and Andre Agassi have also used the two-hand backhand very effectively. On the other hand (pun intended), John McEnroe and Pete Sampras have done very well with a one handed backhand motion (see Figure 2-24).

This example shows that it is sometimes appropriate to have more than one "model technique" for use in instruction and skill evaluation. The tennis backhand is interesting because each of the two possible movement solutions is distinctly different from the other, and each could be studied independently.

Two Handed Backhand

One Handed Backhand

Figure 2-24. Andre Agassi and Pete Sampras use different techniques in the backhand stroke. Photos courtesy of John Yandell, www.tennisplayer.net

Freestyle Swimming Technique

Finally, let's consider the evaluation of swimming technique in freestyle (the front crawl stroke). Research on stroke technique (Schleihauf, 1977) has shown that there are at least three overlapping model techniques that could be used for swimming instruction.

Freestyle Swimming

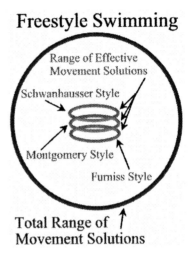

Total Range of Movement Solutions

Figure 2-25. The freestyle swimming stroke provides an interesting example of three overlapping styles of model swimming technique.

The model swimming styles are named after the world-class swimming performers who volunteered to donate their research data to the scientific community. Each of the model performers has a stroke technique that appears different from the others. Carolyn Schwanhausser had a high rate of turnover stroke, with a deep press at the beginning of the pull and an extended upward swept finishing motion. Jim Montgomery had a low rate of turn over style that involved a backward push in the middle of the pull and an upward swept finish at the end. Finally, Bruce Furniss used an "S" pattern underwater pull to generate propulsion.

The swimming examples are interesting because they overlap. Elements of one style are seen in others and there is a continuum of "tendencies" that will often produce skilled swimmers with hybrid techniques. The increased variability of model techniques for swimming indicates that lots of different arm motions can be used to produce equivalent propulsive forces. We will see in the chapter on swimming propulsion that there are still very clear biomechanical principles that can be used to guide the instruction and analysis of swimming.

Biomechanical Database

One of the most interesting questions in biomechanics comes up when we try to distinguish between those movements that are within the range of effective movement solutions and those that are just outside of that range. In order to answer this question, we need to have a *biomechanical database* of information for the skill in question.

We have already mentioned that one of our strategies for the evaluation of skill involves an analysis of the factors held in common across a sampling of skillful competitors. A biomechanical database is simply the collection of these biomechanical measurements. For example, in the tennis serve we may expect that skillful technique will involve a number of variables that can be measured through video analysis. Many of these variables are based upon concepts that will be discussed in the remaining chapters of this book. Some of the variables can be measured very simply however. In a tennis serve, we would expect that the speed of the racket motion would in part be determined by an effective use of the arm segments. The flexion and extension of the elbow will certainly be a factor in an effective arm swing movement. As with the vertical jump example we mentioned above, we should expect that an effective arm motion will involve a specific degree of elbow flexion. Too much flexion will inhibit force production; too little flexion will allow too little time for the development of force.

Tennis Serve Backscratch Position

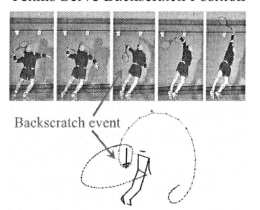

Figure 2-26. The backscratch event in a tennis serve.

We can determine an estimate of the optimal degree of elbow flexion in a tennis serve by measuring the *elbow angle at backscratch* for a sample of highly skilled performers. The backscratch event in a

tennis serving motion occurs when the racket is lowered behind the performer's back just prior to the upswing motion of the racket.

The elbow angle at the moment of backscratch can be determined through video analysis. The measures for every performer in a large sampling of skilled performers can be used to build the biomechanical database. The elbow angle scores for the sample can then be plotted as a frequency distribution. The figure below shows the frequency distribution of the elbow bend at backscratch for a sampling of 25 professional tennis players. The graph is similar to a normal curve graph that you may have seen in a statistics text. You may also have seen normal curves used in classes where your exam scores have been "graded on a curve". The average elbow angle for the professional players was 77°. The standard deviation (a measure of the variability in the elbow angle) is +/- 23°.

Elbow Bend at Backscratch Frequency Distribution

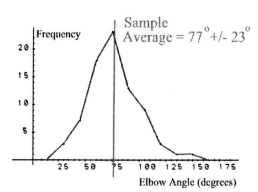

Figure 2-27. A frequency distribution of elbow bend at backscratch scores for skillful tennis players.

We can use the mean and standard deviation measures to "draw the line" between effective technique and flaws in performance. Statistically, 68% of the professional sample elbow angle scores will fall between −1 and +1 standard deviations of the mean.

As an exercise, consider how you can compute the lower number for the -1 and +1 standard deviation range:

Question 5:
What elbow angle is equal to the sample mean minus one standard deviation?

O A. 77°   O B. 54°   O C. 23°

As an exercise, consider how you can compute the upper number for the -1 and +1 standard deviation range:

Question 6:
What elbow angle is equal to the sample mean plus one standard deviation?

O A. 100°   O B. 54°   O C. 23°

We can expect that elbow angle measures between 54° and 100° will be common. However, only 2% of the professional sample will be expected to have elbow angle scores greater than 123° (+2 standard deviations above the mean). It will be safe to identify all scores above +2 standard deviations as flaws in technique.

Biomechanical Database Example

An experienced performer (Subject A) is shown in the figure below. A video analysis of this performer reveals that his elbow angle at backscratch is 98°.

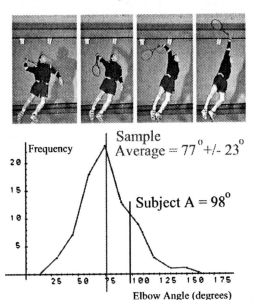

Figure 2-28. A skillful tennis player may be expected to use elbow bend angles that are "typical" of those found in a biomechanical database of skillful tennis players.

Question 7:
Does Subject A's technique fall within the range of effective movement solutions for the elbow bend at backscratch measure?

O A. Yes
O B. No

Because subject A's elbow angle measure falls within +/- 1 standard deviation of the mean, we can safely conclude that his movement is within the range of effective movement solutions, at least as far as the elbow angle variable is concerned.

Let's now consider the data for a less experienced performer (Subject B). The figure below shows that this player has an elbow bend at backscratch measure of 174°.

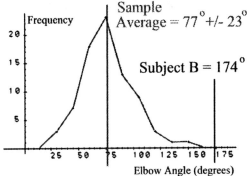

Figure 2-29. Errors in technique may be defined by measures that are outside of the range of those found within a skillful sampling of performers.

Question 8:
Does Subject B's technique fall within the range of effective movement solutions for the elbow bend at backscratch measure?

O A. Yes   O B. No

Because Subject B's elbow angle measure is greater than two standard deviations above the mean, we can safely conclude that his movement is outside of the range of effective movement solutions.

Database Interpretation Issues

Measures that fall between +1 and +2, or –1 and –2 standard deviations represent more of a gray area. It may be best to delay making recommendations for changes in technique based upon "gray area information" until after all other "larger" flaws have been corrected.

The primary advantage of a biomechanical database is that it provides an *objective* basis for the evaluation of skill. If we use well-intended "expert opinion" instead of objective data, we run the risk of placing incorrect weights on stylistic variables. For example, we may find that the height of the ball toss on a tennis serve has a high degree of variability among skilled performers. As a result, only very extreme toss heights would be shown to be flawed in an objective analysis. However, a given expert in tennis instruction may feel that the toss should be thrown to a specific height.

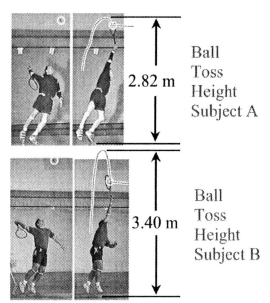

Figure 2-30. The height of ball toss on a tennis serve will vary considerably across skillful performers.

Of course, the "expert opinion" of an effective tennis instructor is often a reflection of years of experience that, in effect, generates a *mental* biomechanical database. Further, a given expert could argue that he has had dozens of world-class pupils and they have all been taught to use a specific toss height. However, if the toss height variable is not really critical in the resulting skill, it could be argued that undue attention to this variable will only produce an unnecessary distraction for the learner. Thus, we see that a biomechanical database can be

used to identify the most important variables for use in instruction. Those with low variability (factors that are held in common, within narrow limits, by skilled performers) should be emphasized heavily in instruction. Those with high variability can be viewed as arbitrary stylistic variables.

The strength of a biomechanical database is derived from the quality of the statistical sample of performers. The statistical treatment of the sample data takes into account that some of the "skilled" members of the sample are not, in fact, using efficient technique. By using a large sample, we can be sure that outliers do not weaken our analysis. In general, it seems appropriate to avoid using the most extreme examples as instructional guides for novice performers.

We must be careful to avoid over-reliance on the biomechanical database statistical data. Flaws in movement technique should be identified on the basis of *two* factors:

1) A movement characteristic represents a flaw in technique if the biomechanical database variable falls outside of the +/- 2 standard deviations range,

and

2) The movement characteristic does not appear to be consistent with the biomechanical principles of skillful movement.

The second criterion above will protect us from errors that will arise from incomplete database information. The following example illustrates the importance of the two-criterion approach.

Imagine that you are coaching track and field and the year is 1964. You have done all of your homework and you have an extensive database of high jump technique performance variables. A new person tries out for your team, but you decide to reject him because of his oddball technique. Later, you see that this person has done so well on another team that they have used his name to identify a very effective style of high jumping – the Fosbury flop.

Figure 2-31. The Fosbury flop technique in the high jump.

Just because a movement style is different, does not by itself, provide proof that the movement is inefficient. An open-minded analysis of the Fosbury flop would show that it involves numerous advantages over the classic straddle style. On the other hand, it would be foolhardy to adopt every unusual style of movement that comes along as the next big thing. By using both an established biomechanical database and an objective analysis of interesting variations on the form of movement, we should be able to provide very good advice to our students.

Video Project Issues

Our discussion of movement analysis issues has been intended to provide you with a general foundation for work in biomechanical analysis. Bear in mind that your term project is intended to be a pilot study report, and it is understood that you may well rely upon theory more that fact in your data analysis. For example, if you do a skilled – novice research design, you can use the ideas behind a biomechanical database, but your sample size for skilled performers will be one. As a result, you will not have any information on the variability of specific measures and you ability to objectively evaluate a flaw will be limited. You can strengthen your analysis by referring to the biomechanics literature to supplement your analysis.

File Library

Figure 2-32. The KAVideo - SFSU Movement Library web page.

As you search your schools library for references, you will find that many movements are not well documented in the scientific literature. You should also check the SFSU Movement Library on the Internet:

http://www.kavideo.sfsu.edu/library.htm

Hopefully, more and more information will be added to the scientific literature and the SFSU

Movement library in the near future. When your work is done on your project, you are encouraged to upload your video images and data to the movement library. This procedure will not only make you famous, it will also help other students around the world who are interested in biomechanics.

Conclusions

Our discussion of the critical issues in movement analysis is now complete. The next chapter will provide a detailed introduction to the Kinematic Analysis software program that you will use on your video analysis project.

References

Higgins, J.R., 1977. "Human Movement: An Integrated Approach" (1977) St. Louis: The C.V. Mosby Co.

Poulton, E.C., 1957. "On Prediction in Skilled Movements", Psychological Bulletin, 54(6), 467-478.

Schleihauf, R.E., 1977. "Swimming Propulsion: A Hydrodynamic Analysis", in Ousley, R. (Ed.), A.S.C.A. Convention, Fort Lauderdale.

Answers to Chapter Questions

Question 1:
Which type of skill would you expect to be the easiest to analyze for your project this semester?

O A. Closed Skill   O B. Open Skill

The correct answer is A. Closed skills will be easier to analyze because the performer will try to perform the movement the same way every time. Note: Open skills are difficult to analyze because the "correct" solution changes from trial to trial.

Question 2:
Can we characterize Arnold Palmer's drive technique as near perfect if he does not hold the world record for the longest drive ever hit?

O A. Yes.   O B. No.

The correct answer is A. The focus in biomechanics is not on the end result, but upon the movement process. Gifted athletes that work for decades developing their skills can develop perfection, in much the same way as a world-renowned artist.

Question 3:
How should we deliver the ball to the novice and skilled performer? After you make your first choice, select the other two possibilities and read their comments.

O A. We should recruit a skilled softball pitcher and pitch the ball exactly as it is done in a game.
O B. We should get a pitching machine and adjust the pitch location to the middle of the strike zone for both participants.
O C. We should put the ball on a tee and set the tee height and position to the middle of the strike zone for both participants.

The correct answer is B. If we find that the swing of the novice performer is poor, we will be sure that the poor swing was not due to a bad pitch.

Response A: Because you will only be able to analyze one swing for each performer, this will be a bad idea. It would be better to control the pitch variability so that difference in the movement trials can be attributed to different swing techniques and not different pitch conditions.

Response C: A batting tee would be a good idea for use with children, but not for use with college age performers. Part of the skill of softball batting revolves around the batters ability to track and react to a moving ball.

Question 4:
Your challenge is to do a vertical jump and jump as high as possible. You will start in a standing position, bend down to a crouch and then jump straight up. How much should you bend your knees when you crouch down to assure the highest possible jump?

O A. You should bend your knees as much as possible to assure a maximal range of motion at the knee.
O B. You should bend the knees about 90 degrees at the bottom of the crouch.
O C. You should bend your knees very little, about 10 degrees will be ideal.

The correct answer is B. A middle size knee bend will allow you to generate a maximal jumping force.

Response A: If you bend down too much, your legs will not be strong enough to generate a maximal force against the ground.

Response C: If you bend down too little, your legs will not have enough time to generate a maximal force against the ground.

Question 5:
What elbow angle is equal to the sample mean minus one standard deviation?
O A. 77°   O B. 54°   O C. 23°

The correct answer is B. The mean elbow angle is 77°. The standard deviation is 23°. One standard deviation below the mean is (77° - 23°) or 54°.

Question 6:
What elbow angle is equal to the sample mean plus one standard deviation?

O A. 100°   O B. 54°   O C. 23°

The correct answer is A. The mean elbow angle is 77°. The standard deviation is 23°. One standard deviation above the mean is (77° + 23°) or 100°.

Question 7:
Does Subject A's technique fall within the range of effective movement solutions for the elbow bend at backscratch measure?

O A. Yes   O B. No

The correct answer is A. On the basis of our professional sample data, Subject A is exhibiting skillful technique on this measure. His elbow angle of 98° falls within the +/- one standard deviation limit and is therefore typical of the technique measures in the skilled sample.

Question 8:
Does Subject B's technique fall within the range of effective movement solutions for the elbow bend at backscratch measure?

O A. Yes   O B. No

The correct answer is B. On the basis of our professional sample data, Subject B is not exhibiting skillful technique on this measure. His elbow angle of 174° falls outside of the +/- two standard deviation limit and is therefore not typical of the technique measures in the skilled sample.

Chapter 3: Kinematic Analysis Software

Introduction to Kinematic Analysis

The Kinematic Analysis (KA) software is a suite of biomechanical analysis programs that can be run on virtually any Windows based PC. We will use the software for three purposes this semester:

1) Many of the examples for the remaining chapters in this book will be drawn from KA research projects. These examples will provide clear illustrations that will help you to visualize the most important theories and biomechanical concepts in this course.

2) KA homework exercises will be included at the end of many of our chapters. These exercises will allow you to use KA to examine how mechanical principles influence "real life" movement examples.

3) You will use KA to perform a complete research project on the movement of your choice. Your course instructor will determine many of the details of this term paper assignment. In many instances, you, and other members of your class, will be able to propose a movement for analysis. You will then collect video data on that movement and capture the video onto your school lab PC. The KA software can then be used to perform a detailed biomechanical analysis of the movement.

This chapter will provide a brief introduction to KA. As you proceed through the remaining chapters in this book, you will gain additional insights into the various KA software programs. You can also use the printed KA Manual for more detailed reference information.

Software Installation

In order to take advantage of the KA software, you should install the software on your home computer.

To perform the software installation, follow the instructions in the Course Guidebook (this guidebook includes general information on the course software, KA installation instructions, and a variety of other course materials). If you do not own a home PC (or if your home PC cannot accommodate the software), you will need to schedule time to do the KA exercises from this book on a "KA equipped" PC at your school (see your course instructor for details).

Quick Tour

Because the KA software and data files will be used extensively in the remaining portions of this course, we will take some time in this chapter to introduce the software and give you a general understanding of its capabilities. This brief introduction will not emphasize the details associated with the various kinematic measurements (i.e., velocity and acceleration curves) shown on the KA screen. We will cover the details behind these measures in the remaining chapters of this book.

The KA suite of programs consists of three main parts: KAVideo, KA2D and KA3D.

KAVideo – This program helps you to transfer video clips from your camcorder to the hard drive on your PC. KAVideo prepares video clip files for analysis and makes it possible for you to "digitize the movement" (determine the XY coordinates of body landmarks) on the PC screen. To digitize the toe point, manually positioning the mouse cursor over the toe and click the mouse. The XY coordinate values will be stored in memory and the next image for the movement will be displayed. This process is repeated for each image in the movement sequence to complete the digitizing process.

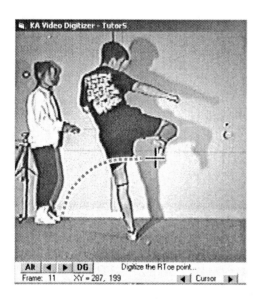

Figure 3-1. The KA Video digitizing program. The right toe point has been digitized for the beginning portion of the movement.

Note: The KA software is designed to run in full screen mode on you PC. For the purposes of this chapter, the KA graphics have been reduced in size to fit within the limits of the columns on this page. Bear in mind that the fine print on these illustrations will be easily read when KA is displayed on a computer screen.

KA2D – This program allows you to inspect the stick figure and video clip animations of the movement. As the video images are "played back" by the software, a wide variety of kinematic measures (i.e., velocity, acceleration, joint angle, etc.) are displayed on the screen.

The figure below shows the KA2D data for a martial arts kicking motion. Because all of the major body landmark points have been digitized, a complete stick figure of the body can be shown.

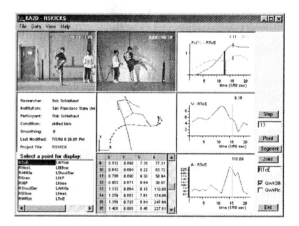

Figure 3-2. A reduced size illustration of the KA2D program screen.

The software also shows a number of kinematic variables (position, velocity and acceleration) in the various viewports within the program window. If the KA2D window is left in "pause" mode, you have ample time to evaluate the data for a single instant in time. You can also place KA in "play" mode to show the *movement* and the associated changes to kinematic variables that occur as the movement progresses. To move forward through the data, position the mouse within a video, stick figure or function plot viewport and press the **left** mouse button. To play the movement backwards, press the **right** mouse button.

The KA2D program can also be used to compare two data sets in side-by-side mode. The figure below shows the data for a "skilled" and "intermediate" level performer in a softball batting motion. The KA2D data can be played back, side-by-side, and differences in the two performers can be identified.

Figure 3-3. The KA2D program screen in "file compare" mode. The video and stick figure data from the four upper left viewports is shown.

KA3D – The KA3D program allows you to combine the information in a pair of front and side view KA2D files to produce a full set of three-dimensional kinematic data. One of the biggest advantages of the KA3D program is that measures of joint angles, point velocity and other kinematic data can be estimated from the full three dimensional range of motion of the performer. Because most human movements occur in three dimensions (and not within a single 2D plane) the KA3D program will often provide the best way to analyze movement data.

The figure below shows the 3D data for a skilled softball batting movement. Notice that the three-dimensional data has been used to generate a stick figure for the overhead view of the movement (in the bottom-middle viewport).

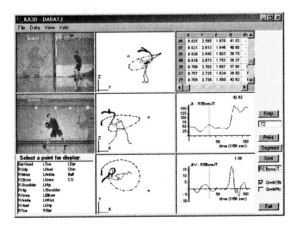

Figure 3-4. A reduced size illustration of the KA3D program screen.

Theory and Practice in Biomechanics

In this course, you will use KA to analyze research data on "real life" examples of human movement. We will also use these KA examples to illustrate many of the most important biomechanical principles in this book. For example, in the linear kinetics chapters we will not only present Newton's second law ($F = mA$), we will also apply it to compute the forces that are generated by research participants as they move. Further, we will watch moving graphical representations of these forces superimposed on computer based stick figure animations. Thus, KA will add an extra dimension to your study of biomechanics that is not present in most "textbook only" courses.

As we progress through the course we will discuss all of the most important *theories* that are relevant to your work in kinesiology. However, we will also try to link these theories to *practice*, and provide you with ample opportunity to apply your knowledge to real world problems. To address the practical aspects of biomechanical analysis, our course will include a special movement analysis project. The project will be unique because you will be given the opportunity to participate in the selection of the movement to be studied. It is our position that the best research assignment grows out of your own interests.

There will be ample room within the project design to allow your course instructor to provide guidance on research design issues. It will also be possible for you to work with other students to increase the depth of analysis and encourage the exchange of ideas. The remaining sections of the chapter will show you how the KA software can be used as a tool in the solution of your research questions.

KA Research Questions

Many of the best biomechanical research projects are generated by simple curiosity. For example, you may wonder what you would need to do to improve your tennis serve. If you have taken an introductory course in kinesiology, you will know that there are no simple answers to this question. There is no *ideal form* model for tennis serves that all performers are expected to follow. Depending upon your strengths, flexibilities and a wide variety of other factors, the best service motion for you will be different from another performer with different characteristics.

There will, however, be a set of biomechanical principles that will be held in common for skilled tennis performers. Thus, your challenge in a tennis serve analysis project will be to distinguish between the idiosyncratic *stylistic* variables in your tennis serve and the *biomechanical factors* in your movement that are related to skillful performance.

The analysis of *skillful performance* is a substantial problem facing researchers in kinesiology. In our course we will focus upon the biomechanical factors associated with skill. We will save the physiological, psychological, neurophysiological and other factors associated with skillful performers for other courses, and we will acknowledge that a broad variety of information must be studied to truly understand skillful human performance. We will, nevertheless, be confident that biomechanical analysis will yield important information that will be useful in understanding skill at the most general level.

The figure below shows stick figure and video data from a tennis-serve analysis project. The experienced performer is shown on the left and the novice performer is shown on the right. If these two trials of data were used for a term project, we would carefully compare the kinematic measures for the performers. We could then make suggestions for changes in the movements of the novice performer. The suggested changes should be based upon biomechanical theories as well as the practical guidelines inherent in the skilled performer's data.

The study of athletic skill often provides clear-cut examples of biomechanical principles. As a result, we will often find it convenient to draw from athletic motions in our study of biomechanics. It is important to note that the more general study of *movement efficiency* and *coordinated movement patterns* is actually more important than the study of athletics for most kinesiologists.

Our goal in kinesiology is not to focus exclusively on elite performers. Instead, we will use biomechanical principles and analysis techniques to study a wide variety of movements; sometimes simply for the purpose of better understanding how human beings solve movement problems. We will acknowledge that the movement is an outward manifestation of the internal motor control processes that generate movement. Further, we will find that a better understanding of skillful / efficient / coordinated movement will often help us to design better instructional and training programs for our clients, students and athletes.

Given our interest in efficiency and coordination, we may find ourselves asking questions such as "I wonder how fatigue will influence the movements of a person who is skipping rope?" Such a biomechanical research project will center upon the *movement process* (not only the movement product) and will be designed to help us to understand issues in human movement coordination and efficiency more than the details associated with "skilled" rope skipping technique.

The figure below shows data from a study of the effects of fatigue on rope skipping technique. Kinematic data on the body's center of gravity is shown on the right and the performer's video and stick figure graphic are shown on the left. Interesting differences will be seen if we compare the same performer under fatigued and non-fatigued conditions.

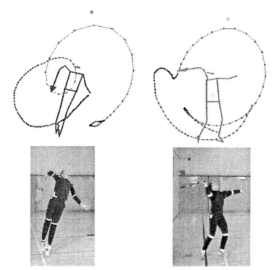

Figure 3-5. A comparison of an experienced and a novice performer in the tennis serve.

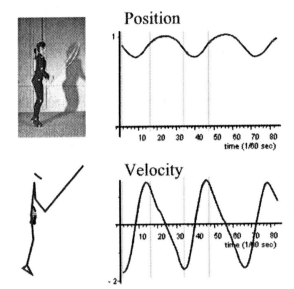

Figure 3-6. Video, stick figure, position and velocity data from an analysis of rope jumping technique.

Individual Research

The tennis serve and skipping rope projects mentioned earlier represent only two examples from a potentially endless list of interesting movement research examples. As a kinesiology major, you undoubtedly have performed, or observed, many movements that you would really like to study and understand in greater depth.

In this course, you will have two options for pursuing a biomechanical research project:

1) If your school's lab has a PC that is set up to support video capture, you can participate in every step of the research process. There are 6 steps in all:

Step 1: Select the movement for analysis
Step 2: Set the research design strategy
Step 3: Shoot the video data
Step 4: Capture the video data onto your Lab PC's hard drive
Step 5: Digitize the XY coordinate data
Step 6: Perform an analysis of the movement data.

2) If your school's lab is not set up for video capture, you can still conduct your own video analysis project. Instead of actually recording video of a movement, you can use a PC with an Internet connection to download video data from the *SFSU Movement Library* web site (www.kavideo.sfsu.edu). This web page includes the video information for many movement analysis

projects. You can select a movement that interests you, and download it to both your school lab PC and your home PC. This will effectively accomplish steps 1-4 above, and you will be able to do steps 5 and 6 under the supervision of your class instructor.

Whether you shoot your own video, or download your video files from the Internet, your course instructor will provide crucial guidance with each step of the research process. There will be plenty of room for variation in the project requirements. For example, your instructor will decide the number of projects that will be done in the course and the number of students that will be assigned to each research idea. You will be able to study either two-dimensional movements (i.e., walking, running) or three-dimensional movements (i.e., baseball batting, throwing). In addition, your instructor may also be able to steer you clear of research ideas that may not lend themselves to video-based biomechanical analysis.

Question 1:
Which of the following research topics seems to be best suited for use in a video based biomechanical analysis project?
Note: After you make your first choice, select the other two answers and read about why they are good or bad choices.

O A. Isometric exercise training.
O B. Dart throwing.
O C. A javelin throw.

Video Tape Data Collection

Once you have selected a movement for analysis, the next step in your project will be to work with your course instructor to collect video data on your project participants. Your primary responsibility during the video sessions will be to help set up the data collection area and prepare the research participants for videotaping. Ideally, your participants should be dressed in dark tight fitting clothing and the joints of the body should be clearly marked.

Figure 3-7. Front and side view video images from a soccer kick analysis project.

Your instructor will need your help on the "video day" because much of the video taping work requires the cooperation of three or more people. If you are collecting data for a three-dimensional movement, two video cameras must be used. The lines of sight of the cameras must be set to intersect at a 90-degree angle, and the distances from the front and side view cameras to the center of the field of view must be measured. Often additional lighting is needed to assure clear and bright images (fast movement must be shot with a high speed shutter and this camera adjustment will make your images appear dark unless plenty of light is available).

As many as 6 students may need to be present when the video data is shot. You may need one student inspecting the side view camera, one student inspecting the front view camera, another student will be needed to bounce a ball at the beginning of each trial and, if the movement involves striking a ball, still other students may be needed to protect flood lights and cameras and retrieve struck balls.

Please see Chapter 2 of the KA Manual for complete details on video data collection procedures.

KAVideo Software

Once you have collected video data, your next step will be to capture the video onto a PC and prepare the video files for use with KA. To run the KAVideo program, activate the **Start, Programs, KAVideo, KAVideo** menu option on your PC.

In many courses, your instructor may do the video capture work, or he/she may assign several of your most "computer savvy" students to assist with the capture work. You should nevertheless understand each step of the data processing work in the KAVideo program. In particular, you should know how to download the captured image set files

from your lab PC hard drive to your home PC and use the digitizing menu option to generate your kinematic data.

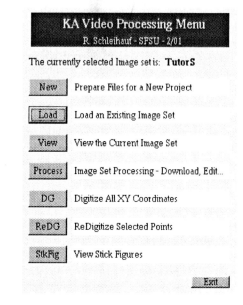

Figure 3-8. The KAVideo main program screen.

We will discuss the function of each option on the KAVideo menu in the following sections.

KAVideo – New Option

The New button is used to begin work on a new project. When **New** is clicked, a submenu screen provides access to video capture, project file definition and related programs.

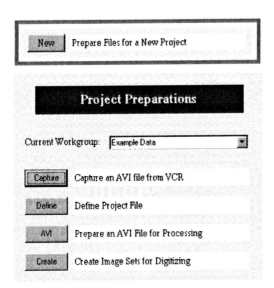

Figure 3-9. The "New Project" sub menu options.

The **New** menu option is unusual in that it presents program options that can only be performed on a PC that has a video capture card installed. Thus, while you can install KA on your home PC, you will only be able to perform the options from this menu on your school lab video capture PC. As a result, for many implementations of this course, the work for the **New** menu option is performed by the course instructor.

While the work that is done on this menu requires extra hardware (a DV or S-VHS video source and a video capture card), it is actually a very intuitive process. Your course instructor will place your video project tape into a VCR and cue the tape up to the beginning of your movement trial. The VCR / camcorder in your lab will be connected to a video capture card inside your lab PC. Video capture software on the PC will allow your instructor to capture a copy of the video stream and store it as an *AVI* file on the PC hard drive.

Note: An AVI file is a standard Windows **A**udio **V**ideo **I**nterleave file that holds video clips. The Media Player program that comes with Windows allows you to play back these AVI format video files.

Figure 3-10. The Windows Media Player program can play back AVI files (like the TutorS.avi file included with the KAVideo program).

The KA software will then allow the AVI file to be trimmed to include only the video frames critical to your analysis. In addition, the software will split the AVI file into a series of *BMP* files. This series of BMP files from your video clip is called a KA *image set.*

Note: A BMP file is a standard Windows *bitmap* file. Bitmap files are used to store graphic images on a PC. The MSPaint program that is included with Windows allows you to load and edit BMP format files. The figure below shows one of the BMP files from the KA tutorial image set loaded into the MSPaint program.

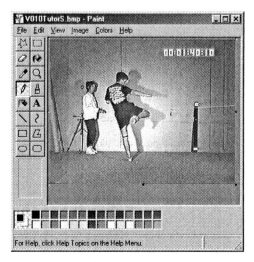

Figure 3-11. The Windows Microsoft Paint program can be used to display and edit the BMP files included in a KA image set.

Video Analysis Basics

Because you will be working extensively with video data, we will go over some of the basics of the video image capture process now. The video information that is recorded on a typical VHS or DV cassette is composed of a stream of *video frames*. In the United States, video is recorded at 30 frames per second (technically the frame rate is 29.97 frames per second, but we will round that number upward for simplicity). Thus, a one second movement will be composed of 30 video frames.

Note: The various countries in the world follow one of two standards for video recording: NTSC and PAL/SECAM. The NTSC video standard is used in the United States and about half of the other countries in the world. The remaining countries, including most countries in Europe, use the PAL standard. PAL standard video is recorded at 25 frames per second.

Each full video frame is best shown on a PC screen as a 640 x 480 pixel image. Each of these pixels (tiny dots) on your computer monitor can display virtually any color visible to the naked eye. Most computer monitors can show photographs in 16-bit mode, where the color of each pixel is selected from a palette of more than 65,000 shades of color.

The apparent quality of any captured video image comes as much from the color depth of the image as from its resolution. The continuous tone of colors in neighboring pixels allows your monitor to show images that appear to be much like a

photograph or slide. One of the shortcomings of a captured video image is the lack of detail available in a 640 x 480 image. The figure below shows a blow up of the researcher's face from the KA Tutor image files.

Blow Up of Video Image

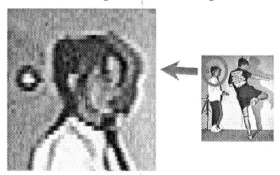

Figure 3-12. A blown up image of a researcher's face shows that the resolution of normal video is limited.

Notice that the researcher's face is not well represented in the blown up image. Further, the white pixels on the edge of her shirt show the individual pixels as blocks, with a staircase-like pattern over the edge of her shoulder. We see that the quality of this video image is not as good as that of a blown-up photographic slide. As a result, it will be important for us to use our camcorder's zoom lens to get "tight shots" of the movement trials we will collect this semester. This will allow us to, at least partially, sidestep the low-resolution problem of video images.

Video Data Collection Sampling Rate

A standard video signal has an additional complication. A full video frame is composed of 480 scan lines, with each scan line composed of 640 pixels. The scan lines are numbered from 0 to 479 with 0 set as the top line. When the video frame is recorded, the scan lines are written in two passes. First, the even scan lines are record (lines 0, 2, 4, 6 … 478). Then the odd scan lines are recorded (lines 1, 3, 5, 7 … 479). The even lines on the frame are called the even *field* or field A. The odd lines on the frame are called the odd field or field B. Because the lines from field A alternate with the lines from filed B, the full video frame is said to be composed of two *interlaced video fields*.

Thus, a full frame of video is actually derived from two separate images: the odd field (on odd line numbers from 1 to 479) and the even field (on even line numbers from 0 to 478). Each individual video field is actually recorded at a rate of 60 fields per second. This increased effective sampling rate of video allows us to analyze faster movements in more detail. The figure below shows the appearance of a fast motion on a normal (interlaced) full frame of video.

Interlaced Video

Figure 3-13. An illustration of two interlaced video fields within a single frame of video.

Notice that the scan lines on the enlarged image clearly show the leg in two positions. The odd lines show the legs position 1/60th second after the even lines. Most VCRs are designed to hide the interlaced pattern that is so obvious in the blown up video image. Thus, when a typical VCR is placed in single frame advance mode, only one field from each full video frame is shown on the television monitor.

If you were to display only the even lines from the interlaced video frame, you would get the information from "Field A". Similarly, the odd lines hold the information from "Field B". The figure below shows the "de-interlaced" information for the KA software TutorS kicking motion.

The upper-left side figure shows just the even lines. The odd lines have been removed and each of the even lines have been shifted upwards to form a solid figure. Similarly, the upper right side figure shows only the odd lines.

Because only half of the lines in the original video frame are shown, the upper two images are only half as tall as they should be. Nevertheless, they clearly show the position of the body at two separate instances in time. These figures show the position of the body at the two 1/60th second intervals that compose the full 1/30th second video frame.

De-interlaced Fields

Field A   Field B

Line Doubled De-interlaced Fields

Figure 3-14. The process of "de-interlacing" a video image produces two half height video images. When these separated video fields are line doubled, the resulting images can be used for motion analysis.

The bottom two "line doubled" fields have been "stretched vertically" to provide an undistorted view of the movement at two successive 60th second intervals. The process of "line doubling" is very simple. Every line from the de-interlaced field is drawn twice. The resulting image is the proper height and we can see 60 "full pictures" of the movement every second. A series of line doubled de-interlaced fields will appear much like the frames of film from a movie camera operating at 60 pictures per second. The film movie camera will of course be sharper than our video data because the full height of every frame is exposed every 1/60th second.

The KA software creates image sets by de-interlacing the original video signal and storing the resulting fields as BMP files on your hard drive. Once these image sets have been generated, the remaining options in the KA Video menu are used to view, digitize and process your project files.

Note that we often use the term "frame" to represent the line-doubled fields that are shown by KA. These images are very much like the film frames that are produced by movie cameras. To avoid confusion, we will use the term "*video* frame" when we are referring to interlaced video images, and we will use the term "frame" when we are referring to line doubled KA images or film frames.

Define Project File

In addition to video capture and processing items, the **New** (Project Preparations) submenu includes the **Define** option.

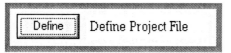

Figure 3-15. The "Define Project File" menu option.

This program allows you to specify many of the details for your project, such as the number of body landmarks and the camera set up information. When a project definition file is first created, a screen similar to the figure below is shown:

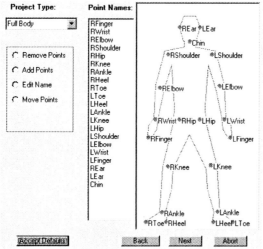

Figure 3-16. The "define" option allows researchers to specify the landmark points for a project.

Your course instructor will use this **Define** program to select a project type and specify all of the remaining critical information for your project. The **AVI** menu option will be used to trim extra frames from the beginning and end of your AVI file, and synchronize the front and side view images for 3D projects. The **Create** option is used to read the information in the AVI files and generate the image sets for each of your video trials. Once your image sets are saved on your lab PC, you will ready to begin your data analysis work.

KAVideo – Load Option

When the image sets for your video project have been generated, you can use the **Load** menu option to read the image sets into memory for review by other KAVideo menu options.

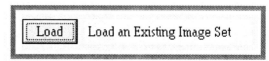

Figure 3-17. The KAVideo, Load menu option.

The figure below shows some of the image sets that are part of the "Example Data" from the KAPro CD-ROM. The researcher's initials are set as the first two characters of each image set name. The remaining characters in the image set name indicate the type of movement, the movement trial number and the view code (S represents the side view; F represents the front view). Note that you can click the code name of the "WorkGroup" for your class (on the left side of the screen) to display the image set names that have been created for your class.

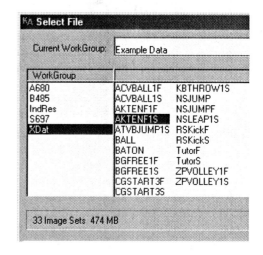

Figure 3-18. The KAVideo File load dialog box.

Question 2:
What would be a good name for the side view of trial 1 in John Smith's study of a long jump?

O A. SideViewLongJump
O B. Long Jump – Side view trial 1
O C. JSLongJump1S

KAVideo – View Option

Once an image set has been loaded for analysis, you can use the **View** option to "play back" the image set.

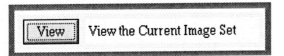

Figure 3-19. The KAVideo, View menu option.

The view option functions like a VCR with a good single frame advance control. If you position the mouse cursor within the picture area, and hold down the *left* mouse button, the video clip will advance. If you position the mouse cursor within the picture area and hold down the *right* mouse button, the video clip will play in reverse.

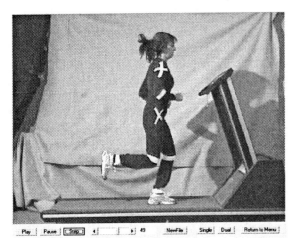

Figure 3-20. The KAVideo, View option program screen.

KAVideo – Process Option

After you view an image set, you may want to **Process** the images through one of the KA – Process sub programs.

Figure 3-21. The KAVideo, Process menu option.

The list of image set processing options is shown in the figure below.

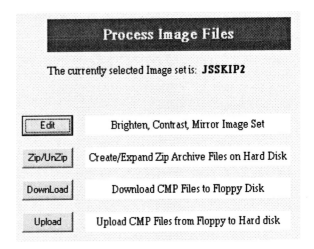

Figure 3-22. The KAVideo, Process sub menu screen.

The **Edit** option allows you to modify the brightness, contract or sharpness of all of the pictures in your image set. You can also use this option to mirror your images or convert them to black and white mode.

The **Zip/UnZip** option allows you to create a compressed (Zip format) file of all of the images in your image set. The resulting ZIP file will usually be too large to fit on a floppy disk. As a result, you should only use this option if you have a recordable CD or DVD drive (or a Zip disk drive) on both your lab and home PCs. If you do have access to one of these high capacity removable drives, the Zip/UnZip option will be faster and more convenient than the floppy disk based Download / Upload option. See the KA Manual for further details on performing the Zip / UnZip file transfer.

The **Download** (copy) image set files to floppy disk(s) option allows you to transfer your image set files from your lab PC to your home PC. Most image sets can be stored on 1 to 3 floppy disks.

Once you have transferred an image set to floppy disk, you can take the disks home and use the **Upload** option to copy the image set files from floppy to your hard disk drive. When this step is accomplished for all of your trials you will be able to do the digitizing and analysis work for your term paper on your home PC. However, the original images will be kept on the lab PC for the full semester in case you want to discuss the meaning of the data with your course instructor or classmates.

Question 3:
You have downloaded the information for an image set onto 2 floppy disks. Will you be able to take these disks to your uncle's house and do your digitizing on his PC this weekend?

O Yes. The disks have all the information you need to do work on any computer.
O No. You uncle's PC will not be able to work with these files.

KAVideo – Digitize Option

The Digitize option allows you to determine the XY coordinates for all of the body landmarks in your project.

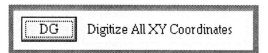

Figure 3-23. The KAVideo, DG menu option. This option is used to digitize body landmark points for a video project.

When the **DG** option is first selected, you will be prompted to enter the *events* for the image set.

Figure 3-24. The "Set Event" screen is typically the first screen shown when the digitize option is selected from the KAVideo menu.

The prompt near the bottom of the screen reminds you to advance the video image until the ball impact event is shown. For example, in the above figure the user must click the scroll bar right arrow, or drag the scroll bar position control to advance the video to show the ball impact frame.

Figure 3-25. When the video image associated with a given event is shown, click the "Set Event" button to store the frame number for the event.

When the video image shows the requested event, click the **Set Event** button to save the event information. If your project involves more than one event, you will be prompted to repeat this process until all events are entered.

The figure below shows the point digitizing stage of the **DG** program. The prompts near the bottom of the screen remind you to digitize the first point in your project. The researcher is being prompted to position the mouse cross hair cursor over the right toe point and click the left button. When the left mouse button is clicked, the video image will advance one frame and the researcher will be prompted to digitize the right toe point again.

Figure 3-26. The digitizer program screen at the beginning of the digitizing process for the TutorS file. The user is prompted to digitize the first frame for the first landmark point (the RToe point).

As you continue to digitize, the right toe pattern of motion will be drawn "behind" the current frame.

Figure 3-27. The digitizing program screen at a point about midway through the RToe digitizing work.

The right toe digitizing process will continue until it is digitized for every frame in the image set. When the last right toe point is digitized, the **DG** program will return the video image to the first frame in the image set and prompt you to digitize the next body landmark.

For the TutorS image set, the right ankle point is digitized after the right toe. The figure below shows that the right ankle joint center is identified by a loop of tape around the ankle. The researcher should use this tape loop marker to estimate the joint center location *inside* the participant's body. Many

students are tempted to use the exact location of a spot on the *outside* of the participant's body to set the digitized XY location. This approach will result in flawed data collection, especially in three-dimensional projects where the same point must be digitized in both the front and side view image sets. Your knowledge of anatomical kinesiology, coupled with a modicum of X-Ray vision, will allow you to use intelligence to obtain the best digitizer values.

Digitize the Joint Center

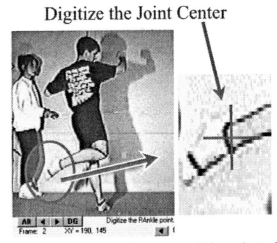

Figure 3-28. The ankle joint point should be estimated as the point inside the body that best represents the joint center.

The digitizing process will continue until all of the points on the body are digitized. Depending upon the number of frames and points in your image set, the total digitizing time may require an hour of your time. To minimize the stress of digitizing, you can exit from the program at the beginning of any point's digitizing sequence and take a break. When you return to your PC, even day's later, the software will remember the last point that you digitized and prompt you to begin work on the appropriate point in the sequence.

The last step in the **DG** option requires you to digitize the scale pole frame for the image set.

Digitize the #1 Scale point...

Figure 3-29. Two points on the scale pole must be digitized at the end of the body landmark point digitizing process.

You are prompted to digitize the top and bottom scale points in turn. When the second point is digitized, the **DG** program saves all of your work to disk and returns you to the KAVideo menu. It would be a good idea to back up your digitizing work at this point. Let's imagine that your trial name is TutorS and your work has been saved to the XDat workgroup folder. To back up your work, run Windows Explorer and show the contents of the C:\KA5\KA2D\XDat folder. (See the figure below.)

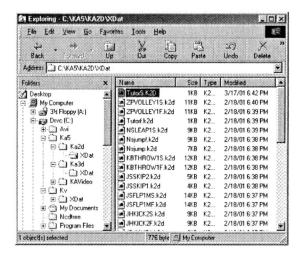

Figure 3-30. The results of all digitizing work are stored in a "K2D" file. Use Windows Explorer to display and back up this file.

The files in the Explorer window figure have been sorted by date, and the most recently digitized file (TutorS.k2d) is shown at the top of the file listing. To back up this file, simply copy it to a floppy disk. Notice that all of the KA2D files in the listing are

very small, with the largest needing only 14 Kb of disk space.

Note: If your instructor has set up a specific workgroup folder for your class, your digitizing work will be saved in that folder.

If you have done your digitizing work on your home PC, you will be able to bring this small K2D format file into your school lab on a floppy disk and copy it to the C:\KA5\KA2D\XDat folder (or the folder for your class). Because your image set will still be on the lab PC, you will be able inspect all of your work both at the lab and at home. This will be very convenient, especially if you would like to consult with your course instructor or your classmates.

Question 4:
You have just completed digitizing the data for both a highly skilled and a novice baseball pitcher. When you inspect the data in KA2D, you are surprised to see that the novice performer has a peak ball velocity that is 50 times greater than that of the skilled pitcher. How do you interpret this "finding"?

O A. This novice pitcher should sign up for the pros right now.
O B. There must be a mistake in the scale factor digitizing for the novice performer.

KAVideo – ReDigitize Option

The Re-Digitize option allows you to quickly correct digitizing errors on selected points in your project.

Figure 3-31. The KAVideo, ReDG program option.

Unlike the **DG** option, that requires you to digitize all of the body landmark points in sequence, the **ReDG** option allows you to digitize any landmark point for any series of frames in your image set. For example, suppose you have finished digitizing a side view trial for a soccer kick motion. When you inspect the data in KA2D, you notice that the right knee point pattern of motion has an unexpected discontinuity and the velocity curve for the right knee has a large unexpected "spike".

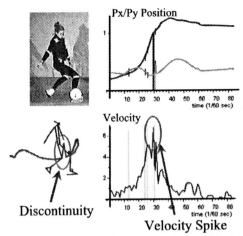

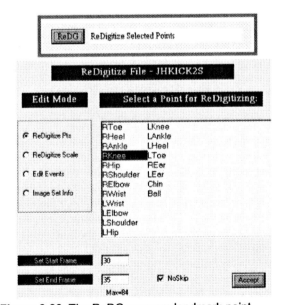

Discontinuity

Velocity Spike

Figure 3-32. KA2D velocity data can be used to identify body landmark points in need of re-digitizing.

It is clear from the picture below that the right knee point has not been correctly digitized at about frame 32 (the frame number for the velocity spike is shown on the horizontal axis of the "V – RKnee" curve).

To correct this digitizing error, we *do not* have to go back and repeat all of the digitizing work for this file. We can use the KAVideo **ReDG** option to limit our re-digitizing work to just the right knee for the frames 30 – 35 (we will digitize several frames before and after the apparent error as a precaution).

The **ReDG** initial program screen is shown below.

Figure 3-33. The ReDG program landmark point selection screen.

The **ReDG** start up screen prompts you to specify the point name and the start and end frame number for the re-digitizing work. When the **Accept** button is clicked the re-digitize program screen shows us the knee pattern of motion for the full movement and prompts us to re-digitize frames 30 – 35.

When the knee is re-digitized for frame 35, we can return to the KAVideo menu and inspect the results of our re-digitizing work with the Stick Figure option.

Figure 3-34. The ReDG program screen shows the complete pattern of motion for a selected landmark point.

KAVideo – StkFig Option

The **StkFig** (view stick figure) option allows you to quickly inspect the stick figure data for any image set that has been completely digitized. This option cannot be used with an image set that has only been partially digitized (i.e., if only 8 of 15 body landmark points have been digitized, the stick figure for the data cannot be generated).

Figure 3-35. The KAVideo, Stick Figure menu option.

The stick figure program screen is shown below. You can animate this figure forward by positioning the mouse within the stick figure area and pressing the **left** mouse button. To animate the figure backward, position the mouse within the stick figure area and pressing the **right** mouse button.

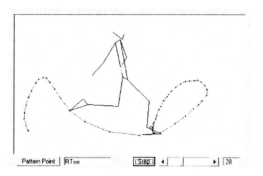

Figure 3-36. The Stick Figure option program screen.

The default pattern of motion is shown when the stick figure program is first run. For the soccer kick study, the right toe is the default pattern of motion point. If unexpected discontinuities are shown in the pattern, you should use the **ReDG** option to correct the apparent digitizing error(s). To inspect the digitizing work for the other points on the body, click on the **Pattern Point** button and select a new point from the list.

You may also want to use the KA2D program to inspect your digitizing work and determine if any re-digitizing is necessary. The KA2D program shows the velocity curve for each point as well as the stick figure and video image. This additional

information may be helpful for spotting digitizing errors.

KA2D Software

The KA software includes a two dimensional movement data visualization program to assist you in your study of human movement. To run the KA2D program, activate the **Start, Programs, KAVideo, KA2D** menu option on your PC.

The figure below shows how the KA2D software allows you to visualize the relationships between the outwardly observable movement characteristics from a research video and the more detailed kinematic information that is associated with the movement.

Notice that the figure shows nine "panes" of information for a soccer kick. KA2D allows you to "step through" a movement and view the changes in the video images, stick figures and related data. Note that the title bar (at the upper left corner of the window) shows that the file JHKick2S is selected for analysis.

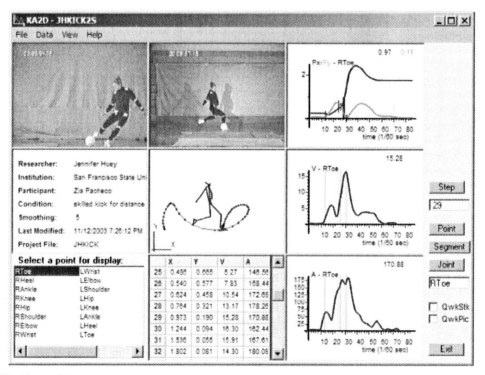

Figure 3-37. The KA2D program screen.

File Info Viewport

The illustration below is taken from SFSU student Jennifer Huey's study of the soccer kick. The kinematic data for the side view of the second trial is shown in the KA2D window. The KA file name for the study (JHKick2S) includes abbreviated information for each of these bits of information (Jennifer Huey Soccer **Kick** trial **2** Side view). Notice that the middle row pane on the left side of the screen shows more detailed information on this study:

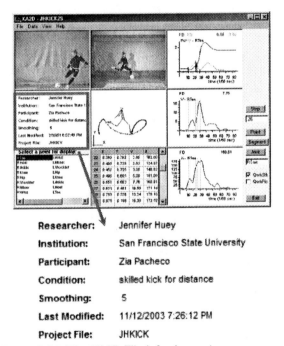

Researcher:	Jennifer Huey
Institution:	San Francisco State University
Participant:	Zia Pacheco
Condition:	skilled kick for distance
Smoothing:	5
Last Modified:	11/12/2003 7:26:12 PM
Project File:	JHKICK

Figure 3-38. The KA2D File Info viewport.

Notice that the name of the skilled performer is listed as well as that of the researcher. Perhaps, as a result of your work in this course, you too will become famous and have your name or pictures published as scientific data on the Internet!

Video Image Viewports

Because this side view file (JHKick2S) is part of a three-dimensional study, both the front view and the side view video images are available for review in the upper left side of the program window. These video images are synchronized to assure that both of the video images represent nearly the same instant in time.

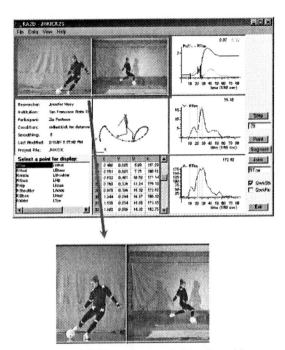

Figure 3-39. KA2D front view and side view video image viewports.

Position Data Viewport

The X and Y *position* data is plotted as a function of time in the upper right viewport of KA2D. The two curves show the data for the currently selected pattern of motion point. In the figure below, the right toe point data is shown. The dark shaded curve shows how the X coordinate values of the right toe vary as a function of time. The lightly shaded curve shows the Y coordinate values.

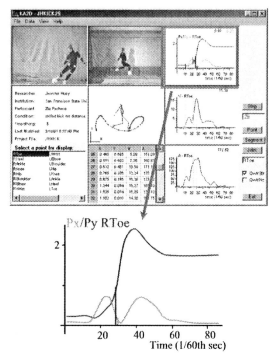

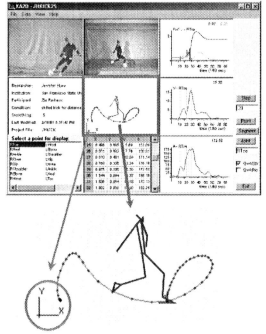

Figure 3-40. The KA2D Position data viewport.

Stick Figure Viewport

The XY values are expressed with respect to an origin point that is illustrated in the bottom left hand corner of the stick figure viewport.

Figure 3-41. The KA2D Stick figure viewport.

As the toe moves to the right in the stick figure (in the plus X direction) the values of X get larger. Similarly, as the toe moves from low to high (in the plus Y direction) the values of Y increase. All of the kinematic measures on the KA2D screen are expressed in metric units. Thus, the X and Y position curve information is expressed in meters.

The pattern of motion for the right toe point is shown on the stick figure illustration. Each black dot on the curve represents the location of the toe at each successive instant in time during the course of the movement. Because the interval between each image is set as a constant value (usually 1/60th second) the distance between each dot on the pattern can be used to estimate the velocity of the toe. When the dots are far apart, the toe is moving quickly. When the dots are close together, the toe is moving more slowly.

Velocity Curve Viewport

The right toe velocity data is shown in the middle row, right side viewport.

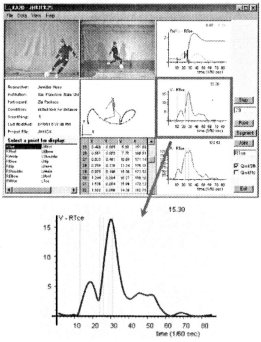

Figure 3-42. The KA2D Velocity curve viewport.

The toe velocity curve shows that the foot is moving very quickly near the moment of ball impact. The stick figures and the video images for the figure below show the position of the body for the 29th frame in the image set. At the moment illustrated in the stick figure, the toe velocity is nearly at a peak value. A yellow highlight bar shows the toe velocity value for frame 29. The value of the toe velocity, expressed in meters per second, can be read from the vertical axis on the velocity curve. The numerical value for the velocity at the currently shown frame is also shown at the upper right portion of the velocity curve viewport.

Note that the scale for the velocity curve has been set to fit the data for the currently selected point. If a different, slower-moving point were selected for display, the velocity curve height would be scaled up to fit the new data. As a result, when you compare the size of different variable plots in KA, be sure to note the vertical scale on the left side of the curve.

As the stick figure advances, the highlight bar on the velocity curve moves to the right. When frame 31 is shown, the stick figure and video images show the toe making contact with the ball. The velocity curve highlight bar also advances to the ball impact event. Notice that a vertical line is shown on the velocity curve plot to indicate the ball impact event. An abbreviated code for each event name is shown at the upper left side of the velocity curve viewport whenever an event frame is reached. Notice that the letters "BI" (for Ball Impact) are shown in the figure below.

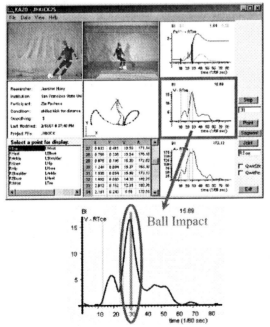

Figure 3-43. Event markers in the velocity curve viewport.

Three other events occurred earlier in the soccer kick motion: right Toe Off, leg Back Swing End, and left Foot Down. The vertical lines on the velocity curve indicate the frame numbers for these events.

Acceleration Curve Viewport

The KA2D software shows point acceleration data at the bottom right viewport.

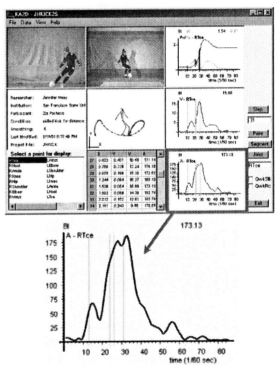

Figure 3-44. The KA2D Acceleration curve viewport.

We will see in Chapter 11 that acceleration measures can often be used to calculate the forces that are generated during human movement.

Numerical Data Viewport

The bottom row middle viewport shows the numerical data associated with the currently selected point.

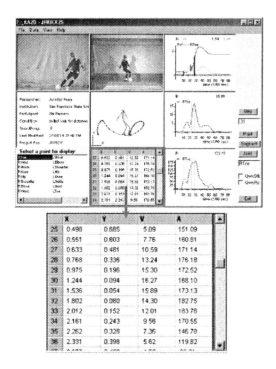

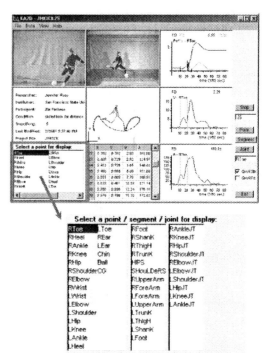

Figure 3-45. The KA2D Numerical data viewport.

Figure 3-46. The KA2D quick pick viewport.

The left-most column shows the frame numbers for the image set. The remaining columns show the X coordinate, Y coordinate, Velocity and Acceleration data respectively. The X and Y coordinate values are expressed in meters. The origin for the XY reference frame is typically placed at the bottom left corner of the stick figure motion. As the stick figure is animated forward and back on the screen, a yellow highlight bar indicates the numbers for the currently shown frame. The scroll bar on the right side of the viewport can be dragged up and down to quickly jump to a given frame in the image set

Quick Pick Viewport

The lower left "Quick Pick" viewport can be used to quickly select new points, segments or joints for review.

The amount of information that can be shown in the Quick Pick viewport depends upon the resolution of your PC display. The upper portion of the figure below shows KA2D in 640x480 reduced size mode. The lower portion of the figure shows the quick pick information from KA2D in 1024x768 mode. The higher screen resolution allows room to display all of the point names, segment names and joint names associated with the project.

To select a new point for review, click on the point name in the Quick Pick viewport. The figure below shows the KA2D screen with the body's center of gravity (CG) point selected for display.

When you click the mouse on the "CG" point name in the Quick Pick viewport, the stick figure pattern of motion shows the pattern for the body CG point. In addition, the position, velocity and acceleration curve viewports all change to show the data for the CG point. Thus, the Quick Pick viewport allows us to show the kinematic data for any body landmark point in our project with a single click of the mouse.

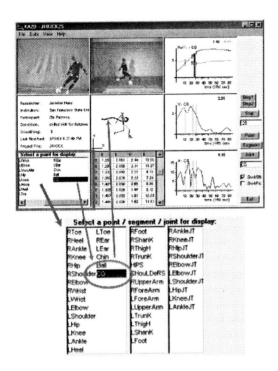

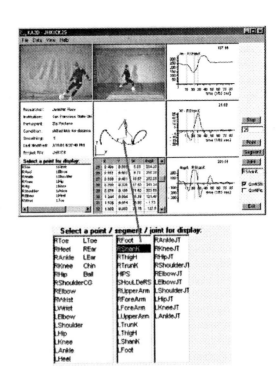

Figure 3-47. Selecting a new point from the quick pick viewport causes changes to the stick figure, numerical data, position, velocity and acceleration display areas.

Figure 3-48. Selecting a new segment for display causes all data viewports to display angular kinematic data.

If sufficient space is available, the Quick Pick viewport will also show the segments associated with a project. If you click the **RShank** segment name in the middle list, the *angular* kinematic data for the right shank will be shown. The right shank segment will be shown as a "fat" green line on the stick figure and the *angular* position, *angular* velocity and *angular* acceleration for this segment will be shown on the right side viewports. Angular kinematics will be discussed in detail in Part 4 of this book.

Measures for the various joints in your project are shown when a given joint is selected from the quick pick viewport. The figure below shows the joint angle and rate of change of joint angle data for the right knee. Chapter 18 will cover the details associated with joint angle measures.

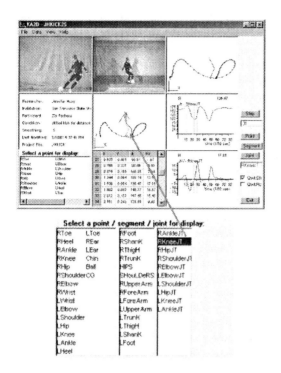

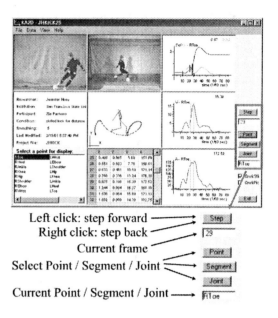

Figure 3-49. Selecting a new joint for display causes all data viewports to display joint angle data.

Right Side Controls

The controls on the right side of the KA2D window provide access to commonly used program features. The **Step** button is used to step forward or back exactly one frame at a time. If you Left click **Step** the KA2D data will animate forward one frame. If you right click the **Step** button the KA2D will animate backward one frame at a time.

Figure 3-50. KA2D right side controls.

The **Point, Segment,** and **Joint** buttons provide access to the various kinematic measures in your project, much like the Quick Pick viewport. The name of the currently selected point, segment or joint is shown in the text box below these buttons.

The lower section of the right side control area includes check boxes that allow you to modify the playback speed of the software.

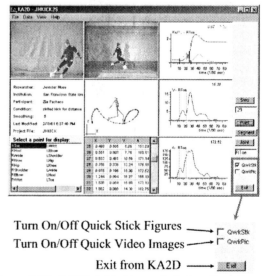

Figure 3-51. KA2D right side controls (continued).

The **QwkStk** (quick stick figure) checkbox, if checked, will allow the stick figure graphics to be animated as quickly as possible. If you find that some of the lines on a stick figure overlap and disappear, un-check this box to improve the stick figure appearance. The **QwkPic** (quick picture) checkbox, if un-checked, will allow the software to display every video image as the KA2D program is played forward or back. If the **QwkPic** checkbox is checked, the stick figure will animate very quickly, but the video images will only be updated when the mouse button is released. The **QwkPic** feature should be left on to increase the performance of a "slow" PC in normal operations, and turned off when you need to step slowly and carefully through the data. If you have a "fast" PC, you may find it convenient to leave **QwkPic** off all of the time.

Menu Commands

The File, Data, View and Help KA2D menu items can be accessed like those of any Windows program. You can activate the KA Help menu option anytime to read about all of the other KA menu options.

The **File, Secondary File** command is one of the most important program options in KA2D. With this command you can perform side-by-side comparisons of two trials of movement data. The figure below shows a comparison of a skilled and an intermediate level performer in a soccer kick. Notice that when two files are loaded, the KA2D screen configuration changes. The first performer's video and stick figures are shown in the upper left side. The stick figure and video data for the second performer is shown in the upper middle portion of the screen. The velocity and acceleration curves for both performers are combined in the lower right side viewports. The first performer's data is shown in blue on the computer screen, while the second performer is shown in the pink.

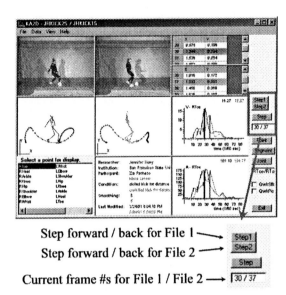

Step forward / back for File 1 ⟶
Step forward / back for File 2 ⟶
Current frame #s for File 1 / File 2 ⟶ 30 / 37

Figure 3-52. KA2D – dual file display mode right side controls.

When data from two different subjects or trials of data are compared, you will often find that the duration of the movements and the location of critical events will not be identical. As a result, you may need to *synchronize* the data for both performers by advancing the stick figures independently to a common event marker. The **Step1** and **Step2** buttons have been used to advance each trial separately to "equivalent" frame numbers in the above figure.

KA3D Software Overview

To run the KA3D program, activate the **Start, Programs, KAVideo, KA3D** menu option on your PC. The KA3D software allows you to combine the data from a pair of front and side view 2D trials into a single three-dimensional trial. For example, the JHKick2F and JHKick2S 2D soccer kick trials can be processed with the KA3D **File, Create 3D File** menu option to generate a single JHKick2 three-dimensional data file. The figure below shows the 3D data for the JHKick2 file.

The layout of the KA3D data viewports is very similar to that of the KA2D program. The KA3D program shows the video and stick figures for the front and side views of the movement in the upper left viewports. The overhead view of the movement is determined from a mathematical analysis of the data and shown in the bottom-middle viewport.

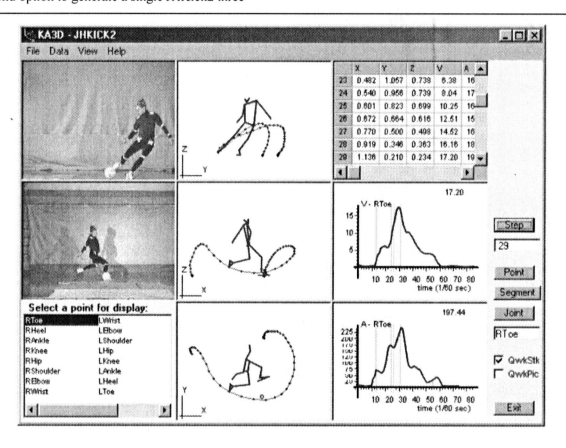

Figure 3-53. The KA3D program screen.

All of the kinematic measures in the KA3D program are more accurate than those in the original 2D data sets. For example, the right toe velocity at frame 38 is measured as 3.59 mps by the KA2D software. The toe velocity for the same frame is computed as 9.76 mps by the 3D software. The KA2D software has underestimated the toe velocity because it considers only the two-dimensional side view data in its calculations. As a result, any motion into or out of the side view plane is ignored in the two-dimensional analysis. The overhead view of the movement shows that there is considerable side-to-side motion of the toe at frame 38. The three-dimensional analysis takes this motion into account and computes the toe velocity as a larger, correct, value. Many other kinematic measures, particularly joint angle, angular velocity and angular acceleration, are often inaccurately measured by 2D calculations. For example, in order to get good estimates of joint angles from two-dimensional data, both of the limb segments associated with the joint must be isolated in the side view plane.

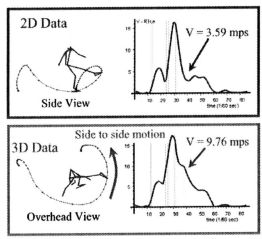

Figure 3-54. A comparison of toe velocity data as measured by the KA2D and KA3D software.

If you are interested in only the peak velocity of the kicking motion, the two-dimensional data provides a reasonable estimate of the true toe movement. Because the motion of the foot is well isolated in the side view plane at the moment of ball impact, the 2D and 3D calculations for velocity are nearly the same (15.89 mps and 16.24 mps respectively).

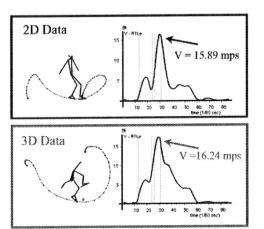

Figure 3-55. A comparison of toe velocity data for a movement that is well isolated in the side view plane.

XYZ Reference Frame Convention

The upper right viewport of KA3D shows the XYZ coordinate data for the currently selected point. This XYX data is expressed with respect to a standard three dimensional reference frame where:

1) The +X axis is set in the horizontal plane and aimed forward.
2) The +Y axis is set in the horizontal plane and aimed to the left of the line of motion.
3) The +Z axis is aimed upward.

	X	Y	Z	V	A
1	0.293	1.051	0.045	0.42	6.23
2	0.293	1.048	0.038	0.33	6.64
3	0.293	1.047	0.034	0.21	6.47
4	0.294	1.046	0.032	0.10	5.25
5	0.294	1.046	0.031	0.02	2.83
6	0.293	1.046	0.032	0.02	1.36
7	0.293	1.046	0.032	0.02	4.08
8	0.293	1.046	0.032	0.10	4.78
9	0.294	1.047	0.031	0.19	2.26
10	0.295	1.047	0.028	0.20	11.09

Figure 3-56. The KA3D numerical data viewport.

Given this reference frame, the front view stick figure is generated by plotting the Y data along the horizontal axis and the Z data along the vertical axis. Similarly, the side view stick figure is generated by plotting the X data along the horizontal axis and the Z data along the vertical axis. The overhead view, while not seen by any physical camera, can be generated by plotting the X data on the horizontal and the Y data on the vertical axis.

3D Reference Frame

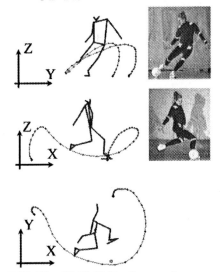

Figure 3-57. The KA3D XYZ reference frame convention.

Question 5:
The XYZ coordinates of the right toe of a soccer kick performer are shown below for frames 40 and 34:
Frame 40: (2.62, 0.99, 0.65)
Frame 34: (2.34, 0.16, 0.27)

How far did the toe travel in the forward direction between frames 34 and 40?

O A. 0.28 meters   O B. –0.28 meters   O C. 2.62 meters

Question 6:
The XYZ coordinates of the right toe of a soccer kick performer are shown below for frames 40 and 34:
Frame 40: (2.62, 0.99, 0.65)
Frame 34: (2.34, 0.16, 0.27)

How far did the toe travel in the *upward* direction between frames 34 and 40?

O A. 0.28 meters   O B. 0.38 meters   O C. 0.83 meters

KA3D File Compare Mode

If the **File, Secondary File** menu option is used to compare two 3D data files, a screen similar to the figure below is shown.

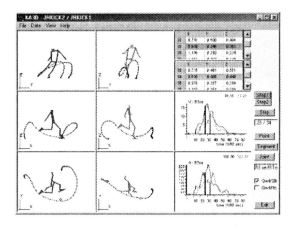

Figure 3-58. KA3D file compare mode.

Notice that the front, side and overhead stick figures for the first and second file are shown in the left side and middle columns of viewports respectively. As with the KA2D program, the stick figure and kinematic data for the first file are shown on the computer screen in blue, while the secondary file color is set as pink.

Because the KA3D program has a lot of information to display, the video images for the movements are not shown by default. The side view images are shown when the **View, Compare Mode, Side View Pic** menu option is selected (or when the <F7> function key is pressed).

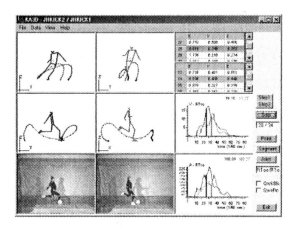

Figure 3-59. KA3D file compare mode with side view picture option activated.

The remaining program options are virtually identical to those of the KA2D program. See the printed KA Manual for details.

Supplemental KA Programs

In addition to the three main KA programs (KAVideo, KA2D and KA3D), there are a number of supplemental programs that will also be used in this course:

BallFlight Software

The BallFlight program is used to display projectile motion problems. To run BallFlight, activate the Windows **Start, Programs, KAVideo, BallFlight** menu option.

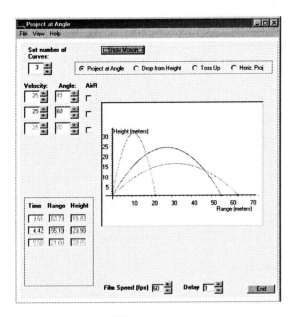

Figure 3-60. The BallFlight program screen.

BallFlight allows you to simulate the movement of projectiles (kicked balls, performers of a dance leap or long jump, etc.) on the PC screen. You can compare the motion of as many as 6 projectiles at once. In addition, you can modify the take off velocity and angle of projection of any projectile and observe the resulting movement. You will use this program to study uniformly accelerated motion in Chapter 8.

JtCalc Software

JtCalc allows you to display important forces and torques (the effect of forces that cause rotation) for running, dance leap and jumping movements. The program allows you to observe ground reaction forces and leg joint torques as they change as a function of time during the course of the movement. The figure below shows the data for a runner on a treadmill. The stick figure in the left side viewport shows the forces that are acting between the performer's foot and the ground. The right column of figures shows estimates of the bone on bone joint reaction forces at the leg joints as well as the leg joint torques. We will use this software to supplement our study of kinetics in Parts 3 and 5.

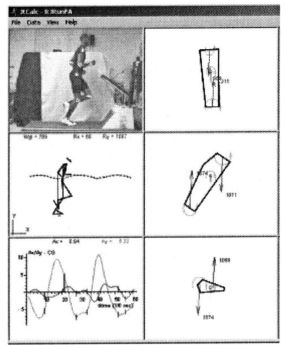

Figure 3-61. A portion of the JtCalc program screen.

Hydrodynamic Analysis Software

The Hydrodynamic Analysis (HA) software is used to display the hand forces involved in human swimming movements. The figure below shows the three-dimensional movement data for a skilled freestyler. The wire frame figures in the right column show the hand, forearm and upper arm positions during the course of the underwater pull. The hand propulsive forces are represented by the three force vectors shown on the wire frame figures. We will use the HA software to supplement our study of fluid mechanics in Chapter 25.

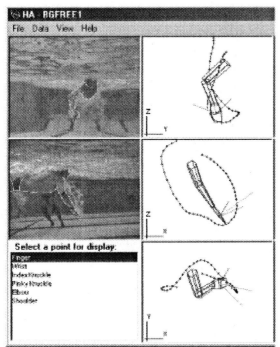

Figure 3-62. A portion of the Hydrodynamic Analysis (HA) program screen.

Conclusions

Our introduction to the KA software is now complete. The meaning of all of the kinematic measures mentioned in this chapter will be discussed in detail in the remaining chapters of this book. The course CD-Rom includes KA exercises at the end of most chapters. These exercises will help you to integrate theory and practice as you proceed with the work in your course.

Answers to Chapter Questions

Question 1:
Which of the following research topics seems to be best suited for use in a video based biomechanical analysis project?

O A. Isometric exercise training.
O B. Dart throwing.
O C. A javelin throw.

The correct answer is C. The javelin throw is a "maximal force output skill" that could be studied with as few as two 3D video trials.

Response A: Because isometric exercise does not involve *movement*, it would be a very poor choice for a video based analysis project. You should bear in mind

that this same topic would be very good for an EMG based study in an Exercise Physiology class.

Response B: Skill in dart throwing involves accuracy and consistency. In order to acquire information on consistency, we would need to collect and analyze multiple trials of video data and then perform a statistical analysis of the results. Because collecting large quantities of video information on a computer can place heavy demands on your hardware, it would be best to save this project idea for a more advanced class in movement analysis, ideally with access to automatic digitizing hardware/software. (KA supports automatic digitizing, but this software is more advanced than the standard KA software modules.)

Question 2:
What would be a good name for the side view of trial 1 in John Smith's study of a long jump?

O A. SideViewLongJump
O B. Long Jump – Side view trial 1
O C. JSLongJump1S

The correct answer is C.

Response A: This name does not include information on the researcher's name. If another student in the class also studies a long jump, her files will write on top of the John Smith files. In addition, the S character at the end of the file name must be present in order for KA to "know" that the file is part of a 3D study. KA will look for a file name starting with the same first characters and ending in F when it tries to compute 3D data.

Response B: This name does not include information on the researcher's name. If another student in the class also studies a long jump, her files will write on top of the John Smith files. In addition, the S character at the end of the file name must be present in order for KA to "know" that the file is part of a 3D study. KA will look for a file name starting with the same first characters and ending in F when it tries to compute 3D data.

Question 3:
You have downloaded the information for an image set onto 2 floppy disks. Will you be able to take these disks to your uncle's house and do your digitizing on his PC this weekend?

O Yes. The disks have all the information you need to do work on any computer.
O No. You uncle's PC will not be able to work with these files.

The correct answer is B. Your uncle almost certainly does not have KA installed on his PC. You must use the KAVideo, Process, Upload program option to gain access to the image files on the floppy disks. Further, note that the disks with your image files have only the image files on them. The KA program is much too large to fit on 2 floppy disks.

Response A: Sorry, your uncle's PC will not allow you do work with these disks unless he has installed the KA software on his system. We are sure that your uncle is a savvy computer user, but most people do not have KA installed on their systems. Thus, you will have to bring your KAPro CD-ROM with you and install the software if you want to work on his PC.

Question 4:
You have just completed digitizing the data for both a highly skilled and a novice baseball pitcher. When you inspect the data in KA2D, you are surprised to see that the novice performer has a peak ball velocity that is 50 times greater than that of the skilled pitcher. How do you interpret this "finding"?

O A. This novice pitcher should sign up for the pros right now.
O B. There must be a mistake in the scale factor digitizing for the novice performer.

The correct answer is B. The scale factor determines the size of objects (i.e., the performer's height, expressed in meters) and related measures such as velocity.

Response A: Every number that appears on a computer screen is not necessarily absolutely true. If you make a mistake in digitizing the scale factor for a trial, every measure in the trial could be scaled up to an unrealistic value.

Question 5:
The XYZ coordinates of the right toe of a soccer kick performer are shown below for frames 40 and 34:
Frame 40: (2.62, 0.99, 0.65)
Frame 34: (2.34, 0.16, 0.27)

How far did the toe travel in the forward direction between frames 34 and 40?

O A. 0.28 meters   O B. −0.28 meters   O C. 2.62 meters

The correct answer is A. The forward motion of the toe is given by the X coordinate data. The X coordinate at frame 34 is 2.34. The X coordinate at frame 40 is 2.62. As a result the toe moves +.028 meters forward.

Response B: The forward motion of the toe is given by the X coordinate data. The X coordinate at frame 34 is 2.34. The X coordinate at frame 40 is 2.62. As a result the toe moves +.028 meters forward.

Response C: The distance between the origin of the reference frame and the toe at frame 40 is 2.62 meters in the forward direction. However, the forward motion of the toe between frame 34 and 40 is given by the difference in the X coordinate values for those two frames. The X coordinate at frame 34 is 2.34. The X coordinate at frame 40 is 2.62. As a result the toe moves +.028 meters forward.

Question 6:
The XYZ coordinates of the right toe of a soccer kick performer are shown below for frames 40 and 34:
Frame 40: (2.62, 0.99, 0.65)
Frame 34: (2.34, 0.16, 0.27)

How far did the toe travel in the *upward* direction between frames 34 and 40?

O A. 0.28 meters   O B. 0.38 meters   O C. 0.83 meters

The correct answer is B. The upward motion of the toe is given by the Z coordinate data. The Z coordinate at frame 34 is 0.27. The Z coordinate at frame 40 is 0.65. As a result the toe moves +0.38 meters upward.

Response A: The upward motion of the toe is given by the Z coordinate data. The Z coordinate at frame 34 is 0.27. The Z coordinate at frame 40 is 0.65. As a result the toe moves +0.38 meters upward.

Response C: In a 3D movement problem, the Y component of motion represents side-to-side motion. The upward motion of the toe is given by the Z coordinate data. The Z coordinate at frame 34 is 0.27. The Z coordinate at frame 40 is 0.65. As a result the toe moves +0.38 meters upward.

Part 2 - Linear Kinematics

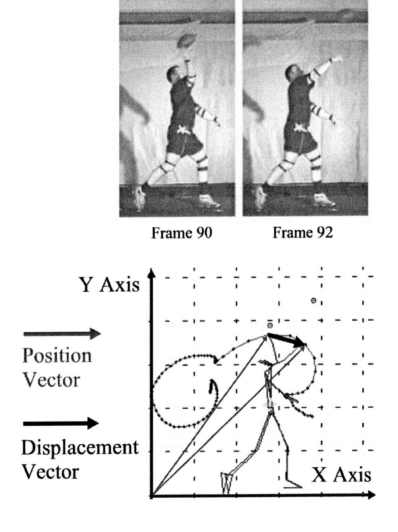

Frame 90   Frame 92

Chapter 4: Introduction to Linear Kinematics

Linear Kinematics

As students of human movement, we are concerned with a wide array of motions, ranging from simple pointing tasks to the advanced skills of an Olympic gymnast. Because movement analysis problems can become complex, our first order of business will be to take advantage of strategies that will simplify our analysis task. As mentioned in Chapter 2, reductionism can be used very well to isolate the *mechanical* factors associated with human movement. Further, the physical aspects of human motion can, in turn, be studied through numerous levels of analysis and each level can be studied separately with no loss of information.

For example, suppose we are interested in the performance of a tennis serve. We may elect to focus our attention, at least initially, on the motion of a single point. By comparing the rackethead motion of two performers in the serve we provide an objective basis for evaluation of the movement.

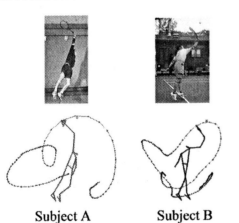

Subject A   Subject B

Figure 4-1. Tennis serve rackethead pattern of motion data for two different examples of tennis serve technique.

Question 1:
Inspect the spacing between the dots on the rackethead pattern of motion curve. Which performer has the fastest racket motion?

O A. Subject A
O B. Subject B

Reductionism is a Plan, not a Goal

The speed of motion of the rackethead will clearly be important in the skillful performance of the tennis serve. However, because we are interested in the *process* of skillful movement (and not simply the movement *product* such as ball velocity or racket velocity) we will want to know where the high racket velocity of subject A "came from". Was it simply a result of superior strength? Or did subject A coordinate the arm and body motion more efficiently that subject B? To answer these questions we will need to consider the motions of other points (the wrist, elbow, shoulder, etc.) and body segments (the hand, forearm, upperarm, trunk, etc.) in our tennis serve analysis.

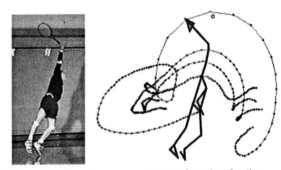

Figure 4-2. Tennis serve patterns of motion for the shoulder, elbow, wrist and rackethead points.

We see from this example that reductionism will allow us to focus our attention and quantify critical aspects of human movement. Given knowledge gained at a first level of analysis, we can move on to study other aspects of the movement, much like a detective following a thread of evidence. For us, reductionism is *not* the end goal of our analysis, it is a plan inherent in our research strategy. It would be foolhardy to expect that we could use reductionism to establish a *single* measurement that could be used to define the intricacies of skillful and efficient behavior. Instead, reductionism allows us to "divide and conquer" difficult problems *without* resorting to oversimplified and subjective interpretations.

It is interesting to note that the motion of a single point provides critical information in our tennis serve analysis. In fact, it follows that if we were to perform an analysis of each individual body landmark point (wrist, elbow, shoulder, etc.) we could generate an extensive quantitative description of the body's motion. As a result, we see that any human movement, no matter how complex, can be broken down and studied on a point-by-point basis. Given this approach, our analysis techniques do not need to be as complex as you might expect. If we can analyze the motion of a single point effectively, we will have the ability to study a complete body motion, at least at the linear kinematic level. Our work in this chapter will focus upon *kinematics*:

Kinematics

Kinematics is the branch of mechanics that describes motion (in terms of position, displacement, velocity and acceleration). Kinematics is traditionally broken into two areas, *Linear* Kinematics and *Angular* Kinematics:

Linear kinematics

Linear Kinematics is the study of the linear and curvilinear motion of a particle (a single point) in terms of position, displacement, velocity and acceleration. For example, the motion of a runner's center of gravity point will provide information that can be used to compare and evaluate the performances of a variety of performers.

Linear Kinematics

Figure 4-3. The first stride out of the blocks on a track strart.

Angular Kinematics

Angular Kinematics is the study of rotational motion (for solid bodies) in terms of angular position, angular displacement, angular velocity and angular acceleration. A giant swing in gymnastics provides a good example of a movement that can be very well described by angular kinematic variables.

Angular Kinematics

Figure 4-4. A giant swing in gymnastics.

For this chapter, we will focus upon linear kinematics only. It is interesting to note that the order of presentation in this book reflects the same reductionism that we will apply to the analysis of human motion. Our study of linear kinematics in this chapter will allow us to define the motion of critical body landmarks objectively. Given this knowledge, we will be prepared to study the forces that cause motion in Chapter 11. Further, we will be prepared to study the kinematics of solid bodies (rather than individual points), in Chapter 14.

Measurements of Human Motion

Our work in linear kinematics will allow us to describe and quantify human motion. In particular, we will define the motion of a point through measures of its *position, displacement, velocity* and *acceleration*. The following sections describe each of these terms in detail.

Position and Displacement

Linear kinematics is synonymous with the term *particle* kinematics. Many people prefer the term "particle kinematics" because it focuses our attention on the study of motion of a single point. A *particle* is defined as an infinitely small point that we can study as it moves about in two and three-dimensional space. Our discussions in Chapter 3 illustrated how we can inspect the motion of different body points with biomechanical analysis software. The figure below shows three different patterns of motion for a golf drive. KA will allow us to study the linear kinematics data (i.e., position, displacement, velocity and acceleration) for these three points and any other points digitized for this image set.

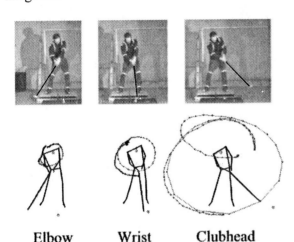

Elbow   Wrist   Clubhead
Figure 4-5. Golf drive patterns of motion.

It should be noted that the word "linear" in linear kinematics does not limit our study to motions on a straight line. The skills we develop in this chapter will allow us to study the motion of a point within any two or three dimensional reference frame (X and Y for two-dimensional data, or X, Y, and Z for three dimensional data).

Question 2:
In a 2D analysis, what dimension of the movement represents vertical motion?

O A. the X axis   O B. the Y axis

Measures of Position

Position provides information on the location of a point at any instant in time. Measures of position are provided by the XY (or XYZ) coordinate values for the point at a given instant in time. The following figure shows the two-dimensional position data for the right toe of a soccer player.

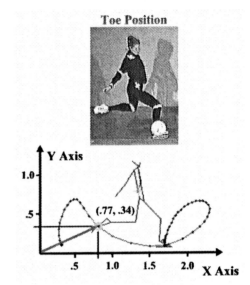

Figure 4-6. Soccer kick; toe position data.

Note that the units along the X and Y-axes are expressed in meters. The position of the toe point is given by the XY coordinates (.77, .34).

Question 3:
The above figure shows the toe at frame 28 for the image set. Three frames later, the toe reaches the lowest point in the pattern of motion arc. To the nearest .1 meters, what is the approximate coordinate value of the toe at frame 31?

O A. (2.0, .2)   O B. (1.5, .1)   O C. (0.5, .9)

Measures of Linear Displacement

Change in position, or *displacement*, provides information about the direction of motion and distance between two specified locations. Mathematically, displacement (**D**) is defined as change in position:

$$\mathbf{D} = (\mathbf{P_f} - \mathbf{P_i})$$

Where:
$\mathbf{P_f}$ final position
$\mathbf{P_i}$ initial position

Very simple studies of motion will look at only the start and end positions of a moving point. If we study a moving point on video, we will have many measures of the position of the point (one for each field in the video). Under these circumstances, the initial and final instances of time can be taken to mean the first and last video field for any portion of the movement that we choose to analyze.

The figure below shows a measure of displacement for the right toe point of a soccer player. The lower portion of this illustration shows two stick figures superimposed upon one another. Note that the frame numbers (28 and 31) of each stick figure are shown next to the two toe point locations. We see that the displacement arrow indicates the approximate distance traveled and direction of motion of the toe. If we were to look at shorter intervals of time (i.e., between images 28 and 29) the estimate of toe motion would be even better.

Image 28   Image 31

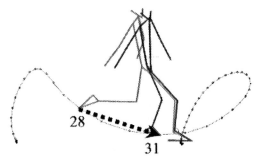

Displacement

Figure 4-7. A measure of soccer kick toe displacement.

Technically, *displacement* is the straight-line distance between two points (i.e., the dotted line arrow shown above) and *distance* is the true curved line distance followed by the toe. As a result, for video data on a movement, the distance traveled between two video fields will be slightly longer than the displacement between the two points. However, if we collect our position data from every field on the video (i.e., at $1/60^{th}$ second intervals) displacement will very closely approximate distance.

Measures of Velocity

We will see in the next chapter that the terms *velocity* and *speed* can be used synonymously for typical problems in biomechanics. Velocity (**V**) provides a measure of the *rate of change* of position:

$$\mathbf{V} = (\mathbf{P_f} - \mathbf{P_i}) / \text{time}$$

Velocity can also be expressed as displacement divided by time:

$$\mathbf{V} = (\mathbf{D}) / \text{time}$$

You have probably seen this velocity equation expressed with other terminology (speed, distance and time).

Question 4:
Imagine that you have just completed a trip in a car. You traveled 150 miles in three hours. What is your average speed?

O A. 150 mph   O B. 65 mph   O C. 50 mph

Question 5:
What equation did you use to compute your average speed in the last question?

O A. Speed = Distance / Time
O B. Speed = Distance * Time
O C. Speed = Time / Distance

Velocity is a crucially important measurement in the study of human movement. In fact, in order to have movement, velocity must be a non-zero value. Our life experiences involve lots of situations where the appreciation of velocity is essential. Often, we find ourselves moving at high velocity as indicated by the speedometers on our cars (but hopefully not on the radar gun measurements of law enforcement officials). At other times we experience objects moving at high velocity as we play tennis, softball, baseball, soccer and other sports.

Figure 4-8. Examples of high-speed athletic movements.

Self Experiment (If you cannot do this exercise, try to image what it would feel like): Go to your neighborhood Olympic swimming pool and experience a variety of velocity measures by jumping into the water from a variety of heights: From the side of the pool; from the 1 meter diving board; from the 3 meter board, from the 5 meter platform and finally from the 10 meter platform. (The last four parts of this experiment are recommended for good swimmers only!). Note that as you approach the water from the 10 meter platform jump you will see the objects around the pool move rapidly in your field of view, and you may well see parts of your life flash before your eyes.

Figure 4-9. Velocity Self-Experiment.

Because we all have an intuitive understanding of velocity, it will be a fundamentally important measurement in any biomechanics research project. We will see in the angular kinematics chapters that the concept of velocity will be extended to help us to understand the angular velocity of rigid bodies and the joint velocities of various joints (elbow, knee, hip, etc.) of the human body.

The units of velocity are expressed as: *length / time*. In biomechanical studies velocity measures are typically reported in meters per second. It is not uncommon to see velocity measured in feet per second, miles per hour or kilometers per hour. The following table compares the speeds of four different movements in terms of meters per second, miles per hour and kilometers per hour:

Peak Movement Speed	Value Units
Swimming stroke:	
Hand	4.0 mps
(Slow)	8.9 miles/hr
	14.4 Km/hr
Volleyball serve:	12.0 mps
Fingertip	26.8 miles/hr
(Moderate)	43.2 Km/hr
Tennis serve:	40.0 mps
Rackethead	89.5 miles/hr
(High)	144.0 Km/hr
Golf drive:	50.0 mps
Clubhead	111.8 miles/hr
(Very High)	180.0 Km/hr

It will be a good idea for you to become familiar with the range of expected velocities for any movement that you study. Armed with this information, you will be able to recognize unexpectedly high values for velocity and trace them back to errors in your video digitizing work.

Velocity Curves

In typical human motions, the velocity of a given point is rarely a single fixed value. Because the size of velocity changes from instant to instant it is best plotted as a function of time. The following curve shows the toe velocity curve for the soccer kick performance we discussed above:

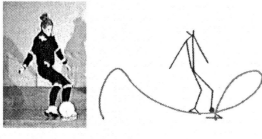

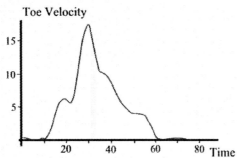

Toe Velocity

Figure 4-10. Soccer kick – toe velocity curve.

The velocity curve function plot on the lower portion of the figure shows how the speed of the right toe changes during the course of the kicking motion. The horizontal axis shows the time period for the soccer kick. The units of measure on the time axis represent the video field numbers for each image. The time for the kicking motion required a total of 86 video fields (or 1 and 26/60th seconds).

The units on the vertical axis represent toe velocity, expressed in meters per second. The velocity curve shows changes in the toe velocity as the kicking movement proceeds. The highlight bar in the velocity curve shows the velocity value at the instant in time shown by the stick figure and video field. We see that this skillful soccer player has timed her kicking motion to assure that a high toe velocity is reached very close to the instant of ball impact. We will see that many "striking" movements involve a peak in the velocity curve very close to the moment of impact.

Frequently asked question: How much time is there between two successive video fields?

Answer: Normal NTSC video cameras (used in the North and South America, Japan and about half of the world) record video at the rate of 30 frames per second. Each frame is composed of two interlaced video fields. Thus, there are 60 video fields in a second of video data. Note: the PAL/SECAM format for video (used in Europe, Asia and Africa) records 50 interlaced fields per second.

Measures of Linear Acceleration

Acceleration is a critical measure in kinematics that defines the rate of change of velocity. We will see in our chapters on kinetics that acceleration is critical to the measurement and evaluation of the forces that act upon the body.

The equation for acceleration is:
$$A = (V_f - V_i) / time$$

Thus, acceleration is a measure of the rate of change of velocity. Note that this equation is very similar to the velocity equation (velocity is defined as the rate of change of *position*). The highest values of acceleration are often associated with high speed motions. However, peak measures of acceleration and peak measures of velocity never occur at the same instant in time. We will see that peak values for acceleration always precede peak values in velocity. For example, when you pull away from a stop sign in your turbo-charged sports car, you will accelerate over the first few seconds and then arrive at your peak cruising velocity (we assume no greater than 55 mph) after that.

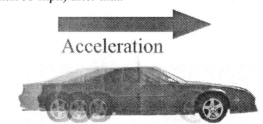

Acceleration

Figure 4-11. An example of acceleration.

Let's assume that your car accelerates from 0 to 25 meters per second (this is about equal to 55 mph) in a time period of 5 seconds. Your change in velocity will be:

Change in velocity = $(V_f - V_i)$
Change in velocity = $(25 - 0)$
Change in velocity = 25 m/s

The *rate of change* of velocity (or acceleration) is obtained by dividing the change in velocity by the time interval:

$A = (V_f - V_i) / time$
$A = (25 \, m/s) / 5$
A = 5 meters per second per second

Note that if the units for *change in velocity* are meters per second, then the units for *rate* of change of velocity must be meters per second *per second*. A convenient shorthand expression for the units of acceleration is m/s^2 (meters per second squared).

Center of Gravity Acceleration

The examples we have seen so far in the KA software have included information on three types of points: 1) body landmark points (wrist, elbow shoulder etc.); 2) points on implements (ball, tennis racket head, etc.); and 3) the body center of gravity (CG) point. The third item, center of gravity, is particularly valuable in studies of the overall representative motion of the human body. Data on the CG acceleration will be very important in our discussion of the net force that acts upon the body in Chapter 11.

We will perform a detailed analysis of the center of gravity and specify the procedure needed to calculate its exact location in Chapter 21 (Angular Kinetics). For now it will be important for us to become comfortable with the center of gravity concept and its value in the kinematic level analysis of human motion.

The center of gravity location for a simply shaped object can be visualized as the "balancing" point of the object:

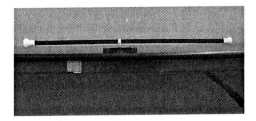

Figure 4-12. A balanced baton.

For an object that has uniform density, the CG location will be at the geometric center of the object shape.

Figure 4-13 shows the motion of a baton that has been tossed across a room. The baton is both rotating about its center of gravity point and progressing forwards and down during the last portion of its flight. The stick figure shows the pattern of motion for a point on the end of the baton as well as the position of the baton at several instances in time. The velocity curve (at the bottom right corner of the figure) shows that the end point

on the baton experiences an irregular fluctuation in velocity.

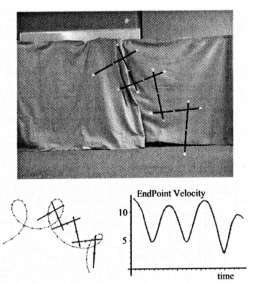

Figure 4-13. Baton end point motion and velocity curve.

The figure below shows the motion of the *center of gravity* point for the baton. Note that the pattern of motion is much simpler; it follows a smooth curved line. In addition, note that the velocity curve for the CG point is also very simple. It shows that the CG speed increases steadily as the baton falls toward the floor.

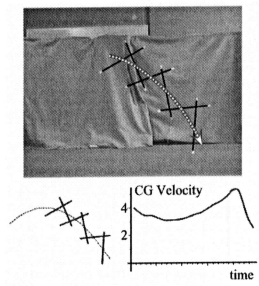

Figure 4-14. Baton center of gravity point motion and velocity curve.

The *linear* kinematics of the baton is perfectly represented by the center of gravity pattern of motion. The *angular* (rotational) component of motion for the baton is effectively removed from the data when the center of gravity point is studied.

If you were to replace the baton with a ball of the same weight and throw it with the same speed and angle of projection, the ball pattern of motion would be the same as that of the baton's CG point. The figure at right shows a comparison of the baton motion and that of a ball that is tossed with about the same speed and angle of projection.

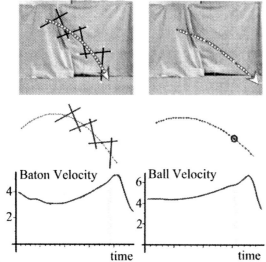

Figure 4-15. A comparison of the center of gravity motion of a baton and a ball.

Notice that the both the flight path and the velocity curve for the tossed ball are about the same as that of the baton. The small differences are a result of differences in the way the objects were thrown. We see that the center of gravity point data allows us to use reductionism to replace the complex motion of a solid object with that of a single point.

The center of gravity becomes even more valuable in the analysis of human motion. For example, when the body is in flight, the center of gravity will follow a predictable flight path in spite of the independent motions of the arms and legs. Note the similarity in the CG flight path of the skilled diver in figure 4-16 and the motion of the baton from our previous example:

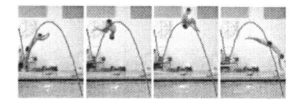

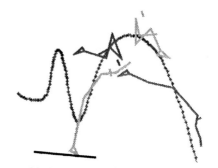

Figure 4-16. The center of gravity motion of a diver performing a 1.5 somersault front dive.

We will see in Chapter 9 that all objects (animate or inanimate) are influenced by the pull of gravity in a very predictable way. Data for the center of gravity point will allow us to measure the overall effect of gravity on the full human body and greatly simplify our analysis task.

Conclusions

Our discussion of the fundamentals issues related to measures of position, displacement, velocity and acceleration is now complete. We have seen that measures of position are analogous to the XY coordinate locations that are studied in basic math courses and geometry. Measures of displacement are used to define the changes in position, or the distance associated with a given motion. Velocity provides information on the rate of change of position. Velocity is fundamentally important in the analysis of motion – if a body has zero velocity it has no motion at all. Finally, we have seen that measures of acceleration (the rate of change of velocity) can be useful in the analysis of the net force that acts on a body in motion.

Answers to Chapter Questions

Question 1:
Inspect the spacing between the dots on the rackethead pattern of motion curve. Which performer has the fastest racket motion?

O A. Subject A
O B. Subject B

The correct answer is A. The wider spacing between the dots on the racket pattern of motion implies that the racket is moving faster for subject A.

Question 2:
In a 2D analysis, what dimension of the movement represents vertical motion?

O A. the X axis   O B. the Y axis

The correct answer is B. In a two-dimensional study, X represents the horizontal dimension and Y represents the vertical dimension.

Question 3:
The above figure shows the toe at frame 28 for the image set. Three frames later, the toe reaches the lowest point in the pattern of motion arc. To the nearest .1 meters, what is the approximate coordinate value of the toe at frame 31?

O A. (2.0, .2)   O B. (1.5, .1)   O C. (0.5, .9)

The correct answer is B. In a two-dimensional study, X represents the horizontal dimension and Y represents the vertical dimension.

Question 4:
Imagine that you have just completed a trip in a car. You traveled 150 miles in three hours. What is your average speed?

O A. 150 mph   O B. 65 mph   O C. 50 mph

The correct answer is C. If you drive at a speed of 50 miles per hour for a period of three hours, you will cover a distance of 150 miles.

Question 5:
What equation did you use to compute your average speed in the last question?

O A. Speed = Distance / Time
O B. Speed = Distance * Time
O C. Speed = Time / Distance

The correct answer is A. Your average speed (50 mph) is equal to the total distance traveled (150 miles) divided by the time for the trip (3 hours). Note that the units of speed (miles per hour) indicate that distance is in the numerator and time is in the denominator of the speed measurement.

Chapter 5: Vectors and Scalars

Our work with movement analysis data will involve an integration of theoretical evaluation and quantitative analysis skills. The quantitative aspects will, in large part, be performed with the aid of computer programs such as KA, spreadsheet software and a hand calculator. We should, nevertheless, thoroughly understand each detail in the analysis process. In particular, we should be prepared to express the fundamental equations that are used in movement analysis and solve these equations with short sets of example data.

The mathematics skills that are essential for biomechanical analysis are a direct extension of the skills developed in high school algebra and trigonometry. We will see in this chapter that working with velocity and force vectors is as easy as solving triangle problems in trigonometry.

Vector Quantities

Many of the biomechanical variables that we have already discussed (position, displacement, velocity and acceleration) are *vector quantities*:

Vector - a quantity that possesses both magnitude and direction. A vector is graphically represented as an arrow. The arrow length indicates the magnitude (size) of the vector. The direction of the vector is indicated by the angle of the arrow.

As our work in this course proceeds, we will study a wide variety of vector quantities. For example, we will work with force, momentum, angular velocity, angular acceleration, angular momentum and torque vectors.

Vectors can be used to define both three-dimensional and two-dimensional quantities. For the sake of simplicity, we will focus upon two-dimensional vectors in this chapter. These 2D vectors will help us to solve problems in uniformly accelerated motion (Chapter 8), ground reaction forces (Chapter 11) and torques (Chapter 21).

In contrast to vectors, many of the quantities that you have worked with in basic math courses are known as *scalars*:

Scalar - a quantity that can be completely described in terms of size.

Examples of scalar quantities are your age, your height, and the number of apples in a bowl. Scalar quantities that are often used in biomechanics are: mass, time, speed and angle.

Trigonometry Review

This section provides a brief review of trigonometry. (If your math skills are strong, you can skim this section quickly.)

Hypotenuse Calculation

The figure below illustrates a typical problem in trigonometry.

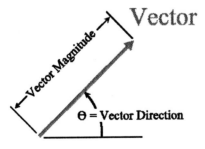

Figure 5-1. A vector is graphically represented by an arrow.

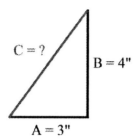

Figure 5-2. A right triangle with sides A and B and hypotenuse C.

Question 5-1:
A right triangle has a horizontal leg (A) of length 3″ and a vertical leg (B) of 4″. What equation is used to solve for the length of the hypotenuse (C)?

○ A. C = A + B
○ B. $C^2 = A^2 + B^2$
○ C. Y = MX + B

Hypotenuse Solution

The solution for the length of the hypotenuse is given below:

$$C^2 = A^2 + B^2$$
$$C^2 = 3^2 + 4^2$$
$$C^2 = 9 + 16$$
$$C^2 = 25$$
$$C = \sqrt{25}$$

C = 5 inches

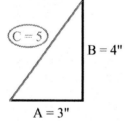

Figure 5-3. A right triangle with sides A = 3 and B = 4, will have a hypotenuse length of 5.

This triangle is unique in that all three of its legs can be expressed as whole numbers (with no decimal point). We will use this triangle in other examples; for short, we will call it a "3-4-5" triangle.

Angle Calculation

Let's now determine the angle between the hypotenuse and the horizontal. For this problem, assume that we are given only the leg lengths A and B:

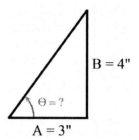

Figure 5-4. If the horizontal and vertical legs of a right triangle are known, the angle formed between the hypotenuse and the horizontal leg can be calculated with trigonometry.

Question 5-2:
A right triangle has a horizontal leg (A) of length 3″ and a vertical leg (B) of 4″. What equation is used to determine the angle between side A and the hypotenuse?

○ A. Tan(θ) = B / A
○ B. Tan(θ) = A / B
○ C. Sin(θ) = B / A

Angle Solution

The solution for the hypotenuse leg angle is given below:

$$Tan(\theta) = B / A$$
$$Tan(\theta) = 4 / 3$$
$$Tan(\theta) = 1.333$$
$$\theta = Tan^{-1}(1.333)$$
$$\theta = 53.13°$$

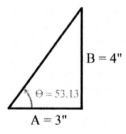

Figure 5-5. If the horizontal leg A and vertical leg B of a right triangle are known, the angle formed between the hypotenuse and the horizontal leg is equal to the $Tan^{-1}(B / A)$.

Calculator Exercise

Let's now try solving the previous problem with the Windows calculator program.

1) Click on the Start button and activate the Accessories, Calculator option.
2) In Calculator, activate the View, Scientific menu option if necessary.
3) Type the text: "4 / 3 =" (without the quotes). The screen should show the result of the calculation as 1.333...3.
4) Click the check box for "Inv" to turn on inverse operations.
5) Click the "tan" button.
6) The inverse tangent of 1.333 will be shown as 53.13 degrees.

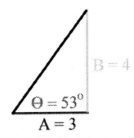

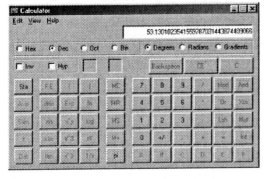

Figure 5-6. The Windows Calculator program can be used to solve problems in trigonometry.

We see that the Windows calculator program makes the calculation of angles from triangle data straightforward. You should also solve this problem on a physical hand calculator. If your course professor will be giving you traditional "in class" exams, you will need to be prepared to work with "old fashioned" technology.

Vertical Leg Length Calculation

Let's now determine the length of the triangle leg B, given only information on the hypotenuse length and the angle between the hypotenuse and the horizontal:

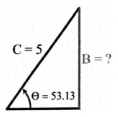

Figure 5-7. A right triangle with angle and hypotenuse data "given" and an "unknown" vertical leg length.

Question 5-3:
A right triangle has a hypotenuse (C) of 5″ and an angle of 53.13° between the hypotenuse and the horizontal. What equation is used to determine the length of the vertical leg (B)?
O A. Cos(θ) = B / C
O B. Sin(θ) = C / B
O C. Sin(θ) = B / C

Vertical Leg Length Solution

The solution for the vertical leg length is given below:

Sin(θ) = B / C
Sin(53.13) = B / 5
B = 5 * Sin(53.13)
B = 5 * .8000
B = 4

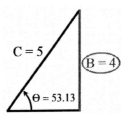

Figure 5-8. Given angle data and the hypotenuse length, the vertical leg length of a right triangle can be computed with the Sin function.

Horizontal Leg Length Calculation

The determination of the length of leg A involves a similar calculation.

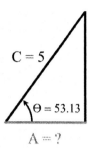

Figure 5-9. A right triangle with angle and hypotenuse data "given" and an "unknown" horizontal leg length.

Question 5-4:
A right triangle has a hypotenuse (C) of 5″ and an angle of 53.13° between the hypotenuse and the horizontal. What equation is used to determine the length of the horizontal leg (A)?

○ A. $Cos(\theta) = A / C$
○ B. $Sin(\theta) = A / C$
○ C. $Tan(\theta) = C / A$

Horizontal Leg Length Solution

The calculation of the leg A length is given below:

$Cos(\theta) = A / C$
$Cos(53.13) = A / 5$
$A = 5 * Cos(53.13)$
$A = 5 * .6000$
$A = 3$

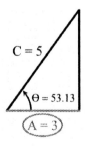

Figure 5-10. Given angle data and the hypotenuse length, the horizontal leg length of a right triangle can be computed with the Cosine function.

Vector Components

The exercises from the last section will help us to make the transition from trigonometry and *triangles* to biomechanics problems and *vectors*. In biomechanics problems, we are sometimes given the magnitude (length) and direction (angle) of a vector and asked to determine the horizontal and vertical vector *components*. The figure below illustrates the velocity vector of a soccer ball:

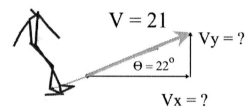

Figure 5-11. A soccer kick ball velocity vector.

The velocity vector magnitude of the ball is 21 mps. The angle of projection of the ball is 22°. The numerical values of the horizontal (Vx) and vertical (Vy) components of the velocity vector (shown by the thin black arrows in the figure) must be computed from the given data.

Horizontal Component Calculation

Question 5-5:
What equation is used to determine the Vx component of the velocity vector?

○ A. $Cos(\theta) = Vx / V$
○ B. $Sin(\theta) = Vx / V$
○ C. $Tan(\theta) = Vx / Vy$

Horizontal Component Solution

The solution for the Vx component is given below:

$Cos(\theta) = Vx / V$
$Cos(22) = Vx / 21$
$Vx = 21 * Cos(22)$

Vx = 21 * 0.934
Vx = 19.6 mps

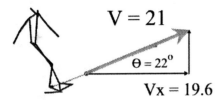

Figure 5-12. The X component of a soccer kick ball velocity vector.

Vertical Component Calculation

The Sine function can be used to determine the vertical velocity component, given the velocity magnitude and the known projection angle:

$Sin(\theta) = Vy / V$
$Sin(22) = Vy / 21$
$Vy = 21 * Sin(22)$
$Vy = 21 * 0.375$
$Vy = 7.9$ mps

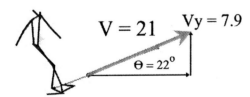

Figure 5-13. The Y component of a soccer kick ball velocity vector.

We see that working with vectors in two dimensions requires no more "math" skill than solving a triangle problem in trigonometry. The only difference (which happens to be very important) is that instead of dealing with triangle leg lengths, we are now able to deal with measures of velocity, acceleration, force, torque, momentum, angular momentum and many other variables that are crucially important in the analysis of human motion.

Vector Magnitude

For some biomechanics problems, we are given the X and Y components of a vector and asked to determine the vector *magnitude*. The illustration below shows a runner on the first stride after a track start. The horizontal and vertical force components acting on the body (R_X and R_Y) are shown. In this analysis we have determined the forces vector components through a separate analysis. At the moment shown, we acknowledge that as the runner pushes down on the ground with his legs, the ground pushes upward on the runner's body. The diagonally upward force acting on the body is called the *ground reaction force*. We will learn much more about ground reaction forces in the linear kinetics chapter. For now, our challenge will be to determine the magnitude of the ground reaction force vector (**R**).

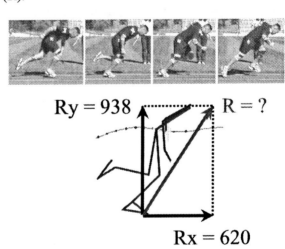

Figure 5-14. The ground reaction force generated during the first stride after a track start.

Question 5-6:
What equation is used to determine the magnitude of the ground reaction force?

○ A. R = Rx + Ry
○ B. R = Tan⁻¹(Ry/Rx)
○ C. R² = Rx² + Ry²

Resultant Force Calculation

The solution for the resultant force calculation is given below:

$$R^2 = (620)^2 + (938)^2$$
$$R^2 = 384440 + 879844$$
$$R^2 = 1264244$$
$$R = \sqrt{1264244}$$
R = 1124.4 Newtons

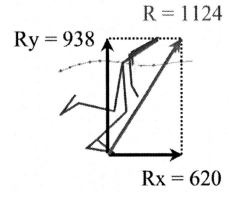

$$R = 1124$$
$$Ry = 938$$
$$Rx = 620$$

Figure 5-15. The magnitude of a ground reaction force is computed with the vector magnitude formula.

Note: a Newton is a unit of force in the metric system of measurements. One Newton is equal to 0.225 pounds.

Calculator Exercise

Run the Windows calculator program and verify that the following solution is correct:

$$R^2 = (620)^2 + (938)^2$$
$$R^2 = 384440 + 879844$$
$$R^2 = 1264244$$
$$R = \sqrt{1264244}$$
R = 1124.4 Newtons

Note: to compute the square root of an entry in the Windows calculator program, click on the "Inv" check box and then click the "X^2" button:

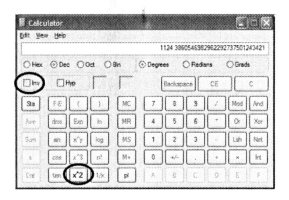

Figure 5-16. The Windows Calculator program can be used to compute square roots.

Note that the line of action of the ground reaction force is directed in front of the runner's center of gravity point. This "off center" ground reaction force helps to generate the "rotation" of the body needed for the runner to attain an upright position during the remaining portion of the run.

Vector Direction

Vectors have *two* important characteristics – magnitude and *direction*. For a two-dimensional vector, direction can be defined as the angle between the line of action of the vector and the positive X-axis. The calculation of vector direction begins with standard operations in trigonometry. The figure below shows the ground reaction force acting on a gymnast during a back somersault motion. The angle of direction is indicated by the θ character in the figure.

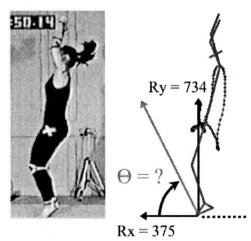

$$Ry = 734$$
$$\theta = ?$$
$$Rx = 375$$

Figure 5-17. Calculation of the angle between the ground reaction force and the horizontal line aimed to the left.

Question 5-7:
What equation is used to determine the angle between the Resultant force vector and the Rx vector?

O A. $Tan(\theta) = Ry / Rx$
O B. $Sin(\theta) = Ry / Rx$
O C. $Tan(\theta) = Rx / Ry$

The solution for the angle θ_1, between **R** and **Rx**, is given below:

$Tan(\theta_1) = Ry / Rx$
$Tan(\theta_1) = 734 / 375$
$Tan(\theta_1) = 1.957$
$\theta_1 = Tan^{-1}(1.957)$
$\theta_1 = 62.9$ degrees

Because trigonometric measures of right triangle angles can never exceed 90°, it is sometimes necessary to perform an additional calculation to determine a given vector's direction angle with respect to the positive X axis. The angle θ_2 (between the **R** vector and the positive X axis) is illustrated below:

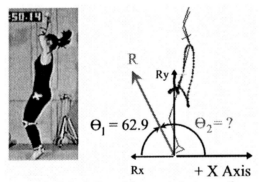

Figure 5-18. Calculation of the angle between the ground reaction force and the horizontal line aimed to the right.

Question 5-8:
The reaction force angle (θ_1), with respect to the negative X axis is 62.9°. What is the vector direction angle θ_2, expressed with respect to the positive X axis? Feel free to use a calculator (software or hardware) to determine the answer.

O A. 27.1°
O B. 117.1°
O C. 62.9°

The calculations for the above reaction force vector angle are provided below:
$\theta_1 + \theta_2 = 180°$

$62.9 + \theta_2 = 180°$
$\theta_2 = 180° - 62.9$
$\theta_2 = 117.1°$

Vectors in Kinematics

Position Vectors

Position vectors indicate the location of a given point with respect to the origin of an XY (or XYZ) reference frame. The figure below shows the coordinates of a football throw fingertip point and the position vector to the point:

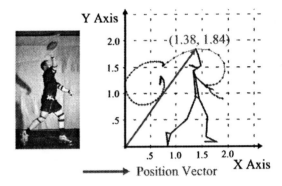

Figure 5-19. The position vector to the fingertip point is shown at a moment during the action phase of a football throw.

Position vectors are unique in that they are *bound* vectors. A bound vector is anchored at a fixed point, in this case, the origin of the XY reference frame. The X and Y components of a position vector are simply the X and Y coordinate values for the point in question. We see that the position vector to any point on the body is simply an arrow that starts at the origin and ends at the location of the point.

Note: the *origin* point of an XY reference frame is at the intersection of the X and Y axes. The coordinates of the origin are (0, 0).

Displacement Vectors

Displacement vectors show the change in position of a point over a specified time interval. The figure below illustrates the change in position between frames 90 and 92 in a football throw image set.

Frame 90　　　Frame 92

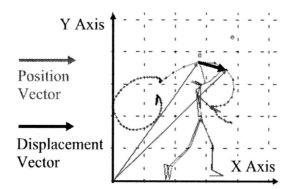

Figure 5-20. A displacement vector of fingertip point motion is shown at a moment during the action phase of a football throw.

Displacement Vector XY Components

The X and Y components of a displacement vector are given by the change in X (or ΔX), and change in Y (or ΔY) between the displacement vector start and end point. The start and end fingertip coordinate values are shown next to the displacement vector:

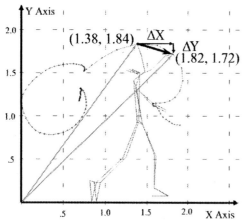

Figure 5-21. The XY coordinate values used in the determination of a displacement vector.

Question 5-9:
If the initial position of a point is (1.38, 1.84) and the final position is (1.82, 1.72), what is the ΔX value (or the displacement vector X component)?

O A. 0.44
O B. 0.46
O C. −0.44

Displacement Vector X Component

The details of the ΔX calculation are provided below:

$$\Delta X = P_{XF} - P_{XI}$$

Where:
P_{XF} = the final position X coordinate
P_{XI} = the initial position X coordinate

For our problem:
$\Delta X = P_{XF} - P_{XI}$
$\Delta X = 1.82 - 1.38$
$\Delta X = 0.44$

Thus, the X component of the displacement vector is aimed in the positive X direction and is 0.44 meters in size.

Displacement Vector Y Component

Let's now determine the Y component of the displacement vector:

Question 5-10:
If the initial position of a point is (1.38, 1.84) and the final position is (1.82, 1.72), what is the ΔY value (or the displacement vector Y component)?

O A. 0.12　　O B. 0.46　　O C. −0.12

Calculations for the Y component of the displacement vector are shown below:

$$\Delta Y = P_{YF} - P_{YI}$$

Where:
P_{YF} = the final position X coordinate
P_{YI} = the initial position X coordinate

For our problem:
$\Delta Y = P_{YF} - P_{YI}$
$\Delta Y = 1.72 - 1.84$
$\Delta Y = -0.12$

Thus, the Y component of the displacement vector is aimed in the negative Y direction and is 0.12 meters in size.

Displacement Vector Magnitude

Given the X and Y components of the displacement vector, we can compute the displacement vector magnitude as follows:

$$|D| = \sqrt{D_X^2 + D_Y^2}$$

Where:
$|D|$ = Displacement vector magnitude
D_X = Displacement vector X component
D_Y = Displacement vector Y component

If you wanted to solve this problem with a spreadsheet program, you could make use of the **Sqrt(..)** function:

$D = Sqrt(0.44^2 + (-.12)^2)$
$D = Sqrt(0.1936 + .0144)$
$D = Sqrt(0.208)$
$D = 0.456$ meters

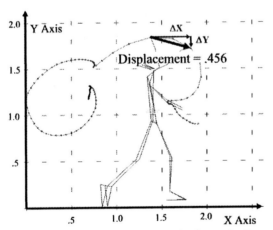

Figure 5-22. A displacement vector is shown for the fingertip point at a moment during the action phase of a football throwing motion.

Vector Equations

Given our introduction to vector quantities, we are now ready to consider some vector operations that will allow us to solve biomechanical problems more effectively. We will discuss vector addition, vector subtraction, and basic vector algebra in the following paragraphs.

Vector Addition

Our work with vector components and vector resultants has already introduced us to the concept of vector addition. Because vectors have both magnitude and direction, the process of adding two vectors together is best done graphically. An example of vector addition is provided in the figure below.

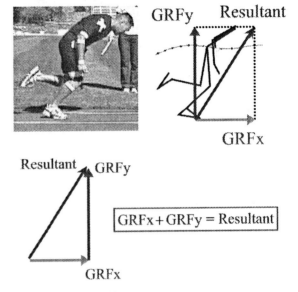

Figure 5-23. Ground reaction force components a shown for a moment during a track start.

The performer in this figure is accelerating out of the starting blocks for a track start. At the moment shown, a large forward force component (GRFx) is acting between his right foot and the ground. This force is causing his body to increase speed in the forward direction. In addition, a large vertical force component (GRFy) is acting upward on his body due to the pressure between his foot and the ground.

In our prior discussions, we have said that the effect of a resultant force is equivalent to its components. This relationship can be expressed as a vector equation:

GRFx + GRFy = Resultant

The above figure illustrates this vector addition process. Graphically, the operation of vector addition is performed as follows:

To add two vectors together, place the tail of the second vector on the head of the first vector. The vector sum is equal to the vector that extends between the tail of the first vector and the head of the second vector.

In the lower portion of the figure, the tail of the **GRFy** vector has been placed on the head of the **GRFx** vector. The sum of **GRFx** and **GRFy** is then given as the **Resultant** vector. Note that it is common practice for a vector to be "picked up and moved" during an addition operation. In our example, the **GRFy** vector from the upper portion of the figure was moved to the right in the lower portion of the figure. Note that the process of moving a vector does not change its magnitude or direction at all.

Vector addition can be performed with any two vectors. For example, the involved vectors do not need to be oriented at right angles to one another. The figure below shows the vector addition of two vectors **A**, and **B**. Both of these vectors are 5 units in length, but their angles of direction are not the same.

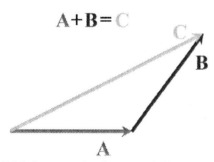

Figure 5-24. An example of vector addition.

Note that the vector **C** is clearly the correct solution to the vector equation. However, because this is a vector equation, it cannot be solved on the basis of vector magnitude information alone:

$$A + B = C$$
$$|A| + |B| \neq |C|$$

The last equation indicates that the magnitude of vector **A** plus the magnitude of vector **B** is *not* equal to the magnitude of vector **C**. The figure below shows the values for the last equation.

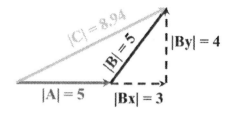

Figure 5-25. The addition of vector components is not equivalent to the addition of vectors.

The vector **B** has an X component of 3 and a Y component of 4. The length of vector **C** can be set as the hypotenuse length of a triangle with a base length of 8 and a height of 4:

$$|C| = Sqrt((8^2) + (4^2))$$
$$|C| = Sqrt((64) + (16))$$
$$|C| = Sqrt(80)$$
$$|C| = 8.94$$

This example shows that vector equations, because they include information on both magnitude and direction, cannot be directly solved with normal scalar math. However, vector equations can be easily solved if they are first broken down into scalar form. For example, the vector equation **A** + **B** = **C** can be broken down into two scalar equations:

$$Ax + Bx = Cx$$
$$Ay + By = Cy$$

These two equations can be used to determine the X and Y component of the two-dimensional vector **C**.

$$Cx = Ax + Bx$$
$$Cx = 5 + 3$$
$$Cx = 8$$

The figure shows that the X component of the **C** vector is, in fact, 8 units long. Similarly, the Y component of **C** must be 4:

$$Cy = Ay + By$$
$$Cy = 0 + 4$$
$$Cy = 4$$

As a result, we see that vector equations can be solved either graphically or through traditional scalar math. We will use both approaches to help us to both visualize and quantify problems in human movement throughout the remaining sections of this book.

Vector Subtraction

We have effectively performed a vector subtraction operation in our prior discussion on displacement vectors. We will use our displacement vector example again in this section to provide a clear illustration of the process of vector subtraction.

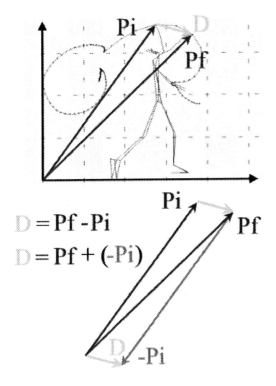

Figure 5-26. Vector subtraction is equivalent to the vector addition of the first vector with the negative value of the second vector.

The figure shows that the displacement vector (**D**) for a body landmark point is equal to the change in position of that point:

$$D = Pf - Pi$$

Where:
D = the displacement vector
Pf = the final position vector
Pi = the initial position vector

The above equation provides a simple example of vector subtraction. It is interesting to note that the above equation can be algebraically manipulated while in vector form. For example, the value of **Pi** can be added to both sides of the equation:

D = Pf - Pi
Pi + D = Pf   (add **Pi** to both sides)
Pf = Pi + D (swap the right and left sides of the equation)

The last equation shows that the vector **Pf** can be visualized as the result of a vector addition of **Pi** and **D**. The upper portion of the figure shows that when the tail of the **D** vector is placed on the head of the **Pi** vector, the resulting vector sum will be **Pf**.

The result of a vector subtraction can be visualized as the vector *addition* of the first vector with the *negative value* of the second. A negative vector can be visualized graphically by simply reversing the direction of the original vector.

The positive **Pi** vector is aimed upward and to the right in the lower portion of the figure. The negative **Pi** vector (**-Pi**) has exactly the same magnitude (length) as the **+Pi** vector but it is aimed in the opposite direction. The vectors in the lower part of the figure form a *vector parallelogram*. The vector sum of the **Pf** and the (**-Pi**) vector results in the **D** vector. The vector **D** shown at the bottom of the parallelogram can be visualized as the result of the vector addition process. Because the opposite sides of the parallelogram are of equal length by definition, the vector between the **Pi** and **Pf** vector arrowheads is also equal to **D**.

Velocity Vectors

Our work with vectors, so far, has not gone much beyond high school trigonometry. Note that our discussions of position and displacement have allowed us to quantify only *locations* and *lengths*. The units of measure of a position or displacement vector are simply meters, feet, inches, etc. As students of biomechanics, we are interested in quantifying *motion,* not just static positions and distances. Thus, we are interested in working with velocity vectors.

The velocity vector of a moving point is aimed in the direction of motion of the point and its length is equal to the velocity magnitude. Thus, slow motions have short velocity vectors and fast motions will have long velocity vectors.

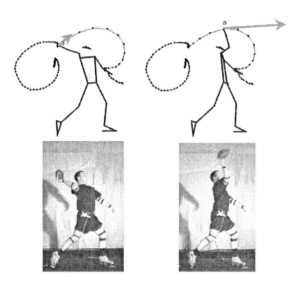

Figure 5-27. The length of a velocity vector indicates the instantaneous value of velocity.

We know from the Chapter 5 that velocity can be computed from displacement:

$\mathbf{V} = (\mathbf{D}) / \text{time}$

In this equation, the "time" value is equal to the time interval between the initial and final positions. If we sample data from every field in a video, the time interval between images is $1/60^{th}$ second and the *effective film speed* is 60 pictures per second.

For the current problem, we are considering the time elapsed between images 90 and 92 (*two* video fields). Thus, the time interval for the displacement is $2/60^{th}$ second and the effective film speed is 30 pictures per second.

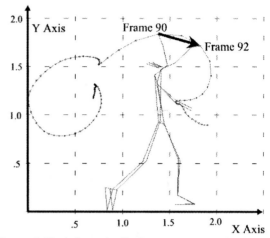

Figure 5-28. A fingertip displacement vector is shown for an instant in time during the action phase of a throwing motion.

Velocity Equation

Because dividing by a fractional time interval and multiplying by the inverse of the time interval are equivalent, we can multiply the displacement by the effective film speed to compute velocity. Because we will use this equation very often, we will call it "the velocity equation":

$\mathbf{V} = (\mathbf{D}) * \text{EFS}$

Where:
EFS = the effective film speed

Vectors carry information about magnitude and direction. Before we can solve the velocity equation, we will need to substitute the numerical values for velocity and displacement *magnitude* into the equation. As a result, we will be removing the "direction" information from the equation to allow the terms to be processed with normal (scalar) mathematics. The following form of the velocity equation emphasizes that scalar values are being used in the calculation:

$|\mathbf{V}| = (|\mathbf{D}|) * \text{EFS}$

Where:
$|\mathbf{V}|$ = the magnitude of the velocity vector
$|\mathbf{D}|$ = the magnitude of the displacement vector

However, the resulting scalar equation can be used to determine only the scalar number for velocity magnitude. Information about the velocity vector direction will need to be computed separately.

$$|V| = (|D|) * EFS$$
$$|V| = (0.456) * 30$$
$$|V| = 13.68 \text{ mps}$$

Note that this equation is equivalent to:

Speed = Distance / time
Speed = (0.456) / (1/30)
Speed = (0.456) * 30
Speed = 13.68 mps

The figure below allows us to visualize the solution of the vector equation for the football throw:

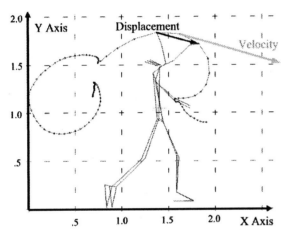

Figure 5-29. The velocity and displacement vectors are shown for an instant in time during the action phase of a throwing motion.

The figure shows that the velocity vector is "equal to" the displacement vector multiplied by the effective film speed number. When we multiply a vector by a number greater than one, we increase the vector length, but we do not change the vector direction. We see that we can *visualize* the magnitudes and directions associated with a vector equation on a stick figure graph. However, we can only solve for the *magnitudes* of the vectors with the velocity equation.

Velocity Curves in KA

The velocity curve for the football trial fingertip value is shown below. We see that the fingertip moves slowly at the beginning of the movement and reaches a peak value of velocity very close to the moment of ball release. When the information for

this curve is computed, the KA software simply takes the digitized XY values, determines displacement vector information and computes the velocity for each frame of data. KA also *smooths* the data to remove the small digitizing errors that are embedded in the XY values.

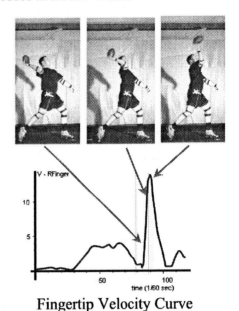

Fingertip Velocity Curve

Figure 5-30. A fingertip velocity curve for a football throwing motion.

Velocity Vectors in KA

KA will also display the velocity vector on the stick figure for any point. The figure below shows velocity vector data for the football throw:

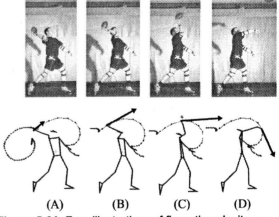

Figure 5-31. Four illustrations of fingertip velocity vectors during the action phase of a throwing motion.

Question 5-11:
For the above figure, which sub-figure (A, B, C or D) shows the velocity vector with the largest vector magnitude?

O A. O B. O C. O D.

Question 5-12:
For the above figure, which sub-figure (A, B, or C) shows the velocity vector with the largest (steepest) direction angle?

O A. O B. O C

Velocity Vector Direction

The direction of the velocity vector is tangent to the pattern of motion of the fingertip point. This will always be the case with velocity vectors. Velocity is parallel to the direction of motion, and the direction of motion is given by the pattern of motion curve.

It is interesting to note that the *scale* for the velocity vectors in the above figure is not the same as that used in our displacement vector figure (in the last section). While the displacement between frame 90 and 92 is 0.456 *meters*, the velocity between these frames is 13.79 *meters per second*. It is not necessary to draw the velocity vector on the same scale that was used for displacement, because the units are not the same. We can use a different scale for velocity to keep the velocity arrow from extending off the page. Thus, a given stick figure illustration may use a scale of one unit per inch on a displacement vector and 4 units per inch on a velocity vector.

Velocity Vector Components

Because velocity vectors typically carry information about two or three dimensions of motion, it will often be convenient to break them down into separate vector components. The vector equation for velocity:

$$\mathbf{V} = (\mathbf{D}) * EFS$$

can be broken down into two scalar equations:

$$V_X = D_X * EFS$$
$$V_Y = D_Y * EFS$$

Where:
V_X is the velocity vector X component
V_Y is the velocity vector Y component

D_X is the displacement vector X component
D_Y is the displacement vector Y component

Note: if the velocity vector is expressed as a three-dimensional vector, the components V_Z and D_Z are added to this set of equations.

The figure below shows that the two-dimensional velocity vector on the football throw example can be broken into two components. The size of the V_X and V_Y vector components can be computed from the known D_X and D_Y terms.

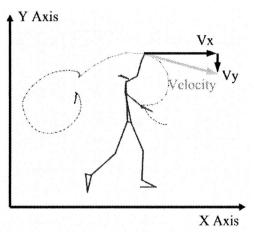

Figure 5-32. A velocity vector and its X and Y components.

The following information is known from our exercise in displacement vector calculation:

$$D_X = 0.44$$
$$D_Y = -0.12$$
$$|\mathbf{D}| = 0.456$$
$$|\mathbf{V}| = 13.68 \text{ mps}$$

We can now compute V_X and V_Y separately and verify that the final velocity magnitude is consistent with the given data:

$$V_X = D_X * EFS$$
$$V_X = (0.44) * 30$$
$$V_X = 13.2 \text{ mps}$$

$$V_Y = D_Y * EFS$$
$$V_Y = (-.12) * 30$$
$$V_Y = -3.6 \text{ mps}$$

$$|\mathbf{V}| = Sqrt(V_X^2 + V_Y^2)$$
$$|\mathbf{V}| = Sqrt((13.2)^2 + (3.6)^2)$$
$$|\mathbf{V}| = Sqrt(174.24 + 12.96)$$

$|\mathbf{V}| = \text{Sqrt}(187.2)$

$|\mathbf{V}| = 13.68$ mps

We see that the calculation of the velocity magnitude from the V_X and V_Y component data yields the same result as computing velocity from displacement magnitude.

V_X and V_Y Information on Direction

Breaking a vector down into components can be very helpful in motion analysis problems. We have noted above that when we solve the equation for velocity, we must convert the vector information into scalar components before the numerical solution can be reached. When we replace vectors with scalars, we effectively remove information about *direction*. We can get this direction information back again by keeping track of the size and sign of the X and Y components of the velocity vector.

If we are told that a velocity values is 13.68 m/s we know that the velocity is "moderately high" but we do not know anything about the direction of motion. If we are told that that a velocity vector has an X component of 13.2 m/s and a Y component of –3.6 m/s, then we know that the velocity is moderately high and it is aimed mainly in the positive X direction.

V_X Plotted vs. Time

If we were to compute the V_X and V_Y data for the full range of motion of a point, we could plot the V_X and V_Y curves as a function of time. The figure below shows the fingertip V_X data for the football throw.

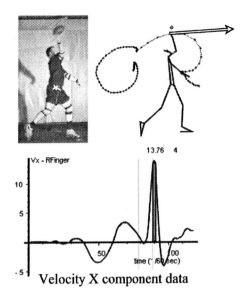

Velocity X component data

Figure 5-33. Velocity data for a football throw. The curve at the lower portion of the figure shows the X component of velocity plotted as a function of time.

Because the velocity vector of the fingertip is large and aimed primarily forward, the velocity curve shows the highlight bar at a high positive peak for the illustrated instant in time. As the throwing motion continues, the X component of velocity changes to a negative value. Note that if the velocity vector points in the backward direction, the X component must be negative.

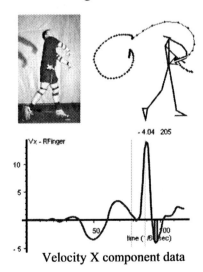

Velocity X component data

Figure 5-34. Velocity data for a football throw. The curve at the lower portion of the figure shows the X component of velocity plotted as a function of time; because the fingertip is moving backward, the Vx component of velocity is negative.

V_Y Plotted vs. Time

The figure below shows the Y component of fingertip velocity for a moment near the beginning of the action phase. Because the velocity vector is aimed upward (in the positive Y direction), the V_Y value is positive.

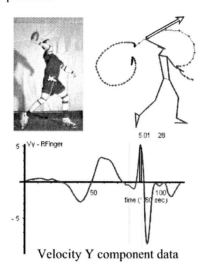

Velocity Y component data

Figure 5-35. Velocity data for a football throw. The curve at the lower portion of the figure shows the Y component of velocity plotted as a function of time.

The next figure shows the Y component of fingertip velocity for a moment after ball release. The fingertip is moving downward (in the negative Y direction) at the illustrated instant in time. As a result, the V_Y curve shows that the Y component value is negative.

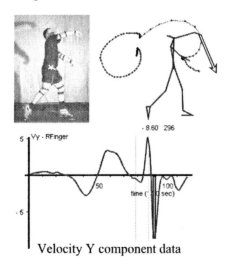

Velocity Y component data

Figure 5-36. Velocity Y component data for a football throw.

Conclusions

Our discussion of vector and scalar quantities in biomechanics is now complete. Given the foundation developed in this chapter, we are ready to move on to discuss velocity vectors in more detail in the next chapter. We will save the discussion of acceleration vectors for Chapter 8.

Answers to Chapter Questions

Question 5-1:
A right triangle has a horizontal leg (A) of length 3″ and a vertical leg (B) of 4″. What equation is used to solve for the length of the hypotenuse (C)?

○ A. C = A + B
○ B. $C^2 = A^2 + B^2$
○ C. Y = MX + B

The correct answer is B. This is the Pythagorean theorem.

Question 5-2:
A right triangle has a horizontal leg (A) of length 3″ and a vertical leg (B) of 4″. What equation is used to determine the angle between side A and the hypotenuse?

○ A. Tan(θ) = B / A
○ B. Tan(θ) = A / B
○ C. Sin(θ) = B / A

The correct answer is A. The tangent of angle θ is defined as the opposite leg (B) divided by the adjacent leg (A).

Question 5-3:
A right triangle has a hypotenuse (C) of 5″ and an angle of 53.13° between the hypotenuse and the horizontal. What equation is used to determine the length of the vertical leg (B)?

○ A. Cos(θ) = B / C
○ B. Sin(θ) = C / B
○ C. Sin(θ) = B / C

The correct answer is C. The sine of angle θ is defined as the opposite leg (B) divided by the hypotenuse (C).

Question 5-4:
A right triangle has a hypotenuse (C) of 5″ and an angle of 53.13° between the hypotenuse and the horizontal. What equation is used to determine the length of the horizontal leg (A)?

O A. $Cos(\theta) = A / C$
O B. $Sin(\theta) = A / C$
O C. $Tan(\theta) = C / A$

The correct answer is A. The cosine of angle θ is defined as the adjacent leg (A) divided by the hypotenuse (C).

Question 5-5:
What equation is used to determine the Vx component of the velocity vector?

O A. $Cos(\theta) = Vx / V$
O B. $Sin(\theta) = Vx / V$
O C. $Tan(\theta) = Vx / Vy$

The correct answer is A. The cosine of the projection angle is defined as the adjacent component (Vx) divided by the velocity magnitude (V).

Question 5-6:
What equation is used to determine the magnitude of the ground reaction force?

O A. $R = Rx + Ry$
O B. $R = Tan^{-1}(Ry/Rx)$
O C. $R^2 = Rx^2 + Ry^2$

The correct answer is C. This is simply the Pythagorean theorem applied to forces instead of triangle legs.

Question 5-7:
What equation is used to determine the angle between the Resultant force vector and the Rx vector?

O A. $Tan(\theta) = Ry / Rx$
O B. $Sin(\theta) = Ry / Rx$
O C. $Tan(\theta) = Rx / Ry$

The correct answer is A. The Tangent of the angle is given by the ratio of the opposite to the adjacent side.

Question 5-8:
The reaction force angle (θ_1), with respect to the negative X axis is 62.9°. What is the vector direction angle θ_2, expressed with respect to the positive X axis? Feel free to use a calculator (software or hardware) to determine the answer.

O A. 27.1°
O B. 117.1°
O C. 62.9°

The correct answer is B. We must subtract θ_1 from 180° to get this result.

Question 5-9:
If the initial position of a point is (1.38, 1.84) and the final position is (1.82, 1.72), what is the ΔX value (or the displacement vector X component)?

O A. 0.44
O B. 0.46
O C. –0.44

The correct answer is A. We must subtract the initial point X value (1.38) from the final X value (1.82).

Question 5-10:
If the initial position of a point is (1.38, 1.84) and the final position is (1.82, 1.72), what is the ΔY value (or the displacement vector Y component)?

O A. 0.12
O B. 0.46
O C. –0.12

The correct answer is C. We must subtract the initial point Y value (1.84) from the final Y value (1.72). Note that the direction of motion (from the initial point to the final point) is in the negative Y direction.

Question 5-11:
For the above figure, which sub-figure (A, B, C or D) shows the velocity vector with the largest vector magnitude?

O A.   O B.   O C.   O D.

The correct answer is C. The velocity vector is longest near the moment of ball release at sub-figure C.

Question 5-12:
For the above figure, which sub-figure (A, B, or C) shows the velocity vector with the largest (steepest) direction angle?

O A.   O B.   O C

The correct answer is A. The velocity vector angle at A is 40°. The vector angles at B and C are 28° and 4° respectively.

Chapter 6: Instantaneous Velocity

The previous chapters in Part 2 of this book have provided us with a good understanding of individual measures of velocity. In this chapter we will extend our knowledge of Linear Velocity further by examining the difference between measures of average and *instantaneous* velocity:

Average Velocity = $(P_F - P_I)$ / Time

Instantaneous Velocity = $(P_F - P_I)$ / Time
Where "Time" is very short.

We see that the two equations are the same with the exception that "time" is defined differently. The obvious question with the second equation is: "how short is a *very short* time interval?" The answer to this question is typical of many *bio*mechanical questions: It depends.

Figure 6-1. Movement speed examples: baseball batting and dance.

If we want to determine instantaneous velocity measures for a slow dance movement, a "very short" time interval may be as long as $1/15^{th}$ second. For most athletic movements a time interval of $1/60^{th}$ second is usually short enough to allow reasonable estimates of instantaneous velocity. The very fastest movements seen in sport (i.e., the golf drive or baseball batting) are better studied with 200 fields per second or better, with high-speed video or film.

Question 1:
The data for a slow dance movement needs to be analyzed so that the time interval between images is $1/15^{th}$ second. Assuming that normal NTSC video is used to collect the video data, how often should the video image data be sampled from the original video?

O A. every single field   O B. every other field
O C. every 3rd field   O D. every 4th field

Average & Instantaneous Velocity

The differences between average and instantaneous velocity are best illustrated by way of example. Let's now consider a variety of ways to measure the velocity of a runner on a track start.

Example: Track Start

In a sprint track start, competitors begin the race with zero velocity and strive to attain a very high velocity in a very brief time. The following figure shows video stills from a high speed video analysis of a track start.

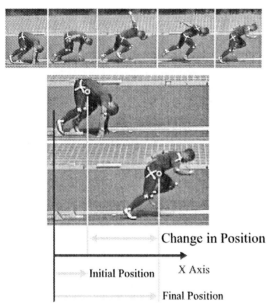

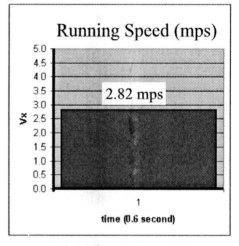

Figure 6-2. The change in position of the body's center of gravity during a track start motion.

The upper portion of the figure shows selected still images from the complete image set. The lower portion of the figure shows the change in position of the runner's center of gravity between images 20 and 140 on the video trial.

Question 2:
The initial position X coordinate value for the runner's CG is 0.80 meters. The final position of the CG is 2.49 meters. What is the change in position of the runner?

O A. 2.49 meters   O B. 1.69 meters
O C. −1.69 meters   O D. 0.8 meters

Question 3:
The change in position of a runner is 1.69 meters. The time period required for the runner's change in position is .6 seconds. What is the average velocity of the runner?

O A. 2.82 m/s   O B. 1.69 m/s
O C. 1.01 m/s   O D. 2.49 m/s

A column chart of the runner's average velocity between frames 20 and 140 is shown below.

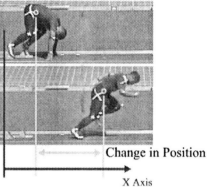

Figure 6-3. An example of the calculation of average running speed.

The running speed column chart provides a concise measure of the movement *product*. Such a chart could be used to compare the overall performance of a number of runners performing the same task. However, the average velocity measure in this single column chart *does not* provide good information on the movement *process* for this skill.

The time interval for the measurement of velocity is too large to permit any detailed understanding of the movement itself. If we were to break the analysis time interval into smaller pieces, we would begin to generate meaningful movement analysis data.

The figure below shows average velocity measures for two time intervals during the course of the movement. The two time intervals span frames (20 to 80) and frames (80 to 140). The time interval between the three photos is the same (60/200th seconds or 0.3 seconds). The average velocity measures shown on the column chart are based upon two sets of change in position data.

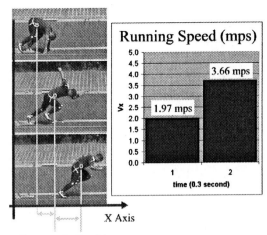

Figure 6-4. An example of running speed calculation for two periods of time during a track start.

The position data for the center of gravity at frame 20, 80 and 140 are as follows:

$P_{20} = 0.802$
$P_{80} = 1.393$
$P_{140} = 2.492$

For the phase between frame 20 and 80, the velocity calculation is as follows:

$V = (P_F - P_I) / Time$
$V = (P_{80} - P_{20}) / Time$
$V = (1.392 - 0.802) / 0.3$
$V = (.591) / 0.3$
$V = 1.97 \ m/s$

For the phase between frame 80 and 140, the velocity calculation is as follows:

$V = (P_F - P_I) / Time$
$V = (P_{140} - P_{80}) / Time$
$V = (2.49l2 - 1.392) / 0.3$
$V = (1.099) / 0.3$
$V = 3.66 \ m/s$

Notice that the runner covers much more ground during the second time interval. As a result, the two-column velocity chart shows that his average velocity is much higher on the second half of the movement than on the first half.

The two-column velocity chart shows that breaking the movement into smaller pieces allows for better information on velocity. In general, we will see that as the time interval between a pair of

"initial" and "final" position values becomes shorter, the estimate of velocity improves.

The figure below shows six estimates of the runner's speed based upon shorter and shorter data *sampling intervals*. The sampling interval is inversely related to the *sampling frequency*. The sampling frequency defines how often data values (in this case, position data) are collected for a movement.

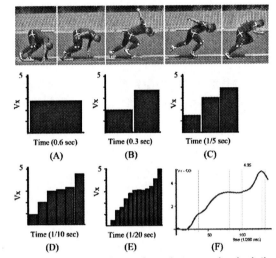

Figure 6-5. A comparison of running speed calculations for shorter and shorter time intervals within the running motion.

We have already seen the data calculations for charts (A) and (B). The column height calculations for the remaining charts are all based upon the same equation for velocity. The only difference between the six charts is the time period represented by each column in the charts. As shown by the width of the columns in charts A – E, the time period for each calculation becomes progressively shorter for each successive graph. Chart F is taken from the KA software and is our best estimate of the instantaneous velocity values for the movement. The time interval for each column in charts A – F is shown on the following table:

| Time interval (seconds) | | | | | |
A	B	C	D	E	F
0.600	0.300	0.200	0.100	0.050	0.005

We see that when the time interval between samples becomes "very small" the velocity curve graphics change from a series of successive *average* velocity measures to a continuous range of *instantaneous* velocity measures.

Position Curves

Given X, Y or Z position data, it is interesting to plot the *position curve* as a function of time. The center of gravity X position data and the position curve for the track start data is shown below.

The curve on the right side of the figure represents instantaneous measures of position sampled at 1/200th second intervals. The stick figures show the body at frames 25, 50, 75, 100 and 125. Notice that the position of the runner's center of gravity increases steadily as he drives off the blocks.

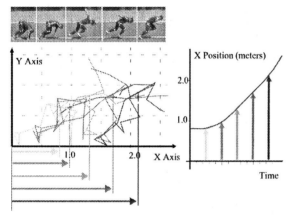

Figure 6-6. A comparison of X coordinate data as taken from a stick figure graphic and from an X position curve.

The first stick figure center of gravity position is just under one meter to the right of the zero mark on the X-axis. The last stick figure is more than two meters away from the origin. Notice that the vertical lines in the position curve show the stick figure CG position data. (The first vertical arrow is just under 1.0 meters and the last vertical arrow is more than 2.0 meters in height).

Question 4:
What is the approximate X coordinate for the CG location of the second stick figure?

O A. 1.0 meters   O B. 2.2 meters
O C. 1.3 meters   O D. 3.0 meters

Question 5:
What is the approximate height of the second vertical arrow on the CG position versus time curve?

O A. 1.0 meters   O B. 2.2 meters
O C. 1.3 meters   O D. 3.0 meters

Slope and Rate of Change

Slope Review

The equation for a line in an XY reference is given by the equation:

$$Y = MX + B$$

Where:
B = the Y intercept, or the Y value of the equation when X is set as zero.
M = Slope
Slope = $\Delta Y / \Delta X$

Slope is defined as the change in Y divided by the change in X. Slope is an indicator of the "steepness" of a line. The figure below shows plots for four lines, each with a different slope.

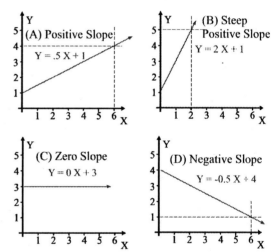

Figure 6-7. A comparison of four different slopes.

The equation in plot A shows a positive slope. The equation for the line, (Y = .5X + 1), indicates that the line will cross the Y-axis where the value of Y = 1. The dotted lines on the chart indicate a point that must be on the line. For example, if the value of X is 6, then the corresponding value of Y can be computed from the equation:

$$Y = .5X + 1$$
$$Y = (0.5 * (6)) + 1$$
$$Y = 3 + 1$$
$$Y = 4$$

As shown in chart A, the point at coordinate (6, 4) is on the line. Plot B shows a line with a steep positive slope. For this equation, the value of "M" (from Y = MX + B) is 2. For the equation Y = 2X + 1, every unit increase in X will be accompanied by a 2 unit increase in Y.

Question 6:
Chart B illustrates the equation Y = 2X + 1. If the value of X is set as 2, what value for Y will satisfy this equation?

○ A. 2   ○ B. 3
○ C. 4   ○ D. 5

Plot C shows a line with a "flat" slope. The equation "Y = 0 X + 3" includes the zero term before the X to make it clear that the value of the slope is zero. This equation could also be written as "Y = 3". The horizontal line for this equation shows that there is no change in Y for any change in X and the value of Y is 3 for all values of X.

Plot D shows a line with a negative slope. The "downhill" slope of this line shows that as X increases, the value of Y decreases.

Slope of the Position Curve

Our knowledge of the slope of lines in an XY plane can be extended to the evaluation of slopes on a position curve. For a plot of a line in the XY plane, slope is defined as the ratio of a change in the vertical (ΔY) divided by a change in the horizontal (ΔX). A position curve is a plot of position (along the vertical axis) versus time (along the horizontal axis). Thus, the slope of a position curve is actually the change in *position* divided by the change in *time*. This definition of slope is identical to our definition of velocity:

$$V = (P_F - P_I) / \text{Time}$$
$$V = \Delta P / \Delta T$$

Where: ΔT is the time period for the change in position interval.

As a result, we can use the slope of the position curve to "visually" determine estimates of velocity. The figure below shows the change in position for the runner between frames 100 and 125. This relatively large change in position has caused the slope of the position curve to be steep and positive.

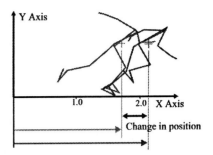

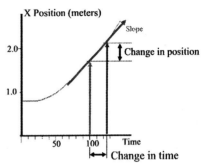

Figure 6-8. A comparison of change in position measures between a stick figure graphic and an X position curve.

The information in the figure can be used to quantify the average velocity between frames 100 and 125. The CG position for the frames is as follows:

$$P_{100} = 1.704$$
$$P_{125} = 2.131$$

The time interval between the two frames is 25/200th second. Velocity can be computed as follows:

$$V = (P_F - P_I) / \text{Time}$$
$$V = (P_{125} - P_{100}) / \text{Time}$$
$$V = (2.131 - 1.704) / (25/200)$$
$$V = (0.427) / 0.125$$
$$V = 3.42 \text{ m/s}$$

The calculations show that, for a given time interval, a steep positive slope will lead to relatively large positive values of velocity.

We see that the *slope* of the position curve indicates the *size* of instantaneous velocity at any instant in time. Further, if a variable is plotted as a function of time, the slope of the curve will provide a measure of *rate* of change. Thus, measures of slope will help us to understand both the rate of change of position (velocity) and the rate of change of velocity (acceleration).

Analysis of Position and Velocity

Let's now take a look at the track start data and investigate the relationship between position and velocity in more detail. The figure below shows still video pictures for frames 10 and 20. The position and velocity curves show the data for the second video still (frame 20).

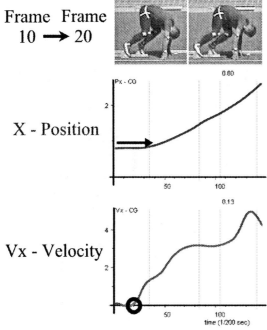

Figure 6-9. X position and Vx velocity data at a moment during the beginning of a track start motion.

Question 7:
What is the value of the slope of the position curve between frames 10 and 20 in the figure above? (Note: on the position curve time axis, each tick mark indicates 10 frames.)

O A. 1   O B. 0
O C. -1   O D. 2

Question 8:
What is the approximate value of velocity for the CG point between frames 10 and 20?

O A. 0   O B. 1
O C. -1   O D. 2

We see that, at the very beginning of the movement, the body has barely begun to move. As a result, the position curve slope is flat and the value for velocity is about zero.

The figure below shows the video stills for frames 50 and 80. The left leg is pushing vigorously during this portion of the movement, and at frame 80, the push is almost over. The position and velocity curves show the data for frames 50 and 80. The position is changing rapidly and the slope is positive at both frames. Because the slope is positive at both frames, the instantaneous velocity (shown by the two circles) is also positive for both. However, the slope is slightly steeper at frame 80 than frame 50, and therefore the velocity value at frame 80 is larger than that at frame 50.

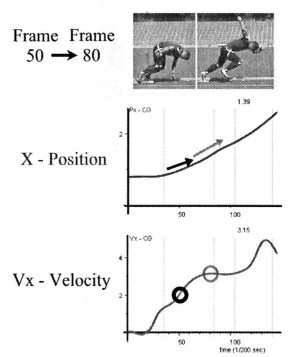

Figure 6-10. A comparison of slope measures from the X position curve and the corresponding Vx velocity values.

The left leg driving action has caused the positive velocity values at frames 50 and 80. Because the leg has pushed longer against the block by frame 80, the velocity has had more time to increase and it has reached a peak near the end of this phase.

The flight phase data is shown in the figure below. Notice that the slope of the position curve is the same at both frame 86 and frame 102. Because the change in position is uniform during this phase, the velocity values for frames 86 and 102 are the same:

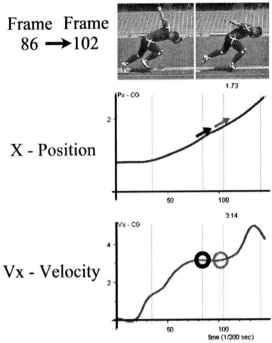

Figure 6-11. A comparison of slope measures from the X position curve and the corresponding Vx velocity values.

Question 9:
The runner's primary goal is to increase his body velocity during the course of the track start. How can we explain the observation that there is no increase in body CG velocity between frames 86 and 102?

O A. This runner's technique is flawed. A more skillful runner would increase speed in this phase.
O B. The data analysis for this runner is incorrect. There must be digitizing errors between frame 86 and 102.
O C. During the flight phase between strides, the runner's feet are not pushing on the ground and he cannot increase his velocity.

It is interesting to note that the body's CG cannot experience an increase in velocity during the flight phase. In order to have a change in velocity (acceleration), a force must be applied to the body. If no force is applied between the feet and the ground, there can be no change in the X component of velocity and, as a result, the V_X values must remain approximately constant.

Self-Experiment: (Just thinking about doing this experiment will be worthwhile). Stand in the middle of a room, at least 20 feet from the nearest wall, and jump up in the air. While you are in the air, think very hard about increasing your forward speed so much that you slam into the wall on the other side of the room.

Normally, it is wise to include a disclaimer for such a "dangerous" experiment but I am hopeful that no one will become injured on this one (with the possible exception of Superman, but he can't get hurt anyway). The point of this thought exercise is to remind us that we cannot increase our velocity in a horizontal direction unless horizontal forces are applied to our bodies.

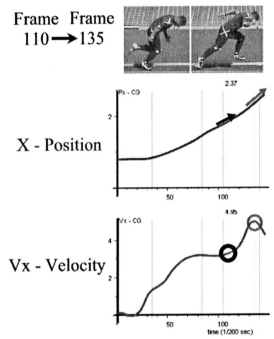

Figure 6-12. A comparison of slope measures from the X position curve and the corresponding Vx velocity values.

Let's now consider the right leg drive phase of the track start data analysis. Between frames 110 and 135, the right leg drives vigorously against the ground to cause an increase in the body's velocity (see figure 6-12 above). This increase in velocity is reflected by the increase in slope on the position curve between frame 110 and frame 135.

The running stride employed by this performer is specifically adapted to the circumstances of the track start. During normal speed running or jogging, many runners will land on the heel first when the foot initially touches the ground. This heel strike is always associated with frictional force and a decrease in running speed. The skilled performer from our video analysis experiences virtually no loss in body speed as he puts his foot down. By putting the toe down first and swinging the leg forcefully backward as soon as the foot touches down, he is able to generate forward propulsive forces almost immediately.

Data Smoothing

We saw in the last section that *very slight* changes in the slope of the position curve can cause substantial changes in the velocity curve. As a result, you may worry that, without absolutely perfect digitizing it will be impossible to get good estimates of movement velocity from video.

While it is true that care must be taken in any video digitizing project, it is also true that mathematical smoothing can be used to remove small digitizing flaws from typical digitizing projects. The position data for the track start example has been taken directly from the work of an undergraduate student who served as his own participant in his biomechanics term paper project. We should be aware that, while the data in the track start file is good, close inspection will show that small flaws exist in the original digitizing work. These small errors have been mathematically *smoothed* in the example figures we have already seen in this chapter. Figure 6-13 shows position data for the right hip point with the KA smoothing factor set as zero (i.e. no smoothing).

The bottom portion of the figure shows a magnified view of the hip pattern of motion data. Each small circle marker on the pattern of motion represents the XY coordinate location of the hip at a given frame in the motion. Note that there is uneven spacing of some of the dots on the line. This uneven spacing is due to normal human errors associated with the digitizing process. Your practice digitizing work on the Tutor files (Chapter 3) has shown that it is difficult to determine the exact location of a body landmark with the mouse cross hair as you perform manual digitizing.

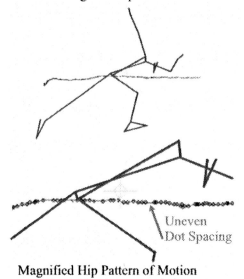

Full Stick Figure / Hip Pattern of Motion

Magnified Hip Pattern of Motion

Figure 6-13. The unsmoothed right hip pattern of motion data for a running motion.

The position and velocity curves for the right hip point are shown in the figure below. Note that the smoothing factor has been set as zero for these curves.

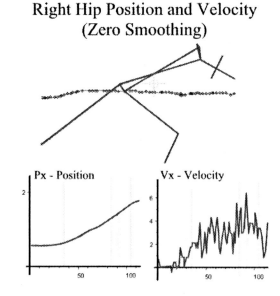

Right Hip Position and Velocity (Zero Smoothing)

Px - Position   Vx - Velocity

Figure 6-14. A comparison of unsmoothed X position data and the corresponding Vx velocity data.

The V_X velocity data is computed on the basis of the velocity equation:

$V = (P_F - P_I) * EFS$
Where: EFS (the effective film speed) = 200

Notice that the uneven pattern of dots in the pattern of motion often shows a wide spacing followed by a very narrow spacing. This pattern will cause the first calculation for velocity to be much larger than the next. This end result of more than 100 such calculations is shown by the jagged velocity curve in the figure. Note that this velocity curve has zero smoothing.

The differences in spacing of the dots cause large fluctuations in the slope of the position curve. Further, when the velocity equation is applied to the data, each slope measure is multiplied by a factor of 200. Thus the slight irregularities in the slope of the position curve lead to large irregularities in the velocity curve.

Digital filter smoothing software routines can be applied to the position and velocity data to remove most of the random "noise" fluctuations in the data (see figure 6-15). The resulting smoothing will yield smoother data that is far easier to interpret, but it will not yield perfect data. In particular, as higher smoothing factors are applied to the data, the "true" peak values in the velocity curve will be "smoothed down" to smaller values.

Right Hip Position and Velocity (Smoothed Data)

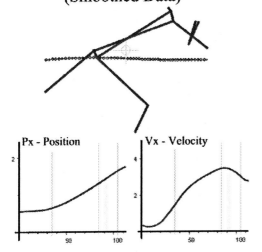

Figure 6-15. A comparison of smoothed X position data and the corresponding Vx velocity data.

The goal of most research projects in biomechanics is not to determine a given velocity value with absolute precision. It is often sufficient to compare "reasonably accurate" measures of velocity across two or more trials or conditions. This can be accomplished by using the *same smoothing factor* for all of the trials in a given research project. With this approach, even if our smoothed data is not exactly correct (as is the case in any project where human beings make use of manual digitizing), the results of several trials will still be comparable to one another. We will discuss the issue of data smoothing in greater detail in Chapter 9.

Conclusions

Our discussion of position and instantaneous velocity is now complete. Our track start example has shown that the use of short time intervals in the calculation of velocity provides us with detailed information on the process of human movement. Further, we have seen that the slope of the position curve can be used in a graphical analysis of velocity. The analysis strategies we have used in this chapter will be very helpful in our analysis of instantaneous measures of acceleration in the next chapter.

Answers to Chapter Questions

Question 1:
The data for a slow dance movement needs to be analyzed so that the time interval between images is 1/15th second. Assuming that normal NTSC video is used to collect the video data, how often should the video image data be sampled from the original video?

O A. every single field   O B. every other field
O C. every 3rd field   O D. every 4th field

The correct answer is D. Normal NTSC video acquires video data at a rate of 60 fields per second. If every forth field is selected for analysis, the effective interval between images will be 4/60 or 1/15th second.

Question 2
The initial position X coordinate value for the runner's CG is 0.80 meters. The final position of the CG is 2.49 meters. What is the change in position of the runner?

O A. 2.49 meters
O B. 1.69 meters
O C. −1.69 meters
O D. 0.8 meters

The correct answer is B. To compute the change in position, we must compute the result of $(P_F - P_I)$ or (2.49 - 0.80).

Question 3
The change in position of a runner is 1.69 meters. The time period required for the runner's change in position is .6 seconds. What is the average velocity of the runner?

○ A. 2.82 m/s
○ B. 1.69 m/s
○ C. 1.01 m/s
○ D. 2.49 m/s

The correct answer is A. To compute the average velocity, we must compute the result of (ΔP / Time) or (1.69 / 0.6).

Question 4:
What is the approximate X coordinate for the CG location of the second stick figure?

○ A. 1.0 meters
○ B. 2.2 meters
○ C. 1.3 meters
○ D. 3.0 meters

The correct answer is A. The cross just in front of the hip for the second stick figure represents the body center of gravity. The vertical line on the second stick figure graphic crosses the X-axis at about the 1.0 meter mark.

Question 5:
What is the approximate height of the second vertical arrow on the CG position versus time curve?

○ A. 1.0 meters   ○ B. 2.2 meters
○ C. 1.3 meters   ○ D. 3.0 meters

The correct answer is A. The height of the position curve is equal to the X coordinate of the CG position at any instant in time.

Question 6:
Chart B illustrates the equation Y = 2X + 1. If the value of X is set as 2, what value for Y will satisfy this equation?

○ A. 2
○ B. 3
○ C. 4
○ D. 5

The correct answer is D. The dotted lines on Chart B show that if X is set as 2, the value for Y must be 5 in order for the point to fall on the line and satisfy the equation.

Question 7:
What is the value of the slope of the position curve between frames 10 and 20 in the figure above? (Note: on the position curve time axis, each tick mark indicates 10 frames.)

○ A. 1
○ B. 0
○ C. -1
○ D. 2

The correct answer is B. The slope of the position curve is very flat at the beginning of the movement.

Question 8:
What is the approximate value of velocity for the CG point between frames 10 and 20?

○ A. 0
○ B. 1
○ C. -1
○ D. 2

The correct answer is A. If the slope of the position curve is zero, there is no change in position over the time period. As a result, velocity must be zero.

Question 9:
The runner's primary goal is to increase his body velocity during the course of the track start. How can we explain the observation that there is no increase in body CG velocity between frames 86 and 102?

○ A. This runner's technique is flawed. A more skillful runner would increase speed in this phase.
○ B. The data analysis for this runner is incorrect. There must be digitizing errors between frame 86 and 102.
○ C. During the flight phase between strides, the runner's feet are not pushing on the ground and he cannot increase his velocity.

The correct answer is C. In order to have a change in velocity (acceleration), a force must be applied to the body. If no force is applied between the feet and the ground, there can be no change in the X component of velocity and, as a result, the V_x values must remain approximately constant.

Chapter 7: Instantaneous Acceleration

Instantaneous Acceleration

Velocity is a fundamentally important measure of human motion. We can often determine a given movement's high and low velocity phases through simple observation. Thus, the evaluation of velocity is relatively easy to perform, especially if we have experience performing or observing the movement in question. In the photo below, the fast moving parts of the body are blurred. In KA, wide spacing on the pattern of motion indicates high velocity.

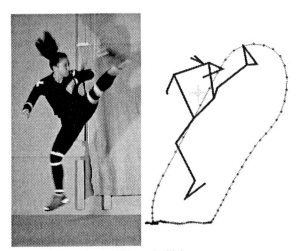

Figure 7-1. A martial Arts spin kick.

Acceleration is mathematically related to velocity. Thus, if we know the velocity of a point's motion, we can calculate the acceleration directly. The determination of acceleration values for a movement is very important because the net force acting on a body at a given instant is directly proportional to the acceleration of the body at that instant. Recall that biomechanics is defined as "the science concerned with the internal and external *forces* acting on the human body…" (Hay, 1993). Our study of acceleration in this chapter will provide us with a foundation for the understanding of force and motion.

Velocity and Acceleration

We will study the relationship between velocity and acceleration in the next example of a volleyball jump. We will make use of the principle of reductionism to isolate only the vertical components of velocity and acceleration for our analysis. This approach will allow us to distinguish between the positive (upward) and negative (downward) velocity and acceleration components.

Example: Volleyball Jump

The volleyball jumping motion will be easy to study because it is one-dimensional. It is primarily an up and down motion and only the Y coordinate data will be critical in our analysis. Even though the volleyball jump occurs in one dimension it is bi-directional. The first half of the jumping motion is upward (from start to peak of flight), and the second half is downward (from peak of flight to the end of the jump).

The following figures illustrate key instances in time during the course of the jump:

Volleyball Jump

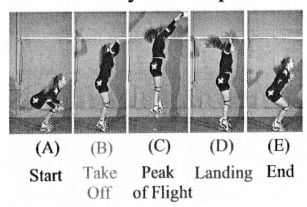

(A) (B) (C) (D) (E)
Start Take Off Peak of Flight Landing End

Figure 7-2. Five critical events during the course of a volleyball jump.

For our example we will consider a simple jump where the body is stationary in picture (A), moving upward in (B), at peak of flight in (C), moving downward in (D) and stationary again in picture (E).

As an exercise, we will estimate the values for velocity at the 5 instances in time A-E and plot the velocity versus time curve. Bear in mind that upward motion is associated with positive values of velocity and downward motion is associated with negative values of velocity. For our exercise, it will be sufficient to identify the possible values for velocity as one of the following 3 possibilities:

1) Zero
2) High Positive
3) High Negative

Question 1:
What is the value of velocity at picture (A)?

O A. Zero
O B. High Positive
O C. High Negative

Question 2:
What is the value of velocity at picture (B)?

O A. Zero
O B. High Positive
O C. High Negative

Question 3:
What is the value of velocity at picture (C)?

O A. Zero
O B. High Positive
O C. High Negative

Question 4:
What is the value of velocity at picture (D)?

O A. Zero
O B. High Positive
O C. High Negative

Question 5:
What is the value of velocity at picture (E)?

O A. Zero
O B. High Positive
O C. High Negative

Velocity Curve Graph

Given estimates of velocity at the 5 instances in time, we can begin to plot velocity as a function of time. The "X" marks on the figure below represent the velocity values of the body at times A – E.

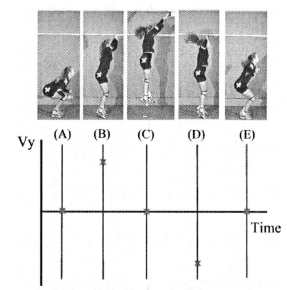

Figure 7-3. Velocity estimates for five instances in time during a volleyball jump motion.

If we "connect the dots" on the curve we can generate the complete graph of the Y component of velocity.

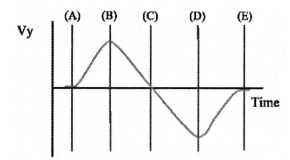

Figure 7-4. The vertical component of the body's center of gravity point velocity curve.

Notice that the Y component velocity curve shows that the upward portion of the motion (A to C) is positive. In addition, notice that the downward portion of the motion (C to E) is negative because it is drawn below the time axis. The velocity curve shows that at the peak of flight (time C), the value of velocity is zero.

Question 6:
Did you expect the value of the curve to be highest at time C?

O A. Yes
O B. No

Estimating Acceleration from Velocity

Our next exercise will be to determine the acceleration curve of the body, given only the information on the velocity as a function of time. We know that, by definition, acceleration is the rate of change of velocity with respect to time:

$$A = (V_f - V_i) / time$$

Thus, the slope of the velocity curve defines the instantaneous value of acceleration at any instant in time. As a first step in defining the acceleration curve for the volleyball jump, let's inspect the velocity curve and identify the times when the slope of the curve is zero:

Question 7:
Which of the following times have a slope of zero?

O A. The slope is zero at time B.
O B. The slope is zero at time C.

The following figure shows horizontal lines at the points on the velocity curve where the slope is zero.

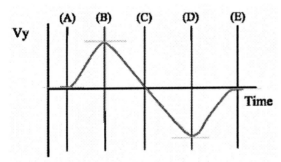

Figure 7-5. Four instances in time with zero change in velocity during a volleyball jump motion.

Because there is no change in velocity when the slope is zero, it follows that the body's acceleration must also be zero at these times.

Our next challenge will be to determine the spots where the slope of the velocity is either at a high positive value or at a high negative value. Note that positive slopes are "uphill" as read from left to right and negative slopes are "downhill".

Consider the following questions:

Question 8:
What is the slope of the velocity curve between moments (A and B)?

O A. Positive
O B. Negative

Question 9:
What is the slope of the velocity curve between moments (B and C):

O A. Positive
O B. Negative

Question 10:
What is the slope of the velocity curve between moments (C and D):

O A. Positive
O B. Negative

Question 11:
What is the slope of the velocity curve between moments (D and E):

O A. Positive
O B. Negative

The figure on the right shows the (+) and (-) markings to indicate the steep positive and negative changes in velocity.

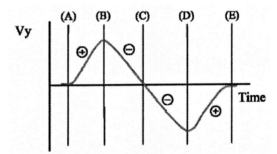

Figure 7-6. The slope of the Vy velocity curve at four during a volleyball jump motion.

We now know the change in velocity (slope) for 8 different instances in time during the volleyball jump: The slope is zero at times A, B, D and E. The slope is (+) between A and B and between D and E. The slope is (-) between B and C and between C and D.

We can begin the plot the approximate acceleration curve by placing "X" marks at the known acceleration values:

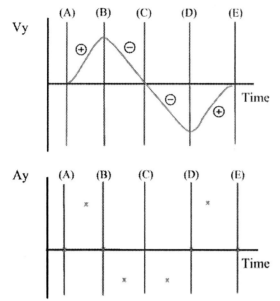

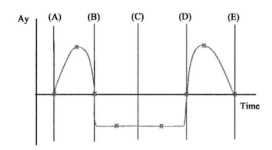

Figure 7-7. A comparison of acceleration values and the slope values for a volleyball jump motion.

The full acceleration curve is shown below.

Figure 7-8. The Y component of the body's center of gravity acceleration curve.

Note that the acceleration curve shows that there is positive acceleration during the "Start -Take Off" phase and during the "Landing – End" phase. The acceleration is negative for the complete "in flight" portion of the jump.

While the body is in the air, gravity acts to cause a uniform acceleration for the time between B and D. Note that the value of acceleration does not change during the time interval from B to D. Do you think an estimate of the numerical value of acceleration is possible given the limited information in the problem?

Question 12:
What is the value of acceleration *while the performer is in the air?*

○ A. The value of acceleration depends upon the size of the performer.
○ B. The value of acceleration depends upon the leg strength of the performer.
○ C. The value of acceleration is 9.81 m/s^2 for all objects in flight.
○ D. The value of acceleration cannot be determined from the supplied information.

The sign (positive or negative) of the body's acceleration can also be determined through inspection of the equation for acceleration:

$$A = (V_f - V_i) / T$$

If we assume that the value of time (T) is a fixed positive value, we see that the sign of acceleration is given by the difference between V_f and V_i. The following equations show the sign of the V_f and V_i terms and indicate the required sign for acceleration. Descriptions of the movement are also provided.

$A = (V_f - V_i) / T$

A-B Speed up upward	$A = (+) - (0) = (+)$
B-C Slow down upward	$A = (0) - (+) = (-)$
C-D Speed up downward	$A = (-) - (0) = (-)$
D-E Slow down downward	$A = (0) - (-) = (+)$

The final description "slow down downward" shows that, mathematically, minus a minus must be equal to a positive value. Logically, if the initial velocity is a negative value and the final velocity is zero, the velocity must have changed in the positive direction, and positive acceleration must have taken place.

Vector Analysis of Acceleration

Acceleration is a measure of the rate of change of velocity. Velocity is a vector that carries information on magnitude and direction. If follows that a careful analysis of velocity vectors can be used in the determination of acceleration. A vector based analysis of acceleration will provide an interesting supplement to our prior discussion because it will allow us to visualize the direction of acceleration vectors at a variety of times during the course of a movement.

Vector diagrams that illustrate velocity vectors are relatively easy to visualize because the velocity vector is always tangent to the pattern of motion. The figure below shows the body's center of gravity velocity information for a martial arts jump kick.

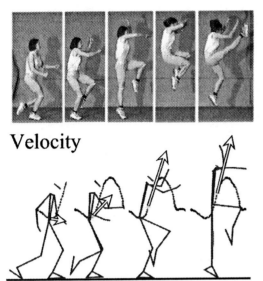

Velocity

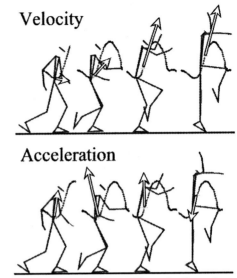

Velocity

Acceleration

Figure 7-9. The center of gravity velocity vector at four instances in time during a jump kick.

Figure 7-10. A comparison of the velocity and acceleration vectors for the body's center of gravity point.

Note that the velocity vectors show the instantaneous directions of motion of the center of gravity point at each instant in time during the movement. In addition, the length of the velocity vector indicates the velocity magnitude.

Figure 7-10 shows a comparison of the center of gravity velocity (in the upper portion of the figure) and acceleration (in the lower portion of the figure) vectors for the jump kick motion.

Note that the acceleration vectors are not aimed along the same direction as the velocity vectors. In fact, the last stick figure shows that at the moment before take off, the velocity and acceleration vectors are aimed in opposite directions. The exact direction of an acceleration vector at a given instant in time can be determined through analysis of the velocity vectors just before and just after the given instant in time.

The upper portion of the figure below shows the velocity vectors for frames 38 and 40 in the jump kick motion. The lower portion of the figure shows a vector analysis of the change in velocity between frames 38 and 40.

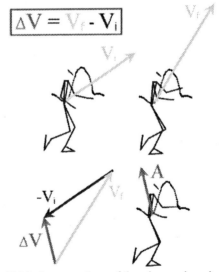

$$\Delta V = V_f - V_i$$

Figure 7-11. A comparison of the change in velocity vector and the acceleration vector for the body's center of gravity point.

Note that the vector subtraction of $(Vf - Vi)$ involves the vector *addition* of the **Vf** vector and the *negative* **Vi** vector (as shown by the opposite direction vector for **Vi**). The vector equation for acceleration is:

A = (Vf – Vi) / time

This vector equation can be broken down into two scalar equations:

Ax = (Vxf – Vxi) / time
Ay = (Vyf – Vyi) / time

These scalar equations can be used to analyze the X and Y components of acceleration for any two-dimensional motion. If the motion in question is clearly one-dimensional, for example, for the case of a volleyball jump, the final equation for Ay can be simplified to the following:

A = (Vf – Vi) / time

However, this last simplified equation can only be used with movements that are clearly one-dimensional. In the case of our two-dimensional jump kick motion, both the X and Y components of velocity must be considered in the calculation of velocity. The vector analysis of the 2D velocity vectors in the figure above allow us to illustrate the change in velocity with a single two-dimensional vector:

ΔV = (Vf – Vi)

This change in velocity vector indicates the direction of the acceleration vector. The acceleration vector can be determined by dividing the ΔV vector by the time interval between frames:

A = ΔV / time

The time interval between frames 38 and 40 is 1/30th second. Dividing a number by a fraction is equivalent to multiplying that number by the inverse of that fraction. As a result, the equation for acceleration can also be expressed as follows:

A = ΔV * 30

This final equation indicates that the acceleration vector will be aimed along the same line as the ΔV vector, although the **A** vector will be 30 times longer. Because the scale for velocity vectors and acceleration vectors is arbitrary, the actual length of the ΔV and **A** vectors in our illustration cannot be directly compared. However, the vector subtraction illustrated in the figure shows us that the direction of an acceleration vector can be visualized through a relatively simple vector subtraction procedure.

Vertical Jump Forces

We will discuss forces very formally in Chapter 11 (linear kinetics). Nevertheless, we can take advantage of our intuitive "feelings" of force to help us to further understand the acceleration of the body in a typical jumping motion.

Flight Phase

It is interesting to note that the only force acting on the body while it is in the air is gravity (as long as we neglect the slight effect of air resistance), and the size of this force is equal to the body weight. The in-flight portion of the movement provides a clear example of the direct relationship between the body's acceleration and an applied force. The body weight is a fixed value and the acceleration is also fixed (at –9.81 m/s^2) while the body is in the air.

Figure 7-12. The flight phase of a volleyball jump motion.

Upward Driving Phase

During the "Start – Take off" phase, very non-uniform forces are acting on the body. Gravity pulls the body down but the legs are driving the body up with more than enough force to offset the body weight. As a result of the leg drive, a peak force is generated near the middle of the upward driving motion. We know that the peak positive force cannot occur too close to the moment of take off because just after take off the body's acceleration will make a smooth transition to negative values. The following figure shows the ground reaction forces that are acting on the body during the upward driving motion. The volleyball player is pushing vigorously down on the ground to generate force for the jump. The arrows show the reaction force of the ground "pushing back" on the body of the performer.

Figure 7-13. The upward driving phase of a volleyball jump motion.

Self experiment: Stand on a bathroom scale, crouch down and remain motionless. The scale will indicate your body weight. Extend your legs forcefully and watch the scale reading rapidly increase. You will be able to feel the increased pressure between your feet and the scale. This pressure is associated with the large positive (upward) force acting on your body.

Frequently Asked Question

Trick question: Is the performer pushing down on the floor or is the floor pushing up on the performer?

Answer: Both things are happening at the same time. In response to the downward drive of the legs, there is a ground reaction force that pushes back up on the body. If you are interested in the motion of the participant's body, it is convenient to show the upward reaction force that is acting upon her to cause her motion. Drawing the force downward would focus our attention on the effect of the leg drive on the Earth. Hopefully, we will not have to concern ourselves with the Earth being pushed out of orbit, even by highly skilled volleyball players!

Landing Phase

Very non-uniform forces are also applied to the body during the "Landing – End" phase. During this phase the legs are flexing and the body is moving downwards into a partial crouch position. The forces acting on the body during the landing must be positive because they must change the negative

velocity of the body (at foot touch down) to zero velocity (at the end of the crouch down phase). Notice that the upward ground reaction force reaches a maximal value in the middle figure as the knees flex to absorb force. At the end of the jump the ground reaction force is equal to the body weight.

Figure 7-14. The landing phase of a volleyball jump motion.

Self experiment: Perform a volleyball jump and make note of the forces that are applied to your feet on the landing. The pressure between your feet and the floor will be very similar to what you felt when you jumped upward on the bathroom scale. In both instances the forces and acceleration of the body are positive.

Question 13:
If velocity is zero, does acceleration have to be zero also?

O A. Yes
O B. No

Bear in mind that any *single* instantaneous measure of velocity can never provide enough information to estimate acceleration. To determine acceleration we need to know the *change* in velocity over the short time period in question. For this, we need at least two values of velocity, one just before and one just after the moment in question. For example, at the peak of flight in the volleyball jump, the velocity is zero but the acceleration is (-9.81 m/s^2).

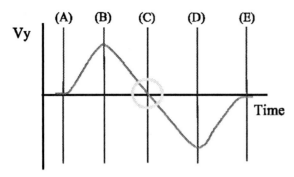

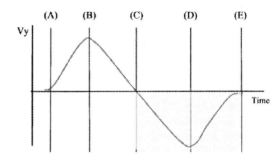

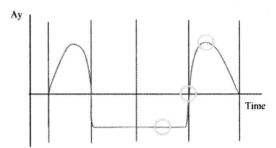

Figure 7-15. The vertical component of the center of gravity point's velocity is 0 mps at the midpoint of the jumping motion. At this same instant, the body's acceleration is -9.81 mps^2

In the figure above, the negative slope of the velocity curve at time C shows that velocity is *changing*. As a result, the value of acceleration at time C cannot be zero.

This example shows the importance of observing the *process* of movement. Information on selected body positions and isolated instances in time will often miss critical information in motion analysis projects.

Question 14:
Can you be moving in a negative direction and have *positive* acceleration?

O A. Yes
O B. No

The sign of the V_Y value indicates the direction of motion at any instant in time. However, the sign of velocity tells us nothing about the slope of the velocity curve. For our volleyball jump example, during the time when velocity is negative (time C-E) the acceleration takes on a wide range of values: negative, zero and positive (see the figure below).

Figure 7-16. A comparison of velocity and acceleration measures for the second half of a volleyball jump motion.

This example also shows that we need to know how velocity is *changing* at the moment in question in order to understand acceleration.

Conclusions

Our discussion of instantaneous acceleration is now complete. We have seen that acceleration values can be determined through a graphical analysis of the slope of the velocity curve. We have also seen that the process of vector subtraction can also be used to visualize the direction of the acceleration vector. Our knowledge of acceleration will be extended in the next chapter, where we will study the details of uniformly accelerated motion.

Answers to Chapter Questions

Question 1:
What is the value of velocity at picture (A)?

O A. Zero
O B. High Positive
O C. High Negative

The correct answer is A. The body is stationary at the beginning of the movement and therefore the velocity is zero.

Question 2:
What is the value of velocity at picture (B)?

O A. Zero
O B. High Positive
O C. High Negative

The correct answer is B. The body is moving very quickly upward at the moment of take off. All of the force from the legs has been transferred to the body to attain peak speed very close to the moment of take off. As are result the velocity is a high positive (upward) value.

Question 3:
What is the value of velocity at picture (C)?

O A. Zero
O B. High Positive
O C. High Negative

The correct answer is A. At the peak of flight the body is momentarily motionless. The body has ceased moving upward and has not yet begun to fall downward. As a result the velocity is zero.

What is the value of velocity at picture (D)?

O A. Zero
O B. High Positive
O C. High Negative

The correct answer is C. The body is moving rapidly downward at landing. As a result the velocity is a high negative (downward) value. The velocity will not diminish to zero until after the legs drive against the ground to absorb the momentum of the body.

Question 5:
What is the value of velocity at picture (E)?

O A. Zero
O B. High Positive
O C. High Negative

The correct answer is A. The body is stationary at the end of the movement and therefore the velocity is zero.

Question 6:
Did you expect the value of the curve to be highest at time C?

O A. Yes
O B. No

The correct answer is B. The body is motionless for an instant at the peak of the jump and the velocity must be zero at time C.

Question 7:
Which of the following times have a slope of zero?

O A. The slope is zero at time B.
O B. The slope is zero at time C.

The correct answer is A. The velocity value is not changing in the vicinity of time B.

Question 8:
What is the slope of the velocity curve between moments (A and B)?

O A. Positive
O B. Negative

The correct answer is A. The slope is "uphill" between A and B.

Question 9:
What is the slope of the velocity curve between moments (B and C):

O A. Positive
O B. Negative

The correct answer is B. The slope is "downhill" between B and C.

Question 10:
What is the slope of the velocity curve between moments (C and D):

O A. Positive
O B. Negative

The correct answer is B. The slope is "downhill" between C and D.

Question 11:
What is the slope of the velocity curve between moments (D and E):

O A. Positive
O B. Negative

The correct answer is A. The slope is "uphill" between D and E.

Question 12:
What is the value of acceleration *while the performer is in the air*?

O A. The value of acceleration depends upon the size of the performer.
O B. The value of acceleration depends upon the leg strength of the performer.
O C. The value of acceleration is 9.81 m/s^2 for all objects in flight.

O D. The value of acceleration cannot be determined from the supplied information.

The correct answer is C. We will see in the next chapter that the pull of gravity causes all objects in flight to experience uniform acceleration (assuming air resistance is negligible).

Question 13:
If velocity is zero, does acceleration have to be zero also?

O A. Yes
O B. No

The correct response is "No".

Question 14:
Can you be moving in a negative direction and have *positive* acceleration?

O A. Yes
O B. No

The correct response is "Yes".

Chapter 8: Uniformly Accelerated Motion

Gravity influences all forms of human motion. At the surface of the earth, the force of gravity is a constant, predictable value. Our ability to anticipate and counteract the force of gravity plays a crucial role in most human motions. From our first steps as infants to our most skillful performances in sport, gravity remains our constant companion.

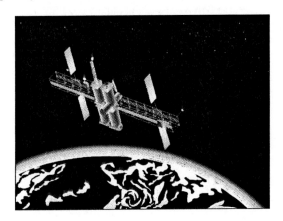

Figure 8-1. A satellite in orbit over the surface of the earth.

Newton's Law of Gravitation

The force of gravity acts straight downward, pulling you and the objects around you toward the center of the earth. At the surface of the earth, the pull of gravity on a given body is directly related to the mass of the body. When an object is moved to a location far above the surface of the earth, the pull of gravity will be greatly reduced. Newton's Law of Gravitation defines the size of gravitational force for any pair of bodies. Let's consider the gravitational force acting on the satellite in the figure above.

$$G \propto (M_1 * M_2) / L^2$$

Where:

$\propto$	is proportional to
G	the force of gravity
M_1	the mass of the earth
M_2	the mass of the satellite
L	the distance between M_1 and M_2

The gravitational force is *directly* proportional to the product of ($M_1 * M_2$) – the bigger the product of the two masses, the bigger the gravitational force will be. The gravitational force is *indirectly* proportional to the distance between the masses – the larger this distance is, the smaller the gravitational force will be. Further, the equation indicates that the gravitational force is indirectly proportional to the *square* of the "L" (distance) term. As a result, if the distance is doubled, the gravitational force will be reduced by a factor of 4. Further, if the distance is multiplied by 3, the gravitational force will be reduced by a factor of 9. Thus, we see that as the L term becomes larger the force of gravity will greatly diminish (i.e. at a given height above the earth, the satellite or space craft will "escape" the pull of gravity).

In the next sections we will consider the influence of gravity on objects in flight, near the surface of the earth. To simplify matters, we will ignore the influence of air resistance (this topic will be covered in our chapter on fluid mechanics). We will talk about many of the same concepts that have been covered in previous chapters, such as instantaneous velocity and acceleration. However, the work in this chapter will be particularly important because it will allow us to use simple mathematical equations to define the motion of a body in flight over a period of time. The practice we get solving these equations will provide us with a foundation for quantifying many other aspects of movement that we will encounter in future chapters.

Uniformly Accelerated Motion

Free falling objects experience uniform (constant) acceleration. As a result, instantaneous acceleration equals average acceleration and:

$$A = A_{Ave} = (V_f - V_i) / T$$
$$AT = V_f - V_i$$
$$V_f = V_i + AT$$

The above "final velocity" equation is simply a rearrangement of the terms in the definitional equation for acceleration. We will refer to this equation as the first equation of uniformly accelerated motion. It indicates that the final velocity of a falling object will change at a uniform rate for every second of its flight. For free fall, the acceleration of gravity ("A") equals -9.81 m/s^2, on or near the surface of the earth and in the absence of other external forces. In our example calculations in this course, we will round the acceleration of gravity term to –9.8 m/s^2.

Velocity of a Falling Object

The following example shows how the speed of an object in flight can be computed on the basis of its flight time.

Example – Ball Drop from Height

Drop a ball from a height; determine the final velocity of the ball at times 1, 2 and 3 seconds after release.

The figure below shows the flight pattern of motion data for the 1-second drop on the left, the 2 second drop in the middle, and the 3 second drop on the right. The solid arrows indicate the distance traveled by the ball. The dots on the pattern of motion lines show the ball locations during the fall at 1/15th second intervals.

Ball Drop from Height

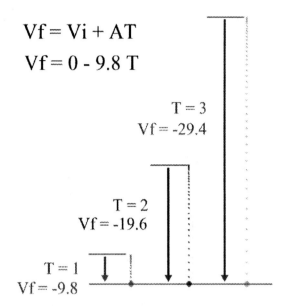

$$Vf = Vi + AT$$
$$Vf = 0 - 9.8 \, T$$

T = 3
Vf = -29.4

T = 2
Vf = -19.6

T = 1
Vf = -9.8

Figure 8-2. Final velocity measures for a ball dropped for 1, 2 and 3 second flight time periods.

The general equation for uniformly accelerated motion is as follows:

$$V_f = Vi + AT$$

For motion near the surface of the earth, the "A" term can be replaced with the constant value "–9.8". If the ball is dropped (and not thrown downward or upward), we can set the Vi term to zero:

$$V_f = 0 - 9.8 \, T$$

The above equation can be used to compute the speed of a dropped ball for any time during the course of its flight. If we solve this equation for T = 1, 2 and 3 seconds we get the following results:

T = 1	V_f = -9.8 m/s
T = 2	V_f = -19.6 m/s
T = 3	V_f = -29.4 m/s

Note: After 1 second of falling, the ball's velocity will change from 0 to -9.8 m/s.
Between 1 and 2 seconds of falling the ball's velocity will change from -9.8 to -19.6 m/s.
Between 2 and 3 seconds of falling the ball's velocity will change from -19.6 to -29.4 m/s.

Question 1:
What is the change in velocity per unit time for each of the intervals (0 – 1), (1 – 2) and (2 – 3) seconds?

O A. -9.8 m/s per second
O B. -4.9 m/s per second
O C. –29.4 m/s per second

The above example shows that the rate of change of velocity (acceleration) during free fall is *uniform* – at a value of -9.8 m/s².

Vertical Projection

Dropping a ball straight down is a very simple example of uniformly accelerated motion. Let's now consider an example where a ball is thrown straight up in the air (vertical projection). We will see that the equations of uniformly accelerated motion will allow us to compute the velocity of this ball both when it is on the rise and when it falls back to the starting position.

Example – Toss Up

Throw a ball straight upwards with an initial velocity = +19.6 m/s and catch it again. Compute the ball's velocity after 1, 2, 3 and 4 seconds of flight. For this problem we will use the first equation of uniformly accelerated motion:

$$V_f = V_i + AT$$
$$V_f = +19.6 - 9.8T$$

The figure below shows an illustration of the ball motion as well as 5 "snap shots" of the ball data at the times T = 0, 1, 2, 3 and 4 seconds. The dotted patterns of motion show the ball positions at 1/10th second time intervals. The filled circles show the ball at the specified instant of time. Finally, the arrows indicates the direction and size of the ball velocity. Note that at time T = 0, the ball has just left the hand of the thrower and the velocity is +19.6 m/s.

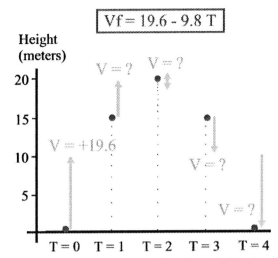

Figure 8-3. Velocity vectors at four times during the flight of a ball that has been thrown straight upward.

We will compute the numerical value of velocity at the one second instant in time in the following question:

Question 2:
What is instantaneous velocity of the ball at instant in time T = 1?

O A. -9.8 meters per second
O B. +9.8 meters per second
O C. +19.6 meters per second

We can use the equation shown at the top of the figure to compute the value of V_f at time T = 1. After one second of flight, the acceleration of gravity has caused the ball's velocity to change from +19.6 m/s to +9.8 m/s. At this instant, the ball is still traveling upward. We will compute the numerical value of velocity at the two second instant in time in the following question:

Question 3:
What is instantaneous velocity of the ball at instant in time T = 2?

O A. -9.8 meters per second
O B. +9.8 meters per second
O C. 0 meters per second

After two seconds of flight, the acceleration of gravity has caused the ball's velocity to change from +19.6 m/s to zero m/s. At this instant, the ball is momentarily at its peak and is just about to begin falling downward. We will compute the numerical value of velocity at the three second instant in time in the following question:

Question 4:
What is instantaneous velocity of the ball at instant in time T = 3?

O A. -9.8 meters per second
O B. +9.8 meters per second
O C. 0 meters per second

After three seconds of flight, the ball has reached its peak and has been falling for a full second. The acceleration of gravity has caused the ball's velocity to change to -9.8 m/s at this instant. We will compute the numerical value of velocity at the four second instant in time in the following question:

Question 5:
What is instantaneous velocity of the ball at instant in time T = 4?

O A. -9.8 meters per second
O B. −19.6 meters per second
O C. +9.8 meters per second

After four seconds of flight, the ball is just about to hit the ground. The ball has been falling for 2 seconds since its peak and the Vf value is -19.6 m/s. Note that, again, the acceleration (change in velocity) remains constant at -9.8 m/s for each one-second time interval of the ball's flight.

Accelerated Motion Equations

So far, we have considered only the first of three equations of uniformly accelerated motion. The complete set of equations is shown below:

In General:
$V_f = V_i + AT$
$D = V_i T + \frac{1}{2} A T^2$
$V_f^2 = V_i^2 + 2AD$

For Free Fall on Earth:
$V_f = V_i - 9.8T$
$D = V_i T - 4.9T^2$
$V_f^2 = V_i^2 - 19.6D$

The equations in the left column are very general, and they can be used to solve movement problems on Earth, Mars, or other planets, provided that the appropriate value for "A" is substituted in the equations. The equations on the right are appropriate only for the study of motion at or near the Earth's surface, because the value of A has been set as -9.8 m/s^2.

Our work with these equations presents us with an interesting *educational* question. We have two choices: 1) We can accept them as complicated and abstract and simply memorize them; or 2) we can study them in detail and arrive at a more complete understanding of their meaning. As biomechanists in training, we will, of course, choose the latter approach.

We have seen above that the first equation in the set is simply a rearrangement of the mathematical definition of acceleration. The second equation, on the other hand, appears to be a bit more complex. We will see in the next exercise that this equation can be derived from a few very basic equations that you probably already know at an intuitive level.

Velocity, Acceleration and Distance

As an exercise, let's answer a number of mathematical questions. Each question will come in two parts. The first part will ask for the numeric answer to a basic problem. The second part will ask you to define the equation you used to solve the first part of the question. During the course of this exercise we will identify three "intuitively correct" equations that can be used to derive the distance equation ($D = V_i T + \frac{1}{2} A T^2$) for uniformly accelerated motion.

Consider the following question on average velocity.

Question 6:
A ball travels 20 meters in 10 seconds. What is its average speed?

O A. 20 meters per second
O B. 2 meters per second

Distance = 20 meters
Time = 10 seconds
Average speed = ?

If a ball travels 20 meters in 10 seconds it will have an average velocity of two meters per second. It is often possible to solve for the answer to a simple mathematical problem without even knowing the exact equation that was used in the solution. Consider the following question:

Question 7:
A ball travels 20 meters in 10 seconds. Its average speed is 2 m/s. What equation is used to solve for average speed, given information on distance and time?

O A. $V_{Ave} = D / T$
O B. $V_{Ave} = D * T$

Given velocity and time, it is possible to easily determine the distance traveled by dividing the distance measure by the time of flight.

Question 8:
A ball travels at a rate of 2 m/s for a time period of 10 seconds. How far does it go?

O A. 20 meters
O B. 2 meters

Velocity = 2 m/s
Time = 10 seconds
Distance = ?

A simple equation that may be used to solve for distance when average velocity and time are known is presented in the next question.

Question 9:
A ball travels at a rate of 2 m/s for a time period of 10 seconds. It goes a distance of 20 meters. What equation is used to solve for distance given information on average velocity and time?

O A. $D = V_{Ave} * T$
O B. $D = V_{Ave} / T$

It is clear that the correct result will be found if we compute the distance traveled as equal to the product of average velocity and the time interval.

Consider the following question on the calculation of the average of two scores.

Question 10:
A basketball player scored 20 points in game #1 and 30 points in game #2. What is his scoring average?

O A. 25 points per game
O B. 50 points per game

Game 1 = 20 points
Game 2 = 30 points
Average = ?

The equation used in the calculation of an average is presented in the next question.

Question 11:
A basketball player scored 20 points in game #1 and 30 points in game #2. His scoring average is 25 points per game. What equation is used to solve for an average of two scores?

O A. Average = (Score1 + Score2) * 2
O B. Average = (Score1 + Score2) / 2

By definition, the average of two scores is equal to the sum of the scores divided by two. The next question computes the average of two velocity measures.

Question 12:
A ball is thrown downward from a height. Its initial speed is -20 mps. Its final speed is -30 mps. Given these two measures, what is its average speed during its flight?

O A. -25 m/s
O B. -50 m/s

V1 = 20 m/s
V2 = 30 m/s
Average V = ?

The equation used in the calculation of an average of two velocity measures is presented in the next question.

Question 13:
A ball is thrown downward from a height. Its initial speed is -20 mps. Its final speed is -30 mps. Its average speed is -25 m/s. What equation is used to solve for average speed given information on initial and final velocity?

O A. $V_{Ave} = (V_i + V_f) * 2$
O B. $V_{Ave} = (V_i + V_f) / 2$

The calculation of the average for two basketball scores and for two velocity measures makes use of the same equation. The average of two velocity measures is equal to the sum of the measures divided by two.

Consider now the calculation of the acceleration of a falling object.

Question 14:
A ball is thrown (downward) with an initial velocity of -20 mps. 2 seconds later the final velocity is -39.6 mps. What is its acceleration?

O A. -9.8 m/s^2
O B. -19.6 m/s^2

Vi = -20 m/s
Vf = 39.6 m/s
Time = 2 seconds
Acceleration = ?

The change in velocity of -19.6 m/s occurs in 2 seconds. The change in velocity per unit time (acceleration) is -9.8 m/s^2. The equation used in the calculation of the acceleration of a falling object is presented in the next question.

Question 15:
A ball is thrown (downward) with an initial velocity of -20 mps. 2 seconds later the final velocity is -39.6 mps. Its acceleration is -9.8 m/s^2. What equation is used to solve for acceleration given information on initial velocity, final velocity and time?

O 1. $A = (V_f - V_i) / T$
O 2. $A = (V_f + V_i) / T$

The change in velocity per unit time (acceleration) is given by dividing the change in velocity by the time interval. Consider now the calculation of the final velocity of an object, given its initial velocity and acceleration:

Question 16:
A ball is thrown (downward) with an initial velocity of -20 mps. It falls for 2 seconds and experiences an acceleration of -9.8 m/s^2. What is its final velocity?

O A. -9.8 m/s
O B. -39.6 m/s

Vi = -20 m/s
Time = 2 seconds
Acceleration = -9.8m/s^2
Vf = ?

The change in velocity for the ball is -19.6 m/s. The final velocity value is determined by adding the change in velocity onto the initial velocity value. The equation used in the calculation of the final velocity of a falling object is presented in the next question.

Question 17:
A ball is thrown (downward) with an initial velocity of -20 mps. It falls for 2 seconds and experiences an acceleration of -9.8 m/s^2. Its final velocity is -39.6 m/s. What equation is used to solve for final velocity given information on initial velocity, acceleration and time?

O A. $V_f = V_i + AT$
O B. $V_f = V_i + A$

The correct answer to the above question is given by the first equation for uniformly accelerated motion.

Derivation: $D = V_i T + ½ AT^2$

The preceding exercises have provided us with three equations that we know intuitively, to be correct. Our challenge in the next exercise will be to use these three equations to derive the distance equation for uniformly accelerated motion.

Given 3 "known" equations:
1) $D = V_{Ave} * T$
2) $V_{Ave} = .5(V_i + V_f)$
3) $V_f = V_i + AT$

Derive the equation:
$D = V_i T + ½ AT^2$

The purpose of this derivation will be to start with known equations (1 – 3 above) and, through mathematical manipulation, arrive at the "new" equation ($D = V_i T + ½ AT^2$). Because we need to solve for distance, the first step in the derivation is "known" equation 1.

$D = V_{Ave} * T$ equation 1)

If we substitute equation 2 for the V_{Ave} term, we will arrive at the next step in the derivation:

$D = .5(V_i + V_f) * T$ substitute 2)

If we substitute equation 3 for the V_f term, we will arrive at the next step in the derivation:

$D = .5(V_i + V_i + AT) * T$ substitute 3)

The last two steps in the derivation involve rearrangement and consolidation of the terms on the right side of the equation:

$D = .5T(2 V_i + AT)$ rearrangement
$D = V_i T + .5 AT^2$ consolidation

This sequence of manipulations "proves" that the distance equation for uniformly accelerated motion is "true". If we substitute –9.8 m/s^2 for the acceleration term, we will arrive at the final form of the distance equation for uniformly accelerated motion:

For free fall on Earth:
$D = V_i T - 4.9 T^2$

Let's now apply this equation to three simple examples. If a ball is dropped from a height and allowed to fall for the time periods of 1, 2 and 3 seconds, how far will it travel? A graphical representation of these examples is provided in the figure below. The arrows indicate the actual distance traveled during the three time periods, although the numeric values for distance are, for now, left open.

Ball Drop from Height

$D = ViT - 4.9 T^2$

$D = - 4.9 T^2$

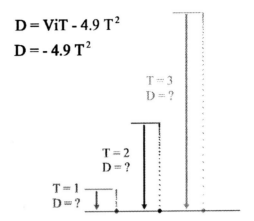

Figure 8-4. The distance of flight for a ball dropped for 1, 2 and 3 second time periods.

Example – 1 Second Drop

If the ball is dropped and falls for 1 second, how far will it travel? In this example the term "dropped" indicates that the initial velocity of the ball is zero. As a result the distance equation simplifies to:

$D = V_i T - 4.9 T^2$
$D = 0 * T - 4.9 T^2$
$D = -4.9 T^2$

The last equation above shows that the distance a dropped ball travels (in the absence of air resistance) will increase with the *square* of the time in flight. For a one second fall, the effect of the square of time will not be apparent.

Question 18:
A ball is dropped and falls for a 1 second time period. What distance does it cover?

O A. –4.9 meters
O B. –9.8 meters

The solution is given by substituting the value of time into the distance equation above. If time is one second, then time squared is equal to one as well and the distance will be computed as -4.9 meters. (D = - 4.9 * 1^2).

Example – 2 Second Drop

Question 19:
A ball is dropped and falls for a 2 second time period. What distance does it cover?

O A. −19.6 meters
O B. −9.8 meters

The solution is given by the equation $D = -4.9 * 2^2$. Thus, distance equals -19.6 meters. Note that the "two second drop" will cover a distance 4 times greater than that of a one second drop.

Example – 3 Second Drop

Question 20:
A ball is dropped and falls for a 3 second time period. What distance does it cover?

O A. −19.6 meters
O B. −44.1 meters

The solution is given by $D = -4.9 * 3^2$. Thus, distance equals -44.1 meters. Note that the "three second drop" will cover a distance 9 times greater than that of a one second drop.

We see from the previous examples that the distance of a uniformly accelerated fall will increase greatly with small increases in time. The non-linear relationship between time and distance traveled is shown in the graph below.

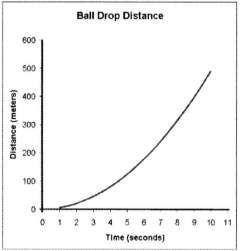

Ball Drop Distance

Figure 8-5. The relationship between falling distance and time in flight for an object falling under the influence of gravity (and without any other force acting, such as air resistance).

Note that in order to experience a free fall lasting 10 seconds, you would need to jump from a height of about 500 meters (more than a quarter mile). Actually, the data in the chart assumes that air resistance can be neglected. This is a reasonable approximation for low speed, short distance movements, but not for activities like skydiving. We will see in the fluid mechanics chapter that a fall from 500 meters can take much longer than 10 seconds, depending upon the techniques employed by the skydiver. Further, we are very hopeful that the skydiver's parachute will add considerable time to the last stages of his or her descent.

Derivation: $V_f^2 = V_i^2 - 19.6D$

The last equation of uniformly accelerated motion can be used to compute information on final velocity, initial velocity or distance, even when no information on time is available. The derivation for this equation is very straightforward, as shown below.

Derive the equation $V_f^2 = V_i^2 + 2AD$

The first step in the derivation is to insert the "known" first equation of uniformly accelerated motion:

$V_f = V_i + AT$ \qquad (Given)

For the second step, square both sides of the equation:

$V_f^2 = (V_i + AT) * (V_i + AT)$
$V_f^2 = V_i^2 + 2 V_i AT + A^2 T^2$ \quad (Square both sides)

The next step involves rearrangement of the terms in the last equation.

$V_f^2 = V_i^2 + 2A (V_i T + .5AT^2)$ \quad (Rearrange)

For the final step of the derivation, we substitute "D" for $(V_i T + .5AT^2)$. These two terms are known to be equal by the second equation for uniformly accelerated motion.

$V_f^2 = V_i^2 + 2AD$ \qquad (Substitute D)

For free fall on Earth:

$V_f{}^2 = V_i{}^2 - 19.6D$

We see from this derivation that the third equation for uniformly accelerated motion is a direct extension of the information in the first two equations of uniformly accelerated motion. Let's now apply the third equation to the solution of a freefall problem.

Example – Ball Drop Velocity

A ball is dropped and falls 44.1 meters downward. What is its final velocity?

The solution begins with the statement of the third equation of uniformly accelerated motion:

$V_f{}^2 = V_i{}^2 + 2AD$

Because the ball is "dropped", the V_i value is zero:

$V_f{}^2 = V_i{}^2 + 2AD$
$V_f{}^2 = 0 + (2 * -9.8 * -44.1)$
$V_f{}^2 = 0 + (-19.6 * -44.1)$
$V_f{}^2 = 864$

To solve for V_f, we take the square root of both sides of the equation:

$V_f = +/- 29.4$ mps

The square root result indicates that either –29.4 or +29.4, when squared, will equal 864. Because we know that the ball is moving downward, the correct answer must have a negative sign.

$V_f = -29.4$ mps

Horizontal Projection

Our analysis of uniformly accelerated motion, thus far, has been limited to the discussion of vertical motion. In this section we will discuss the motion of projectiles that move in both the horizontal and vertical dimensions.

You may worry that the addition of an extra dimension of motion will increase the complexity of our analysis. Fortunately, this will not be the case, because we will use *reductionism* to study the two dimensional motions one dimension at a time. We will see that no information will be lost in our approach and our analysis will be simplified

considerably. As a preparation to our discussion of horizontal projection, consider the following two questions:

Example – Ball Drop

A ball is dropped from a height of 19.6 meters. How long will it take to hit the ground?

The solution to this one dimensional vertical motion problem is given by the distance equation:

$D = V_i T - 4.9T^2$
$-19.6 = 0 - 4.9T^2$
$T^2 = -19.6 / -4.9$
$T^2 = 4$
$T = 2$ seconds.

Now let's consider a very similar problem for horizontal projection:

Example – Horizontal Projection

A ball is thrown *straight* forward at a speed of 10 mps from a platform that is located 19.6 meters above ground level. How long will it take for the ball to hit the ground?

The answer is: $T = 2$ seconds, as indicated by the last example.

The figure below illustrates the movement of both the dropped ball and the ball that is projected horizontally. Note that both balls are released at the same time and they both land at the same time. In fact, the vertical dimension of the motion for the horizontally projected ball is identical to that of the dropped ball at each instant in time. The dots on the curves indicate the ball's location at 1/15th second time intervals.

Drop vs. Horizontal Projection

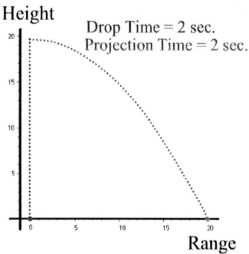

Height

Drop Time = 2 sec.
Projection Time = 2 sec.

Range

Figure 8-6. A comparison of the flight paths of a ball that has been dropped and another ball that has been projected horizontally.

The details of the time calculation for the projected ball are provided below:

$$D = V_i T - 4.9T^2$$

Note that the above equation holds only for the vertical component of motion for the projected ball. In this equation, the V_i term represents the *vertical* component of the initial velocity of the projected ball. Because the ball is being projected *horizontally*, with no upward or downward component of motion at all, the vertical component of the initial velocity is zero:

$$D = V_i T - 4.9T^2$$
$$-19.6 = 0 - 4.9T^2$$

It is very important for us to realize that the *horizontal* component of the velocity vector is *not* appropriate for use in the above equation. If we were to plug in a +10 for the V_i term, we would be indicating that the ball was thrown up with a velocity of 10 m/s. The remaining steps in the calculation are identical to that for the dropped ball:

$$T^2 = -19.6 / -4.9$$
$$T^2 = 4$$
$$T = 2 \text{ seconds.}$$

Once the time in flight for the projected ball is known, the next question to consider is: "How far forward will the ball travel?"
You may be tempted to use the uniformly accelerated motion distance equation to answer this question:

$$D = V_i T + AT^2$$

However, the term "A" in this equation has been used so far to represent the acceleration of gravity, and we must acknowledge that gravity causes objects to be accelerated *downward*, but not *forward*. Technically, the above equation can be applied to our problem, provided that we substitute zero for the horizontal component of acceleration of the ball.

$$D = V_i * T + (0) * T^2 \quad \text{(for horizontal motion)}$$
$$D = V_i * T$$
$$D = 10 * 2$$
$$D = 20 \text{ meters.}$$

The horizontal distance we have computed above is consistent with the data shown for the range of projection in the figure below. This figure also shows the ΔX and ΔY displacement components for the ball at uniformly spaced intervals of time. Note that the ΔX values are the same for every time interval during the flight of the ball.

Delta X and Delta Y Values

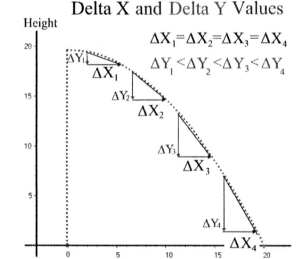

Height

$$\Delta X_1 = \Delta X_2 = \Delta X_3 = \Delta X_4$$
$$\Delta Y_1 < \Delta Y_2 < \Delta Y_3 < \Delta Y_4$$

Range

Figure 8-7. The ΔX and ΔY displacement components for the ball during horizontal projection.

As a result, it is clear that the change in position is constant for each time interval and, therefore, the velocity must also be constant:

$V = (P_F - P_I) / Time$

For the X component data:

$V_X = \Delta X / Time$

The ΔY values for the ball increase during the course of the ball flight. As a result, the Y component of the ball velocity is also increasing. We see that the acceleration of the ball is indicated on the figure by the *change* in length of the ΔY values.

$A = (V_f - V_i) / Time$

Projection at an Angle

Our final analysis of projectile motion will involve the projection of an object at an angle, such as the motion of a soccer ball that is kicked over a long distance. The key to the solution of this problem will again rely upon the use of reductionism to simplify the analysis. We will consider the vertical and horizontal components of motion separately to determine the range of motion, the time in flight and the peak height of the trajectory.

Given Vi and θ:
How far does the ball go?
How long is it in flight?
How high does the ball go?

Figure 8-8. The questions associated with projectile motion problems.

Introduction to the BallFlight Program

The BallFlight program is included as part of your KA Software installation. This program can be used to simulate uniformly accelerated motion of a ball under a variety of conditions. The "Project at Angle" display option will allow us to set the ball's initial velocity and projection angle, and then inspect the resulting "data" for the time in flight, range of motion and height of motion variables.

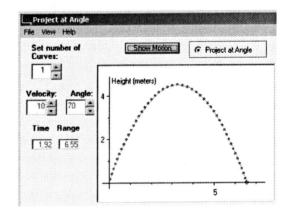

Figure 8-9. The BallFlight software program window.

Let's do a brief review of the features in the BallFlight program. To run the program, click on the Start button and select the KA Video, BallFlight option. When the program is run, the "Project at Angle" display mode is set as active and the data that was entered in the last session with the program is shown. The screen shot above shows the flight path of a ball that has been kicked from ground level at an angle of 70°.

The data shown in this figure was generated in BallFlight by doing the following actions:

1) Set the number of curves (in the upper left corner control) to 1:

2) Set the ball velocity value to 10 m/s and the projection angle to 70 degrees:

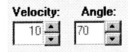

3) Click the "Show Motion" button to animate the ball flight:

Show Motion

The speed of the animation will depend upon the speed of your PC. If the animated motion is too fast, you can change the delay factor (at the bottom of the BallFlight window) to a number larger than zero. If the animation is too slow, you can change the film speed setting to a value less than 60 frames per second.

4) After the ball motion is shown, data on the motion is shown at the bottom left corner of the window.

Time	Range	Height
1.92	6.55	4.50

The total flight time shows the number of seconds required for the "real" flight of the ball, although the effect of air resistance is not included. Note that the Range, or horizontal distance covered by the ball is specified in meters in the text box above and it is also shown by the scale on the X axis of the projection graphic viewport. Similarly, the peak height of the ball flight is shown in the text box and it is also shown by the Y axis in the projection graphic viewport.

The BallFlight program allows you to display the data for as many as 6 ball projections at once. This feature is very handy, because it will allow you to compare two or more ball projections and see how changes in one of the input variables will change the outcome of the ball motion. The figure below shows a comparison of five balls that are all projected with a velocity of 25 m/s. The projection angles for the balls are 15°, 30°, 45°, 60° and 75°. Note that the time in flight data shows that the balls that are projected at the steepest angles stay in the air the longest. Note also that longest range of motion occurs with the 45° projection angle (the range of motion measures are shown on the horizontal axis of the graph). Finally, the figure shows that balls that are projected at angles less than 45° have smaller ranges of motion and shorter flight times.

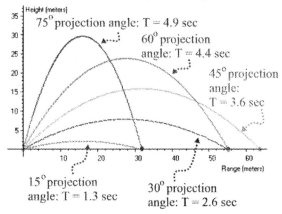

Figure 8-10. The BallFlight software program window with two projectile motions shown.

Projection at an Angle Summary

Our BallFlight program examples have illustrated a number of important principles. For each of these principles, we assume that the initial velocity of each ball is held constant and air resistance, ball spin and wind are not factors.

1) If a ball is projected from one point at ground level to another (as in a soccer kick on a level field), the largest range of ball motion will be produced with a projection angle of 45°.

2) Balls that are projected at angles between 45° and 90° will stay in the air longer than those projected at angles less than 45°.

3) The greater the angle of projection (and therefore, the greater the Y component of the initial velocity vector), the greater the ball's time in flight.

The third principle is very important. It shows that gravity influences only the vertical component of a ball's motion. Thus, it is the vertical component of velocity that determines how long a projected ball will stay in flight. The horizontal component of a ball's initial velocity will *not* be influenced by gravity. However, the higher the horizontal component of velocity, the longer the range will be for any given flight time.

Let's now use our understanding of projection at an angle to compute time in flight, range and height data for a kicked ball.

Example – Soccer Kick

A soccer ball is kicked with a velocity of 22.63 m/s in a direction 60 degrees above the horizontal. How long will the ball stay in flight?

We know that the flight time for this ball will be the same as that of another ball that is thrown straight up with a velocity equal to the vertical component of the projected ball's velocity. As a result, our first step in the solution of this problem will be to determine the velocity vector X and Y components (we will need to know the X component information when we compute the range for the flight).

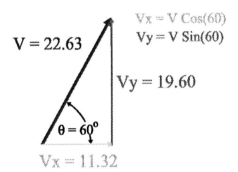

Figure 8-11. The horizontal and vertical velocity components of a ball projected at a 60 degree angle.

The figure above shows the velocity vector and its V_X and V_Y components. The calculation of the component values is shown below:

Compute V_X:
Cos θ = adjacent / hypotenuse
Cos 60 = V_X / 22.63
.500 = V_X / 22.63
V_X = 11.32 m/s

Compute V_Y:
Sin θ = opposite / hypotenuse
Sin 60 = V_Y / 22.63
.866 = V_Y / 22.63
V_Y = 19.6 m/s

A ball that is projected with a velocity of 22.63 m/s at an angle of 60 degrees will stay in the air the same amount of time as another ball that is thrown straight up with a velocity of 19.6 m/s. We can solve this problem with the first equation of uniformly accelerated motion:

$V_f = V_i - 9.8\ T$

In order to solve this equation for the value of "T", we must know values for V_f and V_i. The initial velocity is +19.6 m/s. The final velocity will depend upon the time period of the flight. We know that a ball that is thrown straight up will have a "final velocity" value of zero is we consider the time interval between the toss and the time "peak of flight" occurs. We can therefore solve for the time to peak of flight:

$0 = 19.6 - 9.8\ T$
$9.8\ T = 19.6$
$T_{up} = 2$ seconds. (Time to reach peak)

We know that if it takes 2 seconds for the ball to reach peak of flight, it will take another 2 seconds for the ball to fall back to the ground. Thus the total flight time must equal 4 seconds:

$T_{down} = 2$ seconds. (Time to fall back down)
$T_{total} = 4$ seconds.

We can now determine the range (distance traveled in the horizontal direction). Note that the ball has not accelerated horizontally and the appropriate equation for distance is D = V * T. Note also that the value for time is set to the full 4 seconds that the ball is in the air.

$D_X = V_{Ave} * T$
$D_X = 11.32 * 4$
$D_X = 45.28$ meters

Finally, we can compute the maximum height attained by the projected ball by acknowledging that it will be equal to the height of a ball that is thrown straight upward with the Y component of the projected ball velocity vector. Note that in the following equations, the value of "T" (time) is set to the time to reach peak of flight, or 2 seconds.

$D_{up} = V_i\ T - 4.9T^2$
$D_{up} = 19.6 * 2 - (4.9 * 2^2)$
$D_{up} = 39.2 - 19.6$
$D_{up} = 19.6$ meters.

Conclusions

Our work with uniformly accelerated motion is now complete. We have seen that, while a body is in flight, the motion of its center of gravity will follow a very predictable flight path. Further, the initial velocity of a projected body can be used, along with the equations of uniformly accelerated motion, to define all aspects of the body's flight.

Figure 8-12. An example of projectile motion of the human body.

The examples in this chapter lend themselves to relatively simple solutions because the acceleration of a body in flight can be assumed to be a uniform −9.8 m/s^2. We will see in the Linear Kinetics chapters that the force of gravity is also a factor in the general motion of a body in contact with the ground and other bodies. However, the acceleration of a body in general motion will *not* be −9.8 m/s^2, and the work we have done in this chapter will provide us only with a starting point for the calculation of the forces that cause motion.

Answers to Chapter Questions

Question 1:
What is the change in velocity per unit time for each of the time intervals (0 − 1), (1 − 2) and (2 - 3 seconds?

O A. -9.8 m/s per second
O B. -4.9 m/s per second
O C. −29.4 m/s per second

The correct answer is A. By definition, the acceleration of gravity is the change in velocity per unit time. The change in velocity during each one-second time interval is −9.8 m/s.

Question 2:
What is instantaneous velocity of the ball at instant in time T = 1?

O A. -9.8 meters per second
O B. +9.8 meters per second
O C. +19.6 meters per second

The correct answer is B. After one second of flight, the acceleration of gravity has caused the ball's velocity to change from +19.6 m/s to +9.8 m/s. At this instant, the ball is still traveling upward.

Question 3:
What is instantaneous velocity of the ball at instant in time T = 2?

O A. -9.8 meters per second
O B. +9.8 meters per second
O C. 0 meters per second

The correct answer is C. After two seconds of flight, the acceleration of gravity has caused the ball's velocity to change from +19.6 m/s to zero m/s. At this instant, the ball is momentarily at its peak and is just about to begin falling downward.

Question 4:
What is instantaneous velocity of the ball at instant in time T = 3?

O A. -9.8 meters per second
O B. +9.8 meters per second
O C. 0 meters per second

The correct answer is A. After three seconds of flight, the ball has reached its peak and has been falling for a full second. The acceleration of gravity has caused the ball's velocity to change to −9.8 m/s at this instant.

Question 5:
What is instantaneous velocity of the ball at instant in time T = 4?

O A. -9.8 meters per second
O B. −19.6 meters per second
O C. +9.8 meters per second

The correct answer is B. After four seconds of flight, the ball is just about to hit the ground. The ball has been falling for 2 seconds since its peak and the V_f value is −19.6 m/s.

Question 6:
A ball travels 20 meters in 10 seconds. What is its average speed?

O A. 20 meters per second
O B. 2 meters per second

The correct answer is B. If a ball moves at 2 meters per second for a period of 10 seconds it will cover a distance of 20 meters.

Question 7:
A ball travels 20 meters in 10 seconds. Its average speed is 2 m/s. What equation is used to solve for average speed, given information on distance and time?

o A. $V_{Ave} = D / T$
o B. $V_{Ave} = D * T$

The correct answer is A. The distance traveled, divided by the time period will equal the velocity expressed in meters per second.

Question 8:
A ball travels at a rate of 2 m/s for a time period of 10 seconds. How far does it go?

o A. 20 meters
o B. 2 meters

The correct answer is A. If a ball moves at 2 meters per second for a period of 10 seconds it will cover a distance of 20 meters.

Question 9:
A ball travels at a rate of 2 m/s for a time period of 10 seconds. It goes a distance of 20 meters. What equation is used to solve for distance given information on average velocity and time?

o A. $D = V_{Ave} * T$
o B. $D = V_{Ave} / T$

The correct answer is A. The distance traveled will be equal to the average velocity multiplied by the time period of flight.

Question 10:
A basketball player scored 20 points in game #1 and 30 points in game #2. What is his scoring average?

o A. 25 points per game
o B. 50 points per game

The correct answer is A. For more details see the discussion below.

Question 11:
A basketball player scored 20 points in game #1 and 30 points in game #2. His scoring average is 25 points per game. What equation is used to solve for an average of two scores?

o A. Average = (Score1 + Score2) * 2
o B. Average = (Score1 + Score2) / 2

The correct answer is B. The average is equal to the sum of the scores divided by the number of scores.

Question 12:
A ball is thrown downward from a height. Its initial speed is -20 mps. Its final speed is -30 mps. Given these two measures, what is its average speed during its flight?

o A. -25 m/s
o B. -50 m/s

The correct answer is A. For more details see the discussion below.

Question 13:
A ball is thrown downward from a height. Its initial speed is -20 mps. Its final speed is -30 mps. Its average speed is -25 m/s. What equation is used to solve for average speed given information on initial and final velocity?

o A. $V_{Ave} = (V_i + V_f) * 2$
o B. $V_{Ave} = (V_i + V_f) / 2$

The correct answer is B. The average is equal to the sum of the two velocity measures divided by two.

Question 14:
A ball is thrown (downward) with an initial velocity of -20 mps. 2 seconds later the final velocity is -39.6 mps. What is its acceleration?

o A. -9.8 m/s^2
o B. -19.6 m/s^2

The correct answer is A. The change in velocity of -19.6 m/s occurs in 2 seconds. The change in velocity per unit time (acceleration) is -9.8 m/s^2.

Question 15:
A ball is thrown (downward) with an initial velocity of -20 mps. 2 seconds later the final velocity is -39.6 mps. Its acceleration is -9.8 m/s^2. What equation is used to solve for acceleration given information on initial velocity, final velocity and time?

o 1. $A = (V_f - V_i) / T$
o 2. $A = (V_f + V_i) / T$

The correct answer is A. The change in velocity is -19.6 m/s. The change in velocity per unit time (acceleration) is given by dividing the change in velocity by the time interval.

Question 16:
A ball is thrown (downward) with an initial velocity of -20 mps. It falls for 2 seconds and experiences an acceleration of -9.8 m/s^2. What is its final velocity?

O A. −9.8 m/s
O B. -39.6 m/s

The correct answer is B. The change in velocity is −19.6 m/s. This change in velocity is added onto the initial velocity value.

Question 17:
A ball is thrown (downward) with an initial velocity of -20 mps. It falls for 2 seconds and experiences an acceleration of -9.8 m/s^2. Its final velocity is −39.6 m/s. What equation is used to solve for final velocity given information on initial velocity, acceleration and time?

O A. $V_f = V_i + AT$
O B. $V_f = V_i + A$

The correct answer is B. The change in velocity is −19.6 m/s. This change in velocity is added onto the initial velocity value.

Question 18:
A ball is dropped and falls for a 1 second time period. What distance does it cover?

O A. −4.9 meters
O B. −9.8 meters

The correct answer is A. The solution is given by D = -4.9 * 1^2.

Question 19:
A ball is dropped and falls for a 2 second time period. What distance does it cover?
O A. −19.6 meters
O B. −9.8 meters

The correct answer is A. The solution is given by D = -4.9 * 2^2.

Question 20:
A ball is dropped and falls for a 3 second time period. What distance does it cover?
O A. −19.6 meters
O B. −44.1 meters

The correct answer is A. The solution is given by D = -4.9 * 3^2.

Chapter 9
Video Digitizing and Movement Analysis

Video Digitizing

Video technology allows us to record a continuous stream of information for any human movement. Discussions from prior chapters have shown that human movement can be quantified by digitizing body landmark points and determining their XY coordinate values. However, our measurements so far, have focused upon the analysis of only one or two XY coordinate values at a time. For example, the figure below shows that a displacement vector for a given portion of the movement can be determined if the start and end XY coordinate values are known.

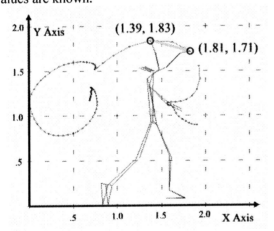

Figure 9-1. Fingertip XY coordinate values and a displacement vector for a moment during the action phase of a throwing motion.

While individual measures of human movement are valuable, they barely scratch the surface of the information available in a video analysis project. For example, the movement for the above throwing motion involves a total of 118 video fields. As a result, a complete analysis of the kinematics of this movement will involve a fairly lengthy (but very repetitious) analysis procedure. To determine the

fingertip velocity and acceleration for the full motion we must perform the following steps:

1) The fingertip point must be manually digitized from the beginning of the wind-up motion through to the end of the follow through. For this throwing motion, the digitizing procedure will provide us with a listing of 118 XY coordinate values.

2) The fingertip XY values will initially be recorded with respect to the rectangular grid of pixels that compose a video image. These pixel-based XY values will need to be rescaled to express the fingertip positions in "real world" units such as meters.

3) The displacement vector components between each successive pair of XY coordinates (i.e., from images 1-2, 2-3, 3-4,...117-118) must be determined next. This stage of the analysis will provide us with a listing of the "change in X" (ΔX) and "change in Y" (ΔY) values.

4) The ΔX and ΔY values can then be divided by the time interval between fields to provide information on the X and Y components of the velocity vectors.

5) Finally, the velocity information can be analyzed to determine the change in velocity (ΔVx and ΔVy) information. These values are then divided by the time interval between fields to compute the X and Y components of the acceleration vectors.

The above five steps allow us to define a complete kinematic description of a given body landmark point. If this procedure is repeated for the other points on the body, we will be able to completely define the linear kinematics of the human movement in question.

This chapter will define the mathematical procedures used to determine a body landmark's position, velocity and acceleration as it progresses from the beginning to the end of a movement. Given an understanding of these foundation analysis procedures, you will be able to understand more fully the results that are "automatically" produced by the KA software.

Quantification of Movement Data

Video Digitizing for 2D Data

The first stage in the quantification of video data involves determining the XY coordinates of selected body landmark points as a function of time. The XY coordinate values are initially expressed as the location of a pixel on the computer screen.

As noted in chapter 3, each video image in a KA image set is stored in bit mapped files that can be displayed in a 640 x 480 format. Because almost all computers have display resolutions considerably higher than 640 x 480, the KA software resizes each video image to nearly fill the screen of your PC. For example, a 17" CRT monitor will typically be set for a 1024 x 768 resolution on a Windows based PC. On such a PC system, KA will enlarge each video image to fill a 960 x 720 pixel portion of the screen. The figure below shows the XY reference frame that is used to digitize the video of a martial arts kicking motion.

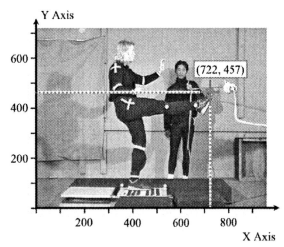

Figure 9-2. The XY coordinate reference frame used for digitizing on a 1024 x 768 resolution Windows desktop.

Note that the origin for the XY reference frame is set at the bottom left corner of the video image. The

scale along the X axis shows that the highest possible X value is 960. Similarly, the highest possible value along the Y axis is 720. At the instant shown, the XY coordinates for the right toe point are (722, 457). When you digitize a body landmark for a KA project, a long list of XY coordinate values (with one pair of XY values for every picture in the image set) are stored on your PC for later processing by the software.

Video Scale Factor

The above figure shows that the toe is 457 pixels above the bottom of the video image. We can use the fine grid of pixels on the video image to make measurements of the movement in much the same way that we can measure the distances between points on a sheet of graph paper. However, the scale of our video based "graph paper" cannot be assumed to be aligned with typical "real world" units of measure. Thus, we can measure the number of pixels that a performer's toe moves between two video fields on the computer screen but we cannot immediately know the "real world" length of the motion (measured in meters).

Question 1:
How much distance is represented by the height of a single line of video pixels in figure 9-2?

O A) About 10 centimeters
O B) Exactly 1 centimeter
O C) Less than one centimeter.

The actual height of a pixel in the figure is about 2.5 millimeters (4 pixels per centimeter). There are about 600 pixels between the supporting foot and the top of the performer's head. This indicates that the standing height at the moment shown is about 1.5 meters.

A quick inspection of the data shows that the height of a pixel must be considerably less than a centimeter. The exact measurement of a pixel's height is given through the calculation of the video's *scale factor*. The scale factor allows us to translate any measure expressed in pixels to an equivalent measure expressed in meters.

The figure below shows a video image of a scale pole with the upper point at pixel coordinate (490, 620) and the lower point at (490, 120). The ΔY for these points is 500. Note that the distance between the scale points and the height of the research participant are about the same. Clearly the number 500 is not a measure of the person's height in real world units (feet, meters, etc.). In order to translate the digitized coordinate data into "real world" unit measures we must calculate the scale factor for the image set.

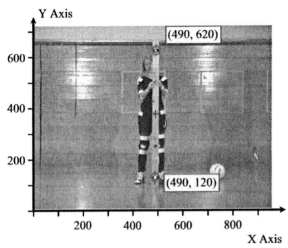

Figure 9-3. An example of a scale pole video image and the XY coordinates of the top and bottom scale pole points.

The equation used in the calculation of the scale factor (SF) is as follows:

$$SF = D_{TRUE} / D_{SCALED}$$

Where: D_{TRUE} (distance true) is the length of the scale pole expressed in real world units (the pole shown above is 1.6 meters long), and D_{SCALED} (distance scaled) is the apparent height of the scale pole expressed in pixels (the distance scaled for the above figure is 500 pixels).

The scale factor is computed as follows:

$$SF = D_{TRUE} / D_{SCALED}$$
$$SF = 1.6 / 500$$
$$SF = 0.0032$$

Thus, the height of a pixel is 3.2 millimeters for the camera distance and zoom lens setting shown in the above figure. Once the scale factor is determined, the distance between any two points in the plane of the video can be readily calculated. For example, if the standing height of a person is determined to be 490 pixels, the true height of the individual is computed as follows:

$$D_{TRUE} = D_{SCALED} * SF$$
$$D_{TRUE} = 490 * 0.0032$$
$$D_{TRUE} = 1.568 \text{ meters}$$

Question 2:
Imagine that the height of two performers is measured with the scale factor information discussed above. The height of participant A is measured as 1.568 meters and participant B's height is measured as 1.566 meters. Given this information, are we sure that participant A is taller than participant B?

O A) Yes.
O B) No.

It should be noted that the computed scale factor is only good for XY coordinates data that are "in the plane" in which the meter stick is held. If you look closely at the above figure, you will notice that the scale pole and the subject's feet are on the floor, but because the subject is standing behind the pole, her foot position appears to be higher.

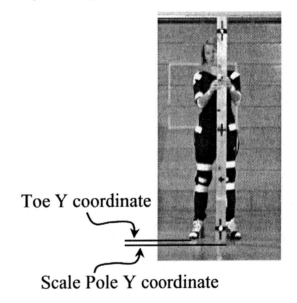

Figure 9-4. An illustration of the apparent differences in the floor level at the bottom of a scale pole and at the toes of a researcher standing behind the pole.

We know, of course, that the subject is not floating above the floor and therefore her true height is actually underestimated from this figure. Similarly, if the subject moves closer to the camera, her image (and corresponding XY coordinate values) will be enlarged on the video screen. A calculation of her standing height will indicate that she "got taller" if the original scale factor is used in the calculation. In fact, a new scale factor will have to be calculated if the participant's position (or the zoom setting of the camera lens) changes between trials of data collection. As a result, we see that our scale factor calculation yields accurate data for points that fall in the vertical plane defined by the scale pole, approximate data for points near this plane and increasingly distorted data for points that fall further from the plane. This observation reminds us that we should be very careful to hold our scale pole in the plane of motion being studied.

If a scale pole is not held up for scale, any known length that is contained in the plane of the video image can be used in the scale factor calculation. Thus, we could use two points on a golf club or even the distance between two spots on the floor in place of a scale pole as long as two requirements are met:

1) The distance between the two points (in real world units) must be known.

2) The two points must be contained within the plane of motion for the two-dimensional trial.

Question 3:
Imagine that after you have recorded video for a movement you realize that you forgot to hold up a scale pole. Can you set the tripod back on the floor, replace the camera on the tripod, and record the scale factor later?

O A) Yes.
O B) Probably not.

Question 4:
Imagine that after you have recorded video for a movement you realize that you forgot to hold up a scale pole. As you inspect the video image you notice that there is a window just behind your participant's line of motion. Through this window you can see a fence post. If you measure the height of this fence post, can it be used to determine the scale factor for your data?

O A) Yes.
O B) No.

Aspect Ratio

Our discussion of scale factor provides a basic foundation for understanding how measurements can be made from video. However, there is one more fine point that must be mentioned before we can proceed further.

The above discussion has implied that a video pixel is "square" - that a pixel's height and width are equal. Actually, this is not exactly true. An original video file will typically be captured with a resolution of 720 x 480 pixels (for NTSC video signals). This original video must be resized to 640 x 480 as a first step in the video analysis process. This resized video image is then approximately correct. These 640 x 480 pixel images may still be slightly "too tall" or slightly "too wide" depending upon slight inconsistencies in the video recording and capture hardware. The KA software uses an "aspect ratio correction factor" to make final adjustments to the height width ratio of a video pixel. These aspect ratio correction factors range from 0.974 to 1.007 for typical camera / capture card combinations.

Two-Dimensional Motion Analysis

The quantitative analysis of video data involves two phases: In phase #1, the video is digitized and XY coordinates are collected for selected body landmarks across a series of video images. In phase #2, the XY data is analyzed and quantitative data on the position, velocity and acceleration values are determined.

We will use the data from a simple martial arts kicking motion to illustrate the "phase #2" motion analysis process. The following illustration shows an image sequence figure for the kicking motion.

Figure 9-5. Martial arts kicking motion image sequence figure.

The complete image set for this movement is stored under the name "TJKickS" on your KAPro CD-ROM. To simplify our work in this chapter, the TJKickS file has been trimmed down to include only 10 images. The figure below shows some of the results of the digitizing work for this image set. The right toe pixel based XY coordinates for pictures 2, 6 and 10 are shown.

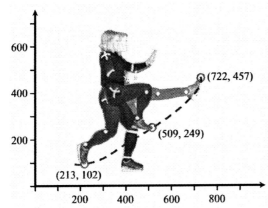

Figure 9-6. The right toe pixel XY coordinates for pictures 2, 6 and 10 in the TJKickS image set.

A complete listing of the pixel based XY coordinates for the full 10 image movement is shown below:

N	Xs	Ys
1	183	75
2	213	102
3	258	138
4	327	168
5	409	201
6	509	249
7	605	318
8	675	399
9	713	444
10	722	457

Given this listing of XY coordinate values, we will be able to use a spreadsheet to compute the toe velocity and acceleration values. To simplify our work, we will compute the X and Y components of velocity and acceleration separately.

X Component Velocity Calculation

The following spreadsheet illustrates a procedure that can be used to calculate the X component of the right toe velocity vector.

	FS=	30	SF=	0.002486902		
N	Xs	Xt	N'	DelX	Vx'	Vx
1	183	0.455				
			1.5	0.075	2.24	
2	213	0.530				2.80
			2.5	0.112	3.36	
3	258	0.642				4.25
			3.5	0.172	5.15	
4	327	0.813				5.63
			4.5	0.204	6.12	
5	409	1.017				6.79
			5.5	0.249	7.46	
6	509	1.266				7.31
			6.5	0.239	7.16	
7	605	1.505				6.19
			7.5	0.174	5.22	
8	675	1.679				4.03
			8.5	0.095	2.84	
9	713	1.773				1.75
			9.5	0.022	0.67	
10	722	1.796				

The top line in the spreadsheet shows the film speed (FS = 30) for the project. To keep this example file short we sampled data from every other field in the video. Thus, the time interval between images is $1/30^{th}$ second and the effective film speed is 30. The scale factor is shown in the upper right corner of the spreadsheet (SF = .002486902).

The lower portion of the spreadsheet is organized into 7 columns of information. A description of the contents of each of these columns is provided below:

Column N: This column holds the picture number of each image in the image set. This number represents the instant in time when each video image was exposed. For this kicking motion, there are ten pictures in the movement sequence. The below illustration shows the toe movement pattern and the picture numbers for each of the 10 images in the TJKickS file.

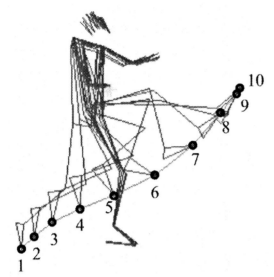

Figure 9-7. Stick figure picture numbers for the TJKickS file.

Column Xs: This column holds the scaled (in pixels) X-coordinate data for the toe. The numbers are produced by the KA manual digitizing process. Note that the X coordinate values for pictures 2, 6 and 10 on the spreadsheet match the values shown in figure 9-6.

Column Xt: This column holds the X "true" values. The numbers in this column have been multiplied by the scale factor to express the toe X coordinates in meters. The equation: Xt = Xs * SF is used to compute the X true values. The units for the X true values are meters, measured as the distance to the right of the XY reference frame origin.

Once the Xs coordinate values are entered into a spreadsheet, the Xt column data can be rapidly computed with spreadsheet formulas. The figure below shows that the Xt value for picture 1 is given by the following spreadsheet formula:

=B3*0.002486902

This formula is stored in cell C3. It causes the contents of cell C3 to be equal to the contents of cell B3 (the Xs value) multiplied by the scale factor value. This formula could also be expressed as:

=B3*E1

The use of an absolute reference to cell location E1 would make it easier to use this spreadsheet as a template for use with different video analysis projects.

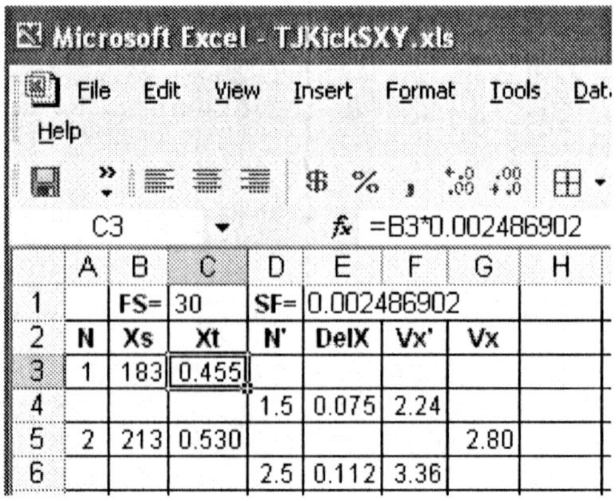

Figure 9-8. The spreadsheet formula used in the calculation of Xt values.

Column N': This column is added to allow us to label the ΔX values with respect to the time line of the image set. Thus, the N' column holds the "shifted picture numbers" for each "between picture" measure on the spreadsheet. For example, the shifted picture number 1.5 represents an instant in time midway between pictures 1 and 2.

Column DelX: The DelX column holds the ΔX measures that are calculated between pictures 1-2, 2-3, 3-4, ..., 9-10. Because these ΔX measures are associated with "between picture" time periods, they are entered on the same row as the N' shifted picture numbers (1.5, 2.5, 3.5, ..., 9.5). The spreadsheet formula for the ΔX calculation in cell E4 is shown below:

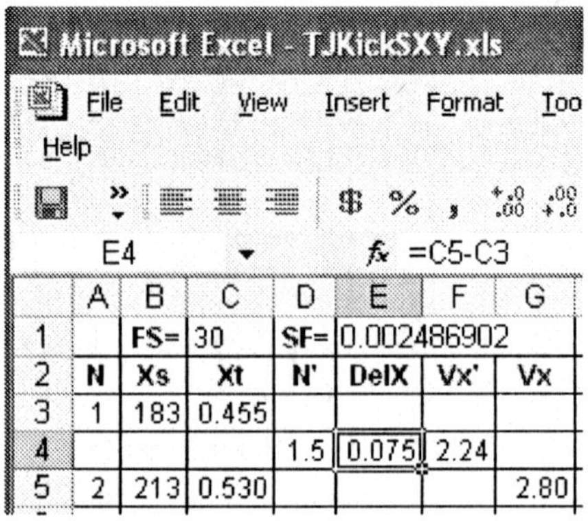

Figure 9-9. The calculation of delta X (the change in X position) is shown in cell E4.

The spreadsheet formula in cell E4 is set as follows:

=C5-C3

This formula computes the ΔX value as the change in X for the interval between pictures 1 and 2. The formula sets the contents of cell E4 to be equal to the difference between cell C5 (the final X coordinate for this interval) and cell C3 (the initial X coordinate for this interval).

Column Vx': The Vx' column holds data for the X component of velocity. These velocity measures are estimates of velocity "between pictures", i.e., between pictures 1-2, 2-3, ..., 9-10. As a result, the Vx' measures are entered on the same row as the N' "shifted" picture numbers. The equation used in the calculation of the X component of velocity is:

$Vx' = \Delta X * FS$
Where: FS = Film Speed

The spreadsheet formula for cell F4 in the figure below is:

=E4*30

This formula multiplies the ΔX value by the film speed (for this image set, the film speed was 30 pictures per second). This formula is equivalent to dividing the ΔX value by the time interval between images ($1/30^{th}$ second).

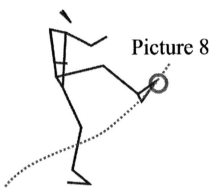

Figure 9-10. The formula for the calculation of Vx' data is shown in the formula bar.

The Vx' value for picture 1.5 represents the X component of velocity for the toe when it is *between* pictures 1 and 2. However, this Vx' value does not provide a good measure of the toe velocity X component at exactly picture 1, or at exactly picture 2. As a result, Vx' velocity measures can be inconvenient.

For example, suppose we want to know the toe velocity for the martial arts kick at the moment of impact with the target. The figure below shows that the toe impacts the target on picture 8.

Figure 9-11. An illustration of the toe impact event for the TJKickS file.

The velocity chart Vx' values will provide us with information on toe velocity at picture 7.5 (just before toe impact) and at picture 8.5 (just after toe impact). However, the Vx' values will not provide information on the toe velocity at the moment shown by video image #8. To get an estimate of the toe velocity at exactly picture 8, or for that matter, at any integer value picture number, we must take one more step in our velocity analysis.

Column Vx: The Vx column holds estimates for velocity at whole integer picture numbers (at exactly picture 2, 3, 4, etc.). To understand how Vx values are calculated, consider this simple example.

Question 5:
The data for a given image set indicates that the Vx' value for picture 1.5 is 3 mps and the Vx' value for picture 2.5 is 5 mps. A plot of these Vx' values as a function of time is shown in the following graph. What is the value of Vx at picture 2 for this data?

Velocity (mps)

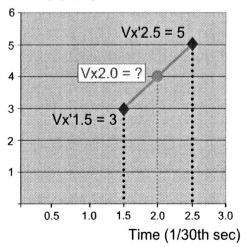

Figure 9-12. Estimation of a Vx value from measures of Vx'.

O A) 3 mps.
O B) 4 mps.
O C) 5 mps.

Question 6:
What formula did you use to compute the Vx value answer for the last question?

O A) $V_{X2} = (V_{X'1.5} + V_{X'2.5}) / 2$
O B) $V_{X2} = (V_{X'1.5} + V_{X'2.5}) * 2$
O C) $V_{X2} = (V_{X'1.5} - V_{X'2.5}) / 2$.

The following figure illustrates the relationship between Vx' (shifted picture) measures of velocity and Vx (centered picture) measures of velocity for the martial arts kicking motion.

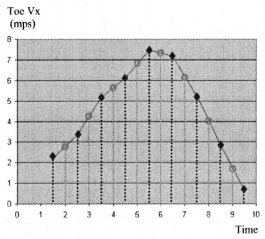

Figure 9-13. A velocity curve graph showing the toe Vx and Vx' values.

The figure shows the velocity curve for the toe motion. The diamond shaped markers represent the Vx' measures as a function of time. The circle markers indicate the Vx values. The horizontal axis represents time, with the spacing between tick marks equal to 1/30th second.

Notice that the Vx' markers are plotted directly above the "shifted picture number" values on the time axis (i.e., above 1.5, 2.5, 3.5, ..., 9.5). The Vx values are plotted half-way between each neighboring pair of Vx' values. Thus, if the Vx' value at picture 1.5 is 2.24 mps and the Vx' value at picture 2.5 is 3.36, the Vx value at picture 2 is half way between these two values, or 2.80 mps. The formula for the calculation of Vx is as follows:

$$VX_N = (VX_{N-.5} + VX_{N+.5}) / 2$$

Where:
VX_N - the toe X component of velocity for a whole integer picture number.
$VX_{N-.5}$ - the toe Vx' value for the interval just before picture N (between picture N-1 and picture N).
$VX_{N+.5}$ - the toe Vx' value for the interval just after picture N (between picture N and picture N+1).

The Vx values are plotted directly above each whole integer picture number on the time axis. These Vx measures provide information on the toe velocity at the moment shown in each successive video image for the movement. Because the Vx measures are "in sync" with the video timeline, they are shown on all KA software X-component velocity curves.

The calculation of Vx within the velocity spreadsheet uses the VX_N formula above. The following figure shows the Vx calculation formula for cell G5.

	A	B	C	D	E	F	G
1		FS=	30	SF=	0.002486902		
2	N	Xs	Xt	N'	DelX	Vx'	Vx
3	1	183	0.455				
4				1.5	0.075	2.24	
5	2	213	0.530				2.80
6				2.5	0.112	3.36	

Microsoft Excel - TJKickSXY.xls — File Edit View Insert Format Tool — 100% — G5 — ƒx =(F4+F6)/2

Figure 9-14. The TJKickS spreadsheet is shown. The formula for the calculation of Vx is shown in the formula bar.

Note that the contents of cell G5 is set equal to the formula:

=(F4+F6)/2

The formula computes the Vx value as the average of the preceding and following Vx' values. The full velocity calculation spreadsheet is shown below.

Y Component Velocity Calculation

The Y component of velocity is computed with a spreadsheet that is virtually identical to that described above. The figure below shows the Y component velocity calculation spreadsheet. Aside from differences in column labels, the only substantive change in this spreadsheet involves the Yt (Y true) calculation formula.

Microsoft Excel - TJKickSXY.xls

File Edit View Insert Format Too

100%

G7 f_x =(F6+F8)/2

	A	B	C	D	E	F	G
1		FS=	30	SF=	0.0024886902		
2	N	Xs	Xt	N'	DelX	Vx'	Vx
3	1	183	0.455				
4				1.5	0.075	2.24	
5	2	213	0.530				2.80
6				2.5	0.112	3.36	
7	3	258	0.642				4.25
8				3.5	0.172	5.15	
9	4	327	0.813				5.63
10				4.5	0.204	6.12	
11	5	409	1.017				6.79
12				5.5	0.249	7.46	
13	6	509	1.266				7.31
14				6.5	0.239	7.16	
15	7	605	1.505				6.19
16				7.5	0.174	5.22	
17	8	675	1.679				4.03
18				8.5	0.095	2.84	
19	9	713	1.773				1.75
20				9.5	0.022	0.67	
21	10	722	1.796				

Figure 9-15. The complete TJKickS Vx spreadsheet.

Given information on Xs data (from the manual digitizing process), film speed and scale factor, the spreadsheet can be used to compute the toe velocity X component as a function of time. The martial arts kicking motion provides us with a very short example of the velocity calculation process. A more realistic "full length" movement will involve many more video images and a longer spreadsheet but the details of the calculation process will not change at all. It is interesting to note that while the KA software can seemingly magically compute kinematic measures, it is really doing nothing more complicated than you could do with an inexpensive hand calculator.

Microsoft Excel - TJKickSXY.xls

File Edit View Insert Format Tools

9   100%

C3 f_x =B3*0.002486902*1.007

	A	B	C	D	E	F	G
1		FS =	30		SF =	0.002486902	
2	N	Ys	Yt	N'	DelY	Vy'	Vy
3	1	75	0.188				
4				1.5	0.068	2.03	
5	2	102	0.255				2.37
6				2.5	0.090	2.70	
7	3	138	0.346				2.48
8				3.5	0.075	2.25	
9	4	168	0.421				2.37
10				4.5	0.083	2.48	
11	5	201	0.503				3.04
12				5.5	0.120	3.61	
13	6	249	0.624				4.40
14				6.5	0.173	5.18	
15	7	318	0.796				5.63
16				7.5	0.203	6.09	
17	8	399	0.999				4.73
18				8.5	0.113	3.38	
19	9	444	1.112				2.18
20				9.5	0.033	0.98	
21	10	457	1.144				

Figure 9-16. The TJKickS Vy spreadsheet. The formula for cell C3 includes an aspect ratio correction factor in the calculation of Yt.

Note that the formula in cell C3 is as follows:

=B3*0.002489602*1.007

This formula computes the Y "true" value as the product of the pixel based Y measure, multiplied by the scale factor (0.002486902), and also multiplied by the aspect ratio correction factor for the video image (1.007). The aspect ratio correction factor adjusts for the "slightly too wide" video image (see the discussion of video aspect ratio at the beginning of this chapter).

Velocity Magnitude

Once the X and Y components of the velocity vector for a point are know, the velocity magnitude is calculated with the following equation:

$$V_{MAG} = \sqrt{V_X^{\,2} + V_Y^{\,2}}$$

Velocity magnitude can be computed rapidly within a spreadsheet. The following figure shows the above formula used in the calculation of velocity magnitude.

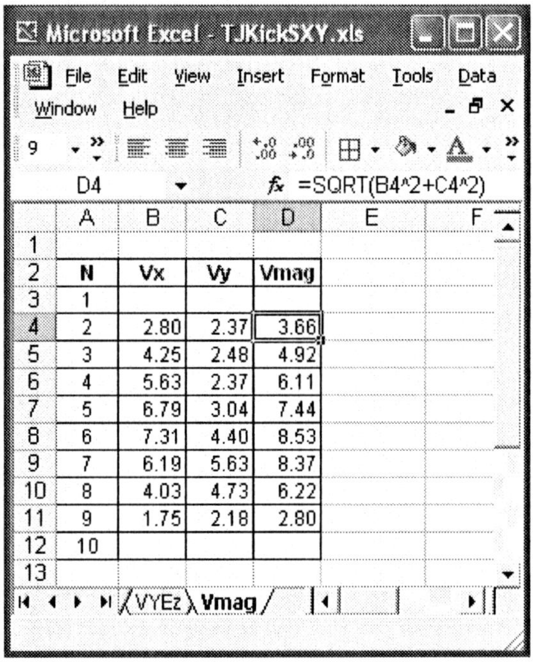

	A	B	C	D
1				
2	N	Vx	Vy	Vmag
3	1			
4	2	2.80	2.37	3.66
5	3	4.25	2.48	4.92
6	4	5.63	2.37	6.11
7	5	6.79	3.04	7.44
8	6	7.31	4.40	8.53
9	7	6.19	5.63	8.37
10	8	4.03	4.73	6.22
11	9	1.75	2.18	2.80
12	10			
13				

Figure 9-17. The TJKickS Vx and Vy data are shown. The spreadsheet formula used to calculate velocity magnitude is shown in the formula bar.

Acceleration Spreadsheet

The calculation procedure for acceleration measures is very similar to that used in the calculation of velocity. Velocity is computed as the change in *position* with respect to time. Acceleration is computed as the change in *velocity* with respect to time. The main difference between a velocity calculation spreadsheet and an acceleration calculation spreadsheet is that the DelX column is replaced with a DelVx column. The spreadsheet for the TJKickS Ax data is shown below:

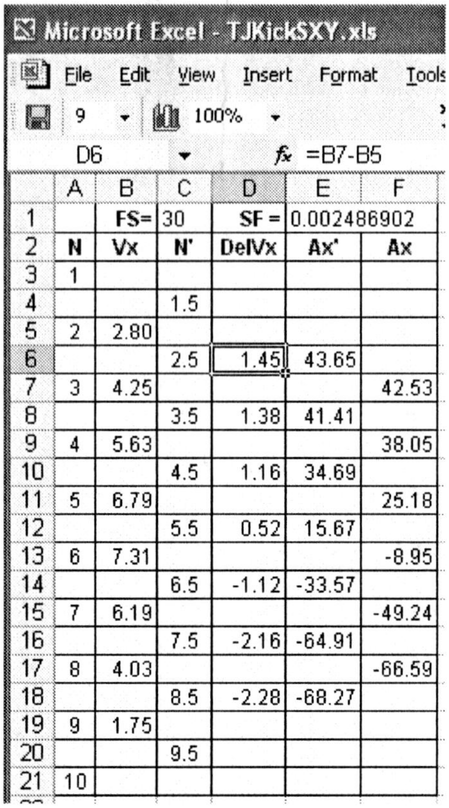

	A	B	C	D	E	F
1		FS=	30	SF =	0.002486902	
2	N	Vx	N'	DelVx	Ax'	Ax
3	1					
4			1.5			
5	2	2.80				
6			2.5	1.45	43.65	
7	3	4.25				42.53
8			3.5	1.38	41.41	
9	4	5.63				38.05
10			4.5	1.16	34.69	
11	5	6.79				25.18
12			5.5	0.52	15.67	
13	6	7.31				-8.95
14			6.5	-1.12	-33.57	
15	7	6.19				-49.24
16			7.5	-2.16	-64.91	
17	8	4.03				-66.59
18			8.5	-2.28	-68.27	
19	9	1.75				
20			9.5			
21	10					

Figure 9-18. The TJKickS Ax spreadsheet.

The formula bar in the figure shows that the DelVx (change in the X component of velocity) for cell D6 is computed with the following formula:

=B7 – B5

This formula computes the change in velocity as the final velocity value for the interval minus the initial velocity value for the interval. The values in the Ax' column are computed with the following equation:

Ax' = DelVx * FS

This equation effectively computes acceleration as the change in velocity per unit time. Note: the time interval between pictures is 1/30th second. Multiplying DelVx by 30 is the same as dividing DelVx by 1/30.

The Ax column in the spreadsheet computes the X component of acceleration at the moment each picture in the image set is exposed.

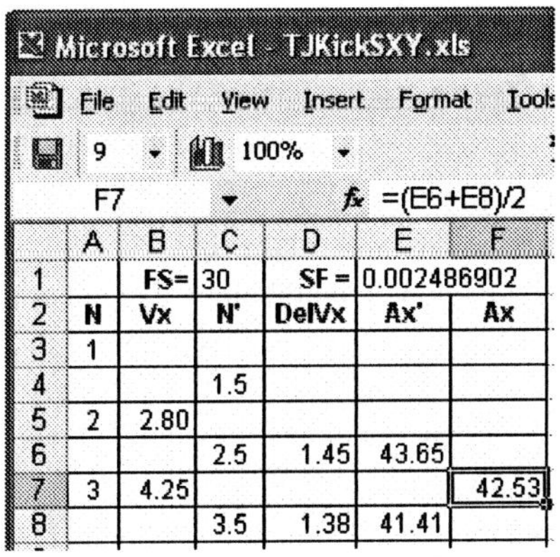

	A	B	C	D	E	F
1		FS=	30	SF =	0.002486902	
2	N	Vx	N'	DelVx	Ax'	Ax
3	1					
4			1.5			
5	2	2.80				
6			2.5	1.45	43.65	
7	3	4.25				42.53
8			3.5	1.38	41.41	

Figure 9-19. The formula for the calculation of cell F7 Ax value is shown in the spreadsheet formula bar.

Note that the value of Ax for each picture is computed as the average of the preceding and following Ax' values. This calculation procedure involves the same approach that was used in the calculation of Vx.

The Y component of acceleration is computed with the exact same formulas as those used in the Ax spreadsheet (Note: The correction for the aspect ratio is not needed in the Ay spreadsheet. The Vy input data is already correct.) The Ay spreadsheet data is shown below.

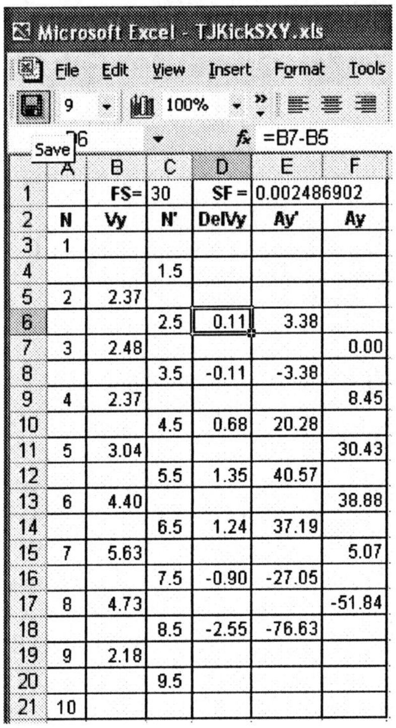

	A	B	C	D	E	F
1		FS=	30	SF =	0.002486902	
2	N	Vy	N'	DelVy	Ay'	Ay
3	1					
4			1.5			
5	2	2.37				
6			2.5	0.11	3.38	
7	3	2.48				0.00
8			3.5	-0.11	-3.38	
9	4	2.37				8.45
10			4.5	0.68	20.28	
11	5	3.04				30.43
12			5.5	1.35	40.57	
13	6	4.40				38.88
14			6.5	1.24	37.19	
15	7	5.63				5.07
16			7.5	-0.90	-27.05	
17	8	4.73				-51.84
18			8.5	-2.55	-76.63	
19	9	2.18				
20			9.5			
21	10					

Figure 9-20. The acceleration Y component spreadsheet.

It is interesting to note that the calculation procedure for acceleration does not provide data for the first and last two pictures in the TJKickS data set (there are no acceleration values shown for pictures 1, 2, 9 or 10). The spreadsheet cannot compute a change in velocity unless velocity data exists for the time periods both before and after an instant in question. This observation has important practical implications.

When an image set is created in the KA software, it is very important to include extra frames of video both before the beginning of the movement and after the end. By adding "padding" video images to an image set we assure that good acceleration information will be available for all critical aspects of the movement.

Issues in Data Analysis

The previous sections of this chapter have shown that the analysis of two-dimensional kinematic data can be done with a relatively simple list of spreadsheet formulas. The XY coordinate values are separated into two charts, and the X and Y components of the velocity vectors are calculated individually. Once the X and Y components are determined, the velocity vector magnitudes are computed on a third chart. This procedure, with only slight adjustments, can be repeated to compute acceleration data.

The KA software uses the same procedures to calculate velocity and acceleration as we have discussed above. KA takes the analysis process one step further by providing options for data smoothing.

Data Smoothing

Data smoothing is almost always required in an analysis of video data. Very small "input errors" – from the manual or automatic digitizing process – will cause relatively large errors in the calculation of acceleration. Digital filter smoothing routines are designed to remove most of the "noise" from digitized video data while leaving the true movement information virtually untouched.

The degree of smoothing can be flexibly controlled within movement analysis software programs. Different movement circumstances will necessitate different levels of noise reduction. The figure below shows the racket-head pattern of motion for a tennis serve. Four levels of smoothing are shown. The upper left corner of the figure shows the racket-head pattern of motion with no smoothing applied to the data. The remaining three portions of the figure show the effects of increased smoothing levels (with KA smoothing factors of 5, 10 and 15). The bottom right corner of the figure (with a smoothing factor of 15) shows the effect of "over-smoothing". In this figure the "rough edges" in the movement pattern have been removed so thoroughly that the true movement information has been distorted.

Smoothing Factor Effects on Pattern of Motion

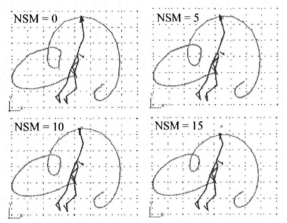

Figure 9-21. A comparison of the effect of four different smoothing factors on the shape of a tennis serve / racket-head point pattern of motion.

The movement pattern with a smoothing factor of 10 is also over-smoothed. The movement pattern with a smoothing factor of 5 is only slightly over-smoothed. The ideal smoothing factor for this point will be between 1 and 4. There are no clear rules that specify the "perfect" smoothing factor for a given point in a data set. It is best to use the lowest smoothing factor that allows easy visualization of the movement data. If measures of velocity are most important in a given research project, relatively low smoothing factors can be used. This is because velocity measures tend to have little noise. On the other hand, if acceleration measures will be critical in a given data analysis, higher levels of smoothing will be necessary. This is because acceleration curves are considerably more noisy than velocity curves.

When the XY coordinate values for a movement pattern are smoothed, irregularities are removed from the movement pattern. When this happens, the velocity and acceleration measures are also affected. The figure below shows a comparison of the velocity curves and ball impact velocity

values for our example tennis serve. Note that the peak velocity values in the movement are progressively "flattened" as smoothing levels increase.

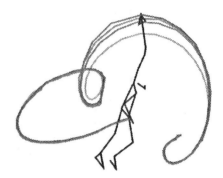

Rackethead Velocity

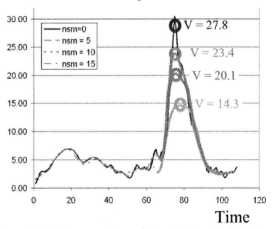

Figure 9-22. A comparison of the effects of smoothing on the pattern of motion and peak velocity measures for the racket-head point on a tennis serve.

Because some smoothing will be necessary for almost all video analysis projects, it will be important to use the same smoothing factor for all trials in a research project. For example, in a tennis analysis project like the one shown above, it would be a good idea to smooth the racket-head point with a factor between 1 and 4. The use of a non-zero smoothing factor will cause the peak racket head velocity value to decrease in all files. However, if the same level of smoothing is applied to all trials, it will be possible to make "fair" comparisons between any trials in the project because the peak velocity values for all trials will be reduced by about the same amount.

Non-Continuous Data

Our discussions, so far, have focused upon the data for continuous movement patterns. The fundamental assumption in data smoothing is that discontinuities in the movement pattern are representative of noise. Smoothing routines specifically seek out irregularities in movement patterns and "smooth them out". On occasion, however, we will observe meaningful movement data that involves discontinuous movement patterns. The motion of a tennis ball just after impact with a tennis racket provides a good example of a discontinuous pattern of motion.

The following figure shows both the pattern of motion of a tennis racket and the pattern of motion of a tennis ball during a serving motion. At the moment of ball impact, the ball's pattern of motion is abruptly changed.

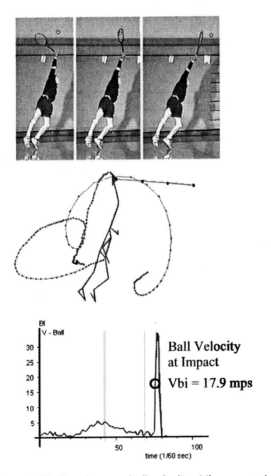

Figure 9-23. Tennis serve ball velocity at the moment of racket impact.

Because the sudden change in the ball velocity is expected, it is a very bad idea to apply smoothing to this ball velocity data. The KA software, by default, sets the smoothing factor for all points that are identified by the name "ball" with a smoothing factor of zero.

The ball velocity curve (shown at the bottom of the figure) indicates that the velocity of the ball changes rapidly at the moment of impact. Just prior to impact, the ball velocity is 1.6 mps. At the moment of impact (picture 76) the ball velocity is 17.9 mps. One field after impact the ball velocity is 34.2 mps.

Because the change in ball velocity happens very rapidly, it is difficult to get a clear indication of the exact timing of the moment of peak ball velocity. In theory, we would expect that peak ball velocity will occur the instant the ball "leaves" the face of the racket after impact. This particular instant in time may not be clearly seen on normal (60 pictures per second) video. The ball impact picture number will simply be selected as the picture that is closest to the moment of impact. For the figure above, the racket appears to be just "touching" the ball at picture 76. It is not clear from this video if the ball has just begun to be "flattened" by the racket at this instant or if the ball is, in fact, just about to be propelled off the strings of the racket. In either case the formula for the calculation of the ball's velocity is as follows:

$$VX_N = (VX_{N-.5} + VX_{N+.5}) / 2$$

This equation shows that the forward component of the ball's velocity will be set as the *average* of the Vx' velocity values just before and just after ball impact. The figure below shows that the ΔX between pictures 75 and 76 (picture 75.5) is very nearly zero. The ΔX between pictures 76 and 77 (picture 76.5) is quite large. As a result, the Vx velocity for picture 76 will be calculated to be about half as large as the Vx' measure for picture 76.5.

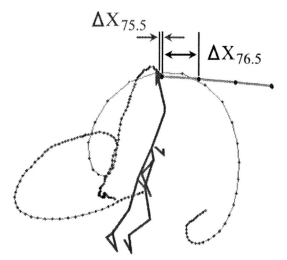

Figure 9-24. Ball pattern of motion ΔX measures just before and just after ball impact.

The velocity one picture after impact will be much larger. The figure below shows that the ΔX values for shifted pictures 76.5 and 77.5 are both very large. As a result, the velocity calculation for the instant in time one picture after impact will be a maximal value.

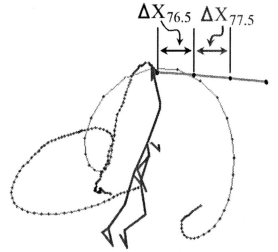

Figure 9-25. The delta X measures for the two intervals just after impact on a tennis serve.

The discussions above shows that, because of the way Vx measures are calculated, the peak ball velocity for a tennis serve should be expected to occur one picture after impact. Technically, this last statement is only true if the ball impact video image actually shows the exact moment of impact. Often, the video camera shutter will not be open at the moment of ball impact. When this happens, the

image set will show a picture of the racket several centimeters behind the ball's location on one image and several centimeters in front of the prior location of the ball on the next. In this circumstance, the peak velocity for the ball may, in fact, occur two pictures after the approximate ball impact picture. Because of the averaging associated with the calculation of Vx, peak ball velocity will not occur until two large displacements are shown in succession after the impact event.

Three-Dimensional Motion Analysis

Our prior discussions have focused upon two-dimensional analysis techniques to simplify our discussion of basic principles. We are now ready to consider several important issues related to the three-dimensional analysis of human movement.

The vast majority of human movements are best analyzed through three-dimensional data. From the standpoint of data collection, the only difference between a 2D and a 3D study is that a second video camera is necessary in the 3D data collection process. Recording data on a second camera adds very little additional work to the *collection* of data for a study. However, the existence of data from a second camera does double the amount of time required for digitizing. The question for the researcher is then: "what will I gain by spending extra time digitizing during the reduction of 3D data?" A short answer to the question is: for most projects you will gain an immeasurable amount - your data and the conclusions you reach from your research will be an order of magnitude better than anything you could possibly achieve with a 2D study. The next section discusses the basics of 3D analysis techniques.

3D Data Analysis Basics

The figure below shows a typical two-camera setup with example data from a swimming motion. The individual front and side view camera are initially used to collect traditional 2D data. When the side 2D data is collected the pattern of motion of the fingertip is projected onto a single plane (see the lower portion of the figure). The front view pattern of motion involves the same "flattening" process.

The upper portion of the figure shows that the true pattern of motion of the fingertip actually occurs within a three-dimensional space that is well approximated by a rectangular solid. The challenge of the three-dimensional data collection process is to take the forward-back X axis and the up-down Z axis information from the side view and combine it with the side to side Y axis information from the front view. When this process is complete a coherent set of XYZ coordinate data values will be available for all landmark points in the project.

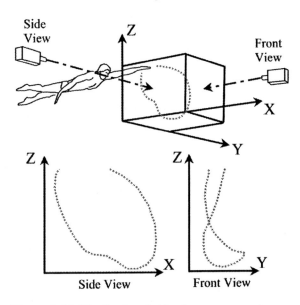

Figure 9-26. The front and side view camera setup used in a three-dimensional data analysis.

Perspective Correction

The analysis of 2D data has one obvious shortcoming. The motion of all landmark points is projected into a single two-dimensional plane. As we have seen above, a single scale factor is calculated for the 2D trial and used to compute the position of all body landmarks. If body landmark points move into or out of the plane of motion, the single scale factor used in the analysis will provide distorted measures of the motion.

Three-dimensional analysis is designed to measure not only the 2D forward-back and up-down dimensions of motion but also the side to side depth of motion that cannot be well seen by a single side view camera. In effect, a 3D analysis can be envisioned as supplying a range of scale factor values to account for all of the various instantaneous planes of motion involved in a human movement.

The following overhead view of a front view / side view camera setup shows how the information from both cameras are used to determine the true XYZ coordinates of a given point.

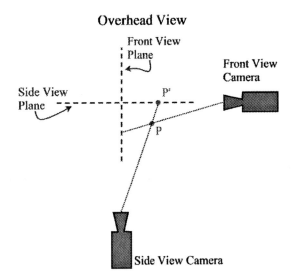

Figure 9-27. An overhead view of a typical front view / side view camera setup. The location of point P in 3D space is determined through information taken from both cameras.

The figure shows the vertical side view and front view planes as dotted lines intersecting at the center of the field of view of the cameras. The point "P" is located in front of the side view plane and also in front of the front view plane. When the side view camera "sees" point P, the 2D data from the point is projected onto the side view plane. Thus, the point P is seen as being located a location P' on the side view plane. However, the front view camera shows that point P is on the left side of the front view plane. As a result, it is clear that the side view camera's estimate of point P's location is too large. The information from both of these cameras is used to determine the exact location of point P in 3D space.

The figure below show the front and side view camera lines of sight and the 3D reference frame setup. The apparent X coordinate of the point P is shown to be at X'p on the side view plane and at Y'p on the front view plane. The true location of the point P is given by the Xp and Yp locations in the figure. Note that the X'p coordinate for the point is larger than the true Xp value. Because point P is closer to the camera than the side view plane, it appears larger than it would if it were on or behind this plane. This distortion in the data is due to perspective error. By mathematically analyzing the information provided by both of the cameras, it is possible to correct for perspective errors and determine undistorted 3D data from a two-camera video analysis.

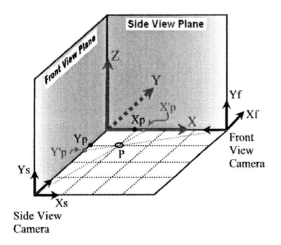

Figure 9-28. The XYZ reference frame of a 3D study is shown with respect to the front view and side view planes of the two cameras.

The following figure shows video images from a special 3D analysis project. The metal structure in the image is known as a direct linear transformation (DLT) reference frame.

Figure 9-29. A picture of a direct linear translation (DLT) calibration frame.

The XYZ positions of the small sphere markers on the frame have been carefully determined in advance. As a result, the exact distances between all of the points on the frame are well known. Note that the shape of this DLT frame is much like a miniature football goal post with a small rectangular

base. The markers on the frame are positioned symmetrically at the top of the two "goal post" bars, at the middle of the cross bar and at the corners of the rectangular base.

The purpose of the above video project was to evaluate the effect of the *perspective correction* software that is used in the KA3D program. The effect of perspective on the video images becomes clear when the DLT frame is made to rotate about a vertical axis set underneath the center of its base.

As we have mentioned above, a photograph of a three-dimensional object will, in effect, project that object onto a 2D plane. Measurements of lengths as seen in the 2D photo will only be accurate if the lengths are well isolated in the plane of the photograph. Perspective errors will be present in measurements of lengths that fall outside of the plane of the photo. Figure 9-30 shows another picture from the DLT frame and a corresponding stick figure from the KA2D software. (Note: this image set is stored with the name DLT03BS on your KAPro CD-Rom).

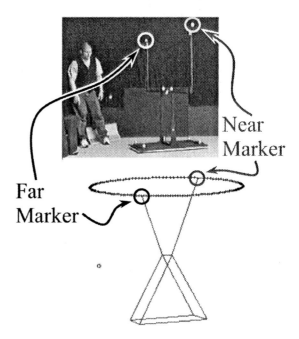

Figure 9-30. The "near" marker in this figure appears to be higher above the floor than the "far" marker as a result of perspective error.

The figure shows that the DLT frame has been made to spin about the vertical axis and one of the upright arms is now closer to the side view camera than before. At the moment shown, the "near maker" at the top of the DLT frame appears to be higher above the floor than the "far marker" on the opposite side of the frame. We know, however, that the apparent extra height of the near marker is a result of perspective error. The DLT frame is, in fact, constructed to be symmetrical and the two top markers are really the same distance above the floor.

It is clear that we cannot get good information on the position of the DLT markers from this 2D video. We must evaluate the motion of this frame in three dimensions (i.e., with the KA3D software) and take advantage of the perspective correction software routines associated with a 3D analysis.

The KA3D three-dimensional analysis software makes use of the information from two cameras to determine the XYZ coordinate values of all landmark points. As discussed above, the software takes into account the information from two cameras to provide an undistorted set of three-dimensional data values.

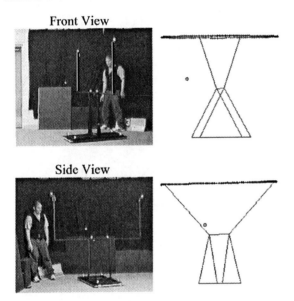

Figure 9-31. Video image and three-dimensional stick figure data for the rotating DLT frame study.

The above figure shows the KA3D data for the rotating DLT frame data. The front and side view stick figures have been constructed from the "perspective corrected" XYZ coordinate data. As a result, the "near" and "far" upright markers are shown to be at the same elevation above the floor. Similarly, the four corner points on the base rectangle are all shown to be at the same level as the floor.

The video images on the left side of the figure show the perspective error that is produced by typical camera lens settings. However, the XYZ coordinate values for all of the landmark points shown in the stick figure have been adjusted to allow accurate measurements to be made from any of the position data in the 3D file.

Given the corrected XYZ data in the 3D file, the process of computing velocity and acceleration data for the file is straightforward. Given X-true, Y-true and Z-true values from the 3D perspective correction software, three standard spreadsheets can be constructed to compute the Vx, Vy, and Vz velocity component data. Three similar spreadsheets are used to compute the Ax, Ay, and Az data. When the three-dimensional vector components are available for the velocity and acceleration vectors, the following formula is used to compute their vector magnitudes:

$$V_{MAG} = \sqrt{V_X{}^2 + V_Y{}^2 + V_Z{}^2}$$

Where:
V_{MAG} = Vector magnitude
V_X = Vector X component
V_Y = Vector Y component
V_Z = Vector Z component

It is interesting to note that the 3D correction process discussed above is completely different from the 3D special-effect film techniques used with some Hollywood movies (the ones that require you to wear special cardboard glasses to appreciate the "3D" nature of the movie). The purpose of the special-effects 3D movie is to exaggerate the size of objects that appear to move off of the movie screen and into the theater. In contrast, the 3D files generated in a biomechanical analysis are specially prepared to *remove* distortions from the data and allow accurate measures to be made along any dimension of the movement.

Conclusions

Our discussion of video digitizing and data analysis procedures is now complete. We have seen that the process of digitizing video data is simply a matter of keeping track of XY coordinate values and their associated scale factor. The calculation of velocity and acceleration for video data involves a series of calculations that can be quickly accomplished with spreadsheet software. An understanding of the calculation procedures themselves provides us with a foundation knowledge that allows us to better interpret the meaning of the data in a video analysis project.

Answers to Chapter Questions

Question 1:
How much distance is represented by the height of a single line of video pixels in the figure above?

- O A) About 10 centimeters
- O B) Exactly 1 centimeter
- O C) Less than one centimeter.

The correct answer is C. If the height of a pixel were 1 centimeter, the height of the toe would be about 4.5 meters above the floor. This kicking height could only be attained if the performer were more than 6 meters tall!

Question 2:
Imagine that the height of two performers is measured with the scale factor information discussed above. The height of participant A is measured as 1.568 meters and participant B's height is measured as 1.566 meters. Given this information, are we sure that participant A is taller than participant B?

- O A) Yes.
- O B) No.

The correct answer is B. The height of a pixel is 3.2 millimeters. This pixel size determines the resolution of our measurements. When the top of a person's head is digitized, we can only click on the pixel that is nearest to the true top of the head. Further, we can expect that we can easily be off by one pixel when we digitize either the head or the toes. Differences in length measurements that are less than one pixel in size should not be considered different in a video analysis.

Question 3:
Imagine that after you have recorded video for a movement you realize that you forgot to hold up a scale pole. Can you set the tripod back on the floor, replace the camera on the tripod, and record the scale factor later?

- O A) Yes.
- O B) Probably not.

The correct answer, in all likelihood, is "B": probably not. To get the correct scale video image you would have to place the tripod in exactly the same position as before and you would have to use the exact same zoom lens setting.

Question 4:
Imagine that after you have recorded video for a movement you realize that you forgot to hold up a scale pole. As you inspect the video image you notice that there is a window just behind your participant's line of motion. Through this window you can see a fence post. If you measure the height of this fence post, can it be used to determine the scale factor for your data?

- O A) Yes.
- O B) No.

The correct answer is B. Because the fence post is not located within the plane of the movement, it cannot be used to set the scale factor.

Question 5:
The data for a given image set indicates that the $V_{x'}$ value for picture 1.5 is 3 mps and the $V_{x'}$ value for picture 2.5 is 5 mps. A plot of these $V_{x'}$ values as a function of time is shown in the following graph. What is the value of V_x at picture 2 for this data?

- O A) 3 mps.
- O B) 4 mps.
- O C) 5 mps.

The correct answer is B. The velocity value that is half way between 3 mps and 5 mps is 4 mps.

Question 6:
What formula did you use to compute the V_x value answer for the last question?

- O A) $V_{x2} = (V_{x'1.5} + V_{x'2.5}) / 2$
- O B) $V_{x2} = (V_{x'1.5} + V_{x'2.5}) * 2$
- O C) $V_{x2} = (V_{x'1.5} - V_{x'2.5}) / 2$.

The correct answer is A. The V_x value is equal to the average of the neighboring $V_{x'}$ values.

Part 3 – Linear Kinetics

Chapter 10: Newton's Laws
Chapter 11: External Forces
Chapter 12: Momentum
Chapter 13: Advanced Topics

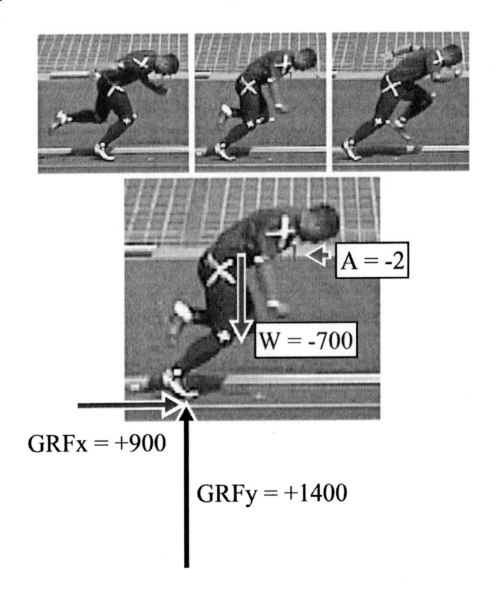

A = -2

W = -700

GRFx = +900

GRFy = +1400

Chapter 10: Newton's Laws

Introduction to Linear Kinetics

Biomechanics is defined as "the science concerned with the internal and external *forces* acting on the human body and the effects these forces produce." (Hay, 1993). Our work in linear kinematics (Chapters 4-9) has provided us with an understanding of the *effects* produced by forces acting on the body. For example, if a volleyball player generates force against the ground in a jumping motion, the effects produced by these forces will be a change in performer's center of gravity position. This change in position will be accompanied by concurrent changes in velocity and acceleration. Our discussions in linear kinematics have noted that the forces acting on the body are proportional to the acceleration experienced by the body. However, our study of human motion, so far, has not discussed the equations used in the calculation of force, or the details involved in the *kinetic level* analysis of human motion.

Linear kinetics is the branch of biomechanics that focuses upon the forces that cause motion. In some cases the calculation of force can be quite simple. For example, if we know the center of gravity acceleration measures for a volleyball jump performance and the body mass of the performer, we can compute the forces generated in the jump at any instant in time with the following equation:

$$F_{NET} = mA$$

Where:
F_{NET} net force acting on the body
m   mass of the body
A   acceleration of the body center of gravity

This equation is Newton's second law, the law of acceleration. We see from this equation that the net force acting on a body is directly proportional to the acceleration experienced by the body. Thus, kinetics and kinematics can be seen as different sides of the same "movement coin." If we know the body mass and the body center of gravity acceleration associated with a jump, we can compute the net force acting on the body. Similarly, if the force acting on a given mass is known at any instant in time, the body's acceleration at that instant can be computed with the above equation.

Figure 10-1 An instant during the upward driving phase of a vertical jumping motion.

Newton's First Law of Motion

Newton's first law of motion, or the law of *inertia,* is defined as follows:

Every body continues in its state of rest or uniform motion in a straight line unless compelled to change that state by external forces exerted upon it.

You have seen and felt the influence of Newton's first law any time your "state of motion" has been changed. For example, as you drive down the highway in a car, you may attain a steady speed of 55 miles per hour. As you drive at this speed, you and the objects around you in the car, for example your school book bag on the passenger seat, are all experiencing uniform motion in a straight line.

Newton's First Law: The law of *Inertia*

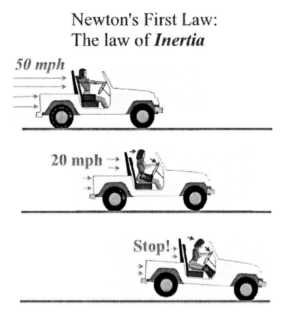

Figure 10-2 A car and driver experiencing rapid deceleration.

If a traffic light ahead of you changes abruptly to red, you will notice that, as you jam on the break, you and the objects in the car have a distinct tendency to keep moving forward at 55 mph. Hopefully, the seat belt will keep you from shifting too far forward, but your book bag could easily fly off of the passenger seat and fall onto the floor.

Let's now consider how Newtons's first law can be applied to the analysis of forces on elevator passengers.

Question 10-1:
Your challenge in this exercise is to make use of the law of inertia to provide evidence that a junk food diet will cause substantial weight loss. Your tools are a bathroom scale and an elevator. You weigh yourself on the stationary scale and then go for lunch at McDonalds. To show your "loss of weight" you get into the elevator, press the button for the top floor and then read the scale at the following instant in time:

O A. Just as the elevator is beginning to move upward.
O B. In the middle of the elevator's trip to the top floor.
O C. Just as the elevator arrives at the top floor.

Elevator Ride Weight Measurement

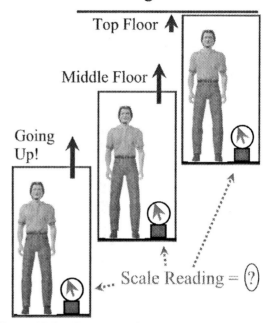

Figure 10-3 A illustration of bathroom scale measures during an upward ride in an elevator.

Inertia

The term *inertia* is defined as the tendency for a body to maintain its given state of motion. A given uniform state of motion of a body is associated with a constant velocity. Thus, an object at rest (with velocity held at a constant value of zero) will have a tendency to stay at rest. If you have ever tried to kick a bowling ball, you know this is true.

Bowling Ball Soccer

Figure 10-4. An illustration of a soccer kick motion applied to a bowling ball.

Internal and External Forces

Similarly, an object in motion (at a uniform, non-zero velocity) will have a tendency to maintain that state of uniform velocity in a straight line, unless an *external force* is applied to the object. This statement implies that, if no external force is applied to a moving object, it will continue to move with uniform velocity on a straight line indefinitely. Note that an external force is any force that is applied to a body by another body or by the surrounding environment.

The idea that an object in motion will continue to move indefinitely was an impressive observation on Newton's part. It is not possible, within the confines of planet Earth, to arrange a situation where no external forces are present. For example, gravity is always present and the pull of gravity will tend to cause an object like a hockey puck to be pressed against the ice and create a frictional force. This frictional force between the hockey puck and the ice, no matter how small, will tend to cause a moving puck to eventually come to rest. However, if the frictional force between the puck and the ice were reduced to zero and if there were no air resistance on the puck, it would move indefinitely with no change in velocity.

While it is very difficult to make direct observations of motions with no external forces on Earth, it is easy to see interesting examples in space travel. Video transmissions from NASA's Space Shuttle, and simulations of these conditions in movies like Apollo 13, show pens and other objects floating and moving uniformly under zero gravity conditions.

An astronaut on a "space walk" provides another very interesting example of uniform motion. If an astronaut were to become separated from the space capsule during a space walk, he/she would run the risk of drifting off into outer space. If the astronaut were to swing her arms and legs in an effort to move back in the direction of the capsule, no progress would be made. The motions of the astronaut's arms and legs would involve *internal force* but not *external forces,* and as a result no change in her state of motion would result. On the other hand, if the astronaut's suit were equipped with small jets capable of propelling gas into space, she could be propelled back to the space capsule due to the *external forces* exerted on her body by the jets.

On Earth, a clown trampolinist can try, for fun, to make use of purely internal forces to generate a change in his state of motion (see figure 10-5). If the trampolinist jumps straight up and at the peak of the jump makes an attempt to run forward through the air, no forward motion will result. This example shows that uniform motion will persist along any component of motion where there is an absence of external forces. While gravity constantly changes the state of motion of the trampolinist in the vertical dimension, the horizontal component of motion will remain unchanged because no horizontal external force components are applied to the body.

Figure 10-5. A gymnast attempting to run in mid-bounce on a trampoline.

Newton's Second Law of Motion

Newton's second law of motion, or the law of *acceleration,* is defined as follows:

The rate of change of momentum of a body (or the acceleration of a body) is proportional to the force causing it, and the change takes place in the direction in which the force acts.

The equation for Newton's second law is:

$$\mathbf{F}_{NET} = m\mathbf{A}$$

Where:
$\mathbf{F}_{NET}$ – is the net force vector applied to a body
m – is the mass of the body
$\mathbf{A}$ – is the acceleration vector of the body's center of gravity

Details of Newton's Second Law

The term "m" in Newton's second law, represents *mass* and is a direct measure of the inertia of a body. The units of mass are kilograms (metric system) or slugs (English system). Further, *linear momentum* is defined as the product of mass times velocity:

Momentum = mV

Newton's second law can be expressed mathematically in terms of change in momentum. In words:

The net force acting on a body is proportional to the rate of change of momentum of the body.

Mathematically:

$$\mathbf{F}_{NET} \propto (m\mathbf{V_f} - m\mathbf{V_i}) / t$$

Where:
$M\mathbf{V_f}$ is the final momentum of the body
$M\mathbf{V_i}$ is the initial momentum of the body
t is the time associated with the change in momentum

This equation can be rearranged as follows:

$$\mathbf{F}_{NET} \propto m (\mathbf{V_f} - \mathbf{V_i})/t$$

Note that the term $(\mathbf{V_f} - \mathbf{V_i})/t$ is equivalent to *acceleration* as defined in Chapter 8. Thus:

$$\mathbf{F}_{NET} \propto m\mathbf{A}$$

Therefore, force is proportional to the product of mass and acceleration. The term *proportional* means, mathematically, that as one side of the equation increases, the other side must also increase, and the ratio of force and acceleration must remain constant. Thus, if the right side of the equation is doubled, the left side must also double. The proportion sign does not, however, require that the left and right side of the equation be exactly equal. The proportional sign can be replaced by an equal sign if a constant "k" is added to the equation:

$$\mathbf{F}_{NET} = k \cdot m\mathbf{A}$$

The above equation states that as $\mathbf{F}_{NET}$ increases, the product of mass and acceleration will also increase but the result will be multiplied by a constant value k. If *consistent units* are used to define the force, mass and acceleration terms, the value of "k" will be 1.0:

$$\mathbf{F}_{NET} = m\mathbf{A} \quad \text{(with consistent units)}$$

The units of measure for force, mass and time are carefully selected in the English and Metric systems of measurements to assure that the "k" value in the above equation is one. Thus, if you express mass in kilograms and acceleration in meters per second[2], you can use the above equation to compute force in *Newtons*.

Reductionism and Newton's Second Law

Newton's second law is a vector equation, where both the **F** and **A** terms are vectors. This vector equation can be broken down into 3 scalar equations:

$$\Sigma F_X = m A_X$$
$$\Sigma F_Y = m A_Y$$
$$\Sigma F_Z = m A_Z$$

Where:
$\Sigma F_{X, Y, Z}$ represent the *summation* of all force components acting in the X, Y, and Z directions.

We see that we can use reductionism to simplify the calculation and analysis of force. A complex three-dimensional set of forces acting on a body can be broken down into an equivalent force vector composed of three force components: F_X, F_Y and F_Z. These individual force components, in turn, can be expected to produce a predictable acceleration along their respective dimension of motion.

Units of Measurement in Kinetics

Examples of consistent units are given in the following table:

	English System	**Metric System**
Force	pound	Newton
Mass	slug	kilogram
Acceleration	Feet/sec/sec	Meters/sec/sec

At the surface of the earth, a fixed and predictable relationship exists between measures of the gravitational *force* of attraction on an object and its *mass*. In the English system, an object that weights 32.2 pounds has a mass of one slug. In general:

Mass (in slugs) = Weight (in pounds) / 32.2

In this equation, the constant 32.2 represents the acceleration of gravity expressed in feet per second per second.

In the metric system, an object that weights 9.81 Newtons has a mass of 1 kilogram. In general:

Mass (in kilograms) = Weight (in Newtons) / 9.81
Weight (in Newtons) = Mass (in kilograms) * 9.81

In this equation, the constant 9.81 represents the acceleration of gravity expressed in meters per second per second.

If we know an object's weight in pounds we can determine the mass of that object in kilograms by dividing by 2.2:

Mass (in kilograms) = Weight (in pounds) / 2.2

For the metric system of units, one *Newton* is defined as the amount of force that will accelerate a 1 kilogram mass 1 meter/sec/sec. Similarly, in the English system, one *pound* is defined as the amount of force that will accelerate a 1 slug mass 1 foot/sec/sec. For both systems of measurement, the value of "k" in the "$F_{NET} = k \bullet mA$" equation is one. However, if you mix units of measurement between the two systems within a single equation your results will be invalid. Thus, you cannot express force in pounds, mass in kilograms and acceleration in mps^2 and get a correct result with the F = mA equation.

Further, it is important to remember that while an object that weights 9.81 Newtons at the surface of the Earth will have a mass of 1 kilogram, the two units of measure are not interchangeable in biomechanical calculations. Mass is a measure of the quantity of matter in an object, and it is therefore independent of any measure of gravitational attraction. A mass of 1 kilogram will weigh 9.81 Newtons at the surface of the Earth, but on the moon, its weight will be only about 1.6 Newtons due to the reduced gravity of the moon. The *mass*, or quantity of matter, remains the same at both locations but the *force* acting on the object (the weight of the object) will depend upon the pull of gravity.

In Biomechanics the metric system of measure is the accepted standard for use in the publication of all measurements. For most students in biomechanics, the units of measure for mass (kilograms), length (meters) and acceleration (mps^2) are reasonably familiar. However, most of us do not frequently encounter measures of force expressed in Newtons. We intuitively know the "feeling" the 10 pounds of force, but we would not immediately know what to expect if we were asked to hold a weight of 44.5 Newtons.

To convert a given measurement expressed in pounds of force to an equivalent measure of force in Newtons, use the following equation:

Force (in Newtons) = Force (in pounds) * 4.45

It is interesting to note that Isaac Newton, an intellectual giant, is given only about one quarter pound of credit in real world terminology!

Question 10-2:
The weight of a given student is 150 pounds. What is the weight force for this student, expressed in Newtons?

O A. The student weight is about 35 Newtons.
O B. The student weight is about 150 Newtons.
O C. The student weight is about 670 Newtons.

The following two examples will help us to understand the relationship between the English and metric systems of measurement.

Example: Weight Lifting

Note: for this example, we will express force in the familiar units of measurement of the English system. We will translate our measures to the metric system in the next example.

Imagine that you are asked to lift a barbell that weighs 161 pounds. If you pull up on the bar with a 151 pound force, it will not move. The upward force acting on the ball does not represent the *net force*. While you pull up with a force of +151 lbs, gravity is pulling down on the bar with a force of –161 lbs. As a result, the effect of these two forces will be -10 lbs. As a result, the bar will still press down against the floor support. If we were to place scales on either end of the bar, their measure of the total weight pressing down would be only 10 pounds. The difference between the upward pull and the weight is –10 lbs, but the floor supports push up with +10 lbs. As a result, the *net* force applied to the bar will be zero (+151 – 161 + 10 = 0). Because the net force is zero, there will be zero acceleration and the bar will not move.

Upward Pull = +151 lbs

Weight = -161 lbs

Figure 10-6. A weight lifter unsuccessfully attempting to lift a barbell.

If you were to pull upward on the bar with 171 pounds of force, a net force of +10 pounds would act on the bar (see the following figure).

Upward Pull = +171 lbs

Weight = -161 lbs

Figure 10-7. A successful attempt at lifting a barbell.

Assuming that the bar is not glued to the floor, the only forces acting will be the weight (-161 lbs) and the upward pull (+171 lbs). As the result, the net force acting on the bar will be +10 lbs. According to Newton's second law, if a +10 pound force acts on the bar, it will experience acceleration in the upward direction. The acceleration can be calculated as shown below. Note that all of the units in these equations are consistent:

$\Sigma F_Y = m A_Y$
$+171-161 = 5 * A_Y$
$10 = 5 * A_Y$
$A_Y = 2 \ fps^2$

Question 10-3:
The numerical value for mass in the above equation is set as 5. What are the units of measurement for this measure of mass?

O A. Kilograms
O B. Slugs
O C. Newtons

Question 10-4:
The value for mass in the above equation is 5 slugs. How was this value determined?

O A. To determine the mass in slugs of a 161 pound object, divide by 32.2.
O B. To determine the mass in slugs of a 161 pound object, divide by 2.2.
O C. To determine the mass in slugs of a 161 pound object, divide by 9.81.

In summary, we see that the +10 pound vertical net force component will result in an acceleration of 2 fps^2.

$\Sigma F_Y = m A_Y$
$171-161 = 5 * A_Y$
$10 = 5 * A_Y$
$A_Y = 2$ fps^2

We should be aware that the barbell will be accelerated at the rate of 2 fps^2 for the time period that a 10 pound net force is applied to the bar. In "real life", the net force applied to the bar will change considerably during the course of the lifting motion. In turn, the acceleration of the bar will also change from instant to instant in time.

For example, we could imagine that early in the lifting motion a net force of +10 pounds may be applied. However, later in the movement, a higher net force may be applied. Suppose that when the weight lifter has lifted the bar half way up, the force of the upward pull is 211 lbs. What will be the bar's acceleration at this instant?

Upward Pull = +211 lbs

Weight = -161 lbs

Figure 10-8. A force exerted during the upward motion of a barbell.

$\Sigma F_Y = m A_Y$
$211 - 161 = 5 * A_Y$
$50 = 5 * A_Y$
$A_Y = 10$ fps^2

We see that a net force of 50 pounds will produce an acceleration that is 5 times greater than that produced by a 10 pound force. As stated in Newton's second law: "The acceleration of a body is *proportional* to the force causing it...".

Example: Weight Lifting – Metric System

Let's now translate the calculation from the last example into the metric system of units. Consider the case where a 211 pound force is applied to a 161 pound barbell. In order to complete this translation we will need to translate 211 and 161 pounds to the metric system measure for force and 5 slugs to the metric system measure for mass.

$\Sigma F_Y = m A_Y$
$211 - 161 = 5 * A_Y$ (expressed in units for the English system)

Question 10-5:
What is the appropriate unit of measurement for force in the metric system?

O A. kilogram
O B. slug
O C. Newton

Question 10-6:
How many Newtons of force are equivalent to 211 pounds?

O A. 939 Newtons (multiply 211 by 4.45)
O B. 47.4 Newtons (divide 211 by 4.45)
O C. 21.5 Newtons (divide 211 by 9.81)

Question 10-7:
How many kilograms of mass are associated with an object that weights 161 pounds?

O A. 16.4 kilograms (divide 161 by 9.81)
O B. 73.2 kilograms (divide 161 by 2.2)
O C. 716 kilograms (multiply 161 by 4.45)

In metric units:

$\Sigma F_Y = m A_Y$
939 Newtons – 716 Newtons = 73.2 kg * A_Y mps^2
223 Newtons = 73.2 kg * A_Y
$A_Y = 3.046$ mps^2

Because one meter is equal to 3.28 feet, a measure of 3.046 mps^2 is equivalent to 10 fps^2 (a length of just over 3 meters is equal to a length of 10 feet).

As a result, we see that the bar's acceleration was computed to be equivalent values: 10 fps^2 in the English system or 3.046 mps^2 in the metric system. Thus, we see that the solution to the equation for Newton's second law produces expected results as long as we use a consistent system of measurement units.

Example: Net Force

Newton's second law indicates that the *summation* of forces applied to a body determine the acceleration of the body along any component of motion:

$$\Sigma F_X = m A_X$$
$$\Sigma F_Y = m A_Y$$
$$\Sigma F_Z = m A_Z$$

Thus, if more than one force is applied to a given body, the net effect of these forces is given by the summation of these forces. For example, if the net force applied to a body in the X direction is known, the X component of acceleration may be readily calculated.

The following figure shows an overhead view of a football linebacker who is being blocked by two offensive linemen. The goal of the linebacker is to drive the two linemen to the left. The two offensive linemen apply forces FA and FB on the linebacker. What is the net force in the +X direction (tending to push the linebacker backward) for this instant in time?

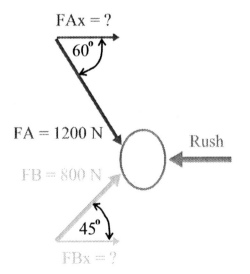

Figure 10-8. An overhead view of the forces acting on a linebacker rushing the quarterback.

Question 10-8:
What is X component of the FA force (use the Windows calculator if necessary)?

O A. 1200 Newtons
O B. 1039 Newtons
O C. 600 Newtons

Question 10-9:
What is X component of the FB force (use the Windows calculator if necessary)?

O A. 566 Newtons
O B. 800 Newtons
O C. 600 Newtons

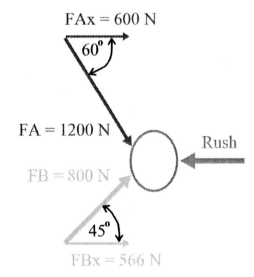

Figure 10-9. A solution of the horizontal force components acting on a linebacker.

The net force applied to the linebacker is therefore +1166 Newtons. To determine the overall result of the linebacker's motion we must specify his mass and the net force produced by his leg drive against the ground. Let's assume that the linebacker has a mass of 100 Kg and is applying a 1200 Newton force in the –X direction. We can now solve for the acceleration of this system of bodies at this particular instant in time:

$$\Sigma F_X = m A_X$$
$$FA_X + FB_X + F_{RUSHX} = m A_X$$
$$600 + 566 - 1200 = 100 * A_X$$
$$-34 = 100 * A_X$$
$$100 * A_X = -34$$
$$A_X = -34 / 100$$
$$A_X = -.34 \text{ mps}^2$$

Thus, the linebacker will advance toward the quarterback. Bear in mind that this value for acceleration will change from instant to instant as the players move.

Newton's 3rd Law: Action Reaction

Newton's third law states:

For every action there is an equal and opposite reaction.

For example, if you perform a vertical jump, the *Action* of your leg drive forces pushes downward on the ground. The floor *reacts* to your leg drive and pushes back up on you as hard as you push down. The figure below shows the Action force vectors as aimed downward and the Reaction force vectors as aimed upward. Note that the Reaction force vector is equal (of the same length) and opposite (upward versus downward) to the Action vector.

Newton's second law indicates that the acceleration due to these jumping forces is inversely proportional to the masses of the bodies (the earth and you). You may jump up 60 centimeters due the *reaction force*. In turn, the earth will be pushed out of orbit by one ten trillionth of an atom's width by the *action* force. (The measure of the earth's displacement has been computed mathematically; this particular measure would be impossible to measure directly!)

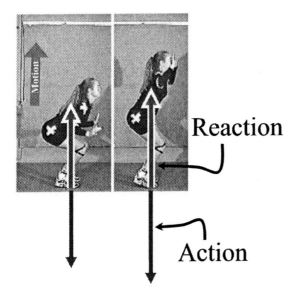

Figure 10-10. The action and reaction forces acting during a vertical jump upward driving motion.

The *action* of the performer's leg drive produces a force downward into the ground. The *reaction* of the rigid ground surface is a force vector that is the same size as the action force but aimed in the opposite direction.

Because we are interested in the motions of humans, and not the motion of the earth, we will be most interested in the reaction force that acts at our feet during the jumping motion. In fact, if we focus our attention on just the forces acting on the human body during the jump, we will be able to graphically represent the system of forces that cause human motion.

Free Body Diagrams

The figure below shows the *free body diagram* of a performer doing a volleyball jump next to a action-reaction force figure.

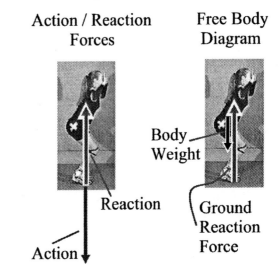

Figure 10-11. A comparison of a diagram with action and reaction forces and a free body diagram.

Note that the free body diagram (right side) shows the forces acting on the performer's body while the action-reaction figure (left side) shows only the forces between the feet and the floor. Note also that the "action" force downward has been removed from the free body diagram figure to emphasize that only one body (that of the volleyball player) is under consideration. The effect of the ground's interaction with the participant is represented by the *ground reaction force* vector.

The forces shown in the free body diagram represent *all* of the forces acting on the body (assuming air resistance is negligible) and therefore can be used to predict the body's acceleration at the selected instant in time. The performer is driving her legs against the ground vigorously and, as a result, the ground reaction force is greater than the body weight force. As a result, the performer will accelerate upward as a result of the system of forces applied to her body. The force, mass and acceleration measures for this particular example are as follows:

Given:
Wgt = -490 N
GRF_Y = 940 N
Mass = 50 kg

$\Sigma F_Y = m A_Y$
$GRF_Y + Wgt = m A_Y$
$940 - 490 = 50 * A_Y$
$450 = 50 * A_Y$
$50 * A_Y = 450$
$A_Y = 450 / 50$
$A_Y = 9 \text{ mps}^2$

Exercise – Free Body Diagram Analysis

The figure below shows the force components acting on a runner near the beginning of a sprint race. The figure shows all of the forces acting on the body at the selected instant of time: the X and Y components of the ground reaction force (GRF_X, GRF_Y), the body weight (W) and the air resistance (A) force. Inspect the data shown in the figure to determine answers to the following questions.

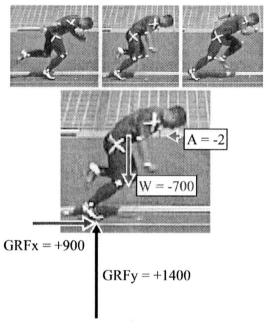

GRFx = +900

GRFy = +1400

Figure 10-12. A free body diagram of the forces acting on a runner performing a track start.

Question 10-10:
What is the net force acting on the body in the horizontal direction?

O A. 900 Newtons
O B. 898 Newtons
O C. 902 Newtons

Question 10-11:
What is the net force acting on the body in the vertical direction?

O A. +700 Newtons
O B. +1400 Newtons
O C. -700 Newtons

Conclusions

Our introduction to Newton's Laws is now complete. We will discuss the application of Newton's laws to the analysis of human motion in much more detail in the remaining chapters of Part 3. In particular, we will discuss the calculation of ground reaction force for a variety of movements in Chapter 11. Given this foundation, we will move on to discuss the impulse momentum relationship in Chapter 12.

Reference

Hay, James G., 1993. The Biomechanics of Sports Techniques. Prentice-Hall Inc., Englewood Cliffs, New Jersey.

Answers to Chapter Questions

Question 10-1:
Your challenge in this exercise is to make use of the law of inertia to provide evidence that a junk food diet will cause substantial weight loss. Your tools are a bathroom scale and an elevator. You weigh yourself on the stationary scale and then go for lunch at McDonalds. To show your "loss of weight" you get into the elevator, press the button for the top floor and then read the scale at the following instant in time:

O A. Just as the elevator is beginning to move upward.
O B. In the middle of the elevator's trip to the top floor.
O C. Just as the elevator arrives at the top floor.
The correct answer is C. At the beginning of the elevator's motion, your body will have a tendency to continue in its state of zero velocity and additional forces (beyond your body weight) will be needed to cause a change in your state of motion. This will cause the scale to measure your weight as a greater value than your true weight.

Question 10-2:
The weight of a given student is 150 pounds. What is the weight force for this student, expressed in Newtons?

O A. The student weight is about 35 Newtons.
O B. The student weight is about 150 Newtons.
O C. The student weight is about 670 Newtons.

The correct answer is C. To convert from pounds to Newtons, multiply the number of pounds by 4.45. There are more than 4 Newtons in a pound. As a result, 150 pounds will have to be equal to more than 600 Newtons.

Question 10-3:
The numerical value for mass in the above equation is set as 5. What are the units of measurement for this measure of mass?

O A. Kilograms
O B. Slugs
O C. Newtons

The correct answer is B. If the English units of measurement are used (i.e., force is expressed in pounds), mass must be expressed in slugs. Kilograms are an appropriate unit of measure for mass only if

forces are expressed in Newtons and acceleration is expressed in mps2.

Question 10-4:
The value for mass in the above equation is 5 slugs. How was this value determined?

O A. To determine the mass in slugs of a 161 pound object, divide by 32.2.
O B. To determine the mass in slugs of a 161 pound object, divide by 2.2.
O C. To determine the mass in slugs of a 161 pound object, divide by 9.81.

The correct answer is A. In the English system, to determine the mass of an object that weights 161 pounds at the surface of the earth, divide that weight (expressed in pounds) by 32.2.

Question 10-5:
What is the appropriate unit of measurement for force in the metric system?
O A. kilogram
O B. slug
O C. Newton
The correct answer is C. In the metric system, the standard unit of measure for force is Newtons.

Question 10-6:
How many Newtons of force are equivalent to 211 pounds?

O A. 939 Newtons (multiply 211 by 4.45)
O B. 47.4 Newtons (divide 211 by 4.45)
O C. 21.5 Newtons (divide 211 by 9.81)

The correct answer is A. To convert from pounds to Newtons, multiply the number of pounds by 4.45 (there are 4.45 Newtons in one pound).

Question 10-7:
How many kilograms of mass are associated with an object that weights 161 pounds?

O A. 16.4 kilograms (divide 161 by 9.81)
O B. 73.2 kilograms (divide 161 by 2.2)
O C. 716 kilograms (multiply 161 by 4.45)

The correct answer is B. To convert from pounds force to kilogram mass, divide the number of pounds by 2.2 (there are 2.2 pounds in one kilogram).

Question 10-8:
What is X component of the FA force (use the Windows calculator if necessary)?

O A. 1200 Newtons
O B. 1039 Newtons
O C. 600 Newtons

The correct answer is C. FAx = FA * Cos(60); FAx = 1200 * .5; FAx = 600.

Question 10-9:
What is X component of the FB force (use the Windows calculator if necessary)?

O A. 566 Newtons
O B. 800 Newtons
O C. 600 Newtons

The correct answer is A. FBx = FB * Cos(45); FBx = 800 * .707; FAx = 566 Newtons.

Question 10-10:
What is the net force acting on the body in the horizontal direction?

O A. 900 Newtons
O B. 898 Newtons
O C. 902 Newtons

The correct answer is B. To determine the net horizontal force, compute the summation of horizontal force components. ΣF_X = GFRx + A; ΣF_X = 900 − 2; ΣF_X = 898

Question 10-11:
What is the net force acting on the body in the vertical direction?

O A. +700 Newtons
O B. +1400 Newtons
O C. -700 Newtons

The correct answer is A. To determine the net vertical force, compute the summation of vertical force components. ΣF_Y = GFR$_Y$ + W; ΣF_Y = 1400 − 700; ΣF_Y = 700

Chapter 11: External Forces

Techniques in Force Analysis

The equation for Newton's second law states, logically, that if a net force is applied to a body, the body will be accelerated. The cause and effect relationship: force *causes* motion, is embedded in the left to right solution of the $\mathbf{F}_{NET} = m\mathbf{A}$ equation. If we know the net force and mass values, we can solve for the value of acceleration:

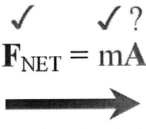

Left to right solution

Figure 11-1. The left to right solution of Newton's second law is shown. Given information on Force and mass, the value of acceleration can be computed.

In Biomechanics, it is often very convenient to solve this equation from right to left.

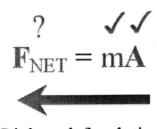

Right to left solution

Figure 11-2. The right to left solution of Newton's second law is shown. Given information on mass and acceleration, the net force can be computed.

Specifically, if we know the mass of the body, and if we know the acceleration of the body's CG at any instant in time, we can compute the net force that caused the acceleration. While this approach is the reverse of the true cause and effect relationship, it is still a very natural and intuitive approach to kinetic level analysis.

In Kinesiology, we are trained to be skilled observers of human motion. Thus, when we see a wide receiver run a crossing pattern and catch a pass, we are impressed with the performer's skill. When we next see a cornerback dart into the path of the wide receiver and deliver a bone crushing tackle, we will say "Ouch! That had to hurt!" Our inference that a large *force* has been delivered is based upon our visual perception of the performer's *motion*. Thus, our day-to-day appreciation of force (kinetics) is derived from our understanding of motion (kinematics).

Figure 11-3. Changes in the state of motion of a body reflect the application of forces to that body.

In this chapter we will focus upon solving the *inverse dynamics problem* by using the details of a performer's motion to determine estimates of the forces associated with the movement. In addition, we will look beyond the calculation of individual forces and consider how the levels of force generated by a movement change continuously as the movement progresses.

Ground Reaction Force Analysis

Our discussions in kinematics emphasized that the motion of a body's center of gravity reflects the net force that is applied to the body. The figure below shows the path of a baton's center of gravity as it is projected across the room. The effect of the net force (in this case, gravity) that is applied to the baton is shown by the curved pattern of motion line.

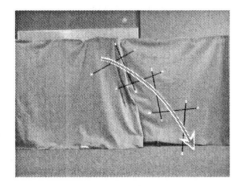

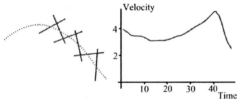

Figure 11-4. The motion of the center of gravity point on a rotating baton as it progresses from left to right across the room.

In this chapter, we will use information on the body's center of gravity acceleration to compute the net force acting on the body at various instances in the course of a movement. This approach will provide us with information on the *process* of human movement. We will see that skillful human movement is a result of the individual's ability to develop force over a period of time. Further, we will see that skillful performers coordinate the movements of their body segments to allow maximal force production at critical instants in time during the course of the movement.

Calculation of Vertical GRF

For general three-dimensional motion, Newton's second law is as follows:

$$\Sigma F_X = m A_X$$
$$\Sigma F_Y = m A_Y$$
$$\Sigma F_Z = m A_Z$$

Where: X represents the forward dimension, Y represents the side-to-side dimension and Z represents the vertical dimension.

For two-dimensional motion, Newton's second law is represented by two equations:

$$\Sigma F_X = m A_X$$
$$\Sigma F_Y = m A_Y$$

Where: X represents the forward dimension and Y represents the vertical dimension.

The volleyball jump provides a good first example for ground reaction force calculations because it is a relatively simple movement that can be studied with two-dimensional data. Further, while the camera will provide information on X and Y components, only the Y (vertical) dimension will be critical for a volleyball jump. Thus, we need to work with only one equation to solve for the critical forces acting on the body:

$$\Sigma F_Y = m A_Y$$

The center of gravity motion for a volleyball jump is shown in the image sequence figure below. Note that the body is a projectile during the flight phase of the jump.

Figure 11-5. A volleyball jump image sequence figure. The dotted line pattern of motion shows the path of the body center of gravity point during the full jumping motion.

The figure below shows the Y component of the body's center of gravity acceleration. During the flight phase, the A_Y values are close to the expected -9.81 mps^2. (Any differences between A_Y and -9.81 are due to small errors in setting the project's scale factor, digitizing errors and/or approximations in the data smoothing procedures.)

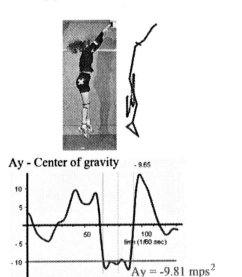

Figure 11-6. The Y component of the center of gravity point acceleration curve is shown at the bottom of the figure. The video and stick figure images for a moment during the flight phase are shown at the top of the figure.

The A_Y curve shows that the acceleration of the body changes considerably over time and large positive accelerations are evident during the upward driving motion and the landing. We will now use the center of gravity acceleration data to compute the ground reaction force at a number of instances during the course of the movement. Our first calculation will be very easy, because we will consider the case when the body is motionless.

The figure below shows the body position and center of gravity acceleration near the very beginning of the jumping motion. Notice that the CG A_Y value at this instant is 0 mps^2.

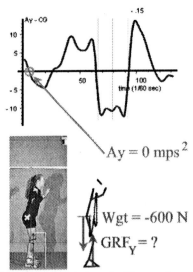

Figure 11-7. The Y component of the center of gravity point acceleration curve is shown at the top of the figure. At the moment shown, the body is experiencing zero acceleration.

The following equations are used to calculate the ground reaction force Y component (GRF$_Y$):

$$\Sigma F_Y = m\, A_Y$$
$$GRF_Y + Wgt = m\, A_Y$$

The equation shows that there are only two forces acting on the participant's free body diagram. The weight force (Wgt) is acting downward and the GRF$_Y$ force is acting upward. The "known" values of the terms in the equation are as follows:

Wgt = -600 Newtons
(equivalent to 134.83 pounds)
m = 61.2 kg
(body mass equals body weight in Newtons divided by 9.81)
A_Y = 0 mps^2
(from the video analysis)

Note that the body weight force (Wgt) is -600 Newtons. The minus sign is important because it indicates that the direction of the weight force is in the *negative* Y direction. If we were to specify the weight force as $+600$ Newtons we would be saying that gravity is constantly pushing the performer upward rather than pulling the body downward.

The solution for GRF$_Y$ is as follows:

$$GRF_Y + Wgt = m\, A_Y \qquad (1)$$
$$GRF_Y = m\, A_Y - Wgt \qquad (2)$$

GRF$_Y$ = (61.2 * (0)) – (-600)   (3)
GRF$_Y$ = (0) + 600   (4)
GRF$_Y$ = +600 Newtons   (5)

- Equation 1 states Newton's second law: the sum of the forces acting on a free body along any given dimension is equal to the product of the body mass and the body's CG acceleration along that dimension.
- Equation 2 is rearranged to show the direct solution for GRF$_Y$. (The variable (–Wgt) is added to both sides of the equation).
- Equation 3 shows the values for each of the "known" terms.
- Equation 4 shows that the product of mass and acceleration must be zero if the A$_Y$ term is zero. In addition, note that the weight term shows that subtracting a negative value is equivalent to adding that value (minus a minus 600 is equal to plus 600).
- Equation 5 shows that the ground reaction force is +600 Newtons.

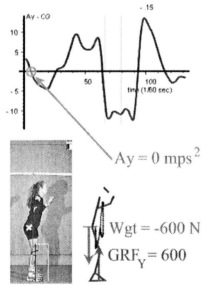

Figure 11-8. The ground reaction force value for a moment in a volleyball motion with zero acceleration.

For the case where the ground reaction force is equal to the body weight, the net force acting on the free body is zero:

Σ F$_Y$ = GRF$_Y$ + Wgt
Σ F$_Y$ = 600 + (-600)
Σ F$_Y$ = 0

This finding follows directly from the fact that the A$_Y$ value for this instant in the movement is zero. If the net force along a given dimension of movement is zero, the acceleration along that dimension must also be zero and vice versa.

The reasoning in this example is analogous to that used for getting your body weight from a bathroom scale. In order to get a "true" weight, you must stand absolutely still (A$_Y$ must be zero). If you move, the mA$_Y$ term in the above equations will be non-zero and the "weight reading" from the scale will be incorrect.

It is interesting to note that your bathroom scale does not actually measure your body weight force. It measures the ground reaction force that is produced by the weight of your body on the scale. If you move while you are being weighted, the scale reading changes but your true weight does not change (assuming that your are not eating lunch at the time).

Let's now compute the ground reaction force during the early portion of the "bend down" phase of the movement. Note that the A$_Y$ value is –4.42 mps^2 when the participant is about half way down on the crouching motion.

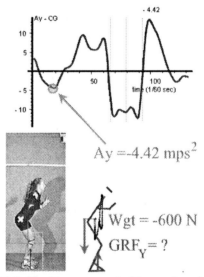

Figure 11-9. The Y component of the center of gravity point acceleration curve is shown at the top of the figure. At the moment shown, the body is experiencing negative acceleration.

The solution for GRF$_Y$ is as follows:

GRF$_Y$ + Wgt = m A$_Y$ (1)
GRF$_Y$ = m A$_Y$ – Wgt   (2)
GRF$_Y$ = (61.2 * (-4.42)) – (-600)   (3)

GRF$_Y$ = (-270.5) + 600   (4)
GRF$_Y$ = +329.5 Newtons   (5)

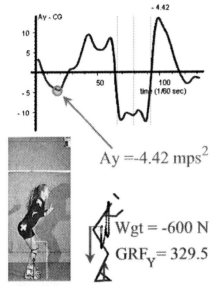

Figure 11-10. The ground reaction force value for a moment in a volleyball motion with a negative acceleration of -4.42 mps^2.

We see that during the early part of the crouch down phase, the participant's ground reaction force is less than the size of her body weight. The negative value for A$_Y$ has caused the mA$_Y$ term to be negative. This in turn causes the GRF$_Y$ value to be less than body weight (GRF$_Y$ = (-270.5) + 600).

The original form of the ground reaction force equation is "mathematically awkward":

GRF$_Y$ = m A$_Y$ – (-Wgt)

The subtraction of a negative value (minus (-Wgt)) at the end of the equation is unnecessarily cumbersome. Because the weight force is always negative, this equation can be simplified as follows:

GRF$_Y$ = m A$_Y$ + |Wgt|

Where:
|Wgt| = the absolute value of the body weight force.

Expressed this way, the numerical value for the |Wgt| term will always be positive. Further we will add this positive number to the value for the (m A$_Y$) term to determine the value for GRF$_Y$. This means that when A$_Y$ is zero, the size of the GRF$_Y$ term will be equal to the size of the body weight.

GRF$_Y$ = m A$_Y$ + |Wgt|
GRF$_Y$ = 0 + |Wgt|
(if A$_Y$ is zero)

Further, if A$_Y$ is negative, the size of GRF$_Y$ will be less than the size of the body weight.

GRF$_Y$ = m A$_Y$ + |Wgt|
GRF$_Y$ = *negative value* + |Wgt|
(if A$_Y$ is negative)

Finally, if A$_Y$ is positive, the size of GRF$_Y$ will be greater than the size of the body weight.

GRF$_Y$ = m A$_Y$ + |Wgt|
GRF$_Y$ = *positive value* + |Wgt|
(if A$_Y$ is positive)

The use of this simplified version of the GRF$_Y$ equation (GRF$_Y$ = m A$_Y$ + |Wgt|) allows us to quickly determine if a given GRF$_Y$ value will be less than or greater than body weight simply by determining the sign of A$_Y$ at any instant in time.

Question 11-1:
The following figure shows the CG A$_Y$ value for a critical moment in a volleyball jumping motion. About how large will the GRF$_Y$ value be at this moment?

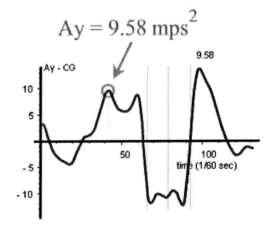

Figure 11-11. A moment in the Ay center of gravity curve with a high positive value for acceleration is shown.

O A. GRF$_Y$ will be less than the size of the body weight.
O B. GRF$_Y$ will be equal to the size of the body weight.
O C. GRF$_Y$ will be greater than the size of the body weight.

It is often convenient to express the size of ground reaction force measures as multiples of the body weight magnitude. For example, the landing phase of some gymnastic stunts will sometimes involve peak ground reaction forces of 5 body weights (BW) or more. By expressing ground reaction forces as a multiple of body weight, we can easily compare the relative size of the forces for a large person to that of a smaller person.

Let's now calculate the exact size of the ground reaction force from the last example. The figure below shows that when the participant is at the bottom of the crouch, the A_Y value is +9.58 mps^2.

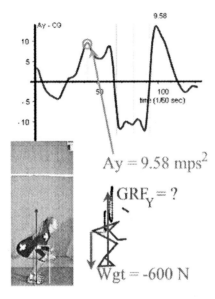

Figure 11-12. The Y component of the CG point acceleration curve is shown at the top of the figure. At the moment shown, the body is experiencing positive acceleration.

The calculation for GRF$_Y$ at this instant in time is shown below.

$GRF_Y = m\ A_Y + |Wgt|$
$GRF_Y = (61.2 * (9.58)) + 600$
$GRF_Y = (585.8) + 600$
$GRF_Y = 1185.8$ Newtons

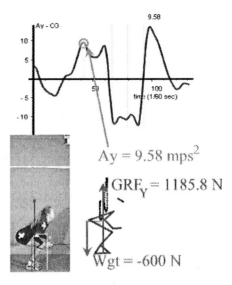

Figure 11-13. The ground reaction force value for a moment in a volleyball motion with a positive acceleration of 9.58 mps^2.

The GRF$_Y$ value is about two times body weight at the bottom of the crouch down phase of the movement. This force is the largest force generated against the ground prior to the landing phase of the movement. It is interesting to note that this large force is associated with a body center of gravity velocity (V_Y) of zero.

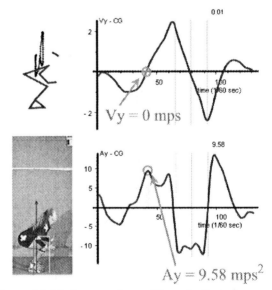

Figure 11-14. A comparison of the velocity and acceleration data at a moment when a large positive ground reaction force is created.

Even though the velocity of the body is zero at the moment shown below, the *rate of change* of velocity is quite high. Notice that the slope of the velocity curve is steep and positive and as the result, acceleration must be large and positive. The fact that a very high ground reaction force is generated at a time in the movement when the velocity is zero is not surprising. The potential for large muscular forces is greater for slow contraction speeds than for high. For example, larger muscular forces can be generated with isometric contractions than with fast concentric contractions.

A second peak in GRF_Y occurs when the performer is about half way up during the driving-up phase of the movement.

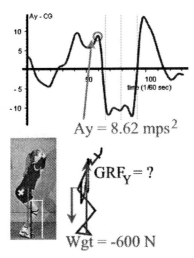

$$Ay = 8.62 \text{ mps}^2$$

$$GRF_Y = ?$$

$$Wgt = -600 \text{ N}$$

Figure 11-15. The Y component of the CG point acceleration curve is shown at the top of the figure. At the moment shown, the body is experiencing positive acceleration and the body moving upward rapidly.

The calculation for GRF_Y at this instant in time is shown below.

$GRF_Y = m\, A_Y + |Wgt|$
$GRF_Y = (61.2 * (8.62)) + 600$
$GRF_Y = (526.9) + 600$
$GRF_Y = 1126.9$ Newtons

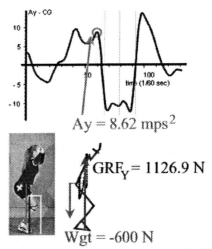

$$Ay = 8.62 \text{ mps}^2$$

$$GRF_Y = 1126.9 \text{ N}$$

$$Wgt = -600 \text{ N}$$

Figure 11-16. The ground reaction force value for a moment in a volleyball motion with a positive acceleration of 8.62 mps^2.

The performer is moving upward rapidly ($V_Y = 8.62$ mps) at the moment shown. This portion of the jumping motion is clearly helping her to attain a high take-off velocity.

Question 11-2:
The following figure shows the A_Y curve for the volleyball performer's CG point. Note that the frame numbers for the movement are shown on the horizontal axis. What frame number is associated with the largest positive ground reaction force during the time course of this movement?

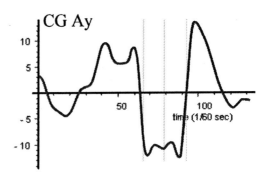

Figure 11-17. The Y component of the center of gravity point acceleration curve.

O A. About frame 40.
O B. About frame 70.
O C. About frame 100.

The CG A_Y curve shows that the landing phase of the volleyball jumping motion involves the largest forces of all in the jump.

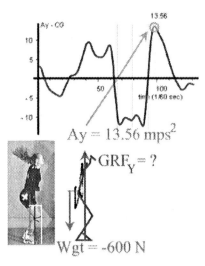

Figure 11-18. The Y component of the center of gravity point acceleration curve is shown at the top of the figure. At the moment shown, the body is experiencing positive acceleration and the body moving downward rapidly.

The calculation for GRF$_Y$ during the most forceful part of the landing phase is shown below.

GRF$_Y$ = m A$_Y$ + |Wgt|
GRF$_Y$ = (61.2 * (13.56)) + 600
GRF$_Y$ = (829.9) + 600
GRF$_Y$ = 1429.9 Newtons

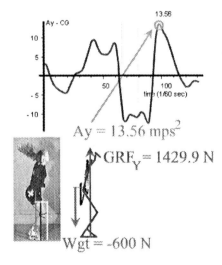

Figure 11-19. The ground reaction force value for a moment in a volleyball motion with a positive acceleration of 13.56 mps^2.

The force produced on landing is about 240% of body weight. In contrast, the largest force produced on the upward driving phase of the movement is only about 190% of body weight. On the driving-up phase, the performer's leg muscles are in concentric contraction. On the landing phase, the participant's legs are in an eccentric (lengthening) contraction. This example reminds us that eccentric muscular contractions can produce greater forces than the most vigorous concentric contractions.

Our detailed analysis of a volleyball jump shows that the ground reaction forces that are generated in forceful human movements can fluctuate dramatically over time. The image sequence figure below shows the GRF$_Y$ force vectors acting upward on the performer's feet. The body weight force is shown acting downward from the body's center of gravity point. Note that the size of the GRF$_Y$ vector changes as the performer moves.

Figure 11-20. A volleyball jump image sequence figure.

Issues in Ground Reaction Force Calculation

Our second example concerns a step-up movement with a simulated foot injury. To create the effect of a foot injury, an old-fashioned metal bottle cap is placed in the participant's shoe. This *antalgic* step is expected to involve less force on the "injured" foot than is seen in the normal (non-injured) condition. The image sequence figure below shows the performer's motion for the "injured" condition.

Figure 11-21. An antalgic step movement.

The bottle cap has been placed inside the shoe and under the right forefoot of the performer, jagged side up. Because the performer is stepping up with the right foot, we can expect that the bottle cap could cause him some minor pain, especially after the trailing left foot leaves the ground. The image sequence figure of the movement shows that the participant is clearly favoring his right foot.

As we have seen with the last example, an analysis of the body's center of gravity acceleration can be used to determine the net force acting on the body. Before we perform the analysis for this step-up movement, we should consider some basic issues in the analysis of ground reaction forces.

The figure below shows the performer in the normal (no bottle cap) condition at a moment when very large center of gravity acceleration measures are created. Notice that the right and left feet are both in contact with the ground or step at this instant in time.

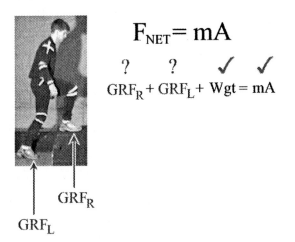

Figure 11-22. The ground reaction forces acting during a step up motion.

In the figure:
GRF_L = the ground reaction force acting at the left foot
GRF_R = the ground reaction force acting at the right foot
Wgt = the body weight
m = the body mass
A = the body's center of gravity acceleration

The equation: $F_{NET} = mA$ can be used to determine the ground reaction forces between the performer's feet and the ground or step, provided enough information is known about the movement. These "known" terms are shown with check marks in the figure. The unknown terms are shown below question mark characters. Notice that we have *two* unknowns (GRF_R and GRF_L) and *one* equation. As a

result, we cannot solve this equation for either ground reaction force. We can use the equation to determine the *sum* of the two forces acting at the feet, but we cannot use the equation to determine the exact size of either of the ground reaction forces with video data alone.

If we elect to study the ground reaction force at a moment when only one foot is in contact with the ground, our analysis will become simplified. The figure below shows the body 3/60ths of a second after the left foot has left the ground.

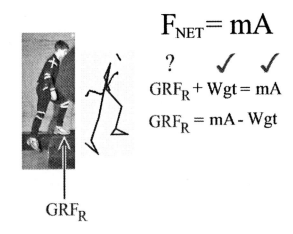

Figure 11-23. The solution for a ground reaction force during a period of single support.

Because the performer is in "single support" – only one foot is in contact with the ground – we can solve the $F_{NET} = mA$ equation. In this case we have one equation and *one* unknown. This example shows that video analysis data can be used to compute ground reaction forces *only* during the single support phase(s) of any given movement. (Note: Later in this chapter we will show how force plate equipment can be used to determine the ground reaction forces for two or more contact points with the ground.)

There is one more crucial issue that must be discussed before we can proceed with our ground reaction force analysis of the step-up motion. The figure below shows the normal and "injured" movement and center of gravity acceleration magnitude data for the movement just after the left foot has left the ground.

Normal   Injured

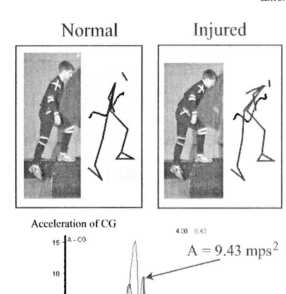

Acceleration of CG

$A = 9.43$ mps^2

$A = 4.00$ mps^2

time (1/60 sec)

Figure 11-24. A comparison of the center of gravity acceleration magnitude values for two comparable moments during a normal and "injured" step up motion.

The acceleration curve at the bottom of the figure shows the body's center of gravity acceleration *magnitude* information. The curve with the lower peaks shows the acceleration for the normal condition and the curve with the higher peaks shows the acceleration for the injured condition. Notice that for the instant in time shown, the injured condition has an acceleration of 9.43 mps^2 and the normal (non-injured) condition has an acceleration of 4.00 mps^2.

Because the performer is in single support for both conditions, we can use the equation $\mathbf{F}_{NET} = m\mathbf{A}$ to compute the ground reaction force acting on the right foot. However, a brief look at the acceleration values indicates that the acceleration of the performer is actually more than twice as large for the injured condition. Does this mean that the force on the right foot is greater for the injured condition?

The following questions will help you to determine the problem inherent in our data presentation.

Question 11-3:
Which of the following equations can be used to compute the vertical component of a ground reaction force?

- A. GRF$_Y$ = mA$_Y$ + |Wgt|
- B. **GRF = mA + Wgt**
- C. GRF$_X$ = mA$_X$

This example shows that acceleration *magnitude* is not appropriate for the calculation of the Y component of the ground reaction force. To solve the *vector* equation $\mathbf{F}_{NET} = m\mathbf{A}$, we must break it down into two scalar equations:

$\Sigma F_X = m A_X$
$\Sigma F_Y = m A_Y$

As a result, to compute the vertical component of the ground reaction force we must use the Y component of the center of gravity acceleration (A$_Y$) information. The figure below shows the A$_Y$ information comparison for the two conditions.

Normal   Injured

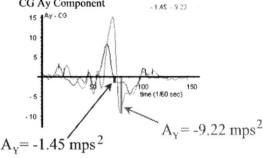

CG Ay Component

$A_Y = -1.45$ mps^2

$A_Y = -9.22$ mps^2

Figure 11-25. A comparison of the Y components of the center of gravity acceleration values for two comparable moments during a normal and "injured" step up motion.

Notice that the CG acceleration Y component is negative for both movement conditions, but it is more negative for the injured condition. Because the injured condition involves a large negative A_Y acceleration, we can expect that the ground reaction force on the right foot will be very small. This, of course, is what we expected to find for the injured condition.

This example shows that acceleration magnitude values should not be used in the calculation of ground reaction forces. In this case, the process of reductionism (breaking the acceleration vector into X and Y components) is a *required* step in the analysis procedure.

The very large negative A_Y value (-9.22 mps^2) for the injured trial causes the GRF$_Y$ force acting on the right foot to be very small:

Given:
|Wgt| = 734.25 N
Mass = 74.85 kg
A_Y = -9.22 mps^2

GRF$_Y$ = m A_Y + |Wgt|
GRF$_Y$ = (74.85 * -9.22) + 734.25
GRF$_Y$ = -690.12 + 734.25
GRF$_Y$ = 44.13 N

Injured

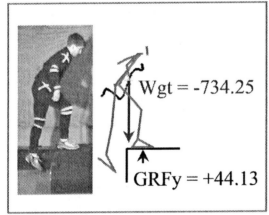

Figure 11-26. A comparison of the body weight force and the ground reaction force at a moment about midway through the "injured" step up motion.

The GRF$_Y$ value of 44.13 Newtons is only 6% of body weight. It is clear that the performer has successfully modified his movement to minimize the load on the injured foot. The non-injured condition involves considerably more force.

Given:
|Wgt| = 734.25 N
Mass = 74.85 kg
A_Y = -1.45 mps^2

GRF$_Y$ = m A_Y + |Wgt|
GRF$_Y$ = (74.85 * -1.45) + 734.25
GRF$_Y$ = -108.53 + 734.25
GRF$_Y$ = 625.72 N

Normal

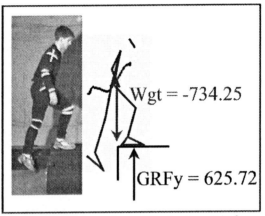

Figure 11-27. A comparison of the body weight force and the ground reaction force at a moment about midway through the non-injured step up motion.

The GRF$_Y$ force for the normal condition is more than 14 times larger than that of the injured condition. By modifying the organization of his movement, the performer has succeeded in minimizing the force to the "injured" right foot as much as possible. As the movement progresses, the load on the right foot must gradually increase for the injured condition. However, the performer has avoided the "sharp" pain that would have been associated with a normal stepping motion.

This movement provides an interesting example of the *movement as an emergent form* principle (Higgins, 1985). The solution to any given movement problem can be expected to change with any alteration to the conditions that regulate the movement. An analysis of the movement process provides us with a clear understanding of the performer's technique modifications.

The figure below shows the stepping motion at a moment early in the step-up movement. The video stills and stick figures show the instant of maximal positive center of gravity A_Y values in the movement. Note that the injured condition involves a larger A_Y peak (15.11 mps^2). In effect, the performer is "jumping up" as a result of the forceful extension of the left leg against the ground. During the following frames, the performer's body is much like a projectile, as he finds himself rising up as a result of the jump.

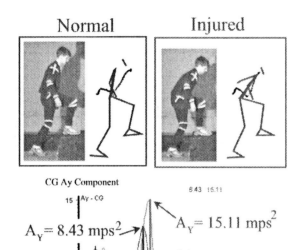

Normal   Injured

CG Ay Component

$A_Y = 8.43$ mps^2 $A_Y = 15.11$ mps^2

Figure 11-28. A comparison of the peak Ay values for the body's center of gravity point for a normal and "injured" step up motion.

In the most extreme case, it would be possible for a performer to accomplish much of the step-up motion with no force at all applied to the right foot. Imagine that the performer has held his right foot 1 mm above the surface of the step and then jumped forcefully upward with his left leg. The right hip and knee angles could be adjusted to keep the foot 1 mm above the step as the rest of the body proceeds upward. The performer in our example has used this type of strategy to successfully minimize the load on the "injured" foot.

Question 11-4:
A marathon runner with an injury to his right foot has decided to continue heavy training in preparation for the "big race". If data were collected on the peak forces generated by his right and left feet, what would you expect to see?

O A. The peak right and left foot forces should be equal.
O B. The peak force on his left foot will be higher than the force on his right.
O C. The peak force on his right foot will be higher than the force on his left.

Question 11-5:
If the potential for injury is directly related to the level of force experienced during training, what can we expect to happen to the left foot of the marathon runner?

O A. The left foot will become stronger as a result of the increased training load.
O B. The left foot will eventually become injured as a result of the persistent high loads that it is forced to absorb during training.

The runner from the previous questions should be careful to avoid too much training while his right foot is injured. If the left foot becomes injured as a result of his continued training, he will have "run out of fresh legs" to absorb the forces of impact with the ground.

Horizontal Ground Reaction Force

Our discussion, thus far, has focused upon the vertical component of the ground reaction force, mainly because this component is often very large. The horizontal component of the ground reaction force (GRF$_X$) is also very important, and we will see that it is even easier to calculate that the GRF$_Y$ value.

As we have mentioned in the previous discussion, the vector equation: $\mathbf{F}_{NET} = m\mathbf{A}$, can be broken into two scalar equations.

$$\Sigma F_X = m\, A_X$$
$$\Sigma F_Y = m\, A_Y$$

The solution of the X component equation from video data is particularly straightforward because the ground reaction force X component is the only horizontal force acting (assuming air resistance is negligible) during periods of single support:

$$\Sigma F_X = m\, A_X$$
$$GRF_X = m\, A_X$$

The figure below shows the injured condition for the antalgic step example. The free body diagram at the lower right section of the figure shows that the GRF$_X$ force is the only horizontal force acting. The body weight force and GRF$_Y$ component are not shown because they have no direct influence on the X component of the body's center of gravity acceleration.

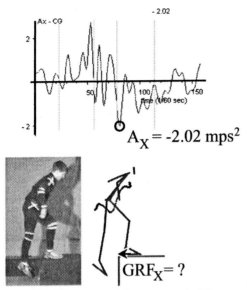

$$A_X = -2.02 \text{ mps}^2$$

$$GRF_X = ?$$

Figure 11-29. The horizontal component of the ground reaction force at a moment during a step up motion.

The calculation for GRF_X is as follows:

$GRF_X = m\, A_X$
$GRF_X = (74.85 * -2.02)$
$GRF_X = -151.19$ Newtons

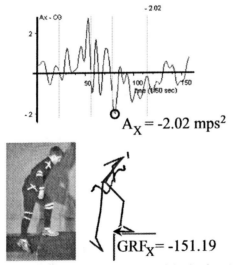

$$A_X = -2.02 \text{ mps}^2$$

$$GRF_X = -151.19$$

Figure 11-30. The calculated value of the horizontal component of the ground reaction force at a moment when the during a step up motion.

The GRF_X vector in the figure is drawn to the same scale as the other force vectors we have seen in this section. The size of this force is relatively small, only 20% of body weight. This GRF_X force acts as a *breaking* force. As the performer steps up, he must accelerate in the forward direction to shift his center of gravity over the step. When the right foot lands

on the step, the body's motion forward must be decelerated. Thus, the movement involves negative acceleration of the body's center of gravity as shown in the figure.

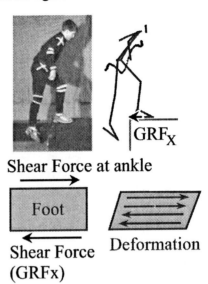

$$GRF_X$$

Shear Force at ankle

Foot

Shear Force   Deformation
(GRFx)

Figure 11-31. The shear force acting on the foot at a moment during a step up motion.

Because the GRF_X vector is applied on a line parallel to the bottom surface of the foot, it creates a *shear* force on the foot. This shear force produces a tendency for the foot to deform slightly, as shown in the figure above.

The rectangular shape below the video image represents the performer's foot. The shear force acting on the lower surface of this box represents the GRF_X force. The shear force acting on the upper surface of the box represents the internal force that is acting at the ankle joint. As the body moves up and forward on the step, its tendency to continue to move forward is represented by this joint reaction force.

The illustration shows that a solid object, such as the foot, will tend to deform when subjected to a shear force. If the shear force is very large, the performer will have a tendency to injure his ankle during the step. Of course, the forces on this motion are very small, and will produce no threat of injury.

However, at the moment shown in the figure, the shear force for this stepping motion is three times larger than the vertical force (GRF_Y). We can assume that the performer is less sensitive to a side-to-side pressure between the bottle cap and his foot than he is to an up-and-down pressure, where the bottle cap is pressed into the sole of his foot. The figure below shows the vertical component of the ground reaction force and the tendency for *compression* that it produces.

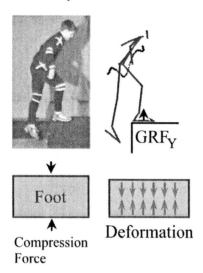

$$\text{GRF}_Y$$

Foot

Deformation

Compression
Force

Figure 11-32. The compression force acting on the foot at a moment during a step up motion.

The vertical force acting upward on the foot represents the GRF_Y force. The force that acts down on the upper surface of the foot represents the weight of the body pressing down on the foot segment. The illustration shows that an object, such as the foot, will tend to deform when subjected to a compression force. If the compression forces are very large, the performer will run the risk of a compression fracture of a bone in the leg or foot. For this particular movement, the performer is purposely minimizing any tendency toward compression in the foot.

Given information on the horizontal and vertical components of the ground reaction force, the resultant ground reaction force can be readily calculated.

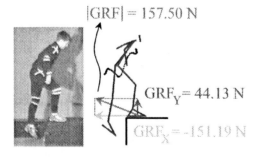

$$|\text{GRF}| = 157.50 \text{ N}$$

$$\text{GRF}_Y = 44.13 \text{ N}$$

$$\text{GRF}_X = -151.19 \text{ N}$$

Figure 11-33. The magnitude of the ground reaction force vector at a moment during a step up motion.

The figure above shows both the GRF_X and GRF_Y vectors. The scale for these vectors has been increased to make them easier to visualize. The diagonal arrow shows the resultant ground reaction force vector. The vector magnitude of the ground reaction force ($|\text{GRF}|$) is shown to be 157.5 Newtons. The calculation for the size of the ground reaction force is based upon the vector magnitude formula. If we know the X and Y components of a given vector, the vector magnitude is calculated as follows:

$$GRF = \sqrt{GRF_X{}^2 + GRF_Y{}^2}$$

GRF = Sqr(-151.19² + 44.13²)
GRF = Sqr(22858 + 1947)
GRF = Sqr(22858 + 1947)
GRF = Sqr(24805)
GRF = 157.5 Newtons

Question 11-6:
Do you think that the body's center of gravity acceleration magnitude value can be used in the $\mathbf{F}_{NET} = m\mathbf{A}$ equation to compute the ground reaction force magnitude?

O A. Yes. A vector equation can be solved just like a scalar equation.
O B. No. A vector equation must be broken into scalar components before it can be solved.

As an exercise, let's compute the resultant ground reaction force from information on vector magnitudes:

$\mathbf{F}_{NET} = m\mathbf{A}$
GRF + Wgt = mA
GRF = mA − Wgt
Given:
$|\mathbf{A}| = 9.43$
$|\mathbf{Wgt}| = 734.25$
m = 74.85

GRF = mA − Wgt
GRF = (74.85 * 9.43) − (734.25)
GRF = (705.8) − (734.25)
GRF = -28.4 Newtons

Of course, the result is incorrect; the correct value for GRF is 157.5 Newtons. This example shows that the ground reaction force magnitude can only be computed from information on its various XYZ components.

Ground Reaction Force Examples

The horizontal ground reaction force components in a dance leap are larger than those from our step-up example. The figure below shows the horizontal ground reaction force component (GRFx) and the vertical component of the ground reaction force (GRFy) at a moment prior to take off.

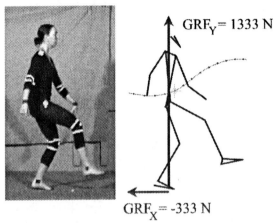

GRF$_Y$ = 1333 N

GRF$_X$ = -333 N

Figure 11-34. The X and Y components of the ground reaction force at the moment prior to take off during a dance leap.

Notice that the horizontal component of the ground reaction force is a "breaking" force that tends to slow the performer's motion in the forward direction. The dancer's goal is to decelerate horizontally to allow more force to be generated in the vertical direction.

The horizontal component of the ground reaction force has been considerably smaller than the vertical component for every example that we have seen so far. Part of the reason for the relatively small size of the horizontal components is that vertical forces are typically greater than body weight at the critical stages of most weight bearing movements. Another reason for relatively small GRF$_X$ components is that there is typically very little resistance to forward motion. The pull of gravity must be continually offset by vertical forces but only air resistance inhibits forward motion in running, dance leap and jumping movements.

Question 11-7:

Imagine that you have data on the center of gravity motion for the world record holder in the 100 meter dash. Analysis of the CG forward velocity indicates that during the middle of the race, the athlete is running faster than any human being has ever run before. At this moment what is the best estimate of the *net force* acting on the performer?

O A. Zero.
O B. A very high positive value
O C. A very high negative value

There are moments during the course of a 100-meter dash when the forward component of the body's center of gravity velocity is increasing. The figure below shows a runner on the first stride after leaving the starting blocks.

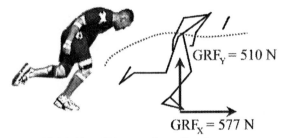

GRF$_Y$ = 510 N

GRF$_X$ = 577 N

Figure 11-35. X and Y ground reaction force components during a moment in a track start motion.

We see that large GRF$_X$ force components are used to increase the performer's speed in the forward direction. At the instant shown, the GRF$_X$ is 0.77 BW and the GRF$_Y$ is 0.87 BW.

Friction

Friction is defined as the force that opposes the motion of one body across the surface of another. Three types of friction are often encountered in typical human movements.

● Static friction - where no sliding occurs between two objects.

● Dynamic friction - where an object slides across the surface of another.

● Rolling friction - where reduced frictional forces are generated through the use of wheels or rollers.

Static Friction

The left portion of the figure below shows the ground reaction force X component at a moment just after heel strike during a running movement. This GRF_X force is a measure of the frictional force between a runner's foot and the ground.

At the moment shown in part A of the figure, the horizontal component of the ground reaction force acts backwards and opposes the forward motion of the runner. About 50 milliseconds later, the body shifts forward over the base of support and the ground reaction force X component becomes positive. This positive GRF_X component (shown in figure B) is used by the runner to generate forward propulsion.

In both of the illustrations, the frictional force opposes the motion of the foot with respect to the ground. In the first case, the frictional force prevents the foot from skidding forward just after the foot "lands" following the flight phase of the stride. In the second case, the frictional force prevents the foot from slipping backwards as the performer accelerates her body in the forward direction.

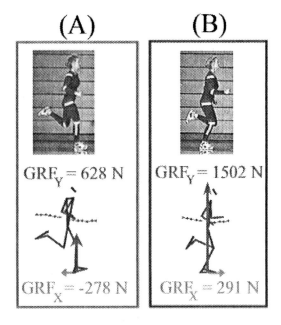

Figure 11-36. A comparison of the horizontal ground reaction force components acting on the foot at a moment just after heel strike (A) and during the support phase (B).

We see from this example that friction can be both "helpful" and "harmful" to the performance of the runner. Sprinters in track events wear spiked shoes to increase their ability to generate large propulsive frictional forces in their movements. By changing the nature of the shoe "surface" that contacts the ground, the potential for larger propulsive forces can be increased.

The following equation can be used to compute the maximal frictional force that can be generated between two surfaces before sliding occurs.

$$F_S \leq \mu_S R$$

Where:
F_S – is the force of static friction
μ_S – is the coefficient of static friction
R – is the normal force

Figure 11-37. The normal force acting on a plastic hockey puck.

In this equation, the normal force is the force that causes the two surfaces (for example, the hockey puck and the board in figure 11-37) to be pressed together. This force acts at right angles to the lower surface (i.e., the puck and the board). For motion across a horizontal surface, the normal force is simply the vertical component of the ground reaction force. For an object that is resting on a horizontal surface, the normal force is equal to the body weight.

The μ_S term in the equation represents the value of the coefficient of static friction. This measure is directly related to the relative "roughness" and "hardness" of the two surfaces. Rough and soft surfaces will produce greater values of μ_S. Smooth and hard surfaces will produce smaller values of μ_S. The value of μ_S for any pair of surfaces is determined experimentally and is typically between 0.1 and 1.0.

Note that the equation for static friction makes use of the "less than or equal to" sign ($\leq$) to indicate that the size of the frictional force between a stationary object and a second surface can take on any value from zero up to a given maximal value. The figure below shows the frictional forces that occur between the puck and the board as a series of pushing forces are applied to the puck.

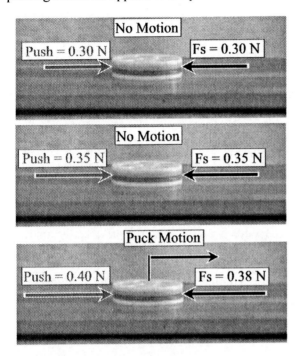

Figure 11-38. The forces of static friction that resist the horizontal motion of a hockey puck.

The upper part of the figure shows that if we push on the puck with a force of 0.30 Newtons, the frictional force will become equal to 0.30 Newtons and no motion will result. The middle portion of the figure shows that if we increase the pushing force to 0.35 Newtons, the frictional force will also increase to 0.35 Newtons, and again, because the net force acting on the puck is zero, no motion will result. The lower section of the figure shows that if the pushing force exceeds the maximal static friction force, a non-zero net force will be applied to the puck and motion will result.

Thus we see that the size of a static frictional force can take on any value from zero up to the product of μ_S and R. Note that the maximal size of static friction is directly proportional to μ_S and R. Thus, if the normal force is doubled, the maximal force of static friction will also double. Alternatively, if the roughness of the surfaces increases, the maximal frictional force will also increase.

The normal force between a given object and an inclined plane surface will change with the angle of inclination of the plane. If a hockey puck is placed on a board and the board is gradually inclined, the puck will eventually begin to slide.

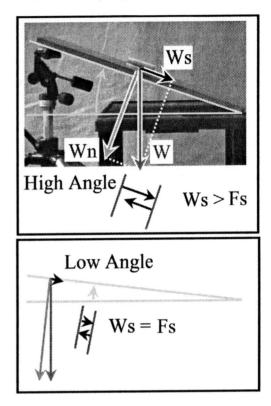

Figure 11-39. A comparison of the force of static friction for a high and low angle of inclination of a plane.

The upper portion of the figure below shows the board angle that is just large enough to cause the hockey puck to slide. The "W" vector represents the weight force for the puck. The "Wn" vector represents the normal component of the weight force. The "Ws" vector represents the shear component of the weight force along the surface of the board. The motion of the puck is a result of two interrelated factors:

1) As the board angle increases, the normal force between the puck and the board decreases. As the size of the normal force gets smaller and smaller, the tendency for the puck to slide increases.

2) As the board angle increases, the component of the puck weight force along a line parallel to the surface of the board increases. Eventually, this Ws force component exceeds the value of the limiting friction force and the puck slides.

For the "High Angle" condition, the board's angle is high enough to cause the Ws force component to exceed the maximal possible static friction force (Ws > Fs). Because the net force acting on the puck exceeds zero, the puck will accelerate down the slope.

The lower portion of the figure shows the forces acting on the puck for a "Low Angle" condition. Because of the small angle of the board, the Ws component of the weight force is small. The static friction force between the puck and the board can easily match the Ws component. As a result, the net force acting on the puck is zero and the puck does not move.

If the value for the coefficient of static friction is known for a pair of surfaces, the critical angle of inclination of the board can be computed mathematically. Conversely, if the coefficient of static friction is not known for the two surfaces, an inclined plane study can be used to determine the μ_S value.

Question 11-8:
A hockey puck weights 0.25 pounds. What equation is used to compute the size of the puck weight force in Newtons?

O A. Force in Newtons = Force in pounds * 4.45
O B. Force in Newtons = Force in pounds / 9.81
O C. Force in Newtons = Force in pounds / 32.2

Question 11-9:
A 1.113 N puck is placed on a board that is inclined at an angle of 19 degrees. What equation is used to compute the component of the puck weight force that is normal to the surface of the board?

O A. Wn = W * Sin(19°).
O B. Wn = W * Cos(19°).

Question 11-10:
Given information on the size of the Ws and Wn forces that are associated with the onset of motion, what equation can be used to solve for the value of the coefficient of static friction?

O A. μ_S = Ws / Wn
O B. μ_S = Wn / Ws

Dynamic Friction

Once an object begins to slide across a surface, the equation for the coefficient of static friction is no longer relevant. The frictional force that acts between a moving object and a given surface is defined by the equation for the coefficient of dynamic friction:

$F_D \le \mu_D R$

Where:
F_D – is the force of dynamic or sliding friction
μ_D – is the coefficient of dynamic friction
R – is the normal force

For typical surfaces, the coefficient of dynamic friction is always less than the coefficient of static friction. As a result, once a hockey puck begins to slide down an inclined plane, it will continue to slide even if the angle is slightly reduced. The figure below shows the puck's motion when the angle of the inclined plane just barely permits motion.

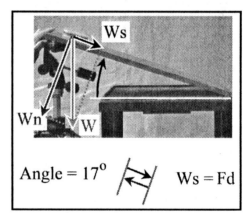

Figure 11-40. An angle of inclination of a plane that is not large enough to cause the puck to slide.

The board angle that is needed to cause the puck to start moving from a stationary position is 19°. When the board is set at 17° and the puck is given a small push, it will continue to move down the slope with a nearly constant velocity.

When the board angle is 17°, the shear force component of the puck weight force is equal to the F_D force, and the puck will move with constant velocity just after the coefficient of static friction is overcome (by the small push). In this special case, the net force acting on the puck is zero (F_D = Ws) and therefore the acceleration is also zero. However this does not imply that the puck velocity is zero. If the puck moves with constant velocity, it will have zero acceleration because the change in velocity will be zero.

The values of the coefficient of static and dynamic friction are very much dependent upon both of the surfaces involved in the sliding motion. For example, the size of the limiting frictional force between a football player's shoes (with quarter inch cleats) and a grass field may be 800 Newtons. If the player generates horizontal ground reaction force components in excess of 800 Newtons, his foot will slip and his ability to accelerate further will be limited.

Note that the football player can increase the size of the limiting frictional force by changing to shoes with one half inch cleats. By increasing the maximal propulsive force that can be generated backward, the player also increases the maximal forward force that can act when he is tackled. If the player receives a forceful blow to the lower leg when tackled, this increased frictional force can increase his chance of sustaining an injury.

Rolling Friction

The frictional forces that resist the motion of a heavy load across a smooth surface can be dramatically reduced through the use of wheels or rollers. The coefficient of rolling friction is 100 - 1000 times smaller than the coefficient of sliding friction. The figure below shows a skateboard push off motion. The performer will glide steadily forward after the push off due to the low frictional force between the wheels and the floor.

Figure 11-41. A skate board "push off" motion.

The velocity of the skateboard will decrease very slowly if the wheels are well lubricated and the floor is smooth and level. The gradual decrease in speed of forward motion that occurs over time is a result of both non-zero values of rolling friction and air resistance.

Relative Motion and Frictional Forces

Efficient technique in running requires the performer to generate large propulsive ground reaction forces and, at the same time, minimize the size of the breaking forces that are generated during each stride. In order to minimize the negative components of the horizontal ground reaction force, skilled performers must adjust their movements to reduce the positive X component of the foot velocity near the moment of impact with the ground.

The figure below shows the toe and hip horizontal components of velocity near the middle of the leg recovery motion and at a moment just before foot strike. Notice that the toe velocity, as measured with respect to the fixed reference frame seen by the camera, decreases from 13.9 mps to 2.0 mps during the last portion of the leg recovery. For the same time period, the hip point forward velocity changes very little, from 8.0 mps to 7.1 mps. The runner uses the large change in the toe forward velocity to minimize the size of breaking forces just after foot touchdown.

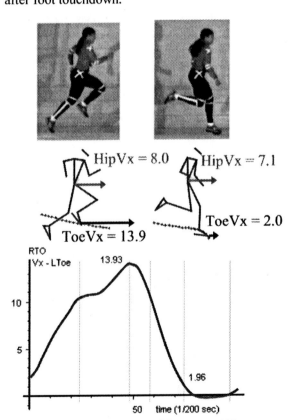

Figure 11-42. A comparison of the toe and hip velocities of a runner at two moments in time during a running stride.

The fact that the toe's velocity approaches zero near the instant of touchdown does not imply that the foot stops moving *with respect to the body*. The figure below shows a comparison of the toe motion from two viewpoints:

● The upper portion of the figure shows the toe velocity as measured with respect to a fixed reference (the stationary floor in the gym)

● The lower portion of the figure shows the toe velocity as measured with respect to the hip.

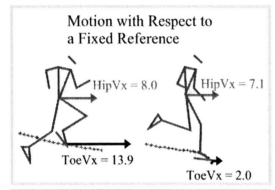

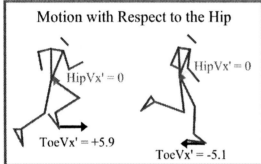

Figure 11-43. A comparison of the toe and hip velocities of a runner expressed with respect to the hip (bottom of figure) and with respect to a fixed reference frame (upper portion of figure).

The lower portion of the figure shows that the toe is moving forward with respect to the hip during the middle portion of the leg recovery. The size of the toe's relative velocity is computed by subtracting the fixed camera hip velocity measure from the toe velocity measure:

ToeVx' = ToeVx – HipVx
ToeVx' = 13.9 – 8.0
ToeVx' = 5.9 mps

Where:
ToeVx' is the toe X component of velocity expressed with respect to the hip.

Near the moment of foot touchdown, the toe is moving *backward* with respect to the hip. By swinging the leg backward with respect to the hip, the performer is attempting to minimize the breaking force that can occur at touchdown.

It is interesting to note that measures that are expressed with respect to a translating reference frame can sometimes reveal important information. For this example, we see that the backward motion of the foot relative to the body must have been produced through extension of the hip joint. The figure below shows the video and stick figure images from a treadmill based study of running.

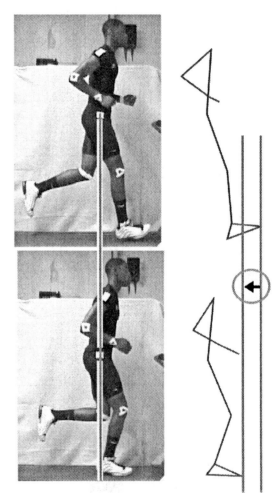

Figure 11-44. Video images and movement data for a runner on a treadmill.

An analysis of the video for this study will isolate the movements of the performer with respect to a translating reference frame. The stick figure data for this study shows that the hip point stays at a nearly fixed X coordinate location throughout the running cycle. The figure shows the backward swinging motion of the foot that occurs near the instant of foot strike.

The video data that is collected for a treadmill running motion from a fixed camera position is equivalent to the collection of over-ground running with a translating camera. For either case, the propulsive and breaking force components generated during the stride cannot be computed without additional mathematical treatment to the data. If all X coordinate values are shifted forward to compensate for the backward motion of the treadmill, data that is equivalent to a "true" fixed camera will result.

This example reminds us that fixed camera positions must be used to generate the data needed for ground reaction force calculations. We also see that measures of movements expressed with respect to the body can also reveal interesting information. We will see in our chapters on angular kinematics that measures of joint angles and rate of change of joint angles will also provide an effective way to evaluate movements with respect to the body.

Force Plate Data Analysis

Our discussions thus far have used examples from video-based projects to emphasize the relationship between center of gravity acceleration and net force. Our study of external forces will not be complete however, until we discuss the use of force plates in biomechanical analysis.

Force plate devices are designed to electronically measure the ground reaction forces that are produced during human motion. The figure below shows an image from a combined force plate and video-based analysis of a golf swing. The study makes use of two force plates, one for each of the performer's feet.

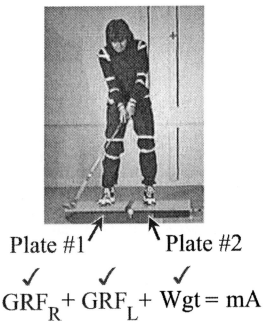

Figure 11-45. Force plate data collection on a golf drive motion.

The force plates can independently record the X, Y and Z components of the ground reaction force for each foot during the golf swing movement. As a result, it is not necessary to use the body's center of gravity acceleration to determine the ground reaction forces. In fact, the center of gravity acceleration could be computed from the force plate data alone, through the left to right solution of the $\mathbf{F}_{NET} = m \, \mathbf{A}$ equation.

Force plate devices, on a simplified level, can be thought of as "very sensitive scales". Thus, while your bathroom scale can be used to measure your body weight as long as you stand perfectly still, a force plate can be used to measure subtle changes in your vertical ground reaction force components while your are moving. Further, while a bathroom scale is used to measure only the vertical component of your ground reaction force, a force plate can measure the forward-back and side-to-side components of any force that is applied to the plate.

The figure below shows a three-dimensional force vector acting on a force plate and the XYZ reference frame convention that is used with typical force plate configurations.

Force Plate Reference Frame

Figure 11-46. The XYZ reference frame used with typical force plate systems.

The readings from a force plate device are sent via electrical cables to a computer for processing by an analog to digital (A/D) data acquisition card. The A/D card, like the sound card or video capture card on your home or lab PC, can accept and process a given "input" signal. The A/D board converts the continuous measures of force from the force plate and converts them to long lists of numbers (the analog signal is converted to digital form). Force plate equipment has three important advantages over the video analysis procedures that we have discussed thus far:

● Higher resolution. Force plates can process upwards of 10,000 samples per second of three dimensional force and moment data. (We will discuss moments in the angular kinetics chapters).

● Higher accuracy. Because force plates are designed specifically for the measurement of force, their final output is considerably more accurate than what we have seen with calculations from video data.

● Ease of processing. Force plate readings are captured "on-line" with very little manual work on the part of the researcher. Once the force plate software is initialized, millions of numbers can be sent to disk with the press of a single keystroke.

There are two disadvantages associated with force plate data collection:

● Force plates do not provide kinematic information on the movements of the performer. The speed of the golfer's club-head and the changes to the angle

of the elbow joint can never be determined from force plate data.

● Force plates are difficult to move to "field based" data collection sites. Almost all force plate data collection is performed within the confines of a laboratory or a specially designed space.

When data can be collected under laboratory conditions, the combination of force plate data and video data provides us with more complete information than would be possible with either mode of data collection alone.

The figure below shows the XYZ reference frame typically used with force plate systems. Notice that the XYZ reference axis convention for force plate devices is different from that commonly used in video analysis. With force plates, the Z-axis is typically taken as perpendicular to the horizontal plane and aimed *downward*. With video analysis, the positive Z-axis is set as perpendicular to the horizontal plane and aimed upward. Thus, the force plate output represents the forces that are applied to the plate, rather than the reaction forces that are applied to the body due to its interaction with the ground. Force plate data can easily be superimposed upon video data however by setting the Z data as upward and swapping the X and Y force measurements.

Force Plate Reference Frame

Video Reference Frame

Figure 11-47. A comparison of a force plate reference frame and traditional video reference frames.

Figure 11-48. An image sequence figure for a back somersault motion. The upward arrows represent the GRFy vector components. The downward arrows represent the weight force vector.

The above image sequence figure shows information from a back somersault motion where data was collected by both force plate and video equipment. Notice that the performer generates a very large ground reaction force just after the moment of landing.

The force plate Z component force measures are shown in figure 11-49. The force plate software collected data before, during, and after the back somersault. The KA software utility program FPView was used to trim off the excess information from the beginning and end of the force plate curves. FPView can also be used to convert the time base of the force plate curves from one measure every 1/500th second to an equivalent curve with measures shown at 1/60th second intervals.

The figure shows a comparison of the force plate data (the smoother curve with zero values for the flight phase time period) and the video analysis data (the curve with more noise and non-zero values for the flight phase time period). Note that the more "noisy" video based data is derived from the center of gravity acceleration data.

These data measures confirm that the force plate data is more accurate than the video based data. Nevertheless, the force measurements from the video data are reasonably close to those generated by the force plate. The video data in the figure has been minimally smoothed (the KA smoothing factor is set as 1). As a result, the "spike" in the ground

reaction force that occurs on the landing (near frame 155) is shown fairly well by the video data curve.

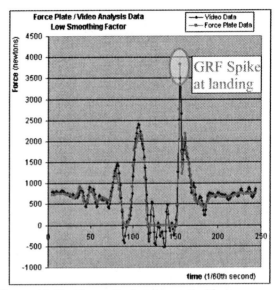

Figure 11-49. The vertical component of force generated during a back somersault motion. The two force curves provide a comparison of ground reaction force as measured by a force plate and through an analysis of the video data.

These data show that video information collected with a sampling rate of 60 hertz (60 fields per second) provides a fair approximation of the "true" ground reaction force measures, as indicated by the force plate output.

Video measures are typically "noisy", and show up and down oscillations where smoother trends in the data are expected. Video analysis software programs like KA include smoothing routines that will mathematically remove much of the noise from the original video data. We have discussed smoothing before in Chapter 9, but we can now use our force plate data to get a better understanding of the influences of smoothing.

If smoothing is applied to data from a video project, the velocity and acceleration curves get smoother, but it is very difficult to know if the data has been "over-smoothed". If too much smoothing is applied to video data, the true values of peak velocity and acceleration are "flattened" as the smoothing routines remove too much of the high and low values in the movement signal. Because we have information on both the "true" movement data from the force plates, and the noisy video data, we can now objectively evaluate the effects of over-smoothing. The figure below shows two graphs comparing the force plate and video based GRF$_Y$ data curves. The upper graph shows the video data with a smoothing factor of one. The lower curve shows the video data with a smoothing factor of 15. Notice that the lower graph provides a pretty good approximation of the force plate data for frames 1 to 150.

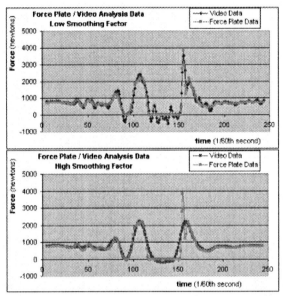

Figure 11-50. A comparison of minimally smooth force data (upper figure) and over-smoothed force data (lower figure). The "true" force data, as given by the force plate, is shown in both portions of the figure.

However, the sharp spike in the force plate curve near frame 155 has been smoothed away within the highly smoothed video data. Thus we see that the smoothed video data has provided reasonable approximations of the real forces acting on the performer for most of the movement. Only the portions of the movement that involve sudden, sharp changes in force are poorly represented by smoothed video data.

Nevertheless, force plates should be included in any research project where sudden changes in force are of interest. It should also be noted that video based estimates of force will be much better for "large" forceful movements than for "small" movements with light forces. Thus, video-based calculations of the relatively small X and Y ground reaction force components in the back somersault will be poor indicators of the true force involved.

Conclusions

Our discussion of the relationships between external forces and human movement is now complete. We have seen that Newton's second law can be used to calculate the ground reaction forces that occur during the single support phase of many movements. We have also seen that force plate equipment can be used to provide very detailed information on the ground reaction forces produced in a wide variety of human movements.

References

Higgins, Susan. "Movement as an emergent form: Its structural limits," Human Movement Science (4), 119-148, 1985.

Answers to Chapter Questions

Question 11-1:
The following figure shows the CG A$_Y$ value for a critical moment in a volleyball jumping motion. About how large will the GRF$_Y$ value be at this moment?

O A. GRF$_Y$ will be less than the size of the body weight.
O B. GRF$_Y$ will be equal to the size of the body weight.
O C. GRF$_Y$ will be greater than the size of the body weight.

The correct answer is C. In order for GRF$_Y$ to be less than body weight, A$_Y$ would have to be negative. Because the A$_Y$ value is positive, the GRF$_Y$ value will be greater than body weight. (GRF$_Y$ = m A$_Y$ + |Wgt|).

Question 11-2:
The following figure shows the A$_Y$ curve for the volleyball performer's CG point. Note that the frame numbers for the movement are shown on the horizontal axis. What frame number is associated with the largest positive ground reaction force during the time course of this movement?

O A. About frame 40.
O B. About frame 70.
O C. About frame 100.

The correct answer is C. Frame 40 has a large positive acceleration, but it is not as high as that for frame 100. In fact, the largest positive A$_Y$ value for acceleration (13.56 mps^2) occurs at frame 98. The equation, GRF$_Y$ = m A$_Y$ + |Wgt| indicates that the largest GRF$_Y$ value will occur at this frame number.

Question 11-3:
Which of the following equations can be used to compute the vertical component of a ground reaction force?

O A. $GRF_Y = mA_Y + |Wgt|$
O B. **GRF = mA + Wgt**
O C. $GRF_X = mA_X$

The correct answer is A. To compute the vertical component of the ground reaction force the center of gravity acceleration Y component must be used.

Question 11-4:
A marathon runner with an injury to his right foot has decided to continue heavy training in preparation for the "big race". If data were collected on the peak forces generated by his right and left feet, what would you expect to see?

O A. The peak right and left foot forces should be equal.
O B. The peak force on his left foot will be higher than the force on his right.
O C. The peak force on his right foot will be higher than the force on his left.

The correct answer is B. It is very unlikely that the runner will maintain a symmetrical stride if pain is present. He will naturally shift the load from the injured leg to the non-injured leg.

Question 11-5:
If the potential for injury is directly related to the level of force experienced during training, what can we expect to happen to the left foot of the marathon runner?

O A. The left foot will become stronger as a result of the increased training load.
O B. The left foot will eventually become injured as a result of the persistent high loads that it is forced to absorb during training.

The correct answer is B. It is very likely that continued training with asymmetrical loads will cause an injury to the left foot.

Question 11-6:
Do you think that the body's center of gravity acceleration magnitude value can be used in the $F_{NET} = mA$ equation to compute the ground reaction force magnitude?

O A. Yes. A vector equation can be solved just like a scalar equation.
O B. No. A vector equation must be broken into scalar components before it can be solved.

The correct answer is B. A vector equation must be broken down into scalar equations before it can be solved.

Question 11-7:
Imagine that you have data on the center of gravity motion for the world record holder in the 100 meter dash. Analysis of the CG forward velocity indicates that during the middle of the race, the athlete is running faster than any human being has ever run before. At this moment what is the best estimate of the *net force* acting on the performer?

O A. Zero.
O B. A very high positive value
O C. A very high negative value

The correct answer is A. At the moment of peak horizontal velocity, the acceleration in the forward direction must be zero. If the velocity is at a peak, the slope of the velocity curve must be zero. If the slope of the velocity curve is zero, acceleration must be zero. If acceleration is zero, net force must be zero.

Question 11-8:
A hockey puck weights 0.25 pounds. What equation is used to compute the size of the puck weight force in Newtons?

O A. Force in Newtons = Force in pounds * 4.45
O B. Force in Newtons = Force in pounds / 9.81
O C. Force in Newtons = Force in pounds / 32.2

The correct answer is A. To covert from pounds to Newtons, multiply by 4.45. The weight of the puck is 1.113 N.

Question 11-9:
A 1.113 N puck is placed on a board that is inclined at an angle of 19 degrees. What equation is used to compute the component of the puck weight force that is normal to the surface of the board?

O A. Wn = W * Sin(19°).
O B. Wn = W * Cos(19°).

The correct answer is B. The triangle formed by the Wn vector, the W vector and the dotted line has a 19° angle. As a result, the Cosine trigonometry function is used because it defines the ratio between the adjacent and "hypotenuse" vectors. Wn = W * Cos(19°); Wn = (1.113)*(0.9455); Wn = 1.052 N

Question 11-10:
Given information on the size of the Ws and Wn forces that are associated with the onset of motion, what equation can be used to solve for the value of the coefficient of static friction?

○ A. μ_S = Ws / Wn
○ B. μ_S = Wn / Ws

The correct answer is A. At the moment when motion
first occurs the equation $F_S \leq \mu_S$ R can be replaced with
Ws = μ_S Wn. As a result, μ_S = Ws / Wn. For the puck
and board in our example, μ_S = 0.344.

Chapter 12: Momentum

Given the foundation knowledge we have developed in Chapters 10 and 11, we are now ready to consider a number of advanced topics in linear kinetics. The remaining sections of this chapter will discuss the impulse momentum relationship and the conservation of momentum principle.

Impulse Momentum Relationship

The formal definition of Newton's second law of motion is as follows:

The rate of change of momentum of a body is proportional to the force causing it, and the change takes place in the direction in which the force acts.

Our introduction to Newton's laws in Chapter 10 has shown that Newton's second law can be expressed mathematically as:

$$F_{NET} = (mV_F - mV_I) / t$$

This equation, and the equivalent $F_{NET} = m\,A$ equation, are very useful in the calculation of *instantaneous* measures of force. We can derive the equation for the impulse momentum relationship by simply multiplying both sides of the above equation by time:

$$F_{NET} \cdot t = (mV_F - mV_I)$$

Where:
t – any time interval of interest
$F_{NET} \cdot t$ – the product of force and time or the impulse of force
$(mV_F - mV_I)$ – the change in momentum over the given time interval

This simple re-expression of Newton's second law provides us with a powerful approach for the analysis of the *impulse of force*. Virtually all human

movements are generated by a series of forces that are developed over a period of time. The image sequence figure below shows the ground reaction forces for a vertical jump. The upward arrows represent the sizes of the ground reaction forces. Note that the ground reaction force vectors change in size to reflect the differences in force levels as the performer moves.

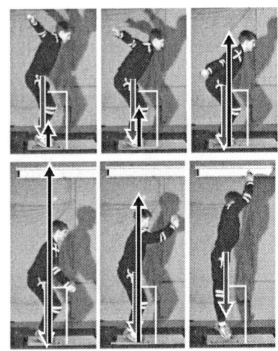

Figure 12-1. The ground reaction forces generated during a vertical jump motion.

We will see in this section that the performer's ability to use well-coordinated full body movements to develop force over a time period is a critical ingredient of skill. Note that the arms are used extensively in a forceful vertical jumping motion. Inspect the arm swing motion in the figure above and answer the following question:

Question 12-1:
Does the arm swing help the performer to jump higher?

O A. Yes.
O B. No.

If you expect that the performer's arm swing has helped him to jump higher you are absolutely right. Bear in mind, the goal of this vertical jump is to achieve as much height as possible, and the full body is used in the generation of force for the jump.

However, a key question still remains. *How* does the motion of the arms allow the performer to jump higher? After all, the arms do not push against the floor directly. Many people may think that the only thing that matters in jumping performance is leg strength. We will see in the remaining parts of this chapter that the skillful coordination of the movements of the entire body is often essential in maximizing performance. Further, we will see that the impulse momentum relationship provides the mechanical rationale for the advantages inherent in well-coordinated whole body motions.

Calculation of the Impulse of Force

The figure below shows the "driving-up" phase of a maximal effort vertical jump.

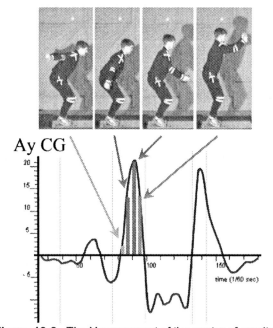

Figure 12-2. The Y component of the center of gravity acceleration (CG Ay) for a vertical jump.

The acceleration curve for the Y component of the body's center of gravity (A_Y CG) is shown at the lower portion of the figure. Note that the positive acceleration phase of the jump takes place in a relatively brief time period. The four colored bars in the figure show the A_Y values for four critical instances in time during the movement.

We will now perform the calculation of the impulse of force generated on this positive acceleration phase of the motion. Remember that the vector equation for the impulse momentum relationship is as follows:

$$F_{NET} \cdot t = (mV_F - mV_I)$$

For a two dimensional data analysis, we can break this vector equation into 2 scalar components:

$$F_{XNET} \cdot t = (mV_{XF} - mV_{XI})$$
$$F_{YNET} \cdot t = (mV_{YF} - mV_{YI})$$

Where:
$F_{XNET} \cdot t$ and $F_{YNET} \cdot t$ - are the net impulse of force delivered to the body along the X and Y dimensions.
$mV_{XF} - mV_{XI}$ - the change in momentum of the body along the X dimension.
$MV_{YF} - mV_{YI}$ - the change in momentum of the body along the Y dimension.

For a vertical jump, we will consider only the component of motion along the Y dimension. Bear in mind that the F_{YNET} term represents the net force acting on the body along the Y dimension. We also know that $F_{YNET} = mA_Y$. Thus, we can begin our solution of the $F_{YNET} \cdot t = (mV_{YF} - mV_{YI})$ equation by determining the mA_Y values.

The figure below shows a plot of the mA_Y values as a function of time for the positive acceleration phase of the jump. The net force curve in this graphic is very similar to the center of gravity A_Y curve information. In the graph, the CG A_Y values have been multiplied by body mass and the function plot has been "zoomed in" to show just the positive acceleration phase of the movement.

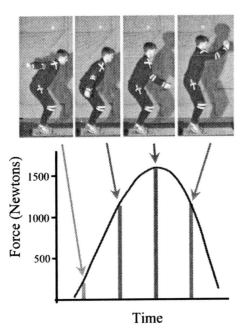

Figure 12-3. The ground reaction force curve for a vertical jumping motion is shown in the lower portion of the figure.

The impulse of force for the jump can be thought of as the area under the force curve in this figure. Note that the horizontal axis represents time, and the vertical axis represents force. As a result, multiplying force by time ($F_{NET} \cdot t$) is equivalent to multiplying the vertical force values by the horizontal time values in this graph.

The figure below shows a column chart with each instantaneous measure for force shown as a vertical bar.

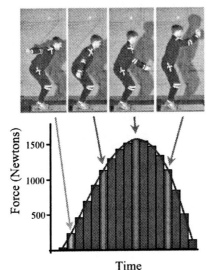

Figure 12-4. The ground reaction force levels for a series of 1/60th second time intervals during a vertical jump are shown.

The area under the force curve can be very well approximated by adding up the areas for each of the rectangular bars in the figure. The area of each bar is given by the formulas:

Rectangular area = Height * Width
Bar Area = Force Level * Time Interval

For each individual bar, the force level, or height of each bar, is the value of the mA_Y term for each frame in the positive acceleration phase of the movement. The time interval, or the width of each bar, is equal to 1/60th second. The figure below shows a table of the force levels and rectangular bar areas for each bar in the graph.

Frame #	Force	F * t
82	25.0	0.42
83	228.8	3.81
84	460.8	7.68
85	703.8	11.73
86	939.0	15.65
87	1150.5	19.17
88	1326.7	22.11
89	1461.2	24.35
90	1550.5	25.84
91	1591.9	26.53
92	1580.9	26.35
93	1510.1	25.17
94	1370.4	22.84
95	1154.5	19.24
96	863.0	14.38
97	509.8	8.50
98	124.2	2.07
Impulse =		**275.85**

Figure 12-5. A spreadsheet table with the forces and impulse measures for the vertical jumping motion.

The net force levels at each frame are shown in the second column. The third column holds the product of each force level and the time interval (1/60th second). Thus, the third column holds the "area" associated with each rectangular bar. The sum of the areas of all of the bars, or the total area under the curve is shown at the bottom of the "F * t" column.

We have now succeeded in computing the value of the impulse for the positive acceleration phase of the movement. Our computed value should theoretically be equal to the change in momentum that is experienced by the body during the time interval:

$$F_{YNET} \cdot t = (mV_{YF} - mV_{YI})$$

The values for the terms on the right hand side of the equation are as follows:

$m = 74.85$ kg
$V_{YF} = 2.82$ mps
$V_{YI} = -0.93$ mps

The calculation of the change in momentum is as follows:

$$F_{YNET} \cdot t = (mV_{YF} - mV_{YI})$$
$$F_{YNET} \cdot t = (74.85 * 2.82) - (74.85 * (-0.93))$$
$$F_{YNET} \cdot t = 211.09 - (-69.71)$$
$$F_{YNET} \cdot t = 211.09 + 69.71$$
$$F_{YNET} \cdot t = 280.80 \text{ Newton-seconds}$$

Our calculated value for the change in momentum (280.8) is very close to our estimation of the impulse of force (275.85). If our digitizing work, assumptions of symmetry and data smoothing procedures were perfect we would expect to get exactly the same result for the impulse calculation and the change in momentum calculation. While the data used for our calculations in this exercise is not perfect, it has nevertheless allowed us to clearly visualize the meaning of an impulse of force. We will use the knowledge that we have gained with this example to help use to evaluate a number of other interesting movements in this chapter.

Arm Swing Effects

Given our understanding of the impulse momentum relationship, we are now in a position to analyze the influence of the arm swing motion in a vertical jump. We have mentioned above that the arm swing helps the performer to jump higher, but we have not defined the mechanism for this improvement in performance.

The image sequence figure below shows the data from an analysis of an "arm swing only" movement.

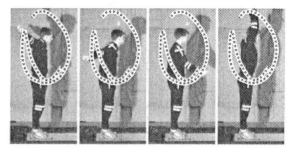

Figure 12-6. An "arm swing only" motion.

In this study, the performer was asked to stand on the force plate and swing his arms with a movement as close as possible to that used in his "real" jump. The performer was reminded to keep his knees as straight as possible during the movement. As a result, his feet never left the ground. However, his center of gravity location shifted within his body as his arms moved.

You may recall from our discussion in Chapter 5 that the center of gravity of a uniformly distributed solid object (i.e., a baton) is located at a fixed spot near the center of the object. The human body, when held in a fixed position, also has a single fixed center of gravity location. However, when any portion of the body moves, the center of gravity of the body must also move. Thus, if the arms are shifted overhead, the center of gravity must shift upward in the body.

Armswing and CG Shift

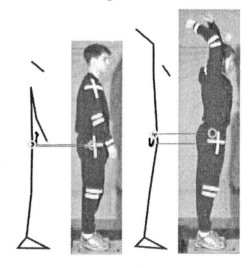

Figure 12-7. The upward center of gravity shift that occurs during an arm swing motion is shown.

The figure above shows video images and corresponding stick figures for the arm swing only movement. The body's center of gravity location is shown as a circle in both the stick figure and video images. Note that the body's CG is at the level of the hip joint marker when the arms are down. When the arms are swung overhead, the center of gravity position shifts upward in the body 10 centimeters above the level of the hip.

The center of gravity of the human body is like a "balancing point" near the middle of the body. The figure below shows a balanced baton and the two body positions for our vertical jump performer. The pivot point is shown at the exact spot where balance is achieved. For the upper figure, the baton was shifted from side to side over the pivot point until the balance point was found. For the lower figures, you can imagine that the same balancing operation was performed on a mannequin that is an exact replica of the performer. Notice that the balance point must shift to the left in the lower figure because the weight of the arms has been moved to the left.

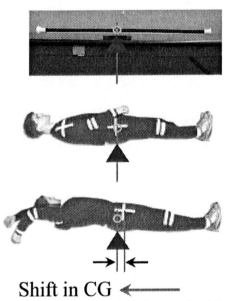

Shift in CG ⟵

Figure 12-8. A comparison of the "balance" point of a baton and a human body with arms up and arms down.

Question 12-2:
Imagine that the baton in the upper portion of the figure is made of wood. Further, suppose that a knife has been used to "whittle" a 8 centimeter x .5 centimeter section from the right side of the baton. The whittled section of wood is then placed on top of the intact baton to the left of the balance point.

What will happen to the baton when the whittled piece of wood is placed on the left side of the baton length?

O A. The baton will tilt to the left.
O B. The baton will tilt to the right.
O C. The baton will stay balanced.

Question 12-3:
Where will the new balance point for the baton be located?

O A. The new balance point will have shifted closer to the right side of the baton.
O B. The new balance point will have shifted closer to the left side of the baton.

Our discussions have shown that the arm swing motion causes the center of gravity point to move within the body. Further, it follows that fast center of gravity movement will follow from fast arm swing motions. Similarly, large center of gravity accelerations will follow from arm swings that involve large changes in movement speed. The figure below shows the center of gravity A_Y curve for the arm swing only motion.

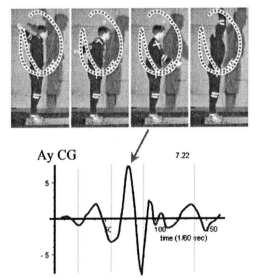

Figure 12-9. The Y component of the center of gravity acceleration data for an arm swing motion analysis.

The peak positive A_Y value for the CG is 7.22 mps^2. This is a relatively large value for the body's CG A_Y. The figure below shows a comparison of the peak positive A_Y values for both the arms-only and full jump trials. Note that the peak A_Y value for the arms-only movement is more than 33% of that found for the full jump motion. (7.2 mps^2 versus 21.3 mps^2).

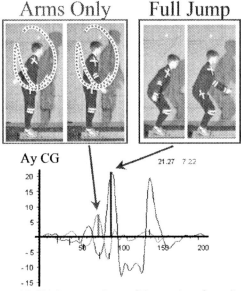

Arms Only   Full Jump

Figure 12-10. A comparison of the center of gravity point Ay data for an "arms only" and a "full jump" motion.

As a result, we see that the arm swing contributes *about* 33% of the center of gravity A_Y value in the jump. Thus, if the arms were not used at all, and all other aspects were held unchanged, the impulse for the jump would be only about 67% of the full body motion value. This reduction in impulse would lead to a reduction in the change in momentum, and the jump height would be greatly reduced.

Technically, the center of gravity acceleration for the "arms-only" movement is derived from both arm motion and a limited amount of trunk flexion and extension. Thus, it may be best to think of the lightly shaded curve A_Y value as being the "non-leg" contribution of whole body motion to the impulse generated on the jump.

A more exact estimate of the non-leg body motion contribution to the jump impulse can be determined from a more detailed analysis of the vertical jump arm swing motion. The 33% estimate that we presented above is based upon two independent movement trials, where the performer was asked to move his arms "the same way". In fact, the performer's movements were not identical and the "arms-only" trial involved a lower peak wrist A_Y value than that used in the full jump trial. The figure below shows that the peak wrist A_Y value for the arms-only trial is 102 mps^2 while the full jump wrist A_Y value is 132 mps^2.

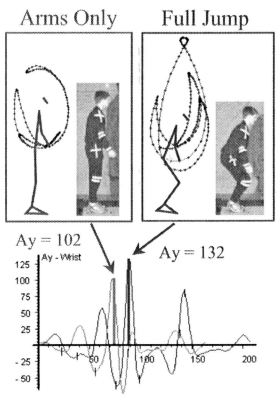

Figure 12-11. A comparison of the wrist acceleration Y component data for an "arms only" and a "full jump" motion.

As a result, our estimate of a 33% non-leg contribution to the body impulse is actually too low. The figure below shows the data from a mathematically generated "arms-only" movement trial with exactly the same wrist, elbow and shoulder movements as those of the full jump trial. The hip, knees and foot points are absolutely still in this simulated movement trial. Notice that the peak center of gravity A_Y value for this trial is 8.60 mps^2.

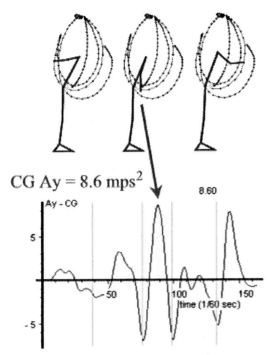

Figure 12-12. Mathematically generated wrist CG Ay data for an arms only movement.

The data from this analysis indicate that the trunk and arm motions generated by the performer contribute about 40% (8.6 / 21.27) to the body's center of gravity acceleration value. This finding shows us that skill in a vertical jump involves much more than strong legs. The well-coordinated movement of the arms and trunk make large contributions to the center of gravity A_Y curve. These A_Y values reflect the large net force being generated by the body motion ($\mathbf{F_{NET}} = m\mathbf{A}$). In turn, the large net forces generate the impulse that causes the change in the body's momentum, and the eventual outcome of the jumping motion.

Easy Jump

We will now use the impulse momentum relationship to compare the movements of a maximal force jump and a less forceful jump. For this example, we asked the participant from the last example to perform an easy jump. The figure below shows that the peak height of the center of gravity above the floor is 16 centimeters less for the easy jump than for the full jump.

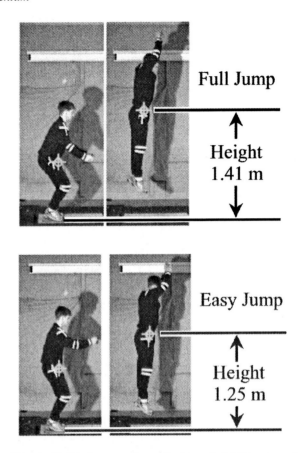

Figure 12-13. A comparison of a "forceful" full jump and an "easy" jumping motion.

The difference in jumping height is relatively large. The easy jump height was 11% less than the full jump height. The lower jumping height for the easy jump is reflected in the peak center of gravity A_Y data. The figure below shows that the easy jump A_Y peak value is 19.7 mps^2, and the full jump A_Y peak value is 21.1 mps^2. Note that the ground reaction force vectors are drawn to the same scale in both video images. Because ground reaction force is directly related to A_Y values, the peak GRF$_Y$ value is also less for the easy jump.

Easy Jump   Full Jump

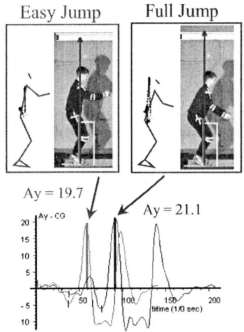

Ay = 19.7

Ay = 21.1

Figure 12-14. A comparison of the peak ground reaction forces and CG Ay values for an "easy jump" and a "full jump".

Thus we see that the easy jump peak center of gravity A$_Y$ value, peak net force and peak ground reaction force are all slightly "scaled down" in size with respect to the full jump. The difference in jumping height is due to both difference in force levels and differences in the time duration of the upward driving phase of the jumps. The figure below shows the positive impulse delivered to the floor for both jumps.

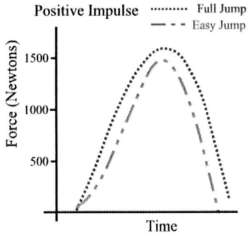

Figure 12-15. A comparison of the impulse curves for a full jump (upper curve) and an easy jump (lower curve).

The area under the finely dotted curve (Full Jump) is clearly larger than that of the lightly shaded curve (Easy Jump). The consistently larger force production of the full jump creates a larger impulse and therefore a higher jumping height.

The reduced time and force levels for the easy jump are a result of alterations in the performer's technique. For the easy jump trial, the performer elected to use less knee flexion. The figure below shows the difference in the knee angle at the moment in the movement where maximal knee bend occurs.

Figure 12-16. A comparison of the maximal knee bend angles for a full jump and an easy jump.

The performer has, at least at a subconscious level, modified his knee bend angle to modulate the degree of force production in his jump. By reducing the amount of knee bend by 12°, the performer has reduced both the movement time of the jump and the peak force level. The purposeful selection of different size knee bend angles in a vertical jump present us with some interesting questions.

The decrease in knee angle from 121° to 109° (a 12° change) produces a larger jumping height for the full jump. What will happen if the performer attempts to jump still higher by using an "extra-deep" knee bend of 80°?

Deep Bend Jump

Maximal Knee Angle = 80°

Normal Jump

Maximal Knee Angle = 109°

Figure 12-17. A comparison of a deep bend jump and a normal jumping motion.

Question 12-4:
The increase in knee angle from 109° to 121° (a 12° change) produces a smaller jumping height for the easy jump. What will happen if the performer attempts to jump still higher than he did in the full jump by bending his knees even more to create a knee angle that is less than 90°?

O A. This greater degree of knee flexion will result in a higher jump height.
O B. This greater degree of knee flexion will result in a lower jump height.

Too much knee bend will certainly hurt the performer's jumping height. The observation that there is an optimal knee flexion angle for a maximal height vertical jump is consistent with our discussion of biomechanical database measures from Chapter 2. Highly skilled performers will find the most effective way to perform any given movement through years of trial and error learning experiences. When we work with individuals and make suggestions to improve their performance, we should make use of Biomechanical Database information whenever possible to be assured that our suggestions are "in the right ballpark". We will often see that changing one aspect of a movement, for example, bending the knees more to increase the time of force application, will often involve undesirable side effects. For the vertical jump,

increasing the time of force application will not benefit the jump if the increased knee bend angles cause disproportionate reductions in force production.

As a result, we see that the range of motion in the bending-down phase of the jump is very important in skillful performance. Another interesting question concerns the time duration of the bending down phase.

Jump from Chair

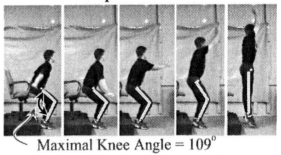

Maximal Knee Angle = 109°

Normal Jump

Maximal Knee Angle = 109°

Figure 12-18. A comparison of a "chair" jump and a normal jump. Both jumps make use of a maximal knee bend of 109°. The chair jump begins from a stationary position.

Question 12-5:
Suppose that an extensive analysis of jumping performance shows that the optimal knee bend angle is 109°. In a research study a skilled performer does a vertical jump two ways. On the first "chair" jump he sits on a chair whose height is set so that the performer's knee angle is exactly 109°, and then jumps up. On the second "normal" jump he bends down with his normal motion to the same knee angle and then immediately jumps up. Which jump will be highest?

O A. The chair jump.
O B. The normal jump.

Performing a jump from a stationary, seated position will produce lower levels of force than a normal jump where the performer "bounces down" to increase the force generation in the jump. The bounce-down phase of the movement creates tension in the leg muscles prior to the upward driving motion. Placing the muscles "on stretch" increases the level of muscular tension that can be generated later in the movement. The timing of the bounce down phase is also critically important, because the muscle's ability to respond to the pre-stretch action is very much dependent on time. Consider the following example.

In a research study a skilled performer does a vertical jump two ways. The first jump is performed with a slow-motion bend down phase, but the final knee flexion angle is made to be exactly 109°. The second jump involves a normal-speed "bounce down" movement that also results in a knee angle of 109°.

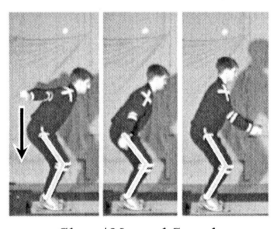

Slow / Normal Speed Bend Down Motion

Figure 12-19. The "bounce down" phase of a vertical jumping motion.

Question 12-6:
Which jump (the slow motion bend down or the normal jump) will be highest?

O A. The normal jump.
O B. The slow-motion bend down jump.

The slow-motion bend down jumping technique will be expected to produce lower levels of tension in the muscle. In addition, the slow-motion technique will also create too much delay between the development of peak tension and the upward driving motion.

In summary, skillful performers utilize the bounce-down movement to accomplish three important outcomes.

● The bounce-down movement must produce the optimal knee flexion angle. Too much or too little knee bend will harm the ultimate outcome of the jump.

● The bounce-down movement must be forceful enough to produce an optimal level of tension in the muscles. Too much tension, for example, that produced with a fall from a height of 2 meters, will harm the outcome of the movement. Too little tension, for example, that produced by a slow motion bounce-down movement will also harm the movement outcome.

● The bounce-down movement must be timed to produce maximal muscle tension at a critical time period just before the upward driving motion. Any delay between the end of the bounce-down phase and the beginning of the upward driving phase will harm the outcome of the movement.

As a result, we see that skill in a vertical jump performance involves many factors that have nothing to do with leg strength. The arm swing must be forceful and properly timed. Further, the bounce-down movement must also be properly timed, while creating an optimal knee angle and muscle tension.

Muscle Force and Contraction Speed

Classic studies of muscular force for isolated muscle fibers by Hill (1970) have shown that the development of forceful muscular contractions is very much dependent upon the speed of contraction. Thus, eccentric (lengthening) muscular contractions are potentially more forceful than isometric contractions. Similarly, isometric contractions are more forceful than isotonic contractions. The figure below shows the muscle force versus speed of contraction curve for isolated (surgically removed) and in-vivo (within the body) muscle. On this graph the vertical axis represents the force of muscular tension and the horizontal axis represents the speed of muscular contraction.

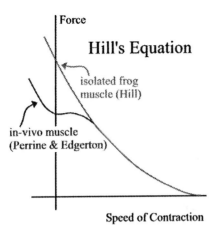

Figure 12-20. The relationship between the force and speed of contraction in a maximal effort muscular action.

The upper curve represents the muscle force velocity relationship for surgically removed frog muscle (Hill 1970). The lower curve shows the muscle force velocity relationship for in-vivo muscle (Perrine and Edgerton, 1978). The "in-vivo muscle" section of the curve shows that there is a reduction in force potential for in-vivo muscle at slow and negative contraction speeds. However, the general trend for the two versions of the curve is the same. The highest possible force production for muscle is associated with eccentric contractions. Further, slow moving concentric contractions are associated with higher levels of force production than fast moving concentric contractions.

Bench Press

Figure 12-21. A bench press motion.

Question 12-7:
A weight lifter's best single repetition lift on the bench press is 250 pounds. He is given a barbell that weights 50 pounds and asked to push the bar upwards as fast and as hard as possible. What is the best estimate of his arm movement speed on this bench press motion?

O A. The bar will move up very quickly.
O B. The bar will move up very slowly.

The figure below shows the muscle force / speed of contraction values that are appropriate for a "light barbell" bench press movement. Note that maximal effort lifting motions are associated with measures that are "on" the Hill's equation curve. The circle represents the fastest possible contraction speed for this performer on a 50 pound bench press.

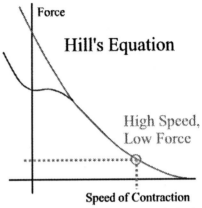

Figure 12-22. Hill's equation indicates that a low force level is associated with a high speed muscular contraction.

If the performer elected to do a very easy, 20% effort bench press with the 50 pound bar, the bar would move up more slowly. The circle on the left side of the figure below shows that a slower contraction speed can be used to lift the 50 pound bar.

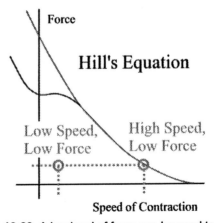

Figure 12-23. A low level of force can be used to generate a low speed (minimal effort) contraction or a high speed (maximal effort) contraction.

For any given force level, the maximal possible speed of contraction is indicated by the intersection of the horizontal "force level" line and the Hill's equation curve. It will not be possible for the performer to generate a movement speed that is faster than the limit set by the Hill's equation curve at any level of force. The figure below shows that contraction speeds to the right of the curve are beyond the capabilities of the performer.

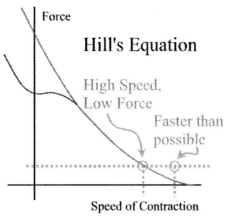

Figure 12-24. For a given muscle, the maximal force available for a given speed of contraction is shown at the point of intersection of the force level and the Hill's equation curve.

If the performer trains extensively, his force of contraction / speed of contraction curve will shift to the right. When this happens he will be able to move faster with a 50-pound load.

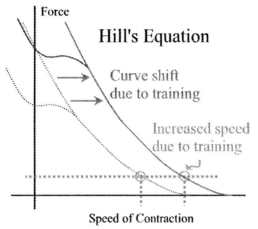

Figure 12-25. The effect of strength training is to cause the Hill's equation curve to shift to the right.

The shift in the Hill's equation curve to the right is the general result of strength training. When people with moderate strength levels train and improve

their maximum lifts, they will be able to move sub-maximal loads faster than before. The observation that stronger muscles will be able to move a given load faster than weaker muscles is generally true for movements with heavy loads. More extreme cases, such as force generation with very light loads, involve complicating factors. For example, an Olympic champion weight lifter may not be expected to throw a fastball as fast as a less strong baseball pitcher. For our purposes in this section, we will only consider the more easily predictable relationships between moderate and heavy loads and muscular contraction speeds.

Question 12-8:
A weight lifter's best single repetition lift on the bench press is 250 pounds. He is given a barbell that weights 240 pounds and asked to push the bar upwards as fast and as hard as possible. What is the best estimate of his arm movement speed on this bench press motion?

O A. The bar will move up very quickly.
O B. The bar will move up very slowly.

The figure below shows the muscle force - speed of contraction values that are appropriate for a "heavy barbell" bench press movement.

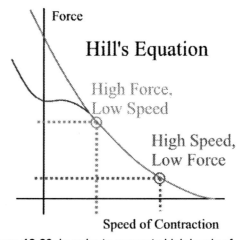

Figure 12-26. In order to generate high levels of muscular force, relatively low muscular contraction speeds must be used.

Because of the shape of the Hill's equation curve, higher levels of force are associated with lower levels of contraction speed. As with the last example, it will be possible for the weight lifter to move the 240 pound bar very, very slowly by using a less than maximal lifting effort. However, he will not be able to generate a movement speed faster than the value indicated by the "high force, low speed" circle on the curve.

Our discussion of Hill's equation has shown that slow movement speeds have very large potentials for force production. We will use our knowledge of the muscle force - speed of contraction relationship to assist in the analysis of skillful performance and the generation of impulse in the next section.

Impulse and Eccentric Contractions

The "bounce-down" phase of movement in a vertical jump is used to place the performer's muscles "on stretch" and increase the potential for force production. This bounce-down portion of the movement also serves to increase the overall positive impulse delivered to the ground.

The figure below shows the impulse information for both the bounce-down and drive-up phases of the vertical jump. For the purpose of simplicity, we have focused on only the positive part of the force curve in our discussions so far. However, the negative portion of the impulse should be considered in any complete analysis of the movement. The negative impulse generated by the bounce-down phase sets up the large positive impulse that follows. Without this negative impulse (i.e., for a jump that is started from a seated position in a chair), the positive impulse would be much smaller and the jumping height would be less.

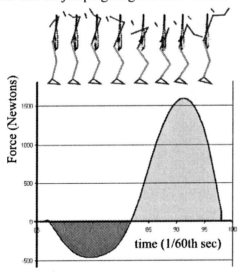

Figure 12-27. The force impulse curve for a vertical jump.

We will now perform a detailed analysis of the force production that is generated as a result of the bounce-down phase. The figure below shows knee joint angle and ground reaction force data for two instants in time near the bottom of the crouch for the vertical jump. The white line scale just above the performer's knees represents one body weight. Notice that the ground reaction forces in the figures are both greater than body weight and are therefore contributing to the positive impulse generated during the jump.

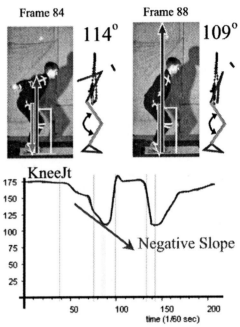

Figure 12-28. The change in knee joint angle during the bounce-down phase of a vertical jump.

The figure shows that the angle between the thigh and shank segment lines (the segment to segment knee joint angle) decreases from 114° to 109° as the movement progresses from frame 84 to frame 88. At the same time that these knee angles are decreasing, large forces are being generated in an effort to drive the body upward. As a result, the knee extensor muscles are undergoing an eccentric muscular contraction. As we have mentioned above, this lengthening contraction is associated with very large potentials for muscular force.

As a result, there is a potential for the development of large ground reaction forces during and immediately following the bounce-down phase. A skilled performer will coordinate his / her overall movement to assure that eccentric contractions are used during critical times in the movement.

The figure below shows the portion of the force curve that is generated through eccentric contractions with darkly shaded columns. The lightly shaded areas show those forces that are generated through concentric contractions.

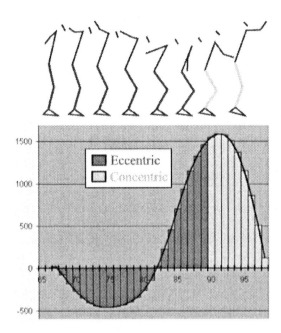

Figure 12-29. A comparison of the impulse of force generated through eccentric contractions (left side of curve) and concentric contractions (right side of curve).

As expected, the negative portion of the impulse is produced entirely by eccentric contractions. The first 38% of the positive portion of the curve is derived from eccentric contractions as well. The last portion of the positive impulse is generated by concentric contractions, although the contraction speeds are still relatively slow for the first several frames (90 – 92) in the lightly shaded area at the right side of the figure. As a result, we see that a great portion of the positive impulse generated in a vertical jump is associated with either eccentric or slow concentric contractions.

The performer has timed his movements to take advantage of the large force production potential associated with slow and negative contraction speeds. The effective use of slow contraction speeds is a clear characteristic of skilled jumping motions. Other movements, such as throwing or kicking also make use of well-timed, full body motions. Baseball pitchers swing their pitching arms in a direction opposite to that of the throw to place the arm muscles on stretch and create a maximal forward impulse to the ball. Soccer kickers, swing their legs

backward to allow for higher levels of force production and longer times for force application to the kicking leg.

Fatigue and Impulse of Force

We will now consider a study of the effects of fatigue on a "box jump". This example will provide additional insight into the value of an impulse momentum based analysis of movement.

The video below shows results from a term paper report from the SFSU Movement Library (Servanda and Strickland, 2001). The paper's authors served as the only participants in the study. We will use the data from Nick Servanda's part of the paper for the following analysis. He performed a jump from floor level onto a 58 cm tall box under two conditions. The first condition involved a normal (non-fatigued) jump. The second jump was performed 10 seconds after a series of nearly exhausting vertical jump exercises. As shown in the figure below, the jumping height for the fatigued condition was 9 cm less than the non-fatigued jump.

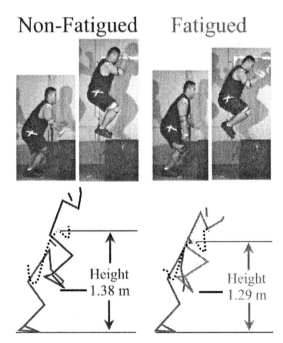

Figure 12-30. A comparison of "box jump" performance under non-fatigued and fatigued conditions.

The difference in jumping height was expected. However, an analysis of the peak ground reaction forces generated during the jump produced unexpected results.

The figure below shows that the peak GRF_Y force was greater for the fatigued jump than for the non-fatigued jump. This finding shows that a single, instantaneous measure of force may not be representative of the overall outcome of a complete movement. However, an analysis of the impulse of force developed for the two jumps provides for a much better understanding of the movement process.

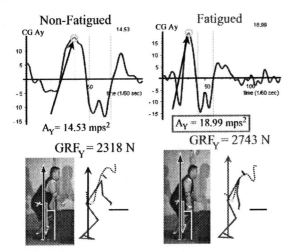

Figure 12-31. A comparison of the peak vertical ground reaction forces produced on a non-fatigued and a fatigued box jump motion.

The peak A_Y value is clearly larger for the fatigued jump, and as a result, the peak ground reaction force is also larger. However, the positive pulse in the acceleration curve is much more narrow for the fatigued jump than it is for the non-fatigued jump. The total time expended for the "bounce-down" and "upward-driving" phase of the movement is only 0.43 seconds for the fatigued jump. The non-fatigued jump developed force over a longer time of 0.63 seconds and therefore produced a larger positive impulse.

The figure below shows the non-fatigued jump impulse curve. The lightly shaded area represents the positive impulse. The darkly shaded area represents the negative impulse that is produced during the early part of the "bounce-down" phase of the movement.

Non-Fatigued Jump

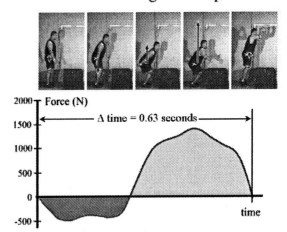

Figure 12-32. The impulse of force curve and time duration of a non-fatigued box jump.

The vertical vectors shown in each video figure represent the net force acting on the performer. These vectors represent the product of mass and the Y component values of the body's center of gravity acceleration.

Similar data from the analysis of the fatigued jump is shown below. Note that the positive area for the fatigued jump is clearly smaller than that for the non-fatigued jump.

Fatigued Jump

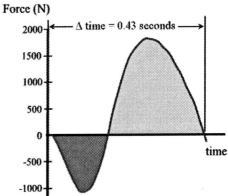

Figure 12-33. The impulse of force curve and time duration of a fatigued box jump.

A comparison of the impulse curves, peak GRF_Y forces and jumping heights for both jumps is shown below. The non-fatigued jump has generated a larger positive impulse because of the relatively long time period of positive force production. The fatigued force curve has a higher peak force but a relatively short time of positive force application.

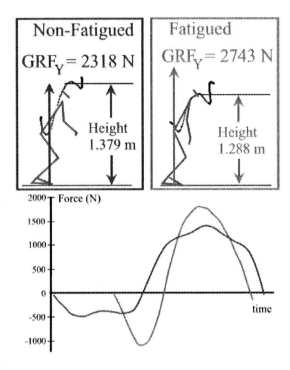

Figure 12-34. A comparison of the peak ground reaction forces and jump height measures for a non-fatigued and fatigued box jump.

The area under each curve, or the impulse of force for both jumps is shown in the figure below. The column graph shown in the bottom of the figure provides a simplified summary of the impulse data. However, the information in the column graph, by itself, could easily cause a misinterpretation of the differences between the two movements. The full impulse curve, shown at the upper portion of the figure, more accurately represents the time duration and force distribution of the two jumps. This more detailed information directs our attention to the changes in movement technique that are responsible for the differences in force development.

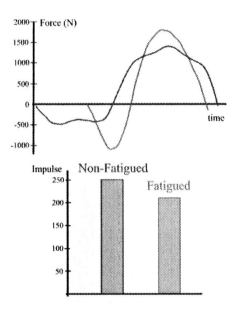

Figure 12-35. A comparison of the impulse generated during a non-fatigued and fatigued box jump.

The figure below shows a comparison of the knee joint range of motion measures for the two jumps in the Servanda and Strickland paper. The knee joint range of motion (ROM) is defined as the difference in knee angles as measured at the moment of take off and the moment of maximal knee flexion at the bottom of the bounce-down phase.

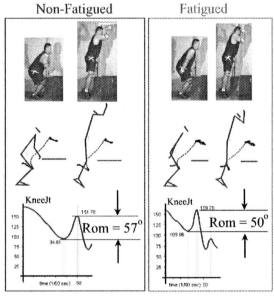

Figure 12-36. A comparison of the knee joint range of motion during a non-fatigued and a fatigued box jump. The joint angle is measured as the angle between the shank and thigh segments.

The non-fatigued jump employed a deeper crouch and a larger ROM than the fatigued jump. This larger range of motion allowed the performer to generate force for a longer time period than was possible in the fatigued jump.

It is interesting to compare the results from this study on the effects of fatigue on jumping performance to the findings we discussed earlier for an "easy" jump. The easy jump involved a movement technique that "scaled down" the peak A_Y, GRF_Y, impulse and knee ROM measures. For the current example, the performer's changes in technique to accommodate fatigue were quite different. Because the performer's legs were severely fatigued, any attempt to produce a normal knee bend caused a tendency for the knees to "buckle". As a result, the performer had no choice but to use a reduced ROM at the knee. Further, the height of the box remained fixed at a difficult level. As a result, the performer had to create very large ground reaction forces in order to generate a successful jump. It is particularly interesting to see how a movement as simple as a jump can be accomplished, very skillfully, with a wide variety of techniques. It is clear that changes in the circumstances surrounding a movement can have important influences on the optimal solution of the movement problem.

Conservation of Linear Momentum

Newton's second law states that the rate of change of momentum of a body is proportional to the net force applied to the body. An interesting special case of this law involves the situation where no external force is applied to a system of two or more bodies. Under these circumstances, momentum is conserved. The formal definition of the conservation of momentum principle is as follows:

> *When the resultant external force acting on a system is zero, the total momentum of the system remains constant.*

The figure below shows an example of the conservation of momentum principle at work. The video image has been taken from the analysis of a wheel chair volleyball serve. The serving motion in this study was performed with the wheelchair brakes off. In the figure, the *system* is defined as the performer, the wheelchair and the volleyball.

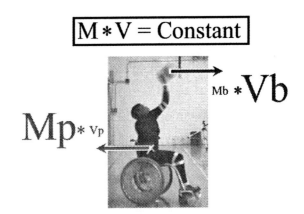

Figure 12-37. A wheelchair bound volleyball serve motion.

During the movement, the performer tosses the ball straight up and then strikes the ball to accomplish the serve. When the performer strikes the ball, her body and the wheelchair have a tendency to roll backward.

The conservation of momentum principle states that the total momentum of the system, along any dimension of motion, will remain constant as long as there is no external force acting on the system along that dimension. Because the wheelchair presents very little resistance to horizontal motion (i.e., friction is negligible), this movement approximates a condition with no applied horizontal force. As a result, the momentum of the system along the horizontal dimension must remain constant (given our assumption of no external force) when the performer strikes the ball.

When the performer strikes the ball, the momentum of the ball portion of the system obviously increases. In order for the horizontal momentum of the total system to be conserved, the remaining portion of the system, i.e., the performer's body and wheel chair, must acquire momentum in a backward direction. Thus the product of mass and velocity for the performer and chair must be equal and opposite to the product of mass and velocity for the ball.

The figure shows the momentum calculation for the ball as Mb * Vb (mass of the ball multiplied by the velocity of the ball). The font size for the Mb term is very small to emphasize that the mass of the ball is relatively small. The font size for the Vb term is large to indicate that the ball acquires a high velocity. The Mp and Vp terms in the figure indicate the mass and speed respectively of the participant-wheelchair portion of the system. The size (both in terms of font size and actual size) of the Mp and Vp terms is reversed from that of the ball. The large mass of the participant-wheelchair must exhibit a small negative velocity in order for the net momentum of the system to remain equal to zero.

In reality, there will be some frictional resistance to the backward motion of the chair and the actual calculation from the video data should not be expected to produce an exact confirmation of the conservation of momentum principle. However, this example does indicate that frictional forces will help the performer to deliver a more forceful blow to the ball (if the wheel chair does not roll backward, the ball will be struck more forcefully). We will further examine the factors that influence the outcome of an impact in the next section.

Conclusions

Our discussion of the impulse momentum relationship and conservation of momentum are now complete. We have seen that the process of skillful human movement can often be better understood through use of the impulse momentum relationship. Skillful performance involves the coordination of multiple segments in the body with precise timing. With jumping movements, we have seen that effective movements are organized to assure maximal force production through both eccentric and concentric muscular contractions.

References

Perrine, J.J. and Edgerton, R. (1978). Muscle force velocity and power velocity relationships under isokinetic loading. Medicine and Science in Sports, 10:159-166, 1978.

Hill, A.V. *First and Last Experiments in Muscle Mechanics.* Cambridge University Press, London, 1970.

Answers to Chapter Questions

Question 12-1:
Does the arm swing help the performer to jump higher?

O A. Yes.
O B. No.

The correct answer is A. There are some types of jumps where jumping height is not as important as quickness of reaction time. For example, some skilled performers in volleyball use very small arm swings when they jump to block a shot. The lack of arm swing in this type of jump detracts from jumping height but enhances response time.

Question 12-2:
Imagine that the baton in the upper portion of the figure is made of wood. Further, suppose that a knife has been used to "whittle" a 8 centimeter x .5 centimeter section from the right side of the baton. The whittled section of wood is then placed on top of the intact baton to the left of the balance point.

What will happen to the baton when the whittled piece of wood is placed on the left side of the baton length?

O A. The baton will tilt to the left.
O B. The baton will tilt to the right.
O C. The baton will stay balanced.

The correct answer is A. In order for the baton to tilt to the right, extra weight would have to be added to the right side of the baton.

Question 12-3:
Where will the new balance point for the baton be located?

O A. The new balance point will have shifted closer to the right side of the baton.
O B. The new balance point will have shifted closer to the left side of the baton.

The correct answer is B. The balance point of the baton will have shifted toward the left side of the baton.

Question 12-4:
The increase in knee angle from 109° to 121° (a 12° change) produces a smaller jumping height for the easy jump. What will happen if the performer attempts to jump still higher than he did in the full jump by bending his knees even more to create a knee angle that is less than 90°?

O A. This greater degree of knee flexion will result in a higher jump height.
O B. This greater degree of knee flexion will result in a lower jump height.

The correct answer is B. The performer for this example is an experienced gymnast and has found the optimal amount of knee bend needed for a maximal height vertical jump. Decreasing his knee angle further will decrease his ability to generate large peak forces on the driving up phase of the movement.

Question 12-5:
Suppose that an extensive analysis of jumping performance shows that the optimal knee bend angle is 109°. In a research study a skilled performer does a vertical jump two ways. On the first "chair" jump he sits on a chair whose height is set so that the performer's knee angle is exactly 109°, and then jumps up. On the second "normal" jump he bends down with his normal motion to the same knee angle and then immediately jumps up. Which jump will be highest?

O A. The chair jump.
O B. The normal jump.

The correct answer is B. The normal "bounce down" jumping motion allows the performer to generate more force on the jump.

Question 12-6:
In a research study a skilled performer does a vertical jump two ways. The first jump is performed with a slow-motion bend down phase, but the final knee flexion angle is made to be exactly 109°. The second jump involves a normal-speed "bounce down" movement that also results in a knee angle of 109°. Which jump will be highest?

O A. The normal jump.
O B. The slow-motion bend down jump.

The correct answer is A. The normal "bounce-down" jumping motion allows the performer to generate tension in the muscles with optimal timing.

Question 12-7:
A weight lifter's best single repetition lift on the bench press is 250 pounds. He is given a barbell that weights 50 pounds and asked to push the bar upwards as fast and as hard as possible. What is the best estimate of his arm movement speed on this bench press motion?

O A. The bar will move up very quickly.
O B. The bar will move up very slowly.

The correct answer is A. A 50 pound bench press will be very easy for this performer. He will be able to lift the bar very quickly.

Question 12-8:
A weight lifter's best single repetition lift on the bench press is 250 pounds. He is given a barbell that weights 240 pounds and asked to push the bar upwards as fast and as hard as possible. What is the best estimate of his arm movement speed on this bench press motion?

O A. The bar will move up very quickly.
O B. The bar will move up very slowly.

The correct answer is B. The weight lifter's maximal lifting weight is 250 pounds. As a result, a 240 pound bar will be very heavy for him. He will be able to lift it, but it will move upward very slowly compared to his prior lift of a 50 pound bar.

Chapter 13: Advanced Topics

Advanced Topics

Given the foundation knowledge we have developed in Chapters 10, 11 and 12, we are now ready to consider a number of advanced topics in linear kinetics. The remaining sections of this chapter will discuss impact, the coefficient of restitution, and measures of work, energy and power.

Impact and Coefficient of Restitution

Many sports related movements involve impacts between a body part or sports implement and a ball. Often, the purpose of the human movement is to maximize the effect of this impact. For example, in a tennis serve, skillful performers coordinate their movements to assure that the peak in racket velocity occurs very close to the moment of racket impact with the ball.

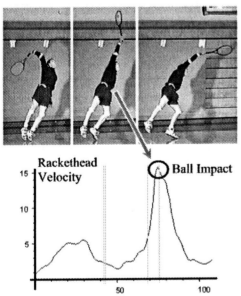

Figure 13-1. The rackethead velocity curve for a tennis serve.

While the speed of the racket is critical in generating a fast serve, the ball itself plays an important role in the outcome of the collision. In general, the velocity imparted to the ball as a result of a collision depends upon the elastic properties of the ball.

Direct Impact

The collision of a dropped ball with the floor represents a simple example of impact. If a tennis ball is dropped from a height, it will deform momentarily when it collides with the floor. During the time period while the ball is deformed, forces are generated between the ball and the floor. When the ball is sufficiently "flattened" to absorb the force of impact, internal forces within the ball cause it to return to its original shape. As the ball's shape returns to normal, additional forces are developed between the ball and the floor. As a result of the forces generated between the floor and the ball during impact, there is a relatively large change in momentum, and the ball bounces upward.

The size of the forces generated between a ball and the floor depend upon the elastic properties of both the ball and the floor. The figure below shows a comparison of bounces for a "lively" handball and a relatively "dead" hockey ball. Note that the motion of the dropped ball is straight up and down. To aid in the visualization of the ball's motion, the video images of the ball are shifted to the right for each instant shown. Both balls were dropped from a height of 1.45 meters. The position curve for the handball (left side) and hockey ball (right side) are shown in the lower portion of the figure. At the peak height of the bounce, the handball bounced up to a height of 1.03 meters while the hockey ball achieved a height after the bounce of only 0.40 meters.

"Lively" Ball   "Dead" Ball

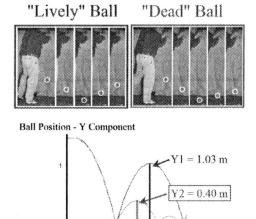

Ball Position - Y Component

Y1 = 1.03 m

Y2 = 0.40 m

Figure 13-2. A comparison of the vertical position data for two dropped balls (a hand ball and a hockey ball).

The figure below shows the peak values for the Y component of the ball acceleration. Because "normal speed" (60 field per second) video was used for these trials, it is likely that the illustrated measures of acceleration underestimate the true values. Nevertheless, the measured A_Y values are much higher than any measures we have seen for human center of gravity motions. In fact, the ground reaction force produced by the handball is equal to 25 multiplied by the "body weight" of the ball.

Notice that the peak A_Y values for the hockey ball is nearly as large as that of the handball, in spite of the fact that the height of rebound is much less for the hockey ball.

"Lively" Ball   "Dead" Ball

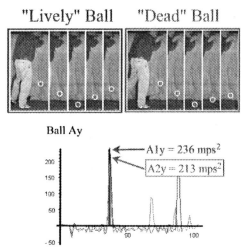

Ball Ay

A1y = 236 mps²

A2y = 213 mps²

Figure 13-3. A comparison of the peak vertical acceleration of two dropped balls (a hand ball and a hockey ball).

The figure below shows the V_Y values for the dropped balls. Notice that the peak negative V_Y value (-5.1 mps) is the same for both balls. This finding is expected because both balls were dropped from the same height.

"Lively" Ball   "Dead" Ball

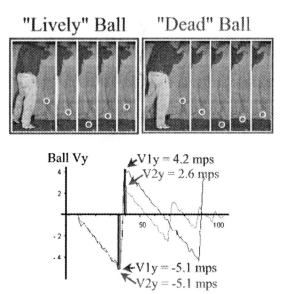

Ball Vy

V1y = 4.2 mps

V2y = 2.6 mps

V1y = -5.1 mps

V2y = -5.1 mps

Figure 13-4. A comparison of the vertical velocity data for two dropped balls (a hand ball and a hockey ball).

However, the peak positive V_Y values that occur just after impact show that the handball is moving 62% faster than the hockey ball. This finding is due to differences in the elastic properties of the balls. The *coefficient of restitution* is a standardized measurement that defines the effect of a collision between two objects. The equation for the coefficient of restitution for collisions between a moving body (for example, a ball) and a fixed object (for example, the floor) is as follows:

$$e = V_F / |V_I|$$

Where:
V_F = the value of the peak post impact velocity
$|V_I|$ = the absolute value of the peak pre-impact velocity

The value of the coefficient of restitution depends upon the two surfaces involved in a collision. Thus, any given ball will have different coefficients of restitution for impacts with different surfaces. For example, a tennis ball will bounce higher on a "hard court" than on a clay court.

Comparisons of coefficient of restitution values can be made between different balls, if the same floor surface is used for all ball drops. For impacts with a hardwood floor, coefficient of restitution values typically range from 0.31 for a softball, to 0.55 for a baseball, to 0.89 for a "Superball".

Our video analysis of a handball provides the following data:

$V_F = 4.22$ mps
$|V_I| = 5.12$ mps

As a result, the coefficient of restitution for a handball collision with a thinly carpeted floor is 0.82:

$e = V_F / |V_I|$
$e = 4.22 / 5.12$
$e = 0.82$

Oblique Impact

Most impacts occur in at least two dimensions. For example, a bounce pass in basketball involves a combination of horizontal and vertical motion. The figure below shows an example of a tennis ball bounce on a thinly carpeted floor.

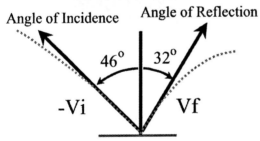

Figure 13-5. The angle of incidence and the angle of reflection for an oblique impact.

As shown in the figure, the *angle of incidence* is defined as the angle between the vertical and the negative ball velocity vector at a moment *before* impact. The *angle of reflection* is defined as the angle between the vertical and the ball velocity vector a moment *after* impact.

The pre-impact and post-impact velocity vectors for the ball can be broken down to their X and Y components. The vertical component of the V_F vector will be determined by the coefficient of restitution for the ball and the floor. The frictional force that acts during the impact will determine the horizontal component of the V_F vector. The combined effect of the angle of incidence, the coefficient of restitution and friction determine the height of the ball bounce.

For a given angle of incidence and ground surface, and for a ball with no spin, the height of the bounce after the impact will be determined by the coefficient of restitution for the ball. The figure below shows that a relatively lively handball has a smaller angle of reflection (27°) than the tennis ball 32° angle that we saw in the last figure.

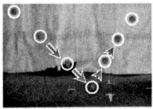

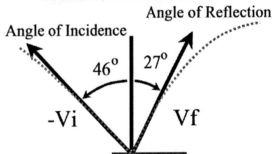

Figure 13-6. The angle of incidence and angle of reflection for a ball bounce with a lively ball.

The effect of friction on the angle of reflection can be shown through a comparison of a given ball bouncing on two different surfaces. The figure below shows data for a tennis ball bouncing on a thin carpet and a lubricated board.

Thin Carpet

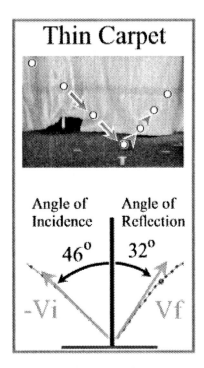

Angle of Incidence   Angle of Reflection

46° 32°

-Vi   Vf

Smooth Board

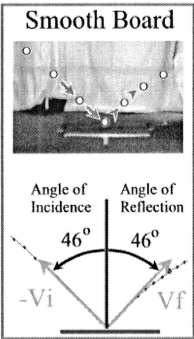

Angle of Incidence   Angle of Reflection

46° 46°

-Vi   Vf

Figure 13-7. The angle of incidence and angle of reflection for a tennis ball bounce on a carpeted surface and a lubricated smooth surface.

Note that the reduced friction produced by the smooth board causes the ball to bounce with a greater angle of reflection. The same "low bounce" will be produced by a softball that is hit onto wet grass in the infield.

While reduced friction will cause a greater angle of reflection, increased friction will cause a smaller angle of reflection and a more upright bounce.

Effects of Spin on Ball Bounce

A tennis ball that is hit with backspin (or underspin), will, in general, produce an increase in the frictional force that is generated between the ball and the ground. As a result, for a given ball and angle of incidence, a ball hit with backspin will tend to bounce up higher as a result of the increased frictional forces. The figure below shows a comparison of a "no spin" bounce and a ball bounce with backspin. (See figure 13-8).

A ball hit with topspin will tend to bounce lower (and have an increased angle of incidence) than an otherwise identical bounce of a "no spin" ball. The topspin will create a reduction in the negative frictional force generated between the ball and the ground. (See figure 13-9).

A ball hit with excessive topspin could, in fact, generate frictional forces that are aimed in the forward direction. Such forward acting frictional forces will tend to increase the angle of reflection even further than that of a ball hit with "normal" topspin.

Effect of Backspin

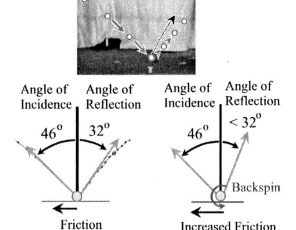

Angle of Incidence   Angle of Reflection

46° 32°

Angle of Incidence   Angle of Reflection

46° $< 32^o$

Backspin

Friction   Increased Friction

Figure 13-8. A comparison of a "no spin" bounce and a ball bounce with backspin.

Effect of Topspin

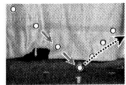

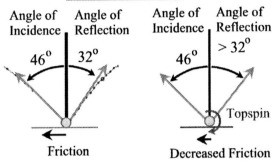

Angle of Incidence
Angle of Reflection

46° 32°

Friction

Angle of Incidence
Angle of Reflection
$> 32^{o}$

46°

Topspin

Decreased Friction

Figure 13-9. A comparison of a "no spin" bounce and a ball bounce with topspin.

Work

Mechanical work is accomplished when an applied force causes an object to move. More specifically, work is defined as the product of force and distance:

Work = Force * Distance

Where:
Force – is the component of the applied force that is aimed in the direction of motion of the object.
Distance – is the magnitude of the displacement vector of the object's motion.

Notice that the work equation does not include any reference to the time period required to accomplish the work. As a result, typical calculations of work involve simplified estimates for force. Figure 13-10 illustrates data for use in the calculation of the work done on a military press.

The work accomplished in the upward pressing motion is equal to the weight of the bar multiplied by the movement distance of the bar. If a bar weighting 800 Newtons is lifted a distance of 0.7 meters, the work is calculated as follows:

Work = Force * Distance
Work = 800 * 0.7
Work = 560 Nm
or
Work = 560 joules

Where:
1 Joule is a unit of measure for work that equals 1 Newton-meter

Figure 13-10. A military press motion.

The actual applied force to the bar will not be exactly equal and opposite to the bar's weight because the bar is accelerated during a typical lifting motion. The use of the bar's weight in the work equation simplifies the calculation considerably. In addition, the comparison of work measurements across individuals is also simplified because different movement techniques, with different bar acceleration values, will all produce the same result as long as the weight and lifting distance are held constant.

It is important to note that work is only accomplished if an object is moved over a distance. If large forces are applied, but no net motion occurs, the mechanical work accomplished is zero. This, however, does not mean that the *physiological* work involved will be zero. In the case of tethered swimming, swimmers are asked to swim while they are held at a fixed distance from the wall of the pool.

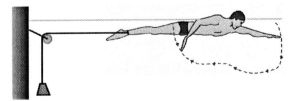

Figure 13-11. A tethered swimming motion.

While this type of swimming exercise can be exhausting, the *mechanical* work accomplished through the training is zero because the body's center of gravity does not undergo displacement.

Negative Work

Our discussion thus far has focused on *positive work* where the force acts in the direction of movement. *Negative work* occurs when the force applied to an object acts in the direction opposite to the displacement vector of the object.

Negative work is associated with eccentric muscular contractions. For example, in a military press, negative work is produced when the bar is lowered from the chest back down to the floor. (See figure 13-12).

Figure 13-12. An example of negative work.

From a purely mathematical standpoint, the act of lifting a barbell from chest level to an overhead position and then lowering it again to chest level results in zero net work. From a more practical standpoint, the work associated with lifting a weight can be set as the positive work associated with one lift multiplied by the number of repetitions. The resultant work calculation will underestimate the energy cost of the weight lifting exercise because it ignores the effort exerted each time the weight is lowered to chest level.

Work Measurement for Running

Running on a grade provides a good example for the calculation of the work produced by full body motion. The figure below shows a "wide angle" side view illustration of a performer running up a slope.

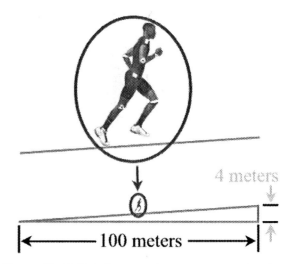

Figure 13-13. Running on a slope causes an elevation of the body's center of gravity.

When the performer reaches the top of the slope, he will have effectively "lifted" his body's center of gravity 4 meters. For this grade of slope, a performer weighing 600 Newtons will accomplish 2,400 joules of work:

Work = Force * Distance
Work = 600 Newtons * 4 meter
Work = 2,400 joules

We see that it is easy to calculate the work done against gravity for a run up a slope. Calculating the work done along the horizontal direction is more difficult however. On an instant-by-instant basis, both horizontal propulsive forces and negative braking forces are applied to the body during each stride. However, if the runner maintains a uniform average running speed, the average acceleration must be zero and as a result, the average force and the average work accomplished must be zero as well.

The work performed against gravity in running can be calculated very easily under laboratory conditions with a treadmill. For example, the treadmill can be set to a speed of 3 mps and a grade of 4%. The work accomplished by the runner during a 10 minute time period can then be computed as shown below.

The equivalent distance run by the performer under these conditions can be computed on the basis of the running speed and the time duration of the run:

Velocity = Distance / time
Distance = Velocity * time
Distance = 3 * (10 x 60)
Distance = 1,800 meters

The distance of the run provides us with the hypotenuse of the "slope triangle" in the figure below. To determine the height of this triangle (and compute the work involved) we must first compute the angle that is equivalent to a 4% grade.

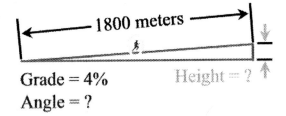

Grade = 4%
Angle = ?

Figure 13-14. An example of running on a slope.

A treadmill percent grade is set as the ratio of the height to the base of the slope triangle, multiplied by 100.

%Grade = (Height / Base) * 100
%Grade = Tan(θ) * 100

The following equation is used to translate from a slope set as a percent grade to a slope angle:

θ = Tan^{-1}(%Grade / 100)

For a grade of 4%, the slope angle is computed as follows:

θ = Tan^{-1}(4 / 100)
θ = 2.3°

Given a "slope triangle" with a hypotenuse of 1800 meters and a base angle of 2.3°, the height can be computed as follows:

Sin(θ) = Height / 1800
Height = 1800 * Sin(2.3°)
Height = 1800 * 0.040
Height = 72 meters

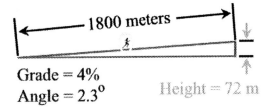

Grade = 4%
Angle = 2.3°
Height = 72 m

Figure 13-15. The calculation of the change in elevation for a performer while running on a slope.

As a result, during the course of the 10 minute long run, the performer's body is effectively elevated a total of 72 meters. The work associated with the run is computed as the product of the performer's body weight and the magnitude of this upward displacement:

Work = Force * Distance
Work = 600 * 72
Work = 43,200 joules

Power

Power is defined as a measure of the *rate* of work production. As a result, the equation for power is as follows:

Power = Work / time

The power generated in our previous running example is computed below:

Given:
Work generated = 43,200 joules
Time duration = 10 minutes

Power = Work / time
Power = 43,200 / (10 * 60)
Power = 72 joules per second = 72 watts

The unit of measurement for power is the *watt*, where 1 watt = 1 joule per second.

In the original example, the treadmill speed was set at 3 mps. If the treadmill speed had been set at 4 mps, the runner would have covered an effective distance of 1800 meters in only 7.5 minutes. Under these circumstances, the work for the run would be the same as before, but the power expended on the run would be 96 watts:

Given:
Work generated = 43,200 joules
Time duration = 7.5 minutes

Power = Work / time
Power = 43,200 / (7.5 * 60)
Power = 96 watts

The increase in power for the 4 mps run is entirely a result of the reduced time interval used to accomplish the work. The increased velocity of the run has increased the rate of work production. Power can be computed directly from the product of force and velocity:

Power = Work / time
Power = (Force * Distance) / time
Power = Force * (Distance / time)
Power = Force * Velocity

Where:
Force – is the component of the applied force that is aimed in the direction of motion of the object.
Velocity – is the magnitude of the velocity vector of the object's motion.

We will now compute the power for the original 3 mps treadmill run using force and velocity. The force term in the equation will remain as 600 Newtons (the weight of the performer). The velocity term must be set as the vertical component of velocity for the runner over the course of the run:

Given:
Vertical displacement = 72 meters
Time duration = 10 minutes

V_Y = 72 / (10 * 60)
V_Y = 0.12 mps

Given the velocity and force measures, the power is calculated as 72 watts:

Power = Force x Velocity
Power = 600 * 0.12
Power = 72 watts

The value computed with the force times velocity equation is, as expected, the same as that determined by the work divided by time equation.

The ability to produce high levels of work in a brief period of time is essential in many athletic motions. The figure below illustrates a critical instant during the course of a shot put movement. In order to maximize the distance of the throw, the performer must generate the highest possible velocity of projection for the shot. (See figure 13-16).

It is interesting to note that maximal values for power are associated with movements that generate high force levels. The achievement of high velocity by itself will not necessarily generate high levels of power. For example, a fastball pitch in baseball will involve very high levels of velocity, but only small levels of force. On the other hand, the very high force levels in the shot put more than make up for the smaller values of velocity for the shot put ball. As we have seen above, Hill's equation indicates that very high levels of muscular force are possible for movements that are relatively slow.

Figure 13-16. A shot put motion.

Energy

Energy is the capacity to do work. In biomechanics, we are primarily interested in *mechanical* energy. Mechanical energy can be broken down into three types: kinetic energy, potential energy and strain energy.

Kinetic Energy

The energy of *motion* is defined as *kinetic energy*:

$$KE = \tfrac{1}{2}\,mV^2$$

Where:
KE - Kinetic Energy
m – is the mass of the object in motion
V – is the magnitude of the velocity vector for the center of gravity of the object

Note that energy is a scalar. As a result, the velocity vector must be converted to scalar form (i.e., the vector magnitude must be used) before a value for kinetic energy can be computed. In addition, note that the above equation indicates that the value of kinetic energy is very sensitive to the value of velocity. For example, if the speed of an object is doubled, the kinetic energy of the object is quadrupled.

Potential Energy

The energy of *position* is defined as *potential energy*:

$$PE = W * Hgt$$
Where:
PE - Potential Energy
W – is the weight of the object
Hgt – is the height of the object above any given reference frame

The *conservation of energy principle* states that, during airborne flight (when gravity is the only force acting) the mechanical energy of the body is constant. The image sequence figure below shows a back somersault movement on a trampoline. The upper portion of the figure shows that the performer moves almost straight up and down. The lower section of the figure shows a series of still image video frames from the movement. Each still shot video image is shifted to the right to allow easy visualization of the performer's various body positions.

Figure 13-17. A back somersault on a trampoline.

Note that when the performer on the trampoline is near the top of the bounce, he will have high levels of potential energy, but low levels of kinetic energy. Conversely, just before impact with the trampoline, the performer will have high levels of kinetic energy and low levels of potential energy. The conservation of energy principle indicates that the sum total of the kinetic and potential energy values will be held fixed at a constant value at any instant in time during the flight phase of the bounce.

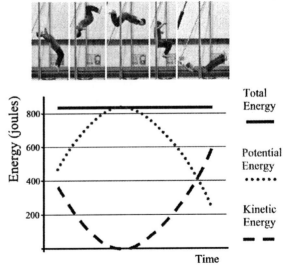

Figure 13-18. A comparison of the kinetic energy, potential energy and total energy associated with a back somersault motion.

The figure above shows the potential energy, kinetic energy and total energy (KE + PE) measures for a performer doing a one and one quarter back somersault on a trampoline.

Notice that the total energy level is held fixed at about 840 joules for the entire flight phase. The potential energy is at its highest when the performer is at the peak of the bounce. Because the body velocity is zero at the peak of the bounce, the kinetic energy is zero there. However, the kinetic energy values are at their highest values when the performer is just "taking off" in the upward direction or is about to land at the bottom of the bounce.

The following example shows that kinetic and potential energy measures can be used to solve problems in uniformly accelerated motion.

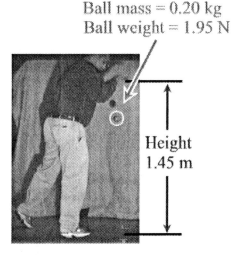

Ball mass = 0.20 kg
Ball weight = 1.95 N

Height
1.45 m

Figure 13-19. The potential energy of a dropped ball.

Question 13-1:
A 7 ounce ball is dropped from a height of 1.45 meters. The ball has a weight of 1.96 Newtons and a mass of 0.20 kilograms. What is the potential energy of the ball when it is initially released?

O A. 2.84 joules
O B. 0.29 joules

The potential energy of the ball is at the peak value of 2.84 joules when it is at its highest elevation. When the ball is first released, its kinetic energy will be zero and the sum of the KE and PE of the ball will be 2.84 joules.

During freefall:
PE + KE = constant

At the beginning of the drop:
PE = 2.84
KE = 0
Total Energy = PE + KE

Total Energy = 2.84

During the flight of the ball the potential energy will diminish while the kinetic energy increases. However, the sum of the kinetic and potential energies will remain constant. When the ball falls and reaches the level of the floor, its potential energy becomes zero. However, just prior to impact with the ground the kinetic energy must be equal to the original potential energy of the ball in order for total energy to be conserved.

At the end of the drop:
PE = W * Hgt
PE = 1.96 * 0
PE = 0

Total Energy = PE + KE = 2.84
PE + KE = 2.84
0 + KE = 2.84
KE = 2.84

If we know the kinetic energy of the ball at the instant of impact, we can compute the final velocity of the ball:

At the end of the drop:
$KE = \frac{1}{2} mV^2 = 2.84$
$V^2 = 2.84 / (.5m)$
$V = Sqrt(2.84 / (.5 * 0.20))$
$V = 5.33$ mps

We can check our energy-based calculation for the final velocity by using a uniformly accelerated motion equation from Chapter 9:

$V_f^2 = V_i^2 - 19.6D$

Because V_I is zero, and the distance of the fall is -1.45 meters, this equation reduces to the following:

$V_F^2 = -19.6 * (-1.45)$
$V_F^2 = 28.42$
$V_F = 5.33$ mps

We see that the result of the uniformly accelerated motion calculation agrees with that from the conservation of energy equation. At first glance, it is surprising that the kinetic energy information can be used to determine final velocity when the acceleration of gravity is not explicitly involved in the calculation. However, the weight term in the potential energy calculation, and the mass term in the kinetic energy equation are related to one another by the acceleration of gravity value:

Mass   =   Weight / Acceleration of Gravity
(kilograms)   (in Newtons)

As a result, the definitions of the kinetic energy and potential energy terms implicitly include information on the acceleration of gravity, and information on energy can be used to solve problems in uniformly accelerated motion.

Strain Energy

In the same way that an object can effectively store potential energy by being raised to an elevation, an elastic object can be made to store energy by being deformed. The energy of *deformation* is defined as strain energy. The figure below shows the storage and release of strain energy through the bending and straightening of a fiberglass pole.

Pole Vault

Figure 13-20. A pole vault motion.

Our discussion of impact and collisions has shown that strain energy is also stored through the compression of the materials in a rubber ball. In addition, the elongation of the elastic materials in the bed of a trampoline is also used to store strain energy. Once an elastic object is bent, compressed or stretched, the stored strain energy is released when the object returns to its original shape.

Work Energy Relationship

Work and energy are closely related. By definition, energy is the capacity to do work. The relationship between work and energy can be expressed mathematically through the work energy relationship:

When work is done on an object, the work done is equal to the sum of the changes in kinetic and potential energies that result.

A mathematical expression of the work energy relationship is provided below:

$$Fd = (\tfrac{1}{2}\,mV_F^2 - \tfrac{1}{2}\,mV_I^2) + ((W * H_F) - (W * H_I))$$

Where:
$(\tfrac{1}{2}\,mV_F^2 - \tfrac{1}{2}\,mV_I^2)$ – is the change in kinetic energy
$((W * H_F) - (W * H_I))$ – is the change in potential energy

This relationship is particularly valuable in an analysis where distances and force levels are of interest. Alternatively, for problems where force levels as a function of time are of interest, the impulse momentum relationship provides the most convenient approach for data analysis.

Figure 13-21. A catcher catching a pitched baseball.

The value of the work energy relationship is best illustrated through an example. Consider the act of catching a pitch in baseball. The approaching ball will have a very high level of kinetic energy. During the catch, work will be performed on the ball to change the kinetic energy level to zero. Figure 13-21 shows a catcher catching a 27 mps pitch.

The initial kinetic energy (at the beginning of the catch) for the 0.19 kg ball is computed as follows:

$KE = \frac{1}{2} mV^2$
$KE = (.5)(0.19)(27)(27)$
$KE = 69.3$ joules

If the catcher's gloved hand shifts backward 0.3 meters during the course of the catch, the average level of force applied during the catch is computed as follows:

$$Fd = (\frac{1}{2} mV_F^2 - \frac{1}{2} mV_I^2) + ((W * H_F) - (W * H_I))$$

In this equation, H_F and H_I are equal and therefore the change in potential energy is zero. In addition, $V_F = 0$ (the ball comes to rest at the end of the catch).

$Fd = -\frac{1}{2} mV_I^2$
$F * (-0.3) = -69.3$
$F = -69.3 / (-0.3)$
$F = 231$ Newtons

This force is equal to about 40% of body weight for a catcher who weights 600 Newtons. If the catcher's gloved hand is allowed to move backward only 0.1 meters during the catch, the average force generated during the catch will be much larger:

$F * (-0.1) = -69.3$
$F = -69.3 / (-0.1)$
$F = 693$ Newtons

This level of force production represents a load on the catching hand that is greater than one body weight. The work energy relationship shows that "soft" hands will allow athletes to more effectively dissipate the forces generated on the hand during catching movements. The technique of allowing the hands to "give" with the catch will minimize the chance of injury for the performer and decrease the likelihood of a dropped ball.

Conclusions

Our discussion of advanced topics in linear kinetics is now complete. We have seen that the process of skillful human movement can often be better understood through use of the impulse momentum relationship. Skillful performance involves the coordination of multiple segments in the body with precise timing. With jumping movements, we have seen that effective movements are organized to assure maximal force production through both eccentric and concentric muscular contractions.

Our discussions of work, power and energy have shown that the outcomes of complex movements can sometimes be analyzed through relatively simple equations. Given an understanding of the impulse momentum relationship and the principles of work, power and energy, we should be well equipped to study human movement under a variety of circumstances.

References

Perrine, J.J. and Edgerton, R. (1978). Muscle force velocity and power velocity relationships under isokinetic loading. Medicine and Science in Sports, 10:159-166, 1978.

Hill, A.V. *First and Last Experiments in Muscle Mechanics.* Cambridge University Press, London, 1970.

Answer to Chapter Question

Question 13-1:
A 7 ounce ball is dropped from a height of 1.45 meters. The ball has a weight of 1.96 Newtons and a mass of 0.20 kilograms. What is the potential energy of the ball when it is initially released?

O A. 2.84 joules
O B. 0.29 joules

Response A: You are correct. Potential energy is equal to the weight of the ball multiplied by the height of the ball.

Response B: The correct answer is A. Potential energy is equal to the weight of the ball multiplied by the height of the ball.

Part 4 – Angular Kinematics

Chapter 14: Measures of Angular Motion

Angular Kinematics

Angular kinematics is the branch of mechanics that focuses upon the study of *rigid body* motion. Our work in *linear* kinematics focused upon the study of individual *particles*, such as a wrist joint center, a ball center point or the body's center of gravity. Our work in angular kinematics will allow us to analyze the motion of solid bodies, such as a baseball bat, a forearm segment, or a foot.

Our work in this chapter will focus on the concepts of angular position and angular displacement. In addition, we will provide a brief introduction to angular velocity and its relation to angular displacement. The following chapters in Part 4 will cover angular velocity (Chapter 15), and angular acceleration (Chapter 16) in detail. The final chapters in Part 4 will discuss circular motion (Chapter 17), joint angle measurements (Chapter 18) and the summation of force principle (Chapter 19).

Examples of Angular Motion

The baseball bat in the figure 14-1 can be considered a separate "body". The forearm and foot in the figure can also be studied as separate "body segments" that happen to be connected to other body segments by hinge or ball-and-socket joints. The motion of any solid body or body segment will typically involve a combination of *translation* and *rotation*. The motion of the given body's center of gravity defines the translation of the body. The change in angular position of the body defines the degree of rotation of the body.

The figure below shows linear and angular data for a golf club. Linear data for the club's center of gravity position and displacement vector are shown in the upper portion of the figure. As we have seen in Chapter 7, the change in position of a given point can be used to compute the displacement and velocity for that point.

Linear Kinematics

Linear Position Data

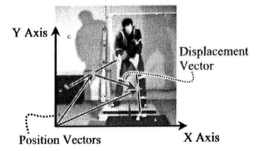

Angular Kinematics

Figure 14-1. A comparison of linear and angular measures of motion.

Angular Position Data

Figure 14-2. A comparison of linear and angular measures of position.

The lower portion of the figure shows the *angular* position of the golf club rigid body at two instances in time. The angular position is measured as the angle between the club's long axis line and the forward direction. We will see in this chapter that given measures of angular position, it is a simple matter to compute measures of angular displacement and angular velocity.

It is important to note that the linear velocity vector alone cannot fully define the movement of the club. The figure below shows that it is possible for a club to have no change in angular position at all and still have a large linear velocity vector. The club in the lower portion of the figure is experiencing pure translation. Note that the linear velocity vector for the "pure translation" club is the same as that for the club in the golf-drive movement.

that it is possible for a club to experience a high level of angular velocity while the club's CG point experiences zero velocity.

Pure Rotation

Figure 14-4. A comparison of the club CG angular velocity vector for a golf club swing and for a pure rotation motion of a club.

The golf club in the lower portion of the figure above is experiencing pure rotation. We will see in this chapter that, in general, problems in human movement involve a combination of translation and rotation. As a result, measures from both linear and angular kinematics must be used to completely describe and understand human motion.

It is interesting to note that data for the angular kinematics of a given segment in the human body is derived from linear kinematic information on the given segment's distal and proximal end points. For example, the trunk segment angular velocity for the back somersault motion shown below can be determined from information on the hip and shoulder point velocity information.

Pure Translation

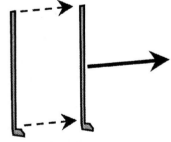

Figure 14-3. A comparison of the club CG linear velocity vector for a golf club swing and for a pure translation motion of a club.

Thus, knowledge of the golf club's CG velocity will tell us nothing about the angular motion of the club. Similarly, data on a golf club's angular velocity will tell us nothing about the linear motion of the club. The figure below shows two club movements that have identical *angular* velocities. The figure shows

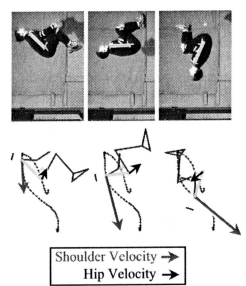

Figure 14-5. Shoulder point and hip point velocity measures during a back somersault motion.

Because angular velocity is derived from linear kinematic measures, you may be tempted to think that angular measures are really unnecessary, and the same information can really be gleaned from segment end point linear velocity data alone. However, the figure below shows that the velocity vectors of the trunk segment end points experience complex changes in both magnitude and direction as the body moves. The interpretation of the relationships between these velocity vectors will be difficult. However, the angular velocity versus time curve shown at the lower portion of the figure will be relatively easy to interpret.

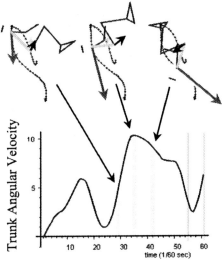

Figure 14-6. The angular velocity curve for the trunk segment of a back somersault performer.

The angular velocity curve is similar to the many linear velocity curves we have seen in Chapter 7. As a result, angular velocity curves will simplify our analysis of movements that involve rotation.

Applications: Angular Kinematics / Kinetics

For most biomechanical analysis problems, it is convenient to model the human body as a system of linked rigid body segments connected by hinge or ball and socket joints. This assumption greatly simplifies the analysis problem. Given only two points on a rigid body segment, for example, the ankle point and the knee point on the shank segment, we will be able to quantify the angular position, angular velocity, and angular acceleration of the segment. The fact that the muscle mass of the shank will change shape slightly as the body moves will be ignored in our analysis. As with other biomechanical measures, such as linear velocity or ground reaction force, our calculated values of angular kinematic variables will include small errors. Nevertheless, these estimates of angular motion will be substantially correct and they will allow us to extend our understanding of the mechanical principles that regulate human motion.

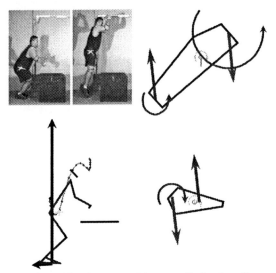

Figure 14-7. The forces and torques that act on the foot and shank segment during a jumping motion are shown.

The quantification of the movements of the various segments of the human body represents an essential step in the analysis of skillful and efficient performance. Our work in linear kinematics and linear kinetics has shown that an analysis of the body's center of gravity point can be used to relate measures of *acceleration* and measures of *force*. Similarly, our work in angular kinematics and angular kinetics will allow us to relate measures of *angular acceleration* and the *torques*, or turning forces, that cause angular motion. Further, we will see that the net muscular actions at the joints of the body (the *joint torques*) can be computed from kinematic variables. Measures of these joint torques will therefore allow us to quantify the *internal forces* that generate human motion. Recall that our definition of biomechanics refers to both internal and external forces:

> *Biomechanics is the science concerned with the internal and external forces acting on the human body and the effects produced by these forces. (Hay, 1993).*

Our work in Chapter 11 has provided us with knowledge of the *external* ground reaction forces that are generated during motion. This information, coupled with measures from angular kinetics, will allow us to evaluate the *internal* forces that act during human motion.

Measures of Angular Position in 2D

Our work in linear kinematics has provided a good foundation for our work in angular kinematics. Linear kinematics, otherwise known as particle kinematics, defines the motion for a single point, or a set of independent points. Particle kinematics involves the calculation of position, velocity and acceleration.

Angular kinematics, otherwise known as rigid body kinematics, defines the motion of "non-deformable" bodies in space. Rigid body kinematics involves the calculation of the angular position (θ), angular velocity (ω), and angular acceleration (α) of the various body segments.

Angular position is a fundamentally important measure that allows us to define the rotation of a body. For two-dimensional motion, the angular position of a given segment is set as the angle between a "representative line" in the segment and the forward direction. The representative line is normally set as the vector between the segment proximal point and the segment distal point. The segment angle is then set as the angle, measured in a counter-clockwise direction, between this segment vector and the positive X-axis. The figure below

shows the segment vector, the positive X-axis and the angular position of a forearm at an instant during a softball pitching motion.

Figure 14-8. The angular position of the forearm segment during the wind up motion of a softball pitch is shown.

Four frames from the action phase of a softball pitch and the associated measures of angular position are shown in the figure below. Notice that each segment angle is measured in a counter-clockwise direction, from the X-axis line to the segment vector line. During the course of the movement, the segment angle increases from 56°, to 143°, to 221°, and then to 340°. Note that the angle between the forearm and the forward direction in figure D is 340°, and not the 20° angle that could have been measured if a *clockwise* direction was used to define the angle between the forward direction and the forearm segment vectors.

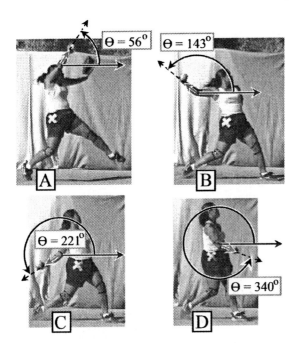

Figure 14-9. Four measures of angular position for the forearm segment.

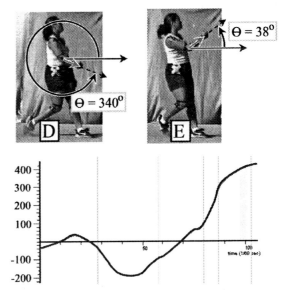

Figure 14-10. The angular position curve for the forearm segment.

It is interesting to note that for two-dimensional motion, angular position can be quantified with a single variable (θ), while linear position requires two variables (X and Y) to define the position of a point. Further, while the direction of positive measures of X is to the right of the origin, positive measures of angular position are measured in the *counter-clockwise* direction.

The convention of defining positive segment angles through counter-clockwise measurements can add complications to the analysis of motions with extended angular displacements. The figure below shows the segment angles for two frames near to the end of the pitching motion. Notice that the segment angle for frame "E" could be set as 38° by the normal rule for defining a segment angle. The angular position curve at the lower portion of the figure shows the forearm angular position data as a function of time. Note that the angular position curve shows the forearm position for frame "E" as 38° + 360° or 398° degrees.

The segment angle data for this movement has been modified to remove discontinuities in the position curve. An angular position measure of 398° for frame "E" indicates that the forearm has gone through more than one complete revolution by the time the pitch has been completed. The KA software automatically performs mathematical shifts to the segment angle data to remove artificial discontinuities.

Note that during the middle portion of the pitching motion, the angular position curve shows that the forearm motion involves negative angles. As shown in the figure below, a segment angular position of -170° is equivalent to a positive angle of 190°. The positive angle is measured in a counter-clockwise direction and the negative angle is measured in the clockwise direction. Both measures represent the same segment angle.

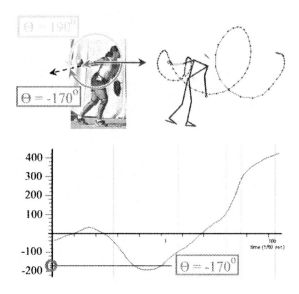

Figure 14-11. Measures of the forearm segment angular position during a softball pitch motion.

The actual values in an angular position curve can be shifted up (by adding 360°) or down (by subtracting 360°) to all values in the curve without changing the form of the curve. Such changes in the angular position curve will not change the angular displacements between frames, the angular velocity or the angular acceleration measures of the movement. As a result, we should remember that any given segment angle measurement is somewhat arbitrary. A given segment angle can be expressed as either θ, $\theta + 360°$, or $\theta - 360°$ with no loss in information.

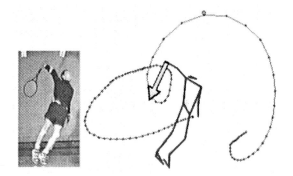

Figure 14-12. The racket segment angular position at a moment just after the back scratch event during a tennis serve motion.

Question 14-1:
The following figure shows the angular position of a tennis racket near the moment of backscratch in a tennis serve.

What is the approximate angular position of the racket?

O A. 65 degrees
O B. 245 degrees
O C. 105 degrees

Angular Displacement in 2D

Angular displacement ($\Delta\theta$) is defined as change in angular position:

$$\Delta\theta = (\theta_f - \theta_i)$$

Where:
θ_f - final angular position
θ_i - initial angular position

While measures of angular position can often exceed 360°, the angular displacement of a body segment between successive fields of video data will almost always be less than 90°. The figure below shows a calculation for an angular displacement that took place over a $1/10^{th}$ second time span.

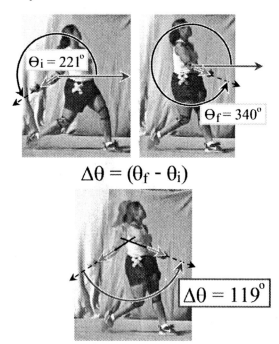

Figure 14-13. An example of the angular displacement of the forearm segment at a moment during a softball pitch motion.

The details for the calculation for the angular displacement are as follows:

$\Delta\theta = (\theta_f - \theta_i)$

$\Delta\theta = (340° - 221°)$

$\Delta\theta = 119°$

Note that the sign of this angular displacement is positive (it is +119°) and the direction of motion for the displacement is counter-clockwise. Because the final and initial angular positions were measured with the "counter-clockwise is positive" convention, the calculated angular displacement will also agree with this convention.

While counter-clockwise angular position measures are set as positive, clockwise angular positions can be set as negative values. The figure below shows another angular displacement calculation. The angular position data in this figure is measured between the forward direction and the forearm segment vector in the *clockwise* direction. As a result, the angular positions are negative.

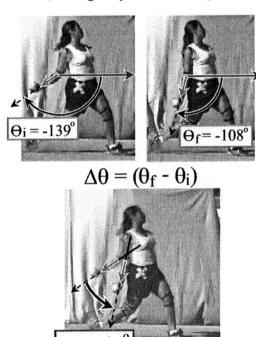

Figure 14-14. The calculation of forearm angular displacement as computed from negative angular position measures.

The calculation of the angular displacement for the forearm using the negative angular position values is as follows:

$\Delta\theta = (\theta_f - \theta_i)$

$\Delta\theta = (-108°) - (-139°))$

$\Delta\theta = 31°$

Note that the sign for this counter-clockwise angular displacement is positive (as expected). Again we see that if consistent measurement conventions are used (in this case, clockwise angular position measures are set as negative) the calculation of angular displacement will yield the correct value for the displacement direction.

Units for Angular Displacement

Linear displacement can be measured with a variety of units, such as centimeters, inches, meters or miles. Similarly, angular displacements are often expressed in terms of degrees, *radians* and *revolutions*.

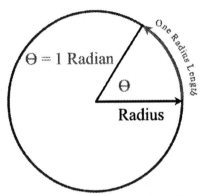

Figure 14-15. An illustration of a single radian angular displacement.

Radians are very commonly used as a basis for measurements of angular displacement, angular velocity and angular acceleration in biomechanics. One radian is equal to the angular displacement associated with a one-radius-length curvilinear distance along the circumference of a circle. The figure below shows a circle, it's radius and a one-radian angular displacement.

In the figure above, the curved arrow on the circumference of the circle is exactly one radius in length. As a result, the angle θ shown in the figure is equal to exactly one radian. To compute the size of this angle in degrees, use the following formula:

Angle (in degrees) = Angle (in radians) * 57.3

Thus, this one radian angle is equivalent to an angle of 57.3 degrees.

The radians-to-degrees conversion factor can also be computed from the formula for the circumference of a circle. The length of the full circumference of the circle is $2\pi R$. As a result, there are 2π radius lengths, or 2π radians associated with a full 360° angle. The relationship between measures in radians and degrees can then be computed as follows:

2π radians = 360 degrees
6.28 radians = 360 degrees
1 radian = 360 / 6.28
1 radian = 57.3 degrees

We will see that it will often be very convenient to use radians as the unit of measure for angular displacements. The KA software expresses angular velocity in radians per second (rad/s), and angular acceleration in radians per second per second (rad/s^2).

The term "revolution" is used to define a full 360° angular displacement. Thus, a 2 and one-half somersault dive involves an angular displacement of 2.5 revolutions. Further, the term revolutions-per-minute (rpm) is sometimes used to quantify angular velocity.

Conclusions

The angular position of any given body segment is set as the angle (measured in the counter-clockwise direction) between the forward direction and a representative line in the segment. Angular displacement is defined as the change in angular position that occurs over a given time period. We will see in the next chapter that the angular velocity of a body segment can be easily computed given information on angular displacement and time.

Answer to Chapter Question

Question 14-1:
The following figure shows the angular position of a tennis racket near the moment of backscratch in a tennis serve.

What is the approximate angular position of the racket?

O A. 65 degrees
O B. 245 degrees
O C. 105 degrees

The correct answer is B. The segment vector is aimed down and to the left. The angle between the segment vector and the positive X-axis direction is 245 degrees as measured in the counter-clockwise direction.

Chapter 15: Angular Velocity

Angular Velocity

Given our understanding of angular position and angular displacement, we are now ready to begin work with measures of angular velocity. We will see in this chapter that many of the concepts that we learned about linear velocity in Chapter 6 will be applied again in this chapter. We will also see that our work with angular velocity vectors will allow us to improve our skills in three-dimensional visualization techniques.

We will discuss angular velocity measures for both two and three-dimensional movements in this chapter. The following section on two-dimensional angular velocity will lay an important foundation that will assist us in the analysis of three-dimensional angular motion.

Angular Velocity in Two Dimensions

Angular velocity is defined as the rate of change of angular position. Two equations that can be used to compute angular velocity (ω) are shown below:

$\omega = (\theta_f - \theta_i) / time$
or,
$\omega = (\Delta\theta) / time$

Either of these equations can be used to compute estimates of instantaneous angular velocity for two-dimensional movement data. The figure below shows the data that is needed to compute forearm angular velocity at a moment during a softball pitching motion.

$$\Delta\theta = 31^\circ$$
$$time = 1/60th\ sec.$$
$$\omega = ?$$

Figure 15-1. The calculation of angular velocity from angular displacement and time data.

The calculation for angular velocity is as follows:

$\omega = (\Delta\theta) / time$
$\omega = (31) / (1/60)$
$\omega = 1860\ degrees / second$
$\omega = 32.5\ rad/s$

The last line in the calculation has converted the angular velocity units from degrees per second to radians per second by dividing by 57.3. Notice that this positive value for angular velocity indicates that the direction of motion for the performer's forearm is counter-clockwise.

Question 15-1:
The following figure shows the angular displacement of a tennis racket during the early part of the action phase in a tennis serve.

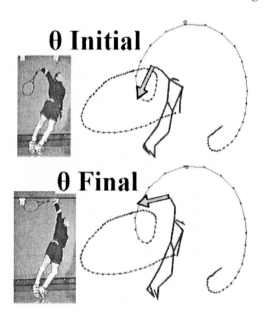

Figure 15-2. A change in angular position of the racket during a tennis serve is shown.

What is the approximate angular displacement of the racket?

O A. 55 degrees
O B. -55 degrees
O C. 190 degrees

Angular Velocity Vectors for 2D Data

Our discussion of angular velocity has so far focused upon two-dimensional movements. These two-dimensional movements make it easy for us to visualize the relationship between measures of angular position and angular velocity. For example, the movement of the forearm in a softball pitch is relatively simple to analyze because, during the action phase of the movement, the full length of the segment is well isolated in the side view plane. Because the pitcher's forearm motion is primarily constrained to the side view plane, it has only two possible directions of motion: counter-clockwise and clockwise.

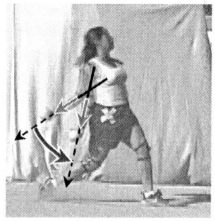

Figure 15-3. The change in angular position of the forearm segment during a softball pitch motion.

Two-Dimensional Motion Examples

The angular velocity vector for a 2D movement can therefore take on only one of two directions. For counter-clockwise motion, the angular velocity vector is defined as being aimed "out of" or above the plane of motion. The figure below shows a diagonal view of a bar shaped object that is rotating in a two dimensional plane.

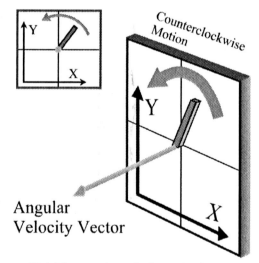

Figure 15-4. The angular velocity vector for a counter-clockwise motion.

The angular velocity vector is aimed along a line that is perpendicular to the plane of motion of the bar. Because the motion of the bar is confined to the XY plane, the angular velocity vector must be directed along a line that is parallel to the Z-axis. You can also visualize the angular velocity vector as being parallel to the axis of rotation of the bar. It is interesting to note that even with a pure 2D motion, it is necessary to make use of 3D visualization in order to understand angular velocity vectors. The use of a third dimension in the definition of an angular velocity vector assures that the given motion will be uniquely identified. The angular velocity vector is directed along the single line that identifies the axis of rotation of the body. Further, the length of the angular velocity vector uniquely identifies the magnitude of the angular velocity.

The Right Hand Rule

The *right hand rule* convention is used to define the direction of any given angular velocity vector. The figure below illustrates the right hand rule.

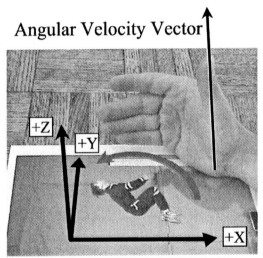

Figure 15-5. The right hand rule for determining angular motion vector direction.

If the fingers of the right hand are aimed in the direction of rotation for a body, the right thumb will be aimed along the line of the angular velocity vector. For a 2D motion, a counter-clockwise motion will have an angular velocity vector that is aimed along the positive Z direction.

It is interesting to note that the right hand rule is also used to define the direction of the positive Z-axis for a three dimensional XYZ reference frame. If the fingers of the right hand are pointed from the X-axis toward the Y-axis, the right thumb will be aimed in the direction of the positive Z-axis. Thus, the positive Z-axis is aimed out of the wall in the lower portion of the figure below, and the negative Z-axis is aimed into the wall.

For a clockwise angular motion, the angular velocity vector should be visualized as aimed "into" or behind the plane of motion. The right hand rule is

applied to the motion of a clock second hand in the figure below. Notice that if the fingers are aimed in the direction of the second hand's motion, the thumb aims into the clock-face. The lower portion of the figure shows that the angular velocity vector for the clock second hand is aimed "into the wall" that holds the clock, and along the negative Z-axis.

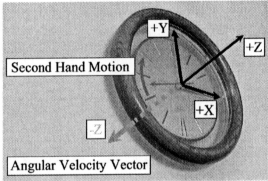

Figure 15-6. The angular velocity vector for a clockwise motion.

As a result, we see that counter-clockwise 2D motions have angular velocity vectors that are aimed "out of the plane", or along the positive Z-axis (see figure 15-7A). Further, clockwise 2D motions have angular velocity vectors that are aimed "into the plane", or along the negative Z-axis (see figure 15-7B).

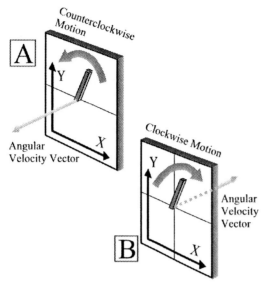

Figure 15-7. The two possible directions of a 2D angular velocity vector.

The following figure shows a screwdriver that is being used to drive a screw into a piece of wood.

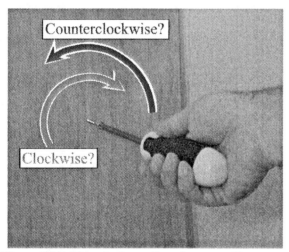

Figure 15-8. The angular motion of a screw driver.

Question 15-2:
Which way should the screwdriver be turned to drive the screw into the board?

O A. Clockwise.
O B. Counter-clockwise.

The screwdriver example shows that the right hand rule is used in "everyday life" examples as well as biomechanics and mathematics problems. Other common examples of the right hand rule include light bulbs and water faucets.

Angular Velocity Vectors & 2D Movement

The visualization of more realistic movement data requires both the side view and the front view, even for a movement that is primarily isolated in the side view plane. The upper portion of the figure below shows the side view of a softball pitching motion. For the purpose of our extended two-dimensional analysis, we will maintain the reference frame convention used in 2D problems. Specifically, we will use the X and Y dimensions to define the side view, and the Z-axis to define the side-to-side dimension.

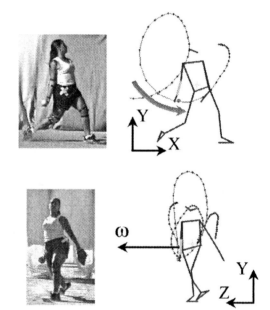

Figure 15-9. The angular velocity vector of the forearm during a softball pitch motion.

The upper portion of the figure shows that, because the forearm is rotating in the counter-clockwise direction, it's angular velocity vector will be aimed "out of" the XY side view plane. The lower portion of the figure shows the front view video and stick figure information for the pitch. Note that the vertical dimension, as represented by the Y-axis, is held in common across the side and front view images. Also note that the positive Z-axis is aimed out of the side view plane, and is therefore directed from the left to the right side of the performer's body.

The angular velocity vector for the forearm is shown in the front view stick figure. For two-dimensional motion, the angular velocity vector can be aimed either straight to the left, as shown in figure 15-9, or straight to the right. We will discuss three-dimensional angular velocity vectors in the next section. These 3D vectors can be aimed along any line in 3D space. When we discuss angular velocity for 3D motion, we will make use of traditional 3D reference frame conventions, with +X taken as forward, +Y taken as to the left of the forward direction, and +Z taken as upward.

Angular Velocity in Three Dimensions

Virtually all human movements occur in three-dimensional space. Angular motions in particular, are often far too complex to be analyzed with only two-dimensional data. Consider the motion of the baseball batting swing shown in the figure below.

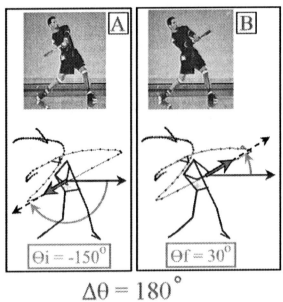

Figure 15-10. Two dimensional measures of the angular position of a baseball bat.

The figure shows two-dimensional angular position data for the bat segment. Figure A shows the bat position a moment before ball impact. Figure B shows the bat 1/30th second later, just after ball impact. Note that the bat head trails the hands in figure A. In figure B, the bat head has rotated around to a position in front of the hands.

The angular position measures for the bat, as defined by *two-dimensional guidelines,* are shown in the figure. The angular displacement for the bat over this brief time interval is shown to be 180°. This two-dimensional measure of the change in angular position of the bat is clearly incorrect. Side view 2D data can be used to compute angular displacement *only if* the segment in question is

isolated in the plane of the video. The motion of the baseball bat in this example is clearly not well isolated in the side view plane. The bat motion occurs primarily in the horizontal plane, especially around the time of ball impact.

Because the baseball bat motion occurs mainly in the horizontal plane, it is best visualized from an overhead view. The overhead view is difficult to capture on video, but quite easy to compute mathematically with the KA3D program. The figure below shows 3D data for the batting motion.

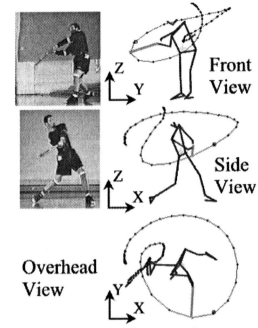

Figure 15-11. Three dimensional data for a baseball batting motion.

As we mentioned in Chapter 9, the KA3D program takes front and side view 2D information and mathematically computes three-dimensional data. Given XYZ coordinate data on the bat head, it is possible to plot the overhead view as well as the front and side views. Note that the overhead view shows that the pattern of motion of the bat head is nearly circular. The front and side view information shows that the action phase of the swing occurs primarily in the horizontal plane.

The upper portion of the figure below shows the bat position for the frame just before ball impact, the frame of ball impact, and the frame just after ball impact. Notice that the motion of the bat is in the counter-clockwise direction as viewed from above.

Overhead View

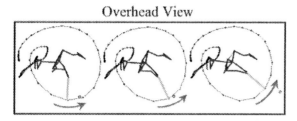

Angular Displacement

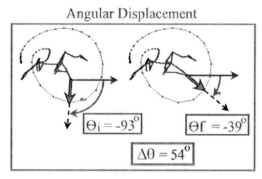

Figure 15-12. Two measures of angular position for a baseball bat as measured within the overhead view plane.

The lower portion of the figure shows the angular displacement of the bat across the 2/60th second interval around ball impact. Note that the angular displacement of 54° is far less than the 180° measure we computed with two-dimensional data. Because the movement of the bat is approximately in the horizontal plane, the angular displacement data from the overhead view provides a much better estimate of the true bat motion than that from the side view.

While we have used the overhead view to illustrate the movement of the bat in this example, it is important to note that the true plane of motion of the bat is angled upward with respect to the horizontal near the moment of ball impact.

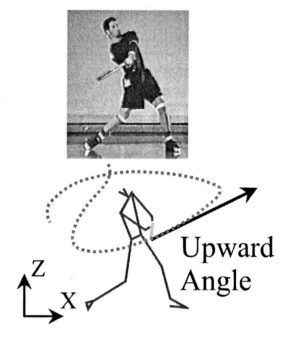

Figure 15-13. The upward angle of a baseball batting motion as seen from the side view.

Because the true plane of motion of the bat is angled upwards above the horizontal, angular displacement measures taken from the overhead view will be slightly distorted. However, the three-dimensional analysis of angular velocity will not be based upon data from any single 2D viewing plane. The 3D data will be based upon the true motion of the bat at every instant in time during the swing. As a result, we can expect that 3D analysis procedures will be superior to 2D analysis for all but the simplest of movements.

The calculation of the bat angular velocity on the basis of the 2D overhead view data is shown below:

$\omega = (\Delta\theta) / time$
$\omega = (54) / (2/60)$
$\omega = 1620$ degrees / second
$\omega = 28.3$ rad/s

The three-dimensional data analysis from KA3D shows that the bat angular velocity is 32.9 rad/s at the frame of impact.

3D Angular Velocity

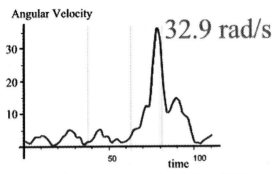

32.9 rad/s

Figure 15-14. The angular velocity of a baseball bat as computed by a three dimensional data analysis.

As a result, we see that the overhead view provides a rough estimate of the true bat angular velocity value. On the other hand, the data from the side view provides a very poor estimate of angular velocity. Because the side view measure of bat displacement was 180°, the calculated value of angular velocity will be very high:

$$\omega = (\Delta\theta) \,/\, \text{time}$$
$$\omega = (180) \,/\, (2/60)$$
$$\omega = 5400 \text{ degrees} \,/\, \text{second}$$
$$\omega = 94.2 \text{ rad/s}$$

The side view based calculation has resulted in an angular velocity measure that is nearly 300% too large. In summary, we see that when 2D data is used in a movement analysis, care should be taken to ignore any angular motion data that is not isolated in the plane of the video. It should be noted that the 2D mathematical calculations for angular velocity shown above were performed properly. However, the 2D calculations are a good illustration of the "garbage in – garbage out" computer principle. When you make use of 2D data, you should be sure to ignore angular measures that are based upon movement values that fall outside of the plane of the video. To avoid confusion with "good" and "bad" measures from 2D data, it would be best to collect

3D data for all movements that cannot be isolated within a single viewing plane.

Angular Velocity Vectors in 3D

For simple, two-dimensional motions, the direction of an angular velocity vector is easily determined. Angular movements are either clockwise or counter-clockwise and the angular velocity vectors are aimed either into or out of the plane of motion. In contrast, more realistic human motions will involve angular velocity vectors that move freely within three-dimensional space. The figure below shows an angular velocity vector associated with the forearm in a football throwing motion.

Figure 15-15. A forearm angular velocity vector at a moment during a football pass motion.

The KA3D software allows you to visualize how the 3D angular velocity vectors change as a function of time. The angular velocity shown above indicates the axis of rotation of the forearm at the instant shown. Further, the length of the arrow indicates the angular velocity magnitude, or how quickly the forearm is changing its angular position.

The angular velocity vector for the forearm changes its direction and length extensively during the course of the football throwing movement. Because the angular velocity vector is three-dimensional, it will have components that fall in front of and behind the front view plane. The figure below shows the angular velocity vector at a moment just before ball release from both the front and side viewing planes.

Front
View

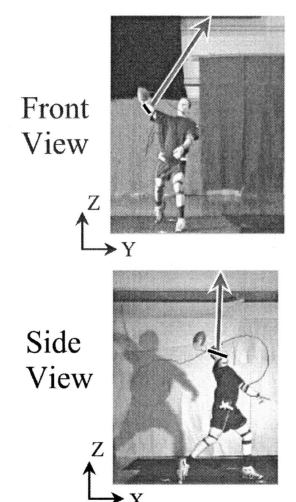

Side
View

Figure 15-16. Front and side view information for the forearm angular velocity vector.

Figure 15-17. The right hand rule applied to the determination of the direction of the forearm angular velocity vector.

The figure below shows the angular velocity vector for the forearm shortly after ball release.

Front
View

Side
View

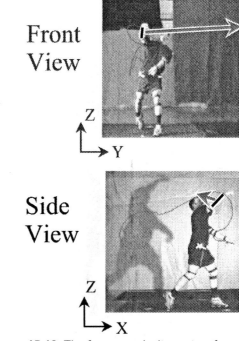

Figure 15-18. The forearm velocity vectors for a moment late in a football pass motion.

The angular velocity vector, as shown in both the front and side view images, is aimed mainly upward (in the Z direction). As a result, we see that the rotation of the forearm is contained mainly in the horizontal plane. The front view shows that the angular velocity vector also has a side-to-side component (along the Y direction). Thus, the forearm is rotating in a plane that is mainly horizontal, but also tilted down toward the performer's left side.

The right hand rule can be used with the angular velocity vector to visualize the direction of rotation for the forearm. The figure below shows a right hand that is positioned around the angular velocity vector with the thumb pointing along the direction of the vector. Given this hand positioning, the direction of motion of the forearm is indicated by the curved arrow pointing toward the fingertips.

Note that the front and side view figures show that the angular velocity vector is aimed mainly to the side (along the Y axis), and it has a small backward component (along the X axis). As a result, the vector shown in the front view picture should be visualized as being aimed slightly behind the front view plane. In summary, the rotation of the forearm occurs primarily in the side view plane at the instant shown above. Because the rotation of the forearm is predominantly clockwise as seen from the side, the angular velocity vector must be aimed *behind* the side view plane. For the vector shown above, the angular velocity vector is aimed behind the side view plane and approximately along the +Y axis. Note that for 3D data, the +Y-axis is aimed toward the performer's *left* side.

Angular Velocity Vector Components

We have seen in Parts 2 and 3 that we can often gain increased insight into skillful performance by focusing upon individual vector components. When the data for a 3D data file is first generated, the XYZ position data for every point, and the angular velocity XYZ components for every segment in the trial are stored as part of the 3D data file. When the KA3D program displays an angular velocity vector, it is simply plotting the information that is stored in the 3D data file. As a result, the X, Y and Z components of any angular velocity vector are readily available for use in the analysis of any 3D human movement.

The figure below illustrates the three dimensional angular velocity vector for the forearm a moment just before ball release on a football throw.

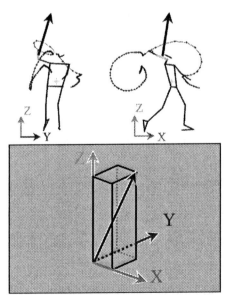

Figure 15-19. The three dimensional components of a forearm angular velocity vector.

Note that the vector has a small component along the positive X-axis, another small component along the Y-axis and a large component along the Z-axis. Any of the angular velocity vector components can be plotted as a function of time to reveal detailed information on the movement process. The figure below shows the values for the Z component of the forearm angular velocity during the course of the full throwing motion. The curve shows that the peak value for ω_Z occurs just prior to ball release.

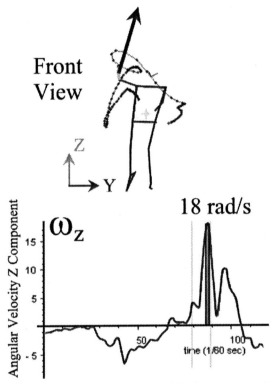

Figure 15-20. The Z component of the forearm angular velocity vector.

The figure below shows plots of all three vector components for the forearm angular velocity. The information in the figure confirms that the Z component of angular velocity is larger (at 18 radians per second) than the X component (at 3 radians per second) or the Y component (at 5 radians per second) for the illustrated instant in time.

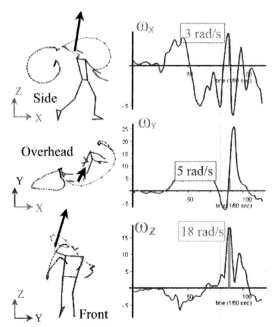

Figure 15-21. The X, Y, and Z components of the forearm angular velocity vector.

The angular velocity information for the performer in the football throw indicates that the rotation of the forearm about the Z-axis is critical in the development of force in the throw. The ω_Z versus time curve shows both the size of the peak angular velocity component and the timing of this peak with respect to the ball release event. This information, coupled with other segment angular velocity measures (and a number of other joint motion measures we will cover in Chapter 18) will help us to identify key factors associated with skillful performance.

Conclusions

Our discussion of topics in angular position, angular displacement and angular velocity is now complete. We have seen how angular position can be measured as the angle between the segment vector and the forward direction for any two-dimensional motion. In addition we have seen that angular displacement and angular velocity can be computed from measures of angular position. The direction of angular motion, whether in 2D or 3D is given by the orientation of the angular velocity vector.

Answers to Chapter Questions

Question 15-1:
The following figure shows the angular displacement of a tennis racket during the early part of the action phase in a tennis serve.

What is the approximate angular displacement of the racket?

O A. 55 degrees
O B. -55 degrees
O C. 190 degrees

The correct answer is B. The final angular position is 190 degrees and the initial angular position is 245 degrees. The angular displacement is equal to (190 − 245) or −55 degrees. Note that the motion of the racket is in the clockwise direction and therefore the sign of the angular displacement must be negative.

Question 15-2:
Which way should the screwdriver be turned to drive the screw into the board?

O A. Clockwise.
O B. Counter-clockwise.

The correct answer is A. In order to drive the screw into the board the screwdriver must be turned in the direction defined by the curved fingers of the right hand. When this is done the screw will be moved in the direction defined by the thumb of the right hand (into the board).

Chapter 16: Angular Acceleration

Angular Acceleration

Our work with angular acceleration will provide us with information that is needed in the calculation of the joint torques that cause human movement. We have seen in Chapter 11 that the linear equation for Newton's second law cannot be solved for unknown values of force unless measures of mass and linear acceleration (**A**) are known:

$$\mathbf{F_{NET}} = m\,\mathbf{A}$$

Similarly, the solution for the net torque acting on a rigid body cannot be accomplished without information on angular acceleration (**α**):

$$\mathbf{T_{NET}} = I\,\boldsymbol{\alpha}$$

We will discuss the net torque (**T**$_{NET}$) and moment of inertia (I) terms in the above equation in detail in Chapter 20. For our purposes in this chapter, however, we will acknowledge that measures of angular acceleration will be critical for our future work in angular kinetics.

Angular Acceleration in 2D

Angular acceleration (α) is defined as the rate of change of angular velocity with respect to time. The equation for angular acceleration is shown below:

$$\boldsymbol{\alpha} = (\omega f - \omega i) / \text{time}$$

Where:
ωf - is the final angular velocity vector
ωf - is the initial angular velocity

This vector equation can be broken down into 3 scalar equations:

$$\alpha_X = (\omega_{XF} - \omega_{XI}) / \text{time}$$
$$\alpha_Y = (\omega_{YF} - \omega_{YI}) / \text{time}$$
$$\alpha_Z = (\omega_{ZF} - \omega_{ZI}) / \text{time}$$

Two-dimensional motion analysis data involves angular velocity vectors that are aimed into or out of the XY plane. As a result, only the Z component of the angular velocity vector will have non-zero values. Because 2D angular velocity vectors can only exhibit change along the Z-axis, the direction of 2D angular acceleration vectors must also be confined to the plus or minus Z direction. As a result, only the third equation above is needed in the analysis of 2D measures of angular acceleration:

$$\alpha_Z = (\omega_{ZF} - \omega_{ZI}) / \text{time}$$

The figure below shows angular acceleration data for frame 82 in a softball pitching motion. The lower portion of the figure shows that the angular velocity for the forearm is 17.3 rad/s at frame 81 and 22.5 rad/s at frame 83.

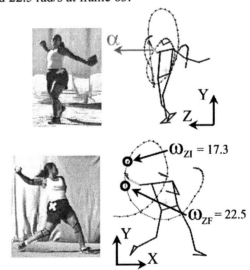

Figure 16-1. Angular velocity measures and an angular acceleration vector for a softball pitch forearm motion.

Because the angular velocity values are increasing over the interval from frames 81 to 83, the forearm is experiencing positive angular acceleration. The calculation for the α_Z is as follows:

$$\alpha_Z = (\omega_{ZF} - \omega_{ZI}) / \text{time}$$
$$\alpha_Z = (22.5 - 17.3) / (1/30)$$
$$\alpha_Z = (5.2) * 30$$
$$\alpha_Z = 156 \text{ rad/s}^2$$

Because the angular acceleration value is positive, the α vector shown in the upper part of the figure is aimed to the player's right, along the positive Z-axis.

The figure below shows the softball pitch data an instant after ball release in the movement. The illustrated instant in time is part of the follow through phase, where the high speeds and forces generated during the action phase are reduced from high values to near zero values.

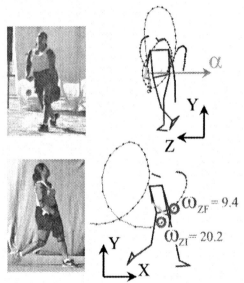

Figure 16-2. An angular acceleration vector associated with decreasing angular velocity values.

The change in forearm angular velocity values for this instant in the pitch is shown in the lower portion of the figure. The calculation for α_Z is as follows:

$$\alpha_Z = (\omega_{ZF} - \omega_{ZI}) / \text{time}$$
$$\alpha_Z = (9.4 - 20.2) / (1/30)$$
$$\alpha_Z = (-10.8) * 30$$
$$\alpha_Z = -324 \text{ rad/s}^2$$

Because the angular velocity of the forearm is decreasing near this moment in time, the numerical value of the α_Z term is negative. This implies that the angular acceleration vector is aimed along the negative Z-axis, or to the player's left, as shown in the upper part of the figure.

Angular Acceleration Curves

Measures of angular velocity can be plotted as a function of time to facilitate the visualization of the movement process. Our discussions above have reinforced the notion that measures of angular acceleration are given by the *rate of change* of angular velocity. As a result, the angular velocity curve can be used to determine measures of angular acceleration. Consider the following question:

Question 16-1:
The 2D angular velocity information for a performer's forearm motion is shown in the figure below. If angular velocity data is shown graphically as a function of time, how can we determine estimates of the angular acceleration of the forearm?

O A. The angular acceleration values are equal to the angular velocity values multiplied by film speed.
O B. The angular acceleration values can be estimated from the slope of the angular velocity curve at any instant in time.
O C. Angular acceleration cannot be determined from data on angular velocity.

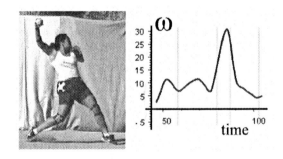

Figure 16-3. The forearm angular velocity curve for a 2D analysis of a softball pitch.

Because angular acceleration is a measure of the change in angular velocity as a function of time, measures of angular acceleration can be determined through analysis of the *slope* of the angular velocity curve. The figure below shows an instant in time where the slope of the angular velocity curve is at a maximal positive value. The angular acceleration curve is therefore at a peak value at the given instant in time.

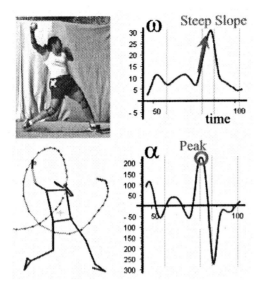

Figure 16-4. The relation between the slope of the angular velocity curve and the magnitude of angular acceleration values are shown.

The relation between angular velocity and angular acceleration is the same as that of linear velocity and linear acceleration. In particular, the slope of the angular velocity curve can be used to determine the value of angular acceleration at any instant in time. When the angular velocity curve slope is zero, the value of α will be zero. When the angular velocity curve slope is steep and negative, the value of α will be at a peak negative value.

Angular Acceleration in 3D

The rate of change of three dimensional angular velocity measures are indicated by the slope of the X, Y or Z component angular velocity curves. We have seen above that this relationship holds for 2D angular data. We will see in this section that the same analysis approach can be applied to the X, Y or Z component curves in a 3D data set.

Angular Acceleration Vectors

The linear velocity vector for a point indicates the instantaneous line of motion of that point. Similarly, the angular velocity vector of a segment indicates the instantaneous axis of rotation and the direction of rotation (by the right hand rule) of that segment. Acceleration and angular acceleration vectors, on the other hand, do not indicate the direction of motion of a point or rigid body segment.

The figure below shows a comparison of an angular velocity vector and an angular acceleration vector for a given instant in time during a football throw. Note that the direction of the angular acceleration vector is not at all similar to the direction of the angular velocity vector. Further, the magnitudes of the two vectors are also very different. The size of the angular acceleration vector is 412 rad/s^2 and the size of the angular velocity vector is 24 rad/s.

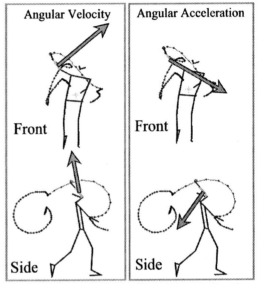

Figure 16-5. A comparison of the size and direction of the angular velocity and the angular acceleration vectors for a given instant in a throwing motion.

The magnitude and direction of the angular acceleration vector can be computed from information on the rate of change of the angular velocity vector. Because angular velocity vectors are typically three-dimensional, their analysis goes one step beyond the examples we discussed in Chapter 7. However, we will see that the calculation of angular acceleration vectors can be accomplished with very basic skills in algebra and vector analysis.

Analysis of Angular Acceleration

In this section we will inspect drawings with angular velocity vectors and determine angular acceleration vectors graphically. This analysis will allow us to visualize and better understand angular acceleration vectors. The vector equation for angular acceleration is as follows:

$\alpha = (\omega f - \omega i)$ / time
or,
$\alpha = \Delta\omega$ / time

Where:
$\Delta\omega$ – is the change in angular velocity over a specified time interval.

A first step in computing the angular acceleration vector will involve determining $\Delta\omega$:

$\Delta\omega = (\omega f - \omega i)$

The upper portion of the figure below shows the forearm angular velocity vector for frames 86 and 88 of a football throwing motion. The lower right hand corner of the figure shows the angular acceleration vector of the forearm at frame 87. The change in angular velocity between frames 86 and 88, divided by the time interval between those frames, will give a good estimate of the angular acceleration at frame 87.

The vector subtraction of $(\omega f - \omega i)$ is shown in the lower left portion of the figure. In this vector diagram the negative value of $-\omega i$ has been added to the ωf vector. Note that the direction of the computed $\Delta\omega$ vector is the same as that of the α vector.

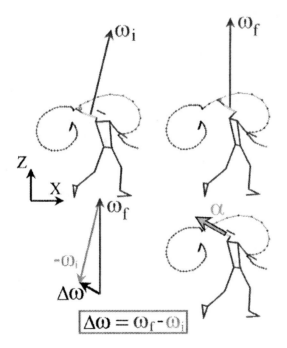

Figure 16-6. The relationship between the change in angular velocity vector and the angular acceleration vector is shown (side view data).

The final step in the calculation of angular acceleration involves dividing the $\Delta\omega$ vector by the time interval between frames 86 and 88:

$\alpha = \Delta\omega$ / time

Because the time interval between the two frames is $1/30^{th}$ second, we will get the same result if the $\Delta\omega$ vector is multiplied by 30 (dividing by a fraction is equivalent to multiplying by the inverse of that fraction).

$\alpha = \Delta\omega * 30$

The process of multiplying a vector by a scalar can be envisioned as lengthening the vector. As a result, we can envision that the α vector will act along the same line as the $\Delta\omega$ vector, although it will be 30 times longer. This 30-fold increase in length is not shown in the figure because the scale for the acceleration vector is not the same as that of the angular velocity vector (if it were, a larger page would be needed to hold the graphic image). The scales for vectors that represent a different unit of measure are almost always different in a well-constructed graphic illustration. For example, the scale for the XZ position values on the stick figure may be set as 1 meter equals one inch on the drawing. On the other hand, the scale for an angular velocity vector may be set as 10 rad/s equals one inch. Finally, a good scale for an angular acceleration vector may be 100 rad/s^2 equals one inch.

The numerical calculation of this angular acceleration value will yield a result that is in agreement with the vector analysis. As a first step, we must break the vector equation into 3 scalar equations:

$\alpha = (\omega f - \omega i)$ / time
$\alpha x = (\omega xf - \omega xi)$ / time
$\alpha y = (\omega yf - \omega yi)$ / time
$\alpha z = (\omega zf - \omega zi)$ / time

Because this example involves side view data, only the X and Z components are needed for the angular acceleration calculation. The following variables are "known" from the KA3D data:

Given:
$\omega xf = 0.68$ rad/s
$\omega xi = 3.96$ rad/s
$\omega zf = 17.73$ rad/s
$\omega zi = 15.36$ rad/s

time = 1/30 s

The αx and αz components of the angular acceleration vector is computed as follows:

$\alpha x = (\omega xf - \omega xi) / time$
$\alpha x = (0.68 - 3.96) / (1/30)$
$\alpha x = -3.28 * 30$
$\alpha x = -98.4$ rad/s^2

$\alpha z = (\omega zf - \omega zi) / time$
$\alpha z = (17.73 - 15.36) / (1/30)$
$\alpha z = 2.37 * 30$
$\alpha z = 71.1$ rad/s^2

The X and Z components of the angular acceleration vector define the direction of the vector as seen in the side view plane. The figure below shows that the angular acceleration vector from our calculations is aimed in the same direction as the $\Delta\omega$ vector.

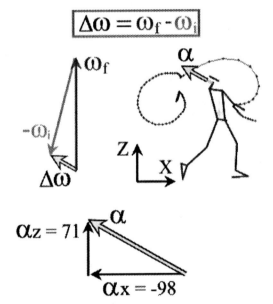

Figure 16-7. The calculation of angular acceleration vector components from change in angular velocity data (side view data).

The analysis of the side view angular acceleration information has provided us with data on the vertical (Z) and forward-back (X) dimensions of the 3D vector. The side view does not, however, provide any information on the side-to-side Y component that is perpendicular to the side view plane. The information on the angular acceleration Y component can be determined through an analysis of the front view data.

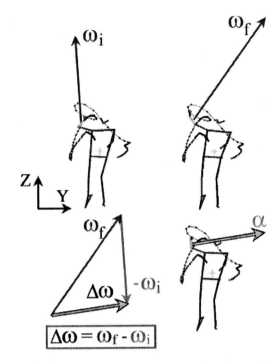

Figure 16-8. The relationship between the change in angular velocity vector and the angular acceleration vector is shown (front view data).

The figure above shows the front view forearm angular velocity vectors for the same frames as that of our side view analysis. The lower left portion of the figure shows the vector subtraction of ($\omega f - \omega i$). The resulting $\Delta\omega$ vector has a large component that is aimed in the positive Y direction. As expected, the $\Delta\omega$ vector is aimed in the same direction as the α vector.

A numerical analysis of the Y component of the angular acceleration vector is provided below:

$\alpha y = (\omega yf - \omega yi) / time$

The following variables are "known" from the KA3D data:

Given:
$\omega yf = 12.11$ rad/s
$\omega yi = -1.79$ rad/s
time = 1/30 s

The αy component of the angular acceleration vector is computed as follows:

$\alpha y = (\omega yf - \omega yi) / \text{time}$
$\alpha y = (12.11 - (-1.79)) / (1/30)$
$\alpha y = 13.9 * 30$
$\alpha y = 417 \text{ rad/s}^2$

The Z component of the angular acceleration vector was computed above:

$\alpha z = 71.1 \text{ rad/s}^2$

The figure below shows that a plot of the angular acceleration Y and Z components produces an acceleration vector that is aimed in the same direction as the $\Delta\omega$ vector.

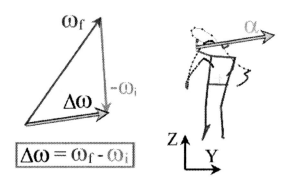

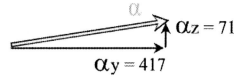

Figure 16-9. The calculation of angular acceleration vector components from change in angular velocity data (front view data).

We see from the above examples that all three dimensions of an angular acceleration vector can be determined through an analysis of both the front and side view angular velocity information.

Conclusions

Our analysis of angular acceleration vectors is now complete. We will see that measures of angular acceleration are very important because they are directly related to the net torque (turning force) that is applied to a segment at any instant in time. The details of the relationship between torque and angular acceleration will be covered in our chapters on angular kinetics. In addition, we will see that the vector analysis skills that we have developed in this

chapter will be very helpful in our analysis of joint angle measurements in chapter 18.

Answer to Chapter Question

Question 16-1:
The 2D angular velocity information for a performers forearm motion are shown in the figure below. If angular velocity data is shown graphically as a function of time, how can we determine estimates of the angular acceleration of the forearm?

O A. The angular acceleration values are equal to the angular velocity values multiplied by film speed.
O B. The angular acceleration values can be estimated from the slope of the angular velocity curve at any instant in time.
O C. Angular acceleration cannot be determined from data on angular velocity.

The correct answer is B. The slope of the angular velocity curve shows the rate of change of angular velocity. As a result, the slope of the angular velocity curve is proportional to the angular acceleration.

Chapter 17: Circular Motion

Circular Motion

A number of human movements involve patterns of motion that are approximately circular. The giant swing motion shown in the figure below is a good example of approximately circular human motion.

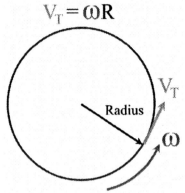

$$V_T = \omega R$$

Figure 17-2. The tangential velocity vector for a point on the end of a radius length rotating with a given angular velocity.

This equation will be exactly correct for purely circular motion and approximately correct for nearly circular motion. While exactly circular human movement is rare, some movements approximate circular motion fairly well. Consider the example of a high bar giant swing.

Figure 17-1. A giant swing on the high bar in gymnastics.

Purely circular motion can be analyzed to show an important relationship between angular and linear motion. In particular, if the angular velocity of a rotating body is measured in terms of radians per second, then the *tangential* velocity (V_T) of a point on the end of the body's length is given by the following equation:

$$V_T = \omega R$$

Where:
V_T = tangential velocity
ω = the angular velocity of the body (measured in radians / second)
R = the radius of the circle

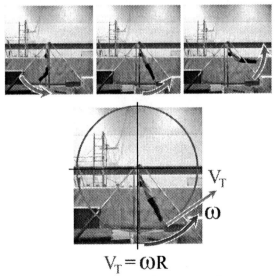

$$V_T = \omega R$$

Figure 17-3. The tangential velocity vector for a gymnast's toe on a giant swing motion.

As an exercise, we will use the KA2D data on the giant swing movement to compare calculation from the $V_T = \omega R$ equation with normal KA2D measures of point velocity. The body's angular velocity and radius length for the moment shown in the lower part of the figure are as follows:

$\omega = 7.59$ rad/s
$R = 1.92$ meters

Given these "known" values, the value of V_T can be computed:

$V_T = \omega R$
$V_T = (7.59) * (1.92)$
$V_T = 14.57$ mps

The actual velocity of the toe point is 14.34 mps. The small difference between the actual velocity measure and the result of the $V_T = \omega R$ equation is due primarily to the fact that the giant swing motion is not exactly circular.

The analysis of movements that are "less" circular than a giant swing will yield less accurate estimates of V_T. The figure below shows data from a baseball batting movement. The upper portion of the figure shows still images taken a moment before ball impact. The lower portion of the figure shows the overhead view of the swing. Note that the swing pattern of motion follows an "approximately" circular path.

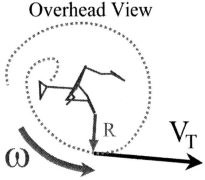

Overhead View

Figure 17-4. The tangential velocity vector for a baseball bat end point on a batting swing.

The "known" values for this batting motion are as follows:

$\omega = 36.2$ rad/s
$R = 0.78$ meters

For this example, the angular velocity and radius length are set for the baseball bat. Given these known values, the value of V_T can be computed as follows:

$V_T = \omega R$
$V_T = (36.2) * (0.78)$
$V_T = 28.2$ mps

The actual value of V_T is 26.6 mps. Again we see that there is a reasonably close agreement between the $V_T = \omega R$ equation and direct measures of point velocity.

Batting movements in softball and baseball provide very interesting examples for the $V_T = \omega R$ equation. For a given bat angular velocity, the outcome of the impact of the ball with the bat will be very much dependent upon the effective radius of the impact point on the bat. Thus, an inside pitch that causes the batter to hit the ball close to the grip, will produce a relatively low ball velocity. In contrast, a pitch that is more "over the plate" will allow the batter to make contact with the ball closer to the end of the bat. By increasing the effective radius of the contact point, the tangential velocity of the bat impact point also increases.

The figure below illustrates the difference in bat speed for two different ball impact points on a simulated baseball batting motion.

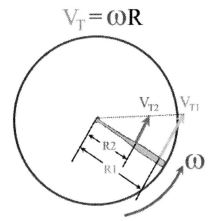

Figure 17-5. The tangential velocity vectors for two points on a baseball bat.

The radius length R1 represents the impact point of a "good hit" near the end of the bat. The radius length R2 is 60% as long as R1, and represents a bat impact with an inside pitch. If the angular velocity of the bat is set as 40 rad/s, the tangential velocity of the impact points can be computed with the $V_T = \omega R$ equation:

Given:
ω = 40 rad/s
R1 = 0.76 meters
R2 = 0.46 meters

The value of V_{T1} for the long radius (R1) is computed as follows:

$V_{T1} = \omega * R$
$V_{T1} = 40 * 0.76$
$V_{T1} = 30.4$ mps

The value of V_{T2} for the shorter radius (R2) is computed as follows:

$V_{T2} = \omega * R$
$V_{T2} = 40 * 0.46$
$V_{T2} = 18.4$ mps

The calculated values show that there is a linear relationship between tangential velocity and the radius of the swing. The reduction in radius length, by 60%, for the R2 radius length has caused a 60% reduction in the tangential velocity value.

Acceleration and Circular Motion

Circular motion provides an interesting example of accelerated motion. Consider the following questions:

Question 17-1:
A weight on the end of a 2 meter long rod is rotated with a fixed angular velocity of 3 rad/s. What is the tangential velocity of the weight?

O A. 6 mps.
O B. 3 mps.
O C. 2 mps.

Question 17-2:
The tangential velocity magnitude of the weight from the above example is held fixed at 6 mps during the complete circular motion. If the velocity magnitude is constant, does this mean that the acceleration of the weight must be zero?

O A. Yes.
O B. No.

The acceleration of an object is equal to the rate of change of velocity with respect to time. Velocity is a vector, and as such, it contains information on magnitude and direction. If the velocity vector of a point does not experience a change in magnitude, but does experience a change in direction over a time interval, then, the velocity vector has changed and acceleration must occur. The figure below shows the change in the tangential velocity vector over a short time period.

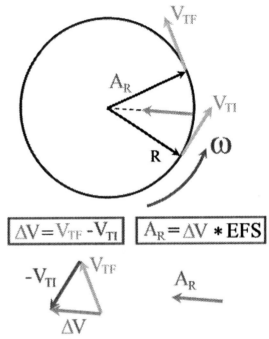

Figure 17-6. The change in velocity vector for a point at the end of a segment of length R.

The change in velocity is illustrated through vector subtraction:

$\Delta V = V_{TF} - V_{TI}$

Where:
ΔV = the change in the velocity vector
V_{TF} = the final tangential velocity vector
V_{TI} = the initial tangential velocity vector

The vector subtraction of $V_{TF} - V_{TI}$ produces a ΔV vector that is aimed to the left and slightly upward, as shown in the figure. The direction of the ΔV vector and the acceleration vector for the point on the end of the rod are identical. Note that for uniform velocity circular motion, this acceleration vector is aimed exactly at the center of the circle. As a result, the acceleration is called *radial* acceleration.

If the weight in our example is rotated with non-uniform angular velocity, there will be both radial and *tangential* components of acceleration. The figure below shows a case where the final tangential velocity magnitude (V_{TF}) is twice as large as the initial tangential velocity (V_{TI}).

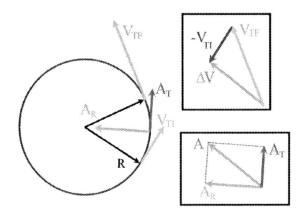

Figure 17-7. The radial and tangential components of an acceleration vector.

The ΔV vector direction is determined through vector subtraction, as shown in the upper right part of the figure. The acceleration vector is shown as acting along the same direction as the ΔV in the lower right side of the figure. This part of the figure also shows how the resultant acceleration vector can be broken down into radial (A_R) and tangential (A_T) components. Once the radial and tangential vector components have been determined, they can be plotted in the original figure.

Conclusions

Our discussion of circular motion, tangential velocity, radial acceleration and tangential acceleration is now complete. While the equations presented in this chapter are only exactly correct with pure circular motion, the principles we have covered will find application in our analysis of joint motions in the next chapter.

Answers to Chapter Questions

Question 17-1:
A weight on the end of a 2 meter long rod is rotated with a fixed angular velocity of 3 rad/s. What is the tangential velocity of the weight?

O A. 6 mps.
O B. 3 mps.
O C. 2 mps.

The correct answer is A. The solution to the equation $V_T = \omega R$ is: $V_T = (3)*(2)$; $V_T = 6$ mps.

Question 17-2:
The tangential velocity magnitude of the weight from the above example is held fixed at 6 mps during the complete circular motion. If the velocity magnitude is constant, does this mean that the acceleration of the weight must be zero?

O A. Yes.
O B. No.

The correct answer is B. The weight must experience acceleration while it is being rotated. See the discussion below for details.

Chapter 18: Joint Angle Measures

Human movement is generated by the actions of the body's joints. From the kinematic level, joint actions can be defined through measures of joint angle, joint range of motion (ROM) and joint velocity (JtV). The remaining sections of this chapter will discuss each of these joint angle measures in turn.

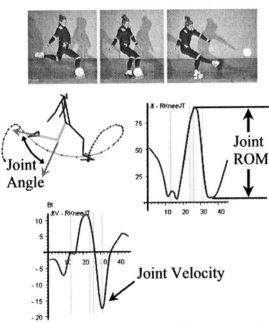

Figure 18-1. Example measures of joint angle, joint range of motion (ROM) and joint velocity (JtV).

Measures of Joint Angle Position

The joints of the human body are all unique in their specific structure. However, for the purpose of biomechanical analysis, it is convenient to break the various joints of the body into two basic classifications: *hinge* and *ball and socket*.

Hinge Joints

Hinge joints are free to rotate about a single axis. The knee, elbow, wrist and ankle can all be approximated as hinge joints in typical biomechanical analysis problems. The following sections will discuss the joint angle measurement conventions used in the analysis of each of these joints.

Knee Joint

The knee joint is an example of a hinge joint. As a result of the structure of the knee, the thigh and shank segments are constrained to move primarily within a single plane of motion. The figure below shows two knee joint angle measures for a walking motion.

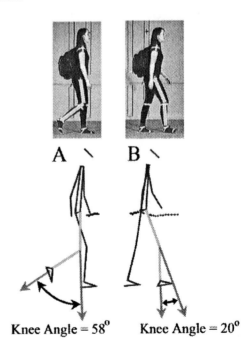

Figure 18-2. Knee angle measurements in walking.

Because the knee joint involves rotation about a single axis, a single numerical value can be used to express the joint's position at any instant in time. For most joints the joint angle is measured as the angle between the distal segment vector and an extension of the proximal segment vector. For figure A above, the extension of the thigh segment vector is shown as a lightly shaded arrow. The knee angle is defined as the angle between the shank segment vector and the thigh extension vector. Note that this measurement convention sets the joint angle as the degree of flexion at the knee joint, where large knee angles are associated with large flexion angles and small knee angles are associated with nearly straight leg positions.

Note: it is also possible to measure joint angles as the angle formed between the two segment lines. If this "segment to segment" joint angle measurement convention is used, a fully extended joint is set as having a 180° joint angle. If the "degrees flexion" joint angle measurement convention is used, a fully extended joint is defined as having a 0° joint angle. The remaining discussions in this book will express joint angles with the "degrees flexion" measurement convention. The KA2D and KA3D software programs also use the degrees flexion joint measurement convention by default, although this setting can be changed to follow the segment to segment measurement convention by changing a setting in the KAVideo software setup program.

Elbow Joint

Elbow joint angles are measured with the same conventions as those used for the knee. Figure 18-3 shows the elbow flexion angle for a moment during a football throwing motion. Because the upper arm and forearm are well isolated in the side view plane, the elbow joint measure shown in the figure provides a very good estimate of the arm's position.

Many movements occur in three-dimensional space and cannot be well approximated by two-dimensional video images. This is especially true for joint angle data. Even though hinge joints allow movement only in a single plane, the plane of motion of a given joint is often *not* the same as the plane of motion of the full body. Figure 18-4 shows the 2D elbow angle data at a moment just prior to release in a football throw.

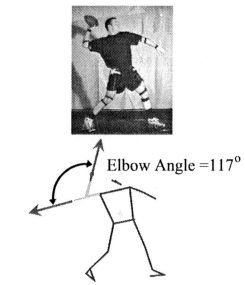

Elbow Angle = 117°

Figure 18-3. An elbow angle measurement from a study of a football pass motion.

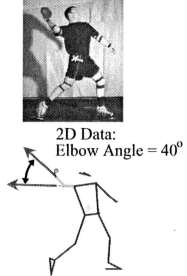

2D Data:
Elbow Angle = 40°

Figure 18-4. A two-dimensional estimate of elbow angle.

The figure shows that the motions of the performer's legs and the ball are well isolated in the side view plane. However, the upper arm and forearm are clearly not contained in the side view. For example, the upper arm should be visualized as "sticking out of" the side view plane. As a result, the estimate of the elbow angle that is provided by this 2D data (i.e., within the KA2D program) will be distorted. The 40° elbow flexion angle shown above underestimates the true elbow angle.

Three-dimensional data for the football throw motion is shown in the figure below. The elbow angle, as measured from the three-dimensional analysis, is shown to be 109°. Note that the front view confirms that the upper arm is "sticking out of" the side view plane and the forearm is angled behind the performer's head. As a result, it is clear that any estimate of the elbow joint angle that is based on side view data alone is likely to be flawed. For this figure, the front view stick figure is more helpful in the visualization of the elbow angle than the side view. However, even the front view data does not perfectly isolate the plane of motion of the elbow joint. For example, if a protractor is placed over the front view stick figure, the elbow angle will not be measured as the "true" value of 109°.

3D Data: Elbow Angle =109°

Figure 18-5. A three-dimensional measure of an elbow joint angle.

The calculation of joint angles in 3D are based upon the XYZ coordinate values for the segment end points. In effect, we can imagine that if a protractor (or goniometer) is positioned in 3D space such that it lies on the plane formed by the upper arm and forearm, it will measure the angle correctly. The figure below shows the instantaneous plane of motion of the elbow. This elbow plane of motion is tilted at an angle with respect to the front view plane. The true elbow angle is measured within the illustrated (tilted) plane.

Elbow Joint Plane of Motion

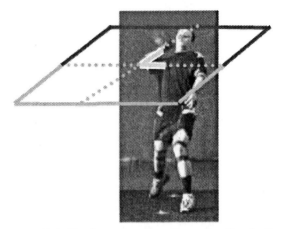

Figure 18-6. The instantaneous plane of motion for the elbow joint.

Wrist Joint

Wrist joint motion can involve radial and ulnar flexion as well as flexion and extension.

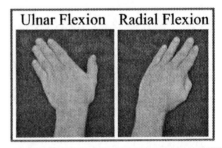

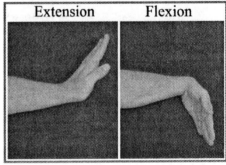

Figure 18-7. Wrist joint angle measurement conventions.

In many instances, the wrist joint can be approximated as a simple hinge joint. Unlike the knee and elbow, wrist motions often involve extension joint angles as well as flexion joint angles. The figure below shows a simplified swimming arm motion. Note that the wrist is flexed during the early part of the pull and extended during the last portion of the pull.

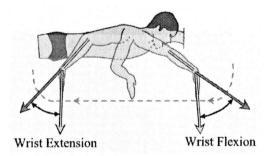

Wrist Extension   Wrist Flexion

Figure 18-8. Wrist joint angles in a swimming arm pull.

A wrist joint angle curve is shown in the lower portion of the figure below. Note that wrist flexion angles are associated with positive joint angle measures and wrist extension angles are associated with negative joint angle measures.

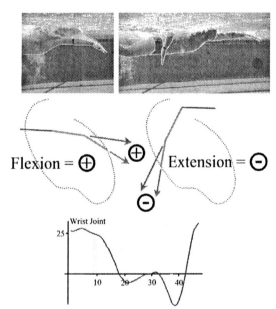

Flexion = ⊕   Extension = ⊖

Figure 18-9. The wrist joint angle curve for a swimming stroke.

Ankle Joint

Ankle joint angle measures are expressed with respect to the neutral position of the foot, where zero degrees flexion occurs when the foot segment forms a right angle with the shank segment. The ankle joint angle is therefore measured as the angle formed between the *shank segment perpendicular vector* (shown as the solid arrow below) and the foot segment vector.

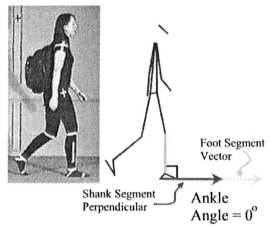

Foot Segment Vector

Shank Segment Perpendicular

Ankle Angle = 0°

Figure 18-10. An ankle joint angle measure for a walking motion.

Movement of the ankle joint beyond the neutral position towards a "pointed toe" position is termed *plantar* flexion. An illustration of ankle plantar flexion is shown below. Because the ankle is extended, the foot segment vector is aimed below the line of the shank segment perpendicular vector.

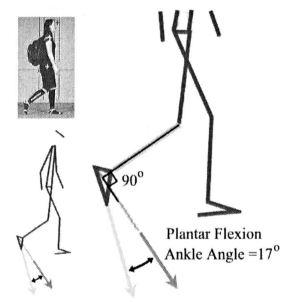

90°

Plantar Flexion
Ankle Angle = 17°

Figure 18-11. An example of plantar flexion of the ankle joint.

Flexion of the ankle joint beyond the neutral position is termed *dorsiflexion.* The figure below shows the ankle joint angle during the latter portion of the stance phase in gait. At the instant shown, the foot is dorsiflexed at an angle of -23°.

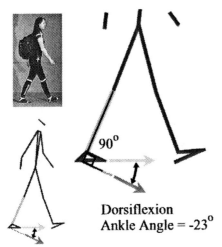

Figure 18-12. An example of dorsiflexion of the ankle joint.

Ball and Socket Joints

A hinge joint can be rotated about a single axis. Thus, if the upper arm is held fixed, the elbow joint allows the forearm segment to be moved only within a fixed two-dimensional plane. In contrast, a ball and socket joint can be rotated about three different axes. If the trunk of the body is held fixed, the shoulder joint allows the upper arm segment to be moved within an extensive three-dimensional range of motion.

Sagital Plane

Frontal Plane

Transverse Plane

Figure 18-13. Three planes of motion for the shoulder joint are illustrated by a standing long jump, cartwheel and Frisbee throw.

Figure 18-13 shows three examples of shoulder joint movement. The upper portion of the figure shows the arm motion used during a standing long jump. The middle portion of the figure shows the arm motion used during a cartwheel. Finally, the lower portion of the figure shows a Frisbee throw arm motion. Note that each of these shoulder motions takes place within a different plane of motion for the body.

The three movements shown in the figure all involve relatively simple shoulder joint actions. In each case, there is minimal trunk motion, while the upper arm moves primarily within a traditional plane. The wide variety of possible shoulder joint angles can be objectively defined through measures made with respect to the 3D reference frame shown in the figure below. Note that the reference frame is aligned with the body's position, with the X-axis aimed forward, the Y-axis aimed to the performer's left, and the Z-axis aimed upward.

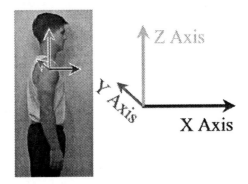

Figure 18-14. The traditional XYZ reference frame for motion analysis.

Given this reference frame, any shoulder joint position can be defined through a combination of three joint angle measures:

Shoulder horizontal abduction / adduction (ab/adduction)
Shoulder internal / external rotation
Shoulder ab/adduction

Horizontal Ab/Adduction

Upper arm motion in the XY plane is defined as shoulder horizontal abduction / adduction (ab/adduction). Zero degrees horizontal ab/adduction occurs when the upper arm is extended directly to the side. Horizontal abduction angles occur when the upper arm is held in a position behind the frontal plane of the body. Horizontal adduction angles occur when the upper arm is held in a position in front of the frontal plane of the body.

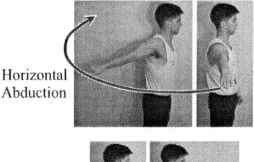

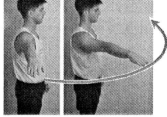

Figure 18-15. Shoulder horizontal abduction and adduction angles.

Horizontal ab/adduction measures are most easily visualized when illustrated with a person in an upright position and with the upper arm moving purely in the transverse plane.

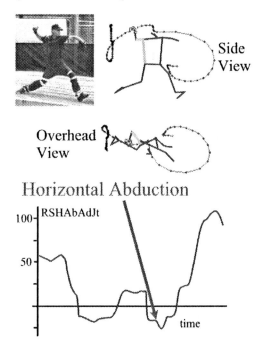

Figure 18-16. The shoulder joint horizontal Ab/Adduction joint angle curve. The highlighted negative value is associated with horizontal abduction.

Figure 18-16 shows an example of horizontal abduction for a pitching motion. In this figure the shoulder joint angle is well isolated in the horizontal plane. As a result, the horizontal abduction angle is well approximated by the angle between the line of the shoulders and the line of the upper arm as seen in the overhead view.

The figure below shows a horizontal adduction angle from a moment later in the pitching motion. In this figure, the joint angle measure is more difficult to visualize because the body is not in an upright position, and the upper arm is not isolated within the transverse plane. Nevertheless the joint angle can be accurately measured by mathematically projecting the line of the upper arm and the line of the shoulders into the transverse plane of the body. The shoulder horizontal adduction angle is then measured as the angle between the projected shoulder and upper arm lines.

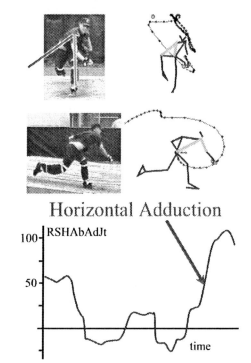

Figure 18-17. The shoulder joint horizontal Ab/Adduction joint angle curve. The highlighted positive value is associated with horizontal adduction.

Internal / External Rotation

Internal and external rotations of the shoulder are generated through rotations about the long axis of the upper arm. Zero degrees internal/external rotation occurs when the forearm is pointed in a forward direction while the upper arm is held to the side. External rotation is associated with "twisting" of the upper arm in the shoulder joint socket like that shown in figure A below. Internal rotation of the shoulder is associated with clockwise twisting of the right upper arm with respect to the shoulder joint (figure C).

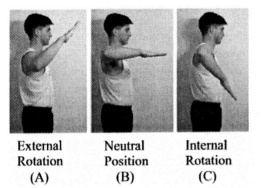

External Rotation (A) Neutral Position (B) Internal Rotation (C)

Figure 18-18. Shoulder internal and external rotation measurement conventions.

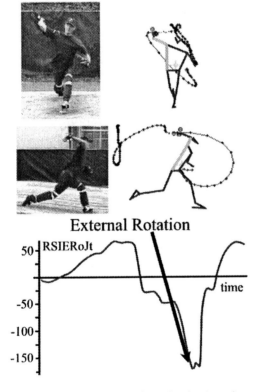

Figure 18-19. An illustration of maximal external rotation during a baseball pitching motion.

Extreme shoulder external rotation angles are often seen in baseball pitching motions. Figure 18-19 shows a skilled pitcher near the beginning of the action phase of a pitching motion. The external rotation angle of -160° allows the pitcher to develop the force of the pitch over an extensive range of motion.

Shoulder Abduction / Adduction

The shoulder ab/adduction angle is measured as the angle between the trunk long axis and the upper arm. Because this angle is measured in three dimensions, it is not associated with any single viewing plane. The figure below shows shoulder ab/adduction angle measures for a long jump and a cartwheel motion. Note that the measure of shoulder ab/adduction is independent of any internal / external rotation or horizontal ab/adduction angle of the shoulder. The shoulder ab/adduction angle is measured as simply the 3D angle that is formed between the upper arm segment vector and the trunk long axis.

Sagital Plane

Frontal Plane

Figure 18-20. Shoulder abduction and adduction as seen from the sagital and frontal planes of the body.

Joint Angles and the Global Reference

We have seen in Chapter 4 that the linear position of a body landmark point is always expressed with respect to a fixed XY or XYZ reference frame. Similarly, in Chapter 14, we defined the angular position of a body segment as the angle between the segment vector and the positive X-axis. The use of a fixed, global reference frame with measures of linear and angular position allows us to relate changes in position (velocity) and changes in velocity (acceleration) to the forces and torques that cause motion.

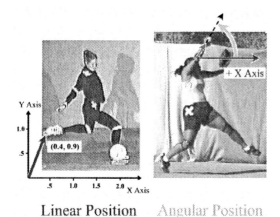

Figure 18-21. Measures of linear and angular position.

Measures of joint angle position, in contrast, are based upon *relative* measurements. For example, the measurement of an elbow joint angle is defined as the angle of the forearm *with respect to* the upper arm. The figure below shows two instances in time during the course of a softball pitch. Note that the elbow angles for both body positions are 70°.

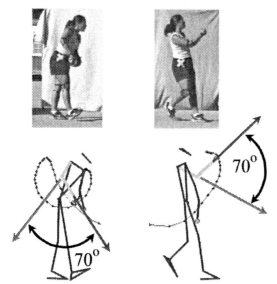

Figure 18-22. A joint angle measure of 70° for two different positions of the body.

The forearm *segment* angle, however, as measured with respect to the positive X-axis will be different for both of these positions. Thus, it is clear that joint angle measures are very different from the segment angles we discussed in Chapter 15. Similarly, joint angle rate of change (joint velocity) and segment angular velocity will also be very different for typical movements.

Because of these differences between joint angle and segment angle measurements, it is not possible to relate joint measures to the forces and torques that cause motion. Measures of the joint range of motion and the rate of change of joint position are nevertheless very important in the *kinematic level analysis* of movement because they objectively describe the joint motions of the body.

Joint Angle ROM

In forceful movements, a full range of motion is often associated with skillful performance. The range of motion (ROM) of a joint is measured as the change in joint angle that occurs during a given phase of a movement. For example, during the extended action phase of a soccer kick, the knee joint undergoes a range of motion of about -77°.

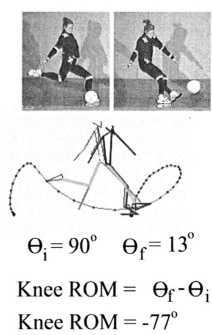

$$\Theta_i = 90^\circ \quad \Theta_f = 13^\circ$$

$$\text{Knee ROM} = \Theta_f - \Theta_i$$

$$\text{Knee ROM} = -77^\circ$$

Figure 18-23. A measure of knee joint range of motion (ROM) for the action phase of a soccer kick motion.

Note that the knee is flexed at a 90° angle at the beginning of the movement phase, and extends to a joint angle of 13° just after impact with the ball. The range of motion calculation is best visualized through inspection of the joint angle curve. The figure below shows the soccer kick stick figures and the joint angle curve for the range of motion in question.

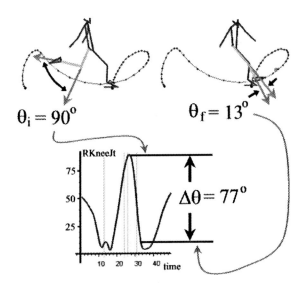

Figure 18-24. The calculation of joint range of motion from the data on a joint angle versus time curve.

The range of motion calculation is shown as the change in height of the joint angle curve for the time period of the extended action phase. The exact time period for the range of motion calculation is, to a certain extent, arbitrary. For the example shown above, the *extended* action phase has been defined as the traditional action phase (from end of backswing to the moment of ball impact) plus the frames of ball impact and one additional frame after ball impact. As a result, this extended range of motion contains part of the follow through phase.

In any biomechanical analysis project, it will be appropriate to compare joint range of motion measures across a range of participants as long as the criteria for comparison is held constant. Thus, we can use either the traditional action phase, or the extended action phase to compare range of motion for different performers.

Question 18-1:
The following figure shows the complete elbow joint angle curve for a skilled softball pitch. Would it be appropriate to use the smallest (θ_{min}) and largest (θ_{max}) elbow angles found in the full movement to define the elbow range of motion?

O A. Yes.
O B. No.

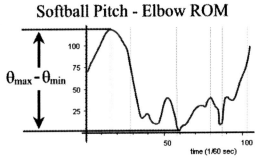

Figure 18-25. The elbow joint angle curve for a softball pitch.

Range of motion measures that are computed across arbitrary time periods in a movement may not yield meaningful information. The figure below shows that the θ_{max} - θ_{min} calculation provides information only on the preparatory phase of the pitching motion. While this calculation of elbow ROM is the largest found in the movement, it actually involves a portion of the movement that involves very low levels of force and speed.

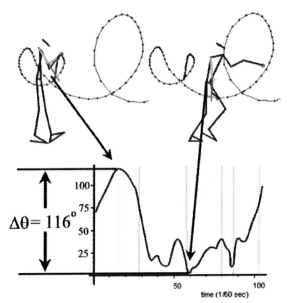

Figure 18-26. The calculation of elbow joint range of motion.

On the other hand, the figure below shows a much more meaningful ROM calculation for the softball pitch. This figure shows the elbow joint action generated during the forceful action phase of the pitch. The relatively small 32° ROM measure from the action phase is far more important than the large 116° angle computed during portions of the wind up motion. This example shows that joint range of motion measures are best taken for critical phases in the overall movement. Comparisons of joint ROM measures made across a variety of performers should focus upon these critical joint action measures and avoid comparisons of the non-critical aspects of the movement.

Elbow ROM - Action Phase

$\Delta\theta = 32^{\circ}$

Figure 18-27. The elbow joint range of motion for the action phase of a softball pitch motion.

Joint Angle Velocity

Joint range of motion measures provide information about the change in position of a joint. The *rate of change* of position of a joint, or the joint angle velocity (JtV) also provides critical information about human movement. Rapid joint actions typically involve both large range of motion measures and large joint angle velocity measures.

The equation used to calculate JtV is as follows:

$$JtV = \Delta\theta / \Delta t$$

Where:
$\Delta\theta$ is the change in joint angle over a specified time interval
Δt is the duration of the time interval

The figure below illustrates the calculation of a joint angle velocity measure. Because the knee joint undergoes a large change in joint angle over a short time interval, the JtV value will be large for this portion of the soccer kick knee motion.

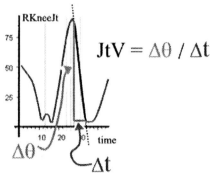

$$JtV = \Delta\theta / \Delta t$$

Figure 18-28. A graphical description of the rate of change of joint angle (JtV) measurement.

The joint angle velocity calculation procedure is the same as that involved in the calculation of linear velocity from linear position data. Thus, the slope of the joint angle curve provides information on the size of the JtV value.

The figure below shows the JtV curve for the soccer kicking motion. Note that the peak JtV value occurs very close to the moment of ball contact. Because the knee joint angle is changing from a high degree of flexion (90°) to a low value close to 0°, the change in knee joint angle is negative and the JtV curve peak occurs below the horizontal time axis. Note also that the JtV values are expressed in radians per second units.

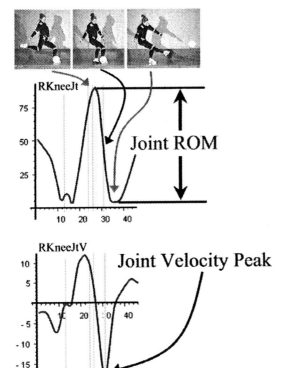

Figure 18-29. A comparison of the joint angle curve and the rate of change of joint angle curve.

Question 18-2:
The following figure shows the knee joint angle position curve for a soccer kick. The instant in time of the peak knee joint angle is indicated by the circle. What is the value of knee joint angle velocity at this moment?

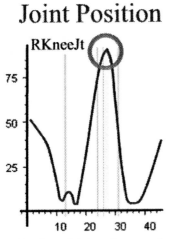

Figure 18-30. The knee joint angle curve for a soccer kick motion.

O A. The JtV is at a positive peak value at this moment.

O B. The JtV is zero at this moment

O C. The JtV is at a negative peak value at this moment.

The figure below shows both the joint position and joint angle velocity curves. Note that when the joint position curve is at a peak value, the slope of the curve must be zero, and as a result, the JtV value must also be zero.

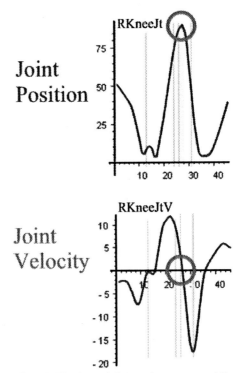

Figure 18-31. The knee joint angle curve, and the rate of change of joint angle curve for a soccer kick motion.

Large measures of joint angle velocity are often correlated with large joint angle ROM values. However, it is possible to have a large joint ROM measure associated with a relatively small JtV measure and vice versa. The figure below shows the early phase of a baseball pitching motion. Note that the pitcher's right elbow undergoes a relatively large joint angle change of 136° during the early part of the wind up motion. Note also that the joint angle velocity peak for this portion of the wind up is only -9 radians per second.

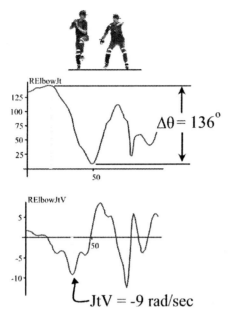

Figure 18-32. A comparison of a large joint angle range of motion measure and its associated rate of change of joint angle measurement.

Later in the pitching motion, the pitcher uses a much more explosive elbow action to generate force on the ball. The figure below shows that a high JtV measure can be associated with a relatively small joint ROM.

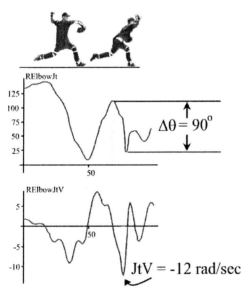

Figure 18-33. A comparison of a relatively small joint angle range of motion measure and its associated rate of change of joint angle measurement.

The very explosive elbow joint action just prior to ball release creates a relatively large joint angle velocity magnitude (-12 radians per second). The large JtV magnitude is generated during a phase of the movement that involves a joint ROM of only 90°. As a result, we see that JtV measures can supply additional insight, beyond that provided by ROM measures, in the analysis of a movement's joint actions.

Conclusions

Our discussion of joint angle measures is now complete. We have seen that human movement can be objectively defined through the use of joint angle, joint range of motion and joint angle velocity measures. In the next chapter, we will see how joint angle measures can be used to gain increased insight into the coordination of skillful human movement.

Answers to Chapter Questions

Question 18-1:
The following figure shows the complete elbow joint angle curve for a skilled softball pitch. Would it be appropriate to use the smallest (θ_{min}) and largest (θ_{max}) elbow angles found in the full movement to define the elbow range of motion?

O A. Yes.
O B. No.

The correct answer is No. Range of motion calculations should be computed for specific phases in a movement. For further details see the next section.

Question 18-2:
The following figure shows the knee joint angle position curve for a soccer kick. The instant in time of the peak knee joint angle is indicated by the circle. What iis the value of knee joint angle velocity at this moment?

O A. The JtV is at a positive peak value at this moment.
O B. The JtV is zero at this moment
O C. The JtV is at a negative peak value at this moment.

The correct answer is B. The rate of change of the knee joint angle is zero at the moment of peak joint angle.

Chapter 19: The Summation of Force Principle

Summation of Force

The goal of many throwing and kicking motions is to maximize the force that is delivered to a ball. In the case of a throwing motion, the end result is a very high hand velocity near the moment of ball release. Our challenge in this chapter will be to evaluate the *process* of human movement that generates the high-speed ball motion. We will see that skillful force development in a throw-like movement is a result of a well-coordinated sequence of joint actions that makes use of trunk rotation as well as shoulder, elbow and wrist joint actions.

Figure 19-1. Three examples of skillfully-timed arm motions.

The *summation of force principle* (Logan and McKinney, 1970) can be used to evaluate the coordination associated with many human movements. This principle states that the high speed generated at the distal end of a chain of body segments, such as the upper arm, forearm and hand in a throw, follows from a sequential development of force. The high levels of force that are generated by each element in the chain of segments are reflected by the peak angular and linear velocity values associated with the motion.

Tennis Serve: Angular Velocity Data

The tennis serve data shown below provides a clear example of the summation of force principle.

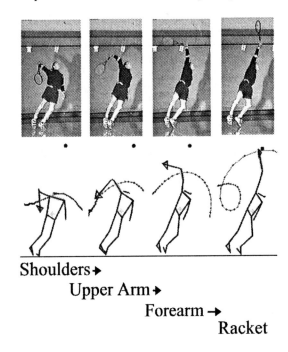

Shoulders →
Upper Arm →
Forearm →
Racket

Figure 19-2. An illustration of the whip-like motion employed within a tennis serve.

At the moment of impact with the ball, the speed of the tennis racket is a result of a well-coordinated sequence of joint actions. First the shoulder segment is rotated about the long axis of the trunk to assist in the racket motion forward. Second, the shoulder joint is extended to cause the upper arm to sweep upward and increase the speed of the racket. Third, the elbow is extended to cause the forearm segment to sweep upward and further increase the speed of the racket. Finally, the wrist joint is flexed to add a final pulse of speed to the racket motion.

The proximal to distal timing of the segmental motions produces a *whip-like* movement. The timing of the movement is critical. Skillful motion is often characterized by a proximal to distal sequence of velocity peaks. In contrast, an out of sequence series of segmental motions, especially in throwing and kicking motions, is often associated with less skillful motion.

The figure below shows the series of angular velocity peak values that occurred during the tennis serve motion. The angular velocity peak values have all been selected from the action phase of the motion (from backscratch to ball impact) only.

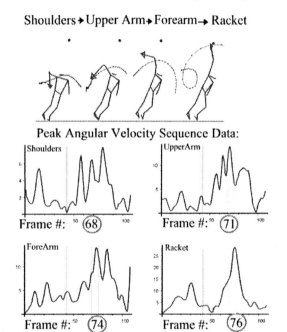

Peak Angular Velocity Sequence Data:

Figure 19-3. The timing of shoulder, upper arm, forearm and racket angular velocity peak values.

Note that the largest shoulder angular velocity that occurs during the action phase is generated at frame 68. The shoulder angular velocity curve shows that numerous peak values are generated during the course of the serve motion. However, the large shoulder angular velocity peak that occurred after impact is not considered in this analysis because it is not logically part of the action phase of the movement. Similarly, the shoulder peak values that preceded the backscratch event are not relevant to our analysis.

The largest upper arm angular velocity value occurs three frames after that of the shoulder at

frame 71. Similarly, the forearm angular velocity peak value occurs 3 frames after that of the upper arm at frame 74. Finally the racket angular velocity peak value occurs 2 frames after that of the forearm.

This sequence of velocity peaks provides a relatively simple way to quantify skill in a tennis serve or other throw-like motions. Our analysis shows that the high velocity value that occurs at the end of a kinetic chain of motion is derived from a carefully timed series of velocity peaks. In particular, the velocity peaks for the more distal segments occur after the peaks of the more proximal segments in the chain.

Tennis Serve: Linear Velocity Data

The summation of force principle can be studied with linear velocity data as well as segment angular velocity values. In fact, linear velocity measures can often provide data that is even easier to interpret. The figure below shows a *peak velocity sequence figure* for the tennis serve movement discussed above.

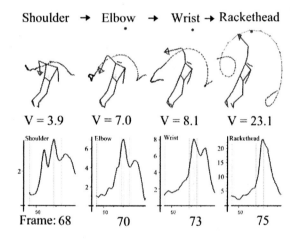

Figure 19-4. The timing of shoulder, elbow, wrist and rackethead peak velocity values.

The peak velocity sequence figure is carefully constructed to focus the reader's attention on only the most relevant information in the analysis. Thus, the figure shows only the relevant portions of the various velocity curves. In addition, the frame number sequence and the peak velocity values are shown in an easily read large font size.

The analysis data confirms that this participant is using a well-coordinated tennis serve motion. Note that the peak velocity frame numbers shown at the bottom of the figure follow the expected proximal to distal sequence. In addition, note that the linear velocity peak values increase steadily from left to right in the figure.

Movement Examples

The summation of force principle has clear applications to tennis serves, throwing and kicking motions. These movements rely upon whip-like motions in order to maximize the generation of speed. It is important for us to note that there are many other movements where the summation of force principle will not apply. For example, movements that tend to maximize force will not rely upon whip-like motions, but will instead make use of nearly simultaneous maximal velocities of the various body segments.

Figure 19-5. A comparison of throwing and striking motions.

Forceful Striking Motions

The figure below shows a peak velocity sequence analysis of a martial arts striking motion. This motion makes use of the development of simultaneous velocity peaks to cause maximal force production.

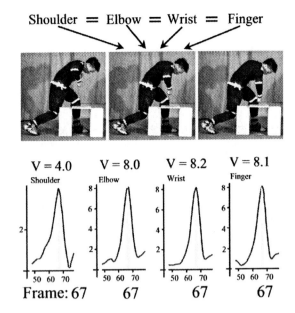

Figure 19-6. The timing of peak velocities for the shoulder, elbow, wrist and finger points.

The video image sequence portion of the figure shows three moments in time just prior to board contact. Only the middle video picture, showing frame 67, is relevant in the peak velocity sequence analysis. The lower portion of the figure shows that the linear velocity peak for the shoulder, elbow, wrist and finger all occur at the same frame number. It is also interesting to note that the elbow, wrist and finger peak velocity values are all nearly identical.

This martial arts striking motion shows that the summation of force principle clearly *does not* apply to all types of movements. However, we should note that the peak velocity sequence analysis we have used in this chapter can be used to study any multi-segment motion. The findings in a peak velocity sequence graphic can be used to compare a variety of performers for any given motion. The velocity sequence data of each performer can be compared to a "model technique" for evaluation purposes. This model technique velocity sequence pattern may be expected to be sequential (for whip-like movements), or simultaneous (for maximal force application). The criteria used to define model technique can be provided from a biomechanical database or, if information is limited, from the data on a single skilled performer.

Golf Drive

The golf drive provides an interesting example of a *non*-whip like movement. The figure below shows a point velocity sequence figure for a skilled golfer. Note that the peak point velocities for the shoulder and elbow occur at the same frame number. This simultaneous timing of the shoulder and elbow peaks is not consistent with the sequential joint action timing we have seen in a tennis serve. Further, the wrist peak velocity occurs only 1/60th second after that of the elbow. The delay between the elbow and wrist peaks in golf is considerably shorter than the 3/60th second delay seen in a tennis serve. The end result of the golf drive is similar to the tennis serve, however, as the club head reaches peak velocity just prior (1/60th second) to impact with the ball.

Shoulder = Elbow ≈ Wrist → Clubhead

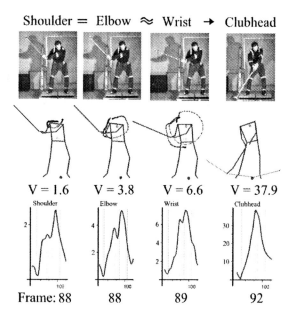

V = 1.6   V = 3.8   V = 6.6   V = 37.9

Frame: 88   88   89   92

Figure 19-7. The timing of the shoulder, elbow, wrist and clubhead velocity peaks for a golf drive motion.

The differences in timing for the tennis serve and golf drive movements are shown in the figure below. The peak velocity values for the shoulder, elbow, wrist and racket / club points are plotted on the vertical axis. The timing of each peak velocity value, expressed as a percentage of time within the action phase, is shown along the horizontal axis.

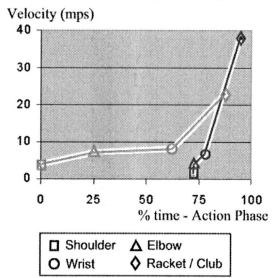

Tennis / Golf
Peak Velocity Timing

Figure 19-8. A comparison of the peak velocity timings employed in a tennis serve and a golf drive.

The tennis peak velocity timing curve (beginning at the left) shows that the final peak racket velocity is developed gradually, over nearly the full time duration of the action phase of the movement. In contrast, the golf peak velocity timing curve (beginning near the right side) shows that the final peak club velocity is developed over a brief portion of time late in the action phase. It is clear that the movement organization is very different for these two movements.

To understand the differences between the golf drive and tennis serve, we must consider the environmental constraints that govern the movements. The golf drive movement must be extremely accurate – a one-centimeter error in club location at the moment of impact can drastically alter the outcome of the swing. In contrast, because the tennis racket face is much larger than the club-face, a similar error in tennis racket location will produce only a minimal change in the serve outcome. In order to maximize the accuracy of the golf drive, skilled performers purposefully minimize the range of motion at the elbows. By "freezing" this degree of freedom, greater swing accuracy is achieved. However, if the elbow range of motion is minimized, its role in the sequential development of club head speed must also be minimal. As a result, a golf drive should not be expected to follow the same movement organization as a tennis serve or throwing motion.

As a result, we see that the traditional summation of force model should not be expected to fit all types of multi-segment motions. This observation is not at all surprising. In Chapter 2, we saw that a single ideal form model cannot be used as a guide for use with all people learning a given skill. Similarly, we should not expect to see that a single movement strategy will be effective for all multi-segment movements.

The summation of force model will nevertheless provide an interesting starting point for the analysis of multi-segment movements. Even if sequential timing is not found to be characteristic of skillful performance in a given movement, the use of peak velocity sequence figures can still be used to quantify the timing associated with model performance.

Conclusions

Our discussion of the summation of force principle is now complete. We have seen that a peak velocity sequence analysis can be used to study a wide variety of movements. For throwing, kicking and other "whip-like" movements, we can expect to see a sequential development of velocity peaks in the movement. For movements that involve maximal force production we can expect to see nearly simultaneous velocity peaks in the movement. Finally, for movements that demand high levels of accuracy, we can expect to see a non-sequential development of movement speed.

Part 5 – Angular Kinetics

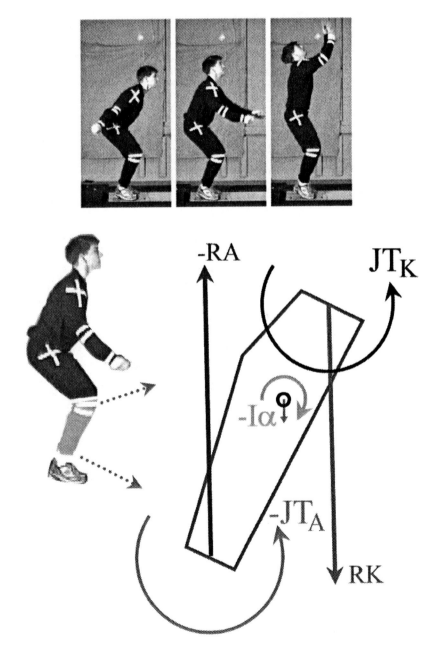

Introduction to Angular Kinetics

Our work in Part 3 – Linear Kinetics - allowed us to relate the *linear* acceleration of a body to the forces that cause human motion. Newton's second law of linear motion was used to compute unknown forces acting on the body from information on the mass of the body and the linear acceleration of the body's center of gravity:

$$F_{NET} = m\ A$$

In this equation, the acceleration term is known through a kinematic level analysis. The mass term represents the body's resistance to linear motion. Knowledge of the values for mass and acceleration allowed us to compute the external ground reaction forces that are associated with human motion.

Newton's second law of *angular* motion can be used to compute the unknown torques acting on a body given knowledge of the body's inherent resistance to angular motion and its angular acceleration. The linear and angular equations for Newton's second law are very similar to one another:

Linear Equation of Newton's Second Law:
$$F_{NET} = m\ A$$

Angular Equation of Newton's Second Law:
$$T_{NET} = I\ \alpha$$

The definitions of the terms in the angular equation are as follows:

- The T_{NET} term represents the net torque or "turning force" applied to the body or body segment.
- The term (I) is the moment of inertia, or the resistance to angular motion of the body or body segment. The moment of inertia value for a body is related to the overall mass of the body, the distribution of that mass within the body and the location of the axis of rotation of the body.
- Finally, the term (α) represents the angular acceleration of the body or body segment.

We will discuss the terms torque and moment of inertia in detail in this chapter. At the onset, we should recognize that the terms force and torque are analogous. We are already well aware that an applied net force will cause linear acceleration of a given body. Similarly, we will see in this chapter that an applied net torque will cause angular acceleration of a body. Further, the terms mass and moment of inertia are also analogous. An object with a large mass will experience less acceleration for a given applied force than an object with a smaller mass. Similarly, an object with a large resistance to angular motion (moment of inertia) will experience less angular acceleration for a given torque than an object with a lower moment of inertia value.

The linear equation for Newton's second law allows us to compute the external forces that are applied to a moving body. For example, information on the body's center of gravity acceleration and mass can be used to compute the ground reaction forces that act during the performance of a volleyball jump.

Ground Reaction Force

Figure 20-1. The ground reaction force generated during a vertical jumping motion.

In biomechanics, we are interested in the both the *internal* and *external forces* that cause human motion. The ground reaction forces shown in the figure above are *external forces*. These external forces are produced as a result of Newton's third law – the *action* of the leg drive against the floor causes a *reaction* that drives the body upward. Measures of ground reaction forces are important in our understanding of human movement, but knowledge of the *internal* muscular forces that generate movement are even more important. We will see in this chapter that Newton's second law of angular motion can be used to study the effects of the internal forces and joint actions that cause human motion.

Joint Torque Basics

Virtually all human movement originates through muscular contractions that cause changes in joint angle positions. These changes in joint angle also create angular acceleration of the associated body segments. For example, in a soccer kicking motion, a joint torque at the knee will cause a change in angular position of the right shank.

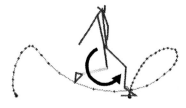

Knee Joint Torque

Figure 20-2. An illustration of the knee joint torque that causes the angular acceleration of the shank during a soccer kick motion.

The muscular actions at the knee joint generate a torque, or turning force, that gives the right shank a tendency to experience angular acceleration. The joint torque shown above is a measure of the net effect of all muscular forces acting at the knee joint.

For a soccer kick motion, the $F_{NET} = m\,A$ equation uses measures of linear acceleration of the body's CG and body mass to compute the ground reaction force components acting on the body. Similarly, $T_{NET} = I\,\alpha$ equation can be used along with information on the angular acceleration of the shank and moment of inertia of the shank to calculate the joint torque acting at the knee. Note: We will discuss the details of the joint torque analysis process in Chapter 23.

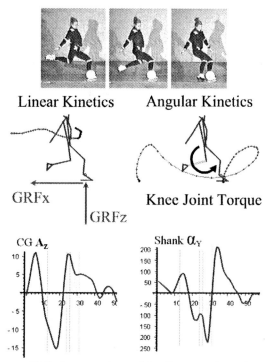

Figure 20-3. A comparison of the linear and angular acceleration values and their relation ship to measures of force and torque respectively.

The knee joint torque that is generated by the kicking leg will generate a high-speed foot motion. In contrast, the torques produced during the support phase of a vigorous jumping movement will be associated with lower foot and shank angular acceleration values, but the knee torque values will nevertheless be very large. In the case of a volleyball jump, the muscular contractions in the ankle, knee and hip joints create the very forceful leg drive that causes the jump. The size of each leg joint torque value will change as a function of time during the course of the jump. The figure below illustrates knee joint torque measures for a volleyball jump movement.

Knee Joint Torque

Figure 20-4. The knee joint torque values produced during a vertical jump.

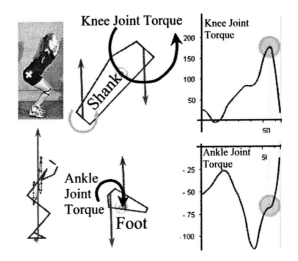

Figure 20-5. Measures of the knee and ankle joint torques produced during a vertical jumping motion.

The curved arrows in the figure represent two-dimensional measures of the knee joint torque vector at the illustrated instants in time. The radius of the circle indicates the size of the knee joint torque. Thus, the largest net muscular action at the knee is generated in the middle picture and the smallest torque is shown in the right-most picture.

The arrowhead on the curved line indicates the direction of the illustrated joint torque vector. All three of the joint torque vectors show that the muscular actions at the knee tend to produce counter-clockwise motion of the shank with respect to the thigh. As a result, the knee is being forcefully extended in each picture.

The KAPro software includes a special program that is designed to illustrate the leg joint torque values that are produced in many human movements. The JtCalc software can be used to analyze the joint torques and ground reaction forces for running, leaping, and jumping motions. The figure below shows information from a typical JtCalc analysis of a vertical jump. Note that the joint torque values for the ankle and knee can be plotted as a function of time, just like the measures of velocity and force that we have seen in prior chapters.

Analysis data, like that shown in the figure above, allow us to evaluate the size and timing of peak joint torque values for the ankle, knee and hip joints during skillful human movement. This type of information can increase the depth of information in the biomechanical database associated with a variety of skills.

One of the most interesting applications of joint torque analysis is in the area of strength training equipment design. Information on the joint torques generated in model technique can be used as a template in the design of highly specific strength training devices. Given devices that mimic the joint torques that are used in skillful human movement, but with variable levels of overload, we can expect that the specificity of strength training programs can be improved.

The figure below shows a breaststroke strength-training device that mimics the hydrodynamic resistance experienced in swimming. Because the joint torques generated during the training motion are similar to the joint torques created in normal swimming, we can expect that the strength gains stimulated by the device will help to create a more powerful arm pull.

Breaststroke Strength Training

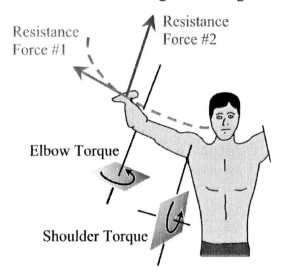

Figure 20-6. The elbow and shoulder joint torques employed in a breaststroke strength training motion.

In summary, we see that an understanding of joint torques will provide valuable information for use in the design of instructional and training programs for a variety of movement tasks. A foundation discussion of the basics of torque calculation is presented in the next section.

Torque Calculation Basics

The calculation of the torque produced by the pull of a number of muscles acting at a joint can be relatively complex. However, the concept of the torque produced by a single force can be quite simple. If fact, most people have an intuitive understanding of torque. Consider the following example.

Example: Seesaw

Question 20-1:
A mother (weight 500 Newtons) takes a child (weight 250 Newtons) to the park to play on a seesaw. The child sits on the right side of the seesaw, 2 meters from the pivot point, as shown in the following figure.

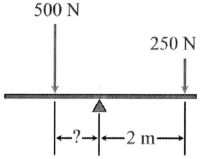

Figure 20-7. A balanced seesaw calculation problem.

Where should the mother sit to allow the seesaw to balance evenly?

O A. 2 meters to the left of the pivot point
O B. 1 meter to the left of the pivot point

Because the parent's weight is twice as large as the child's, she must sit closer to the pivot point to achieve a balanced weight distribution. We should note that the determination of the right place to sit for the parent is very important in both a practical and theoretical sense. For example, if the parent selects the wrong place to sit down, the child could experience projectile motion!

Projectile Motion!

Figure 20-8. A possible result of an unbalanced system of applied torques.

Technically, a torque describes the turning effect produced by an eccentric force (off center force) or force couple. The term *moment* is often used synonymously with the term torque. The equation used to calculate the moment of a force (or the torque produced by a force) is as follows:

$$M = F\ D_P$$

Where:
F is the applied force
D_P = lever arm

Note: The lever arm is equal to the perpendicular distance between the line of action of the force and the pivot point.

For our parent / child seesaw example, the moment produced by the child is:

$M = F\ D_P$

F = -250 Newtons
D_P = 2 meters

M = -250 * 2
M = -500 Newton-meters

Note that the negative sign for the moment (or torque) vector indicates that the turning force will produce clockwise motion.

For the parent, the moment calculation is as follows:

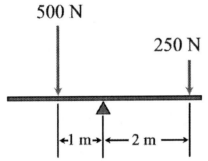

500 N

250 N

|◄1 m►|◄── 2 m ──►|

Figure 20-9. A balanced system of applied toques.

$M = F\ D_P$

F = -500 Newtons
D_P = -1 meters

M = -500 * -1
M = 500 Newton-meters

Note that the sign of the lever arm term for the parent's force is negative because the distance is measured to the left of the pivot point. The positive sign associated with the moment vector indicates that the parent's torque will tend to produce counter-clockwise motion.

Because the torque for the parent is +500 Nm and the torque for the child is –500 Nm, the net torque applied to the seesaw will be zero and there will be no tendency for the seesaw to experience angular acceleration:

$T_{NET} = I\ \alpha$
$T_{CHILD} + T_{PARENT} = I * \alpha$
(-500) + (+500) = I * \alpha
$0 = I * \alpha$

If the product of (I) and α equals zero, and (I) is non-zero, α must be equal zero. We will consider more detailed examples of torque calculations in the next chapter of Part 5.

Eccentric Force

An *eccentric* force is an "off-center" force, or a force that does not project through the center of gravity of an object. If an eccentric force is applied to a body, it will experience both translation *and* rotation. The figure below shows an overhead view of three forces applied to a textbook. Figure A shows a force that is directed straight through the center of gravity point of the book. This force causes the book to translate straight to the right. Figure B shows an eccentric force that is directed above the book center of gravity. This force causes the book to translate to the right and rotate clockwise. Finally, figure C shows an eccentric force that causes translation and counter-clockwise rotation.

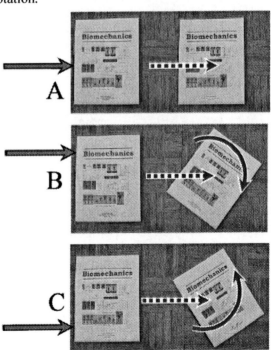

Figure 20-10. The effect of an applied eccentric force is shown in parts B and C above.

Eccentric forces are used in many athletic events where angular motion is important. For example, the performance of a back somersault must involve eccentric ground reaction forces in order to generate the angular acceleration needed to accomplish the movement. The figure below shows a series of ground reaction forces that are generated prior to take off in a back somersault. Note that the line of action of each ground reaction force falls in front of the body's center of gravity. As a result, each force generates a clockwise torque on the body and helps to generate the body's backward rotation. This movement presents the performer with a difficult challenge. His ground reaction force must create both backward rotation and a sufficiently large vertical thrust to propel him into the air for a long time period.

Back Somersault
Eccentric Ground Reaction Forces

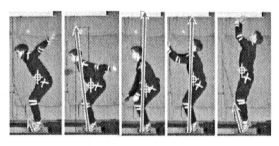

⬧ Center of Gravity Location

⟶ Ground Reaction Force

Figure 20-11. Eccentric ground reaction forces and a back somersault motion.

It should be noted that the term "eccentric" in our above discussions refers to "off-center" forces. The term "eccentric" is also used to denote psychologically "off-center" individuals, such as eccentric millionaires. However, the term "eccentric", when used to define a muscular contraction, takes on a different meaning, as it refers to a lengthening muscular contraction.

Force Couples and Lever Systems

The use of eccentric forces to cause angular motion is so common place that a number of "every day" terms are used to describe their effect. The following sections describe the relationships between eccentric forces, force couples and lever systems.

Force Couple

Any single eccentric force will produce rotation and translation. A combination of two eccentric forces, when properly arranged, will produce a *force couple*. A force couple will produce pure rotation, with no translation at all. The figure below shows an overhead view of a book that is being rotated by two eccentric forces. Because each force is equal in size, opposite in direction, and equidistant from the center of gravity of the book, a pure rotation is produced.

Figure 20-12. The effect of a force couple.

Levers

The effect of an eccentric force is a function of the lever arm system that is involved. The lever system associated with an eccentric force is determined by three factors: 1) the location of the fulcrum or pivot point, 2) the location of the resistance force, and 3) the location of the applied force. The following examples define the arrangement of first, second and third-class levers.

A first-class lever exists whenever the pivot point is located between the resistance force and the applied force. A seesaw and a crowbar are examples of first-class levers.

Resistance Force

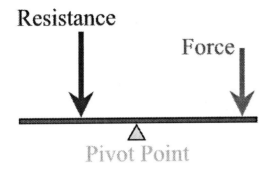

Pivot Point

Resistance Force

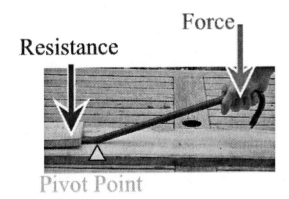

Pivot Point

Figure 20-13. Examples of a first class lever system.

A first-class lever can be used to "magnify" force when the lever arm distance between the pivot point and the applied force is greater than the lever arm distance for the resistance. This is the case with the crowbar shown above. The long lever arm of the applied force allows a relatively small applied-force to generate a force large enough to pry out a nail at the end of the lever.

A first-class lever can be used to "magnify" speed when the lever arm distance between the pivot point and the applied force is smaller than the lever arm distance for the resistance. This is the case with the "test your strength" attractions at amusement parks. Patrons are asked to use a large hammer to hit a lever at the foot of a tall column. When the lever is hit, a weight is propelled up the column. A very strong impact will cause the weight to ring a bell at the top of the column. For this apparatus, the short lever arm of the applied force allows a relatively large force to generate a high speed of motion of the resistance.

Test Your Strength

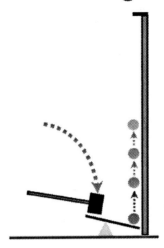

Figure 20-14. An amusement park "test your strength" apparatus is an example of a first class lever system that increases speed.

A second-class lever exists whenever the resistance force is located between the pivot point and the applied force. A wheel-barrow provides a good example of a second class lever system.

Resistance Force

Pivot Point

Force

Resistance

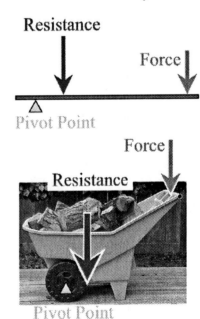

Pivot Point

Figure 20-15. Examples of a second class lever system.

Because the force lever arm must always be longer than the resistance lever, a second-class lever allows magnification of force only.

A third-class lever exists whenever the applied force is located between the pivot point and the resistance force.

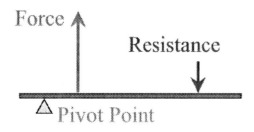

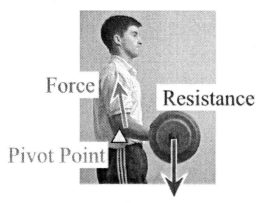

Figure 20-16. Examples of a third class lever system.

The leverage associated with a third-class lever allows relatively large forces to generate high speeds of motion. It is interesting to note that the human body is a system of third-class levers. Figure 20-16 above shows the leverage associated with a barbell curl exercise.

Because the point of attachment of the muscle is close to the axis of rotation of the elbow joint, a large muscular force is needed to overcome a relatively small resistance force. The trade-off for this arrangement is that it supports the potential for very high speeds of motion. With typical human joints, a relatively small change in length of the muscles at the joint can result in a rapid movement of the segment end point. This "design feature" of the human body is certainly not arbitrary. It appears that, in the evolution of mankind and womankind, the importance of a rapid retreat from predators had a strong influence on the "survival of the fittest" process.

Moment of Inertia

The eccentric forces that are applied at the joints of the human body tend to produce angular acceleration. We have mentioned above that the degree of angular acceleration caused by an applied torque will be related to the moment of inertia value for the body:

Moment of Inertia

$$T_{NET} = I \alpha$$

For the movement of many objects, the size of the moment of inertia value can be easily "felt" and understood. Consider the motion of a baseball batting swing. The figure below shows an 0.82 kg baseball bat. Note that the hands are positioned at the bottom of the handle, as would be done on a normal swing.

Figure 20-17. A baseball bat with a "normal" grip.

The moment of inertia of the bat can be "felt" by the batter when the swing is performed. To test your intuitive knowledge of the moment of inertia concept, answer the following question.

Question 20-2:
Imagine that the batter's grip on the bat changes to a "choked-up" position, as shown in the following figure.

Figure 20-18. A choked-up grip on a baseball bat.

How will the resistance to angular motion of the bat change as a result of this new grip?

O A. There will be no change in the resistance of the swinging motion because the mass of the bat does not change.
O B. The choked-up grip will result in a reduction in the resistance to angular motion for the bat.
O C. The choked-up grip will result in an increase in the resistance to angular motion for the bat.

If you have any experience with "America's pastime" you will know that "choking-up" on the bat will reduce the bat's resistance to angular motion and make it easier for you to swing the bat quickly. If you have no experience with batting, try the following experiment:

Borrow a baseball bat, hold the bat by the handle and use your wrists to swing the bat along a circular arc. Feel the resistance of the bat as you increase the angular velocity of the bat. Now switch your grip so that your hands are positioned near the "fat end" of the bat as shown in figure B. Again, swing the bat through a circular motion and note that the resistance to angular motion is greatly reduced.

Bat Grip Differences

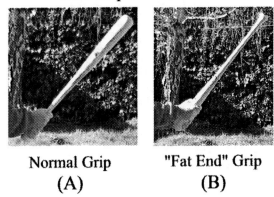

Normal Grip   "Fat End" Grip
(A)   (B)

Figure 20-19. A comparison of a "normal" and a "fat end" grip on a baseball bat.

The specific moment of inertia value of any object is a function of both the body mass and the distribution of that mass with respect to the axis of rotation. When a baseball bat is held normally, a large percentage of the bat mass is positioned far from the axis of rotation. This will cause a relatively high resistance to angular motion. When a baseball bat is held by the "fat end" and rotated, a large percentage of the bat mass is positioned close to the axis of rotation. This will cause a relatively low resistance to angular motion. Thus we see that while a given object can have only one value for mass, it can have a wide range of moment of inertia values.

To simplify our discussion of moment of inertia, let's now consider the example of a single *point* mass. Because a point mass has all of its mass concentrated at a single location, it is very easy to work with mathematically. The calculation of moment of inertia for a point mass is determined by the following equation:

$I = m R^2$

Where:
I - is the moment of inertia value
m – is the mass of the point mass
R – is the radius length between the point mass and the axis of rotation.

The figure below shows a metal sphere on the end of a rod of length "R". This sphere is being rotated in a circular motion. For the purpose of this example, we will imagine that the rod is "weightless" and, as a result, has no influence on the moment of inertia of the sphere and rod motion.

$$I = m R^2$$

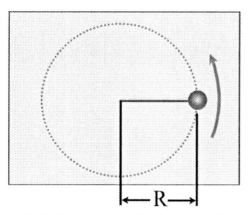

Figure 20-20. The moment of inertia equation for a point mass.

The $I = m R^2$ equation will yield an exactly correct value if the sphere on the end of the rod is infinitely small (that is, if it is a point mass, where a point is infinitely small). The moment of inertia value for a "small" sphere's motion, while not exact, will still be well approximated by this equation. Thus, the resistance to angular motion of this rod/sphere object will increase linearly with the mass of the sphere. Greater masses will involve greater resistance to angular motion. However, the radius (R) term will very dramatically influence the moment of inertia value. Because the moment of inertia size is related to the *square* of the radius term, when the length of the rod is doubled, the value for (I) will quadruple. As a result, we see that the value of the moment of inertia of an object is very sensitive to the distribution of the mass with respect to the axis of rotation.

Question 20-3:
A small, spring driven, "grandfather clock" (see figure 20-21) is running consistently fast. The clock pendulum has an adjustment screw that allows the pendulum bob to be moved further down or further up along the length of the pendulum.

How should you adjust the pendulum to make the clock run slower?

O A. The pendulum bob should be moved further down the length of the pendulum to make the pendulum longer.
O B. The pendulum bob should be moved further up along the length of the pendulum to make the pendulum shorter.

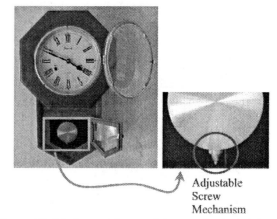

Figure 20-21. A pendulum resistance adjustment for a grandfather clock.

Moment of Inertia – Rigid Body

Most objects involved in biomechanical analysis projects cannot be approximated by a point mass on the end of a weightless rod. However, a solid object like a baseball bat can be thought of as a collection of point masses, distributed at a variety of radius lengths from the bat handle. Thus, the moment of inertia for the bat can be approximated by the sum of the individual point masses:

$$I_{BAT} = \sum m_i R_i^2$$

The figure below shows one mass element of the bat and it's radius length. The moment of inertia for this single mass element is equal to the product ($m_i * R_i^2$). The moment of inertia of the complete bat is approximately equal to the sum of all of the point mass inertia values.

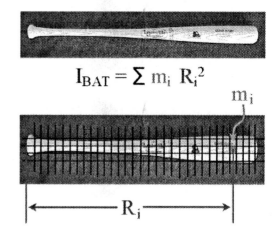

$$I_{BAT} = \sum m_i R_i^2$$

Figure 20-22. An illustration of the moment of inertia calculation for the distributed mass in a baseball bat.

If the bat is swung by the handle end, a large number of mass elements with long R values will be added into the sum total moment of inertia value. If the bat is swung by the fat end instead, the moment of inertia value must decrease because many of the bat mass elements will have small R values. Under this circumstance, note that the mass of the bat does not change, but the resistance to angular motion must change considerably.

We have noted before that the terms for mass and moment of inertia are analogous in the following equations:

$$\mathbf{F}_{NET} = m\,\mathbf{A}$$
$$\mathbf{T}_{NET} = I\,\alpha$$

Note, however, that while mass (m) is unique for a given body, (I) is dependent upon the shape of the body and the location of the axis of rotation. Thus, the moment of inertia of a given rigid body cannot be determined without information on the location of the axis of rotation.

Moment of Inertia – Human Body

A single rigid body, by definition, cannot change its shape. On the other hand, the human body, even when modeled as a collection of rigid bodies connected by hinge and ball and socket joints, can change its shape considerably. The variability in the human body's resistance to angular motion is well illustrated by performers in gymnastics and diving. The degree of difficulty associated with a dive or floor exercise somersault is directly related to the "position" of the body. A somersault in tuck position involves the least resistance to angular motion and is given the lowest weight in performance scoring systems.

A somersault in pike position is more difficult than a somersault in tuck because the legs and arms are extended further from the axis of rotation. Finally, a somersault in layout position is extremely difficult to accomplish because large portions of the arms and legs are very far from the axis of rotation.

Tuck Position

Pike Position

Layout Position

Figure 20-23. Three examples of the body positions used in back somersault motions.

Typical moment of inertia values for an adult male performer in the tuck, pike and layout body positions are shown below (Hay, 1993):

Icg = 3.5 kg m^2 for tuck position
Icg = 6.5 kg m^2 for pike position
Icg = 15 kg m^2 for layout

Note that a very large increase in the moment of inertia value occurs as the body position changes from tuck to pike and then to layout. This non-linear increase occurs because the radius terms for the hands and feet in the layout position are very large. When a large radius term is squared in the $I_{BAT} = \Sigma\, m_i\, R_i^2$ equation, a large contribution to the total moment of inertia value is produced.

Calculation of Moment of Inertia

As mentioned above, the moment of inertia of any rigid body can be approximated mathematically, given knowledge of the body shape and its axis of rotation.

$$I_{BODY} = \Sigma\, m_i\, R_i^2$$

The calculation process is relatively simple for uniformly shaped objects like rectangles and cylinders. However, the calculation process can become complex with irregularly shaped objects and for objects with non-uniform density. Unfortunately for us, the segments of the human body are neither regularly shaped nor of uniform density. As a result, accurate mathematical modeling of human segment moment of inertia values is relatively complex.

Under certain circumstances, an experimental procedure provides the easiest way to determine the moment of inertia of a body. The procedure involves suspending the body from a wire and allowing it to oscillate, like a pendulum. The time required for a full oscillation of the movement can be used to determine the moment of inertia value.

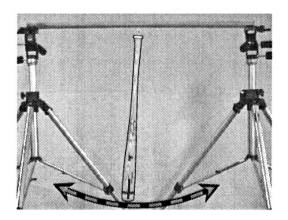

Figure 20-24. The moment inertia calculation for a baseball bat.

The moment of inertia equation is as follows:

$$I_O = WhT^2 / 4\pi^2$$

Where:
I_O – is the moment of inertia of the body about an axis through the point of suspension
W – is the weight of the body
H – is the distance between the center of gravity of the body and the suspension point
T – is the time period for a full oscillation of the pendulum

Figure 20-24 illustrates the moment of inertia measurement process for a baseball bat. Once the time of a full oscillation is determined, the moment of inertia for the bat, expressed with respect to the pendulum pivot point, can be easily calculated. Traditionally, moment of inertia values for commonly studied bodies are published in tables and expressed with respect to an axis through the body's center of mass.

Once the moment of inertia with respect to the center of mass point is known, the moment of inertia of the body expressed with respect to another parallel axis is given by the following formula:

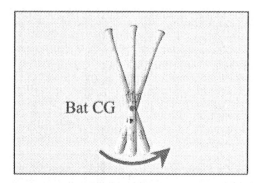

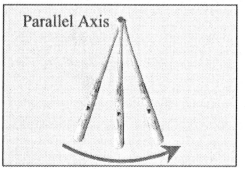

Figure 20-25. The moment of inertia for a bat will be change as the location of the axis of rotation changes.

$$I_O = I_{CG} + mh^2$$

Where:
I_O – the moment of inertia of the body with respect to an axis that is offset from the center of gravity position.
I_{CG} = the moment of inertia of the body with respect to an axis through the center of gravity.
m - the mass of the body
h^2 – the distance between the center of gravity axis and the offset axis of rotation.

Moment of Inertia for Body Segments

It is easy to visualize how the pendulum method can be used to determine moment of inertia values for baseball bats and other inanimate objects. In studies of human movement, however, we need to know the moment of inertia of individual body segments in order to calculate the joint torques that cause motion. For example, the figure below shows that the knee joint torque produced during a soccer kick is related to both the angular acceleration of the shank and foot as well as the moment of inertia of the shank – foot segment.

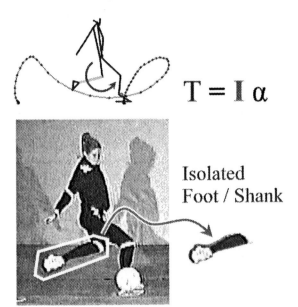

$$T = I\,\alpha$$

Isolated
Foot / Shank

Figure 20-26. A soccer kick motion.

To determine the moment of inertia of the shank and foot with the pendulum method, we need to physically separate those segments from the human body. While the determination of information on separate human body segments is important, most people agree that the separation of body segments from living subjects is taking the principle of reductionism one step too far.

The humane solution to this particular problem has been found through cadaver studies. Researchers have determined valuable biomechanical information on the human body by performing painstaking analysis of carefully dissected, frozen human cadavers. This research has resulted in tables of information on the human body that can be used to approximate the moment of inertia values for every segment of the human body. Our work in Chapter 23 will make use of this information in the calculation of the joint torque measures generated during human movement.

Conclusions

Our introduction to angular kinetics is now complete. The next chapter will focus upon the calculation of torque for a number of simple examples. The remaining chapters in Part 5 will consider torque and angular motion measures for a variety of human motions.

Reference

Hay, James G., 1993. The Biomechanics of Sports Techniques. Prentice-Hall Inc., Englewood Cliffs, New Jersey.

Answers to Chapter Questions

Question 20-1:
A mother (weight 500 Newtons) takes a child (weight 250 Newtons) to the park to play on a seesaw. The child sits on the right side of the seesaw, 2 meters from the pivot point, as shown in the following figure. Where should the mother sit to allow the seesaw to balance evenly?

O A. 2 meters to the left of the pivot point
O B. 1 meter to the left of the pivot point

The correct answer is B. If the parent sits 1 meters from the pivot point the seesaw will be balanced because the torque produced by both weight forces will be balanced.

Question 20-2:
Imagine that the batter's grip on the bat changes to a "choked-up" position, as shown in the following figure. How will the resistance to angular motion of the bat change as a result of this new grip?

O A. There will be no change in the resistance of the swinging motion because the mass of the bat does not change.
O B. The choked-up grip will result in a reduction in the resistance to angular motion for the bat.
O C. The choked-up grip will result in an increase in the resistance to angular motion for the bat.

The correct answer is B. Because the mass elements of the bat are closer to the axis of rotation, the resistance to angular motion will decrease.

Question 20-3:
A small, spring driven, "grandfather clock" is running consistently fast. The clock pendulum has an adjustment screw that allows the pendulum bob to be moved further down or further up along the length of the pendulum.

How should you adjust the pendulum to make the clock run slower?

O A. The pendulum bob should be moved further down the length of the pendulum to make the pendulum longer.

O B. The pendulum bob should be moved further up along the length of the pendulum to make the pendulum shorter.

The correct answer is A. A longer pendulum creates more resistance to angular motion and the clock will run slower.

Chapter 21: Torque Calculations

Torque Calculations

A moment (or torque) describes the turning effect produced by an eccentric force or couple. The "turning" effect of an eccentric force is influenced by two factors:

- The size of the force
- The length of the force lever arm

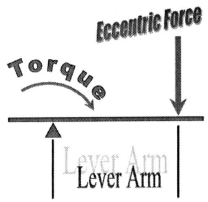

Figure 21-1. The force, lever arm and torque associated with the angular motion of a lever system.

We will consider a number of examples to clarify the role of these factors in the generation of torque. Our first example will consider the details of the parent / child seesaw problem we introduced in the last chapter.

Example: Parent / Child Seesaw

The challenge for this example will be to compute the parent weight lever arm that will result in a balanced system. The "given" information is detailed below:

Parent weight = 112 lbs = 500 Newtons
Child's weight = 56 lbs = 250 Newtons
The child sits 2 meters from seesaw pivot

To solve this problem, we must first compute the child's moment. Then we can determine the parent force lever arm that will create an equal and opposite moment.

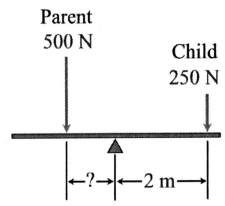

Figure 21-2. A seesaw torque calculation example.

The child's moment is computed from the following equation:

$$M = F \, D_P$$

Note that the D_P term represents the child force lever arm, and it is measured as the perpendicular distance between the line of action of the child force and the pivot point. Note: the line of the *perpendicular* distance must intersect the line of action of the force at a right angle.

The child's force is –250 Newtons (the sign is minus because the force is aimed in the negative Y direction), and the lever arm is 2 meters:

$$M_{CHILD} = F \, D_P$$
$$M_{CHILD} = -250 \, (2)$$
$$M_{CHILD} = -500 \text{ Newton-meters (clockwise)}$$

The negative value of the moment indicates that the child's force gives the seesaw a tendency to rotate in the clockwise direction. The right hand rule sets this clockwise rotation as negative.

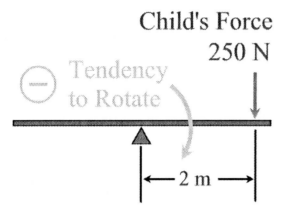

Child's Force
250 N

Tendency
to Rotate

← 2 m →

Figure 21-3. The torque produced by a single applied force.

The lever arm for the parent's force must be selected to assure that the seesaw will be "in balance". Thus, the seesaw net torque and angular acceleration must be zero. This information can be substituted into the equation for Newton's second law of angular motion:

$$T_{NET} = I \alpha$$

The vector equation for Newton's second law can be broken down into scalar form. Because we are considering angular motion in the XY plane only, the angular acceleration and torque vectors are isolated entirely along the Z-axis. As a result, only the Z-axis scalar equation is relevant to our discussion:

$$TZ_{NET} = I_{ZZ} \alpha_Z$$

Where:
TZ_{NET} is the net torque vector component that represents the tendency to rotate about the Z axis.

I_{ZZ} represents the moment of inertia value for the seesaw / parent / child "object" for rotation about the Z axis.

α_Z represents the see saw angular acceleration vector component about the Z axis.

Because all of our work with torque calculations in this chapter will be two-dimensional, we will use the $TZ_{NET} = I_{ZZ} \alpha_Z$ scalar equation for all of our example problems. We can also simplify the notation of the equation to "$T_{NET} = I \alpha$" as long as we remember that this scalar form of the equation is limited to use with two-dimensional problems.

Because the seesaw must remain balanced, its angular acceleration must be zero. If the angular acceleration of the seesaw is zero, the product of (I * α) must also be zero. As a result:

$$T_{NET} = 0$$

Only two moments are being applied to the seesaw. The sum of these two moments, or the net torque, must be zero:

$$M_{PARENT} + M_{CHILD} = 0$$

We know that the moment produced by the child is –500 n-m. We can substitute this value into the above equation and solve for the parent's torque:

$$M_{PARENT} - 500 = 0$$
$$M_{PARENT} = 500$$

We can re-express the parent's moment in terms of the parent's weight and the unknown lever arm length:

$$M_{PARENT} = F * D_P$$

The parent weight, times the D_P value must be equal to 500 n-m:

$$-500 (D_P) = 500$$

We can then use the above equation to solve for the D_P distance:

$$D_P = 500 / (-500)$$
$$D_P = -1$$

Thus, the parent must sit one meter to the left of the pivot point to generate a balanced system.

Unbalanced Moments

Let's now consider the case of a seesaw that has an unbalanced net torque. For this example, we will assume that the parent moves back to a position 1.5 meters to the left of the pivot point.

Parent
500 N

Child
250 N

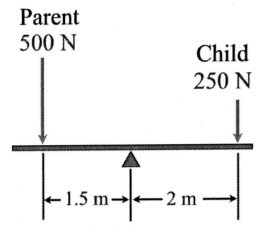

← 1.5 m → ← 2 m →

Figure 21-4. An unbalanced seesaw.

The parent torque is calculated as follows:

$$M_{PARENT} = F * D_P$$
$$M_{PARENT} = -500 (-1.5)$$
$$M_{PARENT} = 750$$

The child torque will be the same as before:

$$M_{CHILD} = -500$$

The net torque applied to the seesaw will be 250 Newton-meters:

$$T_{NET} = I \alpha$$
$$M_{PARENT} + M_{CHILD} = I \alpha$$
$$750 - 500 = I \alpha$$
$$250 = I \alpha$$

Because a non-zero net torque is applied to the seesaw, it will experience angular acceleration. If the seesaw moment of inertia value is known, this equation can be used to compute the seesaw angular acceleration.

Lever Arm and Torque

So far we have considered forces that are applied at right angles to the line of the seesaw. In this section, we will consider how an *angled* line of action of an applied force will influence its lever arm.

Question 21-1:
Suppose that a 100 N force is applied at the end of the seesaw but aimed straight at the pivot point. Will the seesaw rotate?

100 N

Figure 21-5. A seesaw with an applied non-eccentric force.

O A. Yes, the seesaw will rotate clockwise.
O B. No, the seesaw will not rotate.

The seesaw will not rotate because the lever arm (D_P) is zero for this force. Remember that the D_P term is a measure of the perpendicular distance between the line of action of the force and the pivot point. Because the line of action of the force goes through the pivot point, D_P is zero.

Let's now consider the case of a 50-Newton force acting at a 53.1° angle. Because this force acts at an angle, it will not produce the same torque as a 50-Newton force acting straight down.

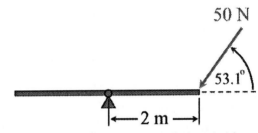

50 N
53.1°
← 2 m →

Figure 21-6. A seesaw with an applied angled force.

If we use reductionism, we can simplify the torque calculation. The following calculations determine the horizontal (F_X) and vertical (F_Y) components of the force.

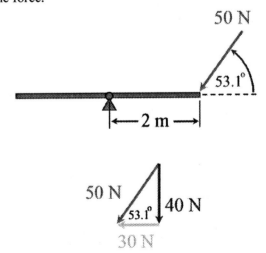

50 N
53.1°
← 2 m →

50 N
53.1°
40 N
30 N

Figure 21-7. The solution to an "angled force" seesaw torque problem.

$Cos (53.1) = F_X / 50$
$F_Y = 50 * Sin (53.1)$
$F_Y = 50 * .8$
$F_Y = 40\ N$

$Sin (53.1) = F_Y / 50$
$F_X = 50 * Cos (53.1)$
$F_X = 50 * .6$
$F_X\ = 30\ N$

The figure below shows the X and Y components of the 50-Newton force. Note that the X component of the force will not produce rotation because its line of action goes through the pivot point. The Y component of the force, however, will certainly cause rotation.

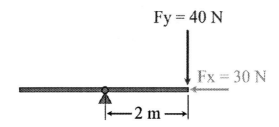

Figure 21-8. The horizontal and vertical components of an angled force.

As a result, the torque produced by the angled 50-Newton force is the same as that produced by a 40-Newton force acting straight down on the seesaw.

$M = F_Y * D_P$
$M = -40 * 2 = -80\ Newton\text{-}meters$

When we broke the 50-Newton force down into its vertical and horizontal components, we simplified the determination of the D_P term in the above equation. The distance perpendicular value is 2 meters for the F_Y component and zero for the F_X component.

We could calculate the torque produced by the full sized 50-Newton force as well, but the determination of the D_P value will be more difficult. The figure below shows the 50-Newton force and several measures of "the distance between the line of action of the force and the pivot point."

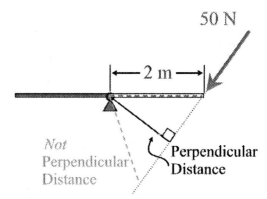

Figure 21-9. The perpendicular distance between a pivot point and the line of action of a force.

The finely dotted line shows the line of action of the action of the 50-Newton force. Note that many distances can be measured from points on this line to the pivot point. For example, both the lightly shaded and darkly shaded lines show distance measures between the line of action of the force to the pivot point. However, only the darkly shaded line shows the *perpendicular* distance between the line of action of the force and the pivot point.

It is possible to determine the exact length of the D_P distance shown in this figure through trigonometry. However, it is easier to determine the 50-Newton force vertical component and use that value along with the given 2-meter lever arm distance to calculate the torque.

Center of Gravity Calculation

We have discussed the concept of the body's center of gravity in prior chapters. In this section we will use our knowledge of torque calculation to determine the body's center of gravity mathematically. Our discussion will begin with a discussion of individual rigid bodies and move on to study the center of gravity location for moving human bodies.

The center of gravity of a body may be viewed as the *balancing point* - or the pivot position that will result in a zero net moment. Symmetrically shaped bodies are particularly easy to analyze. For example, when we balance a baton over a pivot point, we are determining the plane that includes the center of gravity point.

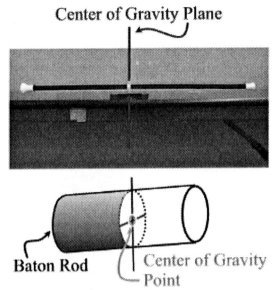

Figure 21-10. The center of gravity point for a baton.

A circular area within the baton is formed by the intersection of the plane directly above the pivot point and the baton itself. Because the mass of the baton rod is uniformly distributed about the baton long axis, the center of gravity point must fall at the center of the circular area of intersection.

Non-symmetrical objects must be balanced at three orthogonal positions to determine the center of gravity point location. Consider the rectangular solid shown below.

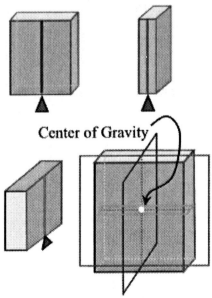

Figure 21-11. The center of gravity point for a rectangular solid.

When the box is held in a given position and balanced over a pivot point, the *balance plane* for that box position is defined. When this balancing exercise is conducted three times, three planes are defined that dissect each side of the box. These planes are illustrated by the lines and rectangles in the figure. The intersection of the planes that define the width and depth of the rectangular solid forms a vertical line that runs down the middle of the box. The intersection of the horizontal plane and the vertical line defines the center of gravity point.

It is important to note that the center of gravity point is a theoretical location that does not need to be located within the physical boundaries of an object. For example, the center of gravity of a hula-hoop is located at the center of the hoop, even though this particular spot is normally occupied by air. It is often convenient to envision a given object as embedded within a "weightless" sheet of glass. Because the envisioned glass has no mass, it will not influence the center of gravity balancing point location. Further, we can more easily see the center of gravity "balancing point" if we visualize the hula-hoop balanced on a pinpoint just underneath the "weightless" sheet of glass.

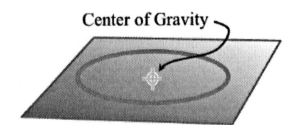

Figure 21-12. The center of gravity point for a hula-hoop.

Center of Gravity: Human Body

The calculation of the center of gravity location for the human body is more complex than that of a fixed shape rigid body. As the body's limbs change position, the center of gravity position will shift in the direction of the shifted body mass. The figure below shows that the body's CG location will shift upward when the arm's are raised overhead.

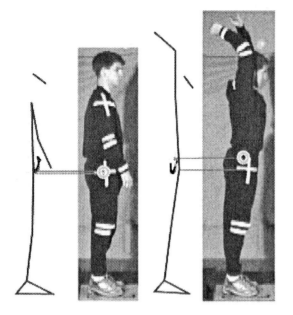

Figure 21-13. The shift in center of gravity location associated with a change in the distribution of mass of a body.

If we envision the body as being "frozen" in a fixed position, we can visualize how the exact center of gravity location could be determined with a simple balanced seesaw mechanism.

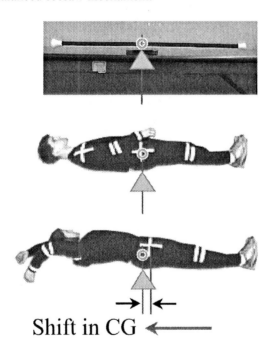

Shift in CG ←

Figure 21-14. The "balance point" for a baton and for two positions of a human body.

The position of the center of gravity for a given body with the arms up or down can be physically estimated by having the participant lie down on a well-balanced seesaw-like apparatus. Such an approach allows us to easily visualize the CG location, but it is awkward to physically shift the body back and forth on a board in an effort to find a balance point. A far easier approach, known as the *reaction board method* is described in the next section.

Reaction Board Method

We can make use of our knowledge of torque calculations to mathematically determine the center of gravity location for any fixed body position. A reaction board is a seesaw-like device that can be used to determine the body's CG position without any need for physically shifting the body to attain a balance. A sketch of a reaction board device is shown below.

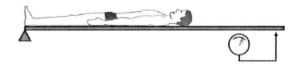

Figure 21-15. A reaction board for use with the measurement of a body's center of gravity location.

Note that there is a scale on the right hand side of the reaction board. Before a participant is asked to lie on the board, the scale must be zeroed to assure that the weight of the board does not influence the CG location calculation.

When a person lies down on the reaction board, with the bottom of the feet carefully positioned above the pivot point, the scale will register a "weight" reading. This weight reading can be used to compute the CG location for the participant. To understand the calculation procedure associated with reaction board readings, we will consider a number of simple examples.

Question 21-2:
Imagine that you are driving down a deserted mountain road and you find that a rockslide has deposited a boulder in the middle of the road. You need to move the boulder off the road by prying at it with a long rod. You have at your disposal, two rods. Rod A is 1 meter long and rod B is 3 meters long (see following figure). Which rod will make your job the easiest?

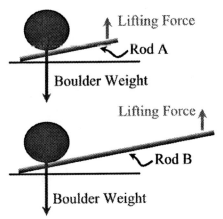

Figure 21-16. Two different lever systems and their effect on a required "lifting" force.

O A. Rod A will be easier.
O B. Rod B will be easier.

The last example shows that the lever arm of an applied force will greatly influence the force needed to overcome a given resistance force. Further, the applied force needed to balance the torque generated by a given resistance will depend upon the lever arm of the resistance. The figure below shows two examples of balanced second-class levers.

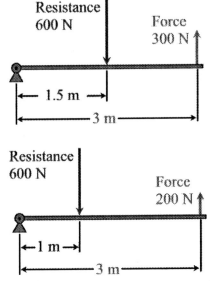

Figure 21-17. The influence of lever arm upon the effect of an applied force.

For both of the lever systems, the resistance force is 600 Newtons. Notice that when the lever arm for the resistance is reduced from 1.5 meters to 1.0 meters, a smaller applied force is needed to balance the lever system.

The upper lever shows that a 300 Newton force, acting over a 3 meter lever arm is needed to balance the effect of a 600 Newton force acting over a 1.5 meter lever arm. For this example the resistance torque is –900 n-m, and the applied force torque is +900 n-m:

$$M_{RESISTANCE} = R * D_P$$
$$M_{RESISTANCE} = (-600) * (1.5)$$
$$M_{RESISTANCE} = -900 \text{ n-m} \quad \text{(clockwise)}$$

$$M_{FORCE} = F * D_P$$
$$M_{FORCE} = (300) * (3)$$
$$M_{FORCE} = 900 \text{ n-m} \quad \text{(counter-clockwise)}$$

The lower lever shows that if the resistance force is moved closer to the pivot point, the needed applied force size drops to 200 Newtons. For this lever system the torque produced by the resistance is a negative 600 n-m. The 200 Newton applied force acts over a 3-meter lever arm and therefore generates a positive 600 n-m torque.

$$M_{RESISTANCE} = R * D_P$$
$$M_{RESISTANCE} = (-600) * (1)$$
$$M_{RESISTANCE} = -600 \text{ n-m} \quad \text{(clockwise)}$$

$$M_{FORCE} = F * D_P$$
$$M_{FORCE} = (200) * (3)$$
$$M_{FORCE} = 600 \text{ n-m} \quad \text{(counter-clockwise)}$$

This example shows that the applied force generated by the scale at the end of a reaction board will change as a function of the lever arm of the resistance force. On a reaction board, the lever arm of the resistance force is simply the height (with respect to the feet) of the body's center of gravity. It is important for us to note that the height of the center of gravity will be different for people with different builds.

Question 21-3:
Your challenge in this question will be to estimate the center of gravity height for two athletes. Both athletes have a body weight of 600 Newtons and a body height of 1.85 meters. Athlete A is a speed skater who has massive legs and narrow shoulders. Subject B is a gymnast who has massive shoulders and thin legs (see following figure). Which athlete will have the lowest center of gravity position?

Gymnast   Skater

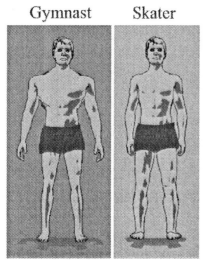

Figure 21-18. Two athletes with identical weight and height but different body mass distribution.

O A. The gymnast will have a lower center of gravity.
O B. The speed skater will have a lower center of gravity.

The last example shows that even though two people have the same body height and weight, their center of gravity position can be different. As a result, when our example's gymnast and skater are placed on a reaction board, the lever arm for their body weight force will be different. Further, the torque produced by their body weight will be different and the scale force measurement at the end of the reaction board must also be different.

The figure below shows reaction board force information for the speed skater and gymnast. In this example, the skater's CG height is 1.0 meters and the gymnast's CG height is 1.2 meters. The lever arm for the reaction board scale force is 3 meters for both athletes. Note that the force that is measured by the scale is different for the two athletes in spite of the fact that both athletes have the same body weight and body height. The speed skater has relatively more mass in his legs and therefore his body's CG point is closer to his feet. The gymnast has relatively more mass in the shoulders and therefore his body's CG point is further from his feet. Because of the differences in body mass distribution, each athlete generates a different torque about the pivot point.

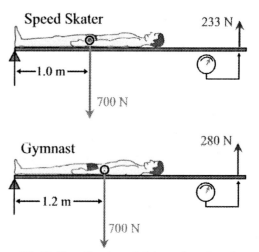

Figure 21-19. Reaction board data and center of gravity location.

The torque calculations for the speed skater are as follows:

$M_{BODYWGT} = W * D_P$
$M_{BODYWGT} = (-700) * (1)$
$M_{BODYWGT} = -700$ n-m   (clockwise)

$M_{FORCE} = F * D_P$
$M_{FORCE} = (233.3) * (3)$
$M_{FORCE} = 700$ n-m   (counter-clockwise)

Note that the force produced by the scale force generates a torque that is equal and opposite to the body weight torque. The torque calculations for the gymnast are as follows:

$M_{BODYWGT} = W * D_P$
$M_{BODYWGT} = (-700) * (1.2)$
$M_{BODYWGT} = -840$ n-m   (clockwise)

$M_{FORCE} = F * D_P$
$M_{FORCE} = (280) * (3)$
$M_{FORCE} = 840$ n-m   (counter-clockwise)

Again, the force from the scale must generate a torque that is equal and opposite to the body weight torque. This must be the case in order for the reaction board to remain in equilibrium.

Let's now consider an example where the reaction board reading is used to determine the *unknown* center of gravity height for a person. For this example, a 800 Newton (180 lb) man lies on a 3 meter long reaction board and produces an adjusted force on the scale of 250 Newtons (56 lbs.). What is the location for the man's center of gravity for this body position?

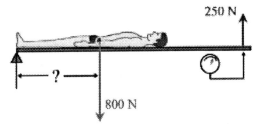

Figure 21-20. An example reaction board problem.

The calculation of the applied force torque is as follows:

$$M_{FORCE} = F * D_P$$
$$M_{FORCE} = 250 (3)$$
$$M_{FORCE} = +750 \text{ N-m}$$

The moment produced by the man's body weight force (which must go through the body's CG position) must be equal and opposite to the scale force moment. The moment produced by the body weight force is equal to body weight multiplied by the unknown distance to the center of gravity (D_{CG}):

$$M_{BODYWGT} = -800 (D_{CG})$$

Because the reaction board is in equilibrium, the net torque must be zero:

$$T_{NET} = 0$$
$$M_{FORCE} + M_{BODYWGT} = 0$$

We can use the above equation to solve for the unknown center of gravity height:

$$+750 + (-800 * D_{CG}) = 0$$
$$(-800 * D_{CG}) = -750$$
$$D_{CG} = -750 / -800$$
$$D_{CG} = .94 \text{ meters}$$

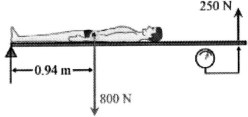

Figure 21-21. The solution to a reaction board CG calculation problem.

The last example shows that the reaction board method can be used to accurately determine the location of the body's center of gravity for any *fixed* position of the body. The next section will describe how the instantaneous location of the body's center of gravity can be computed from video data on human motion.

The Segmental Method

The *segmental method* uses information on each of the body's segments to calculate the center of gravity location for the full body. In order to apply this method to an analysis of human motion, a good approximation of the mass of each body segment and the location of the center of gravity for each body segment must be known. This information is available in the biomechanics research literature from anthropometrical and mathematical modeling research studies. We have mentioned above that cadaver studies can be used to determine the mass and moment of inertia of any body segment through a literal application of reductionism. Further, a small size reaction board can be used to determine the center of gravity location of any isolated body segment simply by following the procedures mentioned in the last section.

Table 21-1. Body segment weight and center of gravity location.

Segment	Weight	CG Location
Head	7.3	46.6
Trunk	50.7	38.0
Upper arm	2.6	51.3
Forearm	1.6	39.0
Hand	0.7	18.0
Thigh	10.3	37.2
Shank	4.3	37.1
Foot	1.5	44.9

Notes:
Weight is expressed as a percentage of total body weight. CG location is expressed as the percentage of the segment length distance, measured from the proximal end.

The information from cadaver and mathematical modeling studies are available in tables from numerous sources (i.e., Dempster, 1955, Clauser et al, 1969). The information in these tables is typically expressed in an abbreviated form. The table above is from Clauser et al, 1969.

The table shows the average information from a sample of adult male subjects. This information provides a reasonable approximation for use with other "typical" adult males and a fair approximation for use with typical adult females. More exact information for use with research on infants and children can be obtained through mathematical modeling software (Hatze, 1980).

The figure below illustrates the calculation procedure used to determine the body's CG location for a moment in a dance leap movement. As a first step, the segment end points for the body must be determined through video digitizing. Given the end point locations, the representative line for each segment in the body is defined.

37%   63%

Right Shank CG Location

Figure 21-23. The application of body segment parameter data to the analysis of the right shank CG location.

The center of gravity location for every body segment is determined by repeating the above procedure. The figure below shows the CG locations for all body segments as squares.

Figure 21-22. The body segments typically used in the calculation of center of gravity location.

The second step in the body center of gravity calculation is shown below. This figure shows the results of a calculation procedure for the right shank segment center of gravity location. Data from body segment parameter tables indicate that the right shank CG is located at a point along the line of the shank that is 37% of the distance between the knee and the ankle. The square on the shank line represents the shank center of gravity location.

Figure 21-24. An illustration of the center of gravity locations for all segments of the human body.

The weight for each body segment is also available in tables. For example, the shank weight is equal to 4.3% of the total body weight. The weight vectors for all body segments are shown in the figure below.

Figure 21-25. The calculation procedure for the X component of the center of gravity position.

Note that an XY reference frame is drawn along the lower edge of the figure and a pivot point is shown at the origin of the reference frame. Imagine that the performer's body is embedded in a "weightless" sheet of glass. This glass / human body object will have a tendency to rotate about the triangular pivot point. The moment produced by the body is equal to the sum of the moments of all of the body segments:

$$T_{BODY} = T_{RFOOT} + T_{RSHANK} + T_{RTHIGH} + \ldots + T_{LHAND}$$

Or:

$$T_{BODY} = \Sigma\, T_{SEGMENTS}$$

Where the torque produced by each body segment is equal to the product of the segment weight and the X-axis lever arm distance between the pivot point and the segment CG location.

The torque produced by the whole body can be expressed as follows:

$$T_{BODY} = WGT_{BODY} * D_{CG}$$

Where:
WGT_{BODY} = the body's weight
D_{CG} = the distance between the body's center of gravity location and the pivot point.
The figure below illustrates the whole body CG torque calculation.

Figure 21-26. The center of gravity location of the human body for a given instant in a dance leap movement.

In the whole body torque equation, the weight of the body is known, but the distance to the whole body center of gravity is unknown. A combination of the last two equations is used to solve for the unknown D_{CG} term:

$$WGT_{BODY} * D_{CG} = \Sigma\, T_{SEGMENTS}$$

In summary, the full body CG location can be computed by setting the moment produced by the full body weight times the D_{CG} distance equal to the sum of the moments produced by the various body segments. Because we know the weight and CG location of every body segment (from the above table), and we know the weight of the body, we can solve for the unknown X coordinate of the center of gravity location.

The Y coordinate of the body's center of gravity is computed with an identical procedure. The figure below shows the body, which we should again envision as embedded in a weightless sheet of glass, rotated 90° with respect to its original position. The sum of the moments about the pivot point for this figure will allow us to determine the Y coordinate of the body's center of gravity.

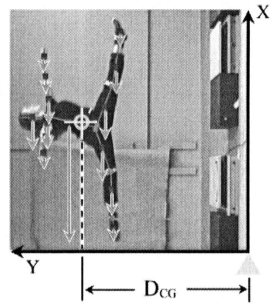

Figure 21-27. The calculation procedure for the Y component of the center of gravity position.

This procedure can be applied a third time, if necessary, to determine the Z coordinate of the body's CG point for a three-dimensional study. The KA software performs the calculations for the X, Y and Z coordinates of the center of gravity point over and over, for every frame in the image set. On a typical PC system, this calculation takes less than one tenth of a second.

Stability

The stability of a body is influenced by the height of the body CG and by the size of the base of support. More stable positions have low CG locations and wide base of support measures. For example, the wrestler shown below has adopted a wide stance to increase his stability.

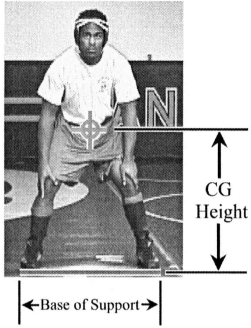

Figure 21-28. An example of a stable stance in wrestling.

To better understand the factors influencing the wrestler's stability, we will consider a specific example. Suppose a 200-Newton force is applied to the wrestler at shoulder level in an effort to tip him over. The turning effect of this applied force will depend upon its lever arm:

$$T_{FORCE} = F * D_P$$

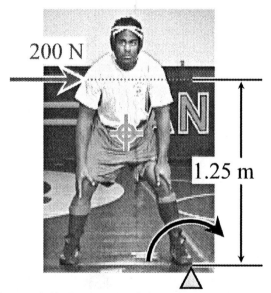

Figure 21-29. An analysis of the stability of a given body position.

The perpendicular distance between the line of action of the force and the pivot point is 1.25 meters. As a result, the torque of the force is 250 Newton-meters:

$$T_{FORCE} = F * D_P$$
$$T_{FORCE} = 200 * 1.25$$
$$T_{FORCE} = 250 \text{ N-m}$$

This applied force is not the only force acting on the body. The body weight force generates a torque that tends to keep the body stable. For the example shown below, imagine that the wrestler's body is embedded in a weightless sheet of glass and suspended over the triangular pivot point. The applied force gives the body a tendency to rotate clockwise. The weight force gives the body a tendency to rotate counter-clockwise.

Figure 21-30. The effect of the body weight torque on body stability.

If the wrestler's weight is 700 Newtons and the distance from the line of action of the weight force and the pivot point is 0.4 meters, the weight torque will be 280 Newton-meters:

$$T_{WGT} = F * D_P$$
$$T_{WGT} = 700 * 0.4$$
$$T_{WGT} = 280 \text{ N-m}$$

Because the body weight torque exceeds the torque from the applied force, the body will remain stable. Note that the relatively low position of the body causes the shoulder to be closer to the floor than when the body is standing erect. The reduction in the shoulder height causes a reduction in the torque produced by the applied force and makes the wrestler more stable. Further, because the wrestler's feet are spread apart, the lever arm for the body weight force is relatively large. This broad base of support increases the body weight torque and makes it more difficult to "tip" the wrestler over.

In many athletic movements, the goal is to produce a rapid change in position. For example, the figure below shows a swimmer just prior to the start of a race. Her starting position has been purposefully adjusted to cause the line of action of her body weight force to fall just barely within the base of support defined by her feet. When the race begins, a small forward motion will cause the swimmer to become "unstable" and begin to fall forward. Further, her "grab start" technique allows her to pull on the starting block to cause even greater acceleration of the body forward than would be possible through the pull of gravity alone.

Grab Start

Figure 21-31. The purposeful minimally stable position of a swimmer on the racing blocks.

Conclusions

Our discussion of torque calculations is now complete. We have seen that the size of a given torque is influenced by both the magnitude of the applied force and the length of the force lever arm.

Further, we have seen that torque calculation procedures can be used to determine the location of the center of gravity of the body. We will extend our knowledge of torque in the remaining chapters in Part 5. Chapter 22 will discuss the importance of torque and selected examples of angular motion. Chapter 23 will complete our discussion of torque with a discussion of the joint torques that generate human motion.

References

Clauser, C.E., McConville, J.T., and Young, J.W. (1969) *Weight, Volume and Center of Mass of segments of the human body.* (Report No. AMRL-TDR-72-5). Wright-Patterson Air Force Base, OH. Aerospace Medical Research Laboratory.

Dempster, W. T. (1955). *Space requirements of the seated operator.* (WADC Technical Report 55-159). Dayton, OH: Wright-Patterson Air Force Base.

Hatze, H. (1980). A mathematical model for the computational determination of parameter values of anthropomorphic segments. Journal of Biomechanics, 13, 833-843.

Answers to Chapter Questions

Question 21-1:
Suppose that a 100 N force is applied at the end of the seesaw but aimed straight at the pivot point. Will the seesaw rotate?

O A. Yes, the seesaw will rotate clockwise.
O B. No, the seesaw will not rotate.

The correct answer is B. Because the line of action of the force goes through the pivot point, the lever arm length is zero and there will be no tendency to rotate.

Question 21-2:
Imagine that you are driving down a deserted mountain road and you find that a rockslide has deposited a boulder in the middle of the road. You need to move the boulder off the road by prying at it with a long rod. You have at your disposal, two rods. Rod A is 1 meter long and rod B is 3 meters long (see following figure). Which rod will make your job the easiest?

O A. Rod A will be easier.
O B. Rod B will be easier.

The correct answer is B. The long lever arm will make it easier to lift the boulder.

Question 21-3:
Your challenge in this question will be to estimate the center of gravity height for two athletes. Both athletes have a body weight of 600 Newtons and a body height of 1.85 meters. Athlete A is a speed skater who has massive legs and narrow shoulders. Subject B is a gymnast who has massive shoulders and thin legs (see following figure). Which athlete will have the lowest center of gravity position?

O A. The gymnast will have a lower center of gravity.
O B. The speed skater will have a lower center of gravity.

The correct answer is B. The athlete's massive legs will keep his center of gravity relatively low in his body.

Chapter 22: Angular Motion

We discussed the general concept of torque in the last chapter. To simplify our initial discussions, we focused on the effects of torques applied to inanimate objects, such as seesaws and reaction boards. In this chapter we will apply our understanding of torque to the analysis of human movement. We will see that many human movements are organized with the express purpose of generating torque. We will also see that many linear forms of motion are organized with an inherent goal of minimizing the turning effects of applied forces.

Eccentric Force & Angular Motion

Movements that must generate large angular displacements typically rely upon large eccentric forces. The figure below shows the forces that are generated during a back somersault take-off movement. Note that the line of the action of the ground reaction force is directed in front of the body's CG location throughout the entire action phase. As a result, a torque is continuously applied to the body and the counter-clockwise angular acceleration needed to assure the completion of the somersault is generated.

Back Somersault
Eccentric Ground Reaction Forces

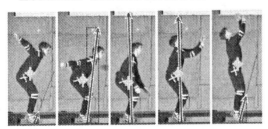

⬩ Center of Gravity Location
⟶ Ground Reaction Force

Figure 22-1. The eccentric ground reaction forces used during the take off phase for a back somersault.

A back somersault is a very challenging movement because it places three difficult constraints on the performer. First, the performer must generate enough vertical force to propel his body into the air long enough to allow completion of the somersault. Second, the performer must shift his body position back and adjust his force production to assure that the line of action of the ground reaction force falls in front of his center of gravity. Finally, the performer must reduce his resistance to angular motion while he is in the air by assuming a tuck body position.

The figure below shows two possible ways to generate force at a key instant during the take-off motion. Figure A shows the force generated during a successful back somersault motion. Figure B shows a technique that will cause pure translation of the body, and no rotation at all.

Tendency to Rotate ↰
Tendency to Translate ↑

A   B

Figure 22-2. The eccentric force (in figure A) produces a tendency for the body to rotate. The force in B goes through the center of gravity and produces no tendency to rotate.

Note that the horizontal component of the ground reaction force in figure A is aimed to the right. As a result, the ground reaction force vector is aimed upward and in front of the body's CG location. This eccentric force generates a counter-clockwise torque on the body. If the ground reaction force had been aimed towards the center of the body, as shown in figure B, the performer would have generated zero torque. If the line of action of the ground reaction force goes through the center of gravity point for the full take-off motion, the performer will not accomplish a somersault. He would simply jump up in the air and then land again on his feet with no change in his angular position. As a result, we see that skill in a back-somersault motion is dependent upon the performer's ability to control both the size and the *direction* of the ground reaction force.

Body Position and Linear Motion

Most movements are organized to assure that the body experiences very little angular displacement. Thus, the inherent goal of linear motion is to *avoid* the production of eccentric forces. This constraint requires the performer to make crucial adjustments in his / her body position. For example, in running, the body must be leaning forward during the early part of a race.

Lean Angle

Figure 22-3. The body lean angle employed on a sprint track start.

The figure shows a runner during the first stride out of the blocks on a sprint start. At this moment in the race, the performer is experiencing near maximal forward acceleration. As a result, the horizontal component of the ground reaction force will be large. The vertical component of the GRF will also be large, because the body is being driven upward as well as forward. In order to understand the importance of the forward "lean angle" in the sprint start, we will need to perform a detailed analysis of the runner's ground reaction force components.

At the moment shown in the figure, the performer is experiencing a horizontal acceleration of 12.39 mps^2 and a vertical acceleration of 6.94 mps^2. The calculation of the horizontal component of the runner's ground reaction force is as follows:

Given:
$|Wgt| = 712$ N
Mass = 72.6 kg
$A_X = 12.39$ mps^2
$A_Y = 2.10$ mps^2

$GRF_X = m\ A_X$
$GRF_X = (72.6 * 12.39)$
$GRF_X = 899$ Newtons

The figure below illustrates the turning effect of the GRF X-component on the runner. To visualize this turning effect, imagine that the runner is embedded in a weightless sheet of glass, and that his body is free to rotate about the center of gravity point only. Thus, the horizontal component of the GRF will cause the runner to rotate in a counter-clockwise direction about the CG point. The size of the counter-clockwise torque will depend upon both the size of the GRF X-component and the lever arm of the force. Note that when the runner leans forward, the length of this lever arm is reduced, and therefore the torque generated by the large GRF X-component force is also reduced.

Tendency to Rotate

Figure 22-4. The horizontal component of the ground reaction force and its lever arm.

Our analysis of the net torque applied to the runner's body cannot be complete until we evaluate the effect of the vertical component of the ground reaction force:

$GRF_Y = m A_Y + |Wgt|$
$GRF_Y = (72.6 * 2.10) + 712$
$GRF_Y = 152 + 712$
$GRF_Y = 864$ N

The figure below shows the vertical component of the GRF. Note that this force produces a tendency for the body to rotate in the clockwise direction. The torques generated by the GRF_X and GRF_Y force components must be about equal and opposite in order to minimize the angular acceleration of the runner's body. Note that the GRF_Y force component is smaller than the GRF_X force (864 N. vs. 899 N.). As a result, the GRF Y-components must be applied over a longer lever arm in order to create a torque that "balances" that of the GRF X-component.

Tendency to Rotate

Figure 22-5. The vertical component of the ground reaction force and its lever arm.

The choice of an appropriate angle of lean is an important aspect of running skill. By adjusting his body position, the performer can create horizontal and vertical lever arms that will generate approximately "balanced" torques on his body. During the first stride out of the blocks the runner's goal is to generate very large horizontal acceleration and GRF_X components. If the runner leans forward, his body will "stay in balance". If the runner were to assume an upright position and apply the same large horizontal ground reaction forces, he could, at least

in theory, cause his body to perform a back somersault. In reality, if a runner selects an angle of lean that is too much upright, it is very unlikely that he will push on the ground hard enough to cause his body to perform a back somersault during the start. However, it is very likely that he will reduce the size of the GRF horizontal component to assure that he does maintain his balance. The result of his upright starting position will therefore not be a back-somersault; it will instead be a slower running performance.

The figure below shows the GRF resultant vector as well as its components. Note that the line of action of the resultant force is directed just below the center of gravity point. At the moment shown, the runner is accelerating forward and upward. He is also experiencing a small tendency to rotate in a counter-clockwise direction. This counter-clockwise rotation will cause him to become more upright as he continues to run forward.

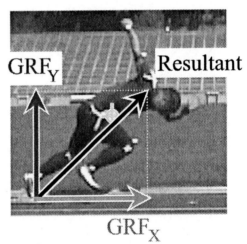

Figure 22-6. The line of action of the ground reaction force vector at a moment during a sprint track start.

When a runner advances further away from the starting line, his body will eventually attain its maximal velocity. When this happens, his body will assume a more upright position. To better understand why this upright body position is characteristic of full speed running technique, consider the following question.

Question 22-1:
At the moment when a runner reaches peak horizontal velocity, what will the horizontal component of his acceleration be?

○ A. Zero.
○ B. The acceleration will be a high positive value.
○ C. The acceleration will be a high negative value.

The figure below shows curves for the X-component of velocity and acceleration for a hypothesized runner. When the runner achieves peak velocity, the slope of the velocity curve is zero. As a result, the rate of change of velocity, and therefore the acceleration value, must also be zero at the moment of peak velocity.

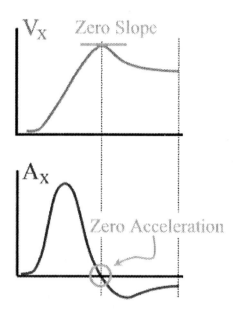

Figure 22-7. The Vx (X component of velocity) and Ax (X component of acceleration) curves for the center of gravity point for a performer on a sprint track start.

During the second half of a 100-meter dash, most runners will have reached peak speed and will be attempting to maintain that peak speed until the end of the race. As a result, most runners will *not* be accelerating on the second half of the race and their net GRF X-component force will be nearly zero. It is important to note that a *net* horizontal GRF component of zero does not indicate that the runner will continuously generate zero GRF X-components. The figure below shows a runner who is "up to speed" and maintaining a steady state running velocity.

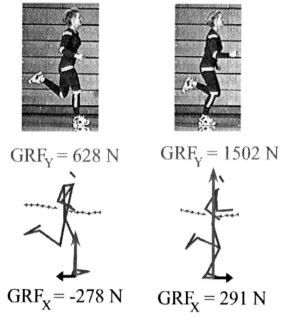

Figure 22-8. The horizontal and vertical components of the ground reaction force during two instants in time during normal running.

Note that the runner is experiencing a negative "braking force" just after the heel strike event and a positive "propulsive force" later in the stride. These two measures indicate that the runner is experiencing a net horizontal force that is approximately zero over the course of each stride.

It is interesting to note that the upright position of the body causes the line of action of the ground reaction force to be aimed along a line that is very nearly through the center of gravity position. In effect, the runner has adjusted her angle of body lean to allow for a balance in the moments applied to the body by the ground reaction force components. As a result, the runner's body experiences only a slight tendency to rotate forward at heel strike and a compensating slight tendency to rotate backward during the propulsive phase of the stride. The upright posture of the runner has clearly been selected for the purpose of keeping the net turning effect of the ground reaction force at a minimum throughout the stride.

Angular Motion in Flight

Angular motion in airborne flight presents a very interesting example for biomechanical analysis. We have seen in prior chapters that the linear motion of a body in flight is well represented by the path of its center of gravity point. This holds true for inanimate objects, as shown by the baton flight path below.

The motion of human beings in flight is also well represented by the center of gravity pattern of motion. Note that the springboard diver below follows the smooth center of gravity pattern of motion even though he is performing one and a half somersaults.

The angular motion of a body in flight takes place about that body's center of gravity point. Thus, the baton's motion is best visualized as a combination of translation along the center of gravity pattern of motion and rotation about the CG point as well.

Baton

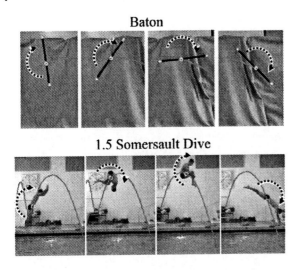

1.5 Somersault Dive

Figure 22-9. A comparison of the flight path and angular motion of a baton and a diver performing a 1.5 somersault front dive.

The previous sections of this chapter have addressed the importance of eccentric forces in the production of angular motion. Let's now consider the effects of the forces that act on the body while in airborne flight.

The figure below shows a free body diagram for the diver from our previous discussion.

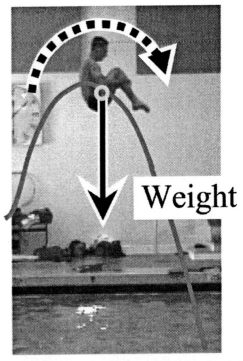

Figure 22-10. The weight force acting on a diver's body at a moment during a 1.5 front somersault dive.

Because the speed of the diver is relatively small, we can ignore the effects of air resistance on the diver's motion. As a result, the only substantial force acting on the body is the force of gravity. Note that this force acts through the body's center of gravity point. Because the body's CG point defines the axis of rotation for the body's angular motion, we must conclude that the torque produced by the body's weight force is zero (because the perpendicular distance between the line of action of the weight force and the pivot point is zero).

While there can be no torque applied to a body in airborne flight, the diver's angular velocity can still change during the course of the dive. However, the change in angular velocity can be predicted on the basis of the body's position. Consider the following example:

Question 22-2:
The following figure shows a springboard diver doing a one and one-half front somersault dive in tuck position. Figure A shows the performer at a moment close to the beginning of the airborne phase of the dive. Figure B shows the mid-portion of the dive. Figure C shows the performer near the end of the flight phase. When will the diver's angular velocity be greatest?

When is angular velocity largest?

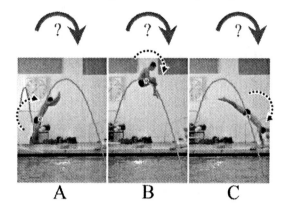

Figure 22-11. An illustration of three time periods during the course of a 1.5 somersault front dive.

○ A. The angular velocity will be greatest at figure A.
○ B. The angular velocity will be greatest at figure B.
○ C. The angular velocity will be greatest at figure C.

It is not uncommon to observe springboard diving motions where the diver's body experiences changes in angular velocity while airborne. This observation presents us with an interesting theoretical question. If no net torque is applied to the body during flight, how can the body's angular velocity change?

We will see in the next sections that the concept of angular momentum will provide critical information that will allow us to answer this question. Further, the conservation of angular momentum principle will provide us with a powerful analysis technique that will help us to better understand skillful airborne motion.

Angular Momentum

The concept of momentum can often be very useful in the analysis of human movement. We have seen in Chapter 10 that the equation for *linear* momentum is equal to the product of mass (the measure of a body's resistance to linear motion) and linear velocity:

Linear momentum = m**V**

The equation for angular momentum is analogous. The measure of resistance to angular motion is (I), or the moment of inertia value. The term used to define angular velocity is (ω). Thus, the equation for *angular* momentum is equal to the product of moment of inertia and angular velocity:

Angular momentum = Iω

The concept of angular momentum is crucially important in the definition of Newton's second law of angular motion:

*The rate of change of **angular** momentum of a body (or the **angular** acceleration of a body) is proportional to the **torque** causing it, and the change takes place in the direction in which the torque acts.*

Newton's second law for angular motion can be expressed mathematically as follows:

$$\mathbf{T}_{NET} = (I\omega_F - I\omega_I) / \text{time}$$

The expression of Newton's second law in terms of momentum is mathematically equivalent to the more familiar $\mathbf{T}_{NET} = I\alpha$ equation. The following equations show that the rate of change of angular momentum is equivalent to the product of moment of inertia and angular acceleration:

$$\mathbf{T}_{NET} = (I\omega_F - I\omega_I) / \text{time}$$

$$\mathbf{T}_{NET} = I(\omega_F - \omega_I) / \text{time} \quad \text{[rearranging terms]}$$

$$\alpha = (\omega_F - \omega_I) / \text{time [the definition of angular acceleration]}$$

$$\mathbf{T}_{NET} = I\alpha \quad \text{[through substitution]}$$

We will see in the next section that the concept of angular momentum will be very helpful in the analysis of in-flight angular motion.

Conservation of Angular Momentum

Newton's second law of angular motion indicates that if a net torque is applied to a body over a time period, the body will experience a change in angular momentum (H). For a given body and time period, larger net torques will cause larger changes in angular momentum. Similarly, smaller net torques will cause smaller changes in angular momentum. Finally, if a *zero* net torque is applied to a body, the change in angular momentum will be zero.

We have noted above that when a diver's body is in the air, a zero net torque is applied to his body. As a result, when the diver is airborne, his angular momentum must remain unchanged. In effect, angular momentum is *conserved* during time periods when the net torque applied to a body is zero.

For a given body & time interval:

$$T_{NET} \propto \Delta H$$

Large | Large

$$T_{NET} \propto \Delta H$$

Small | Small

$$T_{NET} \propto \Delta H$$

Zero | Zero

$$T_{NET} \propto \Delta H$$

Figure 22-12. The relationship between the net torque applied to a body and the change in momentum of that body.

A mathematical proof of the conservation of angular momentum principle is presented below.

In general:
$$T_{NET} = (I\omega_F - I\omega_I) / time$$

For the special case of zero net torque (as in airborne flight):

$$0 = (I\omega_F - I\omega_I) / time$$
$$0 * time = (I\omega_F - I\omega_I)$$
$$0 = (I\omega_F - I\omega_I)$$

The conservation of angular momentum principle can be applied only to the analysis of movements that involve zero net torque. As a result, it can be used to study airborne flight in springboard diving and gymnastics (as long as air resistance is negligible). The conservation of angular momentum principle can also be applied to the analysis of spinning motions in figure skating, because the frictional forces between the skates and the ice are typically very small.

Spin Motion on Ice

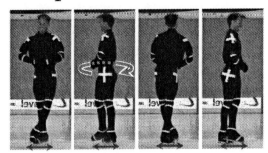

Friction = 0

Figure 22-13. A skilled ice skater performing a high speed spin.

The conservation of angular momentum principle states that the angular momentum of the body will be constant when a zero net torque is applied to the body. However, the conservation of angular momentum principle *does not imply* that the angular *velocity* of a body in flight will remain constant.

Example – 1 ½ somersault dive

Let's now consider our discussion of a one and one-half somersault dive in more detail. During the in-flight portion of the dive, angular momentum (H) must be constant. Thus, any change in moment of inertia (I) will cause a corresponding change in angular velocity (ω). The figure below shows the compensating changes that occur in the angular velocity and moment of inertia values during the dive. Note that the product of (I * ω) is held constant at 32 kg-m^2/sec. during the complete airborne motion.

In effect, the angular momentum of the body is set at the moment of take-off from the diving board. During the springboard take-off phase, the diver must lean forward to cause the line of action of the board reaction force to fall behind his center of gravity point. This eccentric force generates a clockwise angular momentum. When in flight, no moments are applied to the body and the angular momentum value must remain fixed. When the diver assumes a high-resistance layout position, his angular velocity must remain low (2 radians/sec.). When the diver assumes a low-resistance tuck position, his angular velocity must increase to 8 radians/sec in order to maintain the constant angular momentum value.

	Layout	Tuck	Layout
ω	2	8	2
I	16	4	16
H	32	32	32

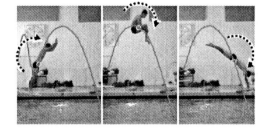

Figure 22-14. The angular velocity, moment of inertia and angular momentum of a diver at 3 instants in time during a 1.5 somersault front dive.

Example – Figure Skating Spin

A figure-skating spin movement provides another interesting example of the conservation of angular momentum principle. The figure below shows three phases from a skilled spin motion. The first, torque generation phase, is used to generate the angular momentum needed for the spin. A large eccentric force is applied to the body as a result of the left leg driving action. The skater extends the arms and gesture leg to the side during the "high moment of inertia spin phase" of the movement. Because a large proportion of the body mass is located far from the axis of rotation of the spin, a large moment of inertia value is generated during this phase. During the final "high angular velocity" phase of the spin, the skater pulls his arms and legs inward, very close to the axis of rotation. The new body position greatly reduces the body's moment of inertia. Because the angular momentum of the body must remain constant, the angular velocity of the body must increase. (Note: The friction between the ice and the skate blade is so small that the frictional torque acting on the body is negligible. As a result, angular momentum must be conserved.)

Torque Generation Phase

High Moment of Inertia Spin

High Angular Velocity Spin

Figure 22-15. Three phases during an ice skating spin motion.

The angular velocity of the body is slow during the first two-thirds of the movement. When the arms are drawn close to the body on the last portion of the spin, the body angular velocity increases dramatically. During this high-speed spin motion, the performer is not able to use his legs to apply a torque on the ice. As a result, the dramatic increase in spin speed must be due to the conservation of angular momentum principle.

High Moment of Inertia Spin

Time for one revolution = 38 fields
Average angular velocity = ?

Figure 22-16. Analysis of the angular velocity of the body during the early portion of a spin motion.

Question 22-3:
The above figure shows the "High moment of inertia spin" phase of the figure skating spin motion. The time required for the skater to accomplish a single revolution is 38 video fields (or 38 * 1/60th second time intervals). What is the average angular velocity of the skater's body for this phase of the movement? Express your answer in radians per second units.

O A. The average angular velocity is 9.9 radians per second.
O B. The average angular velocity is 568 radians per second.
O C. The average angular velocity is 38 radians per second.

The calculation procedure for the skater's average angular velocity is as follows:

Given:
One revolution = 360 degrees
Time for one revolution = 38/60 seconds
Time for one revolution = 0.633 seconds

Angular velocity calculation:
ω_{AVE} = angular displacement / time
ω_{AVE} = 360 / (0.633)
ω_{AVE} = 568 degrees per second
ω_{AVE} = 9.9 radians per second
Note: 1 radian = 57.3°

It will be interesting to compare the average angular velocity values from the "high moment of inertia" and the "high angular velocity" phases of the spin. An inspection of the video data shows that the skater completes one revolution during the high angular velocity phase in 16 video fields.

High Angular Velocity Spin

Time for one revolution = 16 fields
Average angular velocity = ?

Figure 22-17. Analysis of the angular velocity of the body during the last portion of a spin motion.

The calculation of his average angular velocity during this phase is as follows:

Given:
One revolution = 360 degrees
Time for one revolution = 16/60 seconds
Time for one revolution = 0.266 seconds

Angular velocity calculation:
ω_{AVE} = angular displacement / time
ω_{AVE} = 360 / (0.266)

ω_{AVE} = 1350 degrees per second
ω_{AVE} = 23 radians per second

Our analysis shows that the skater is able to more than double his angular velocity by reducing his moment of inertia on the final phase of the spin. This example shows us that relatively small changes in the distribution of a performer's body mass will produce large changes in the body's moment of inertia. The following equation defines the relationship between the body's moment of inertia and the distribution of its mass elements:

$$I_{BODY} = \Sigma \, m_i \, R_i^2$$

If the radius length between a given portion of the body mass and the axis of rotation is reduced by half, the moment of inertia for that body mass will be reduced to one quarter size. For the skater in our example, the distance between the right foot segment and the body's axis of rotation is reduced from 86 centimeters to 12 centimeters when the body position changes to its final spin position. This seven fold reduction in the right foot radius length results in a 49 fold reduction in the moment of inertia contribution of the foot mass. The change in position of the arm segments and right leg shank and thigh segments also contributes to the skater's overall reduction in moment of inertia.

←—86 cm —→

→| |←

12 cm

Figure 22-18. The distance between the foot and the pivot foot for two positions during a skating spin motion.

Moment of Inertia and Swinging Motions

Our analysis of human motion in flight and on ice has shown that a very predictable inverse relationship exists between a body's moment of inertia and angular velocity. However, the movements we have discussed so far have been special case examples that adhere to the assumptions of the conservation of momentum principle. More general examples of angular human motion will typically be generated through the application of applied torques, and the sizes of these torque values can be expected to change as a function of time. For example, the giant swing shown in the figure below is an example of an angular motion that is constantly influenced by the pull of gravity.

Figure 22-19. A giant swing on the high bar.

Question 22-4:
Which way is the gymnast's body rotating in the figure above?

O A. His body is rotating in a clockwise direction.
O B. His body is rotating in a counter-clockwise direction.

To determine the direction of motion of the giant swing, remember that the swing will have both a "downhill" and "uphill" side. Imagine that the gymnast's body is replaced with a rigid block of wood. If the wooden object is suspended above the bar and then given a tiny push to the left, we can expect that the only a partial revolution will be

accomplished. The wood will rotate slowly past the 11 o'clock position, pick up speed at the 9 o'clock position, and achieve maximal angular velocity near the 6 o'clock position. As the wood begins the "uphill" part of the swing, it will be slowed by the pull of gravity. Frictional forces between the wood and the bar will cause further reduction in angular velocity. As a result, the wood will be expected to rotate to about the 1 o'clock position and then fall back and begin to rotate in the clockwise direction.

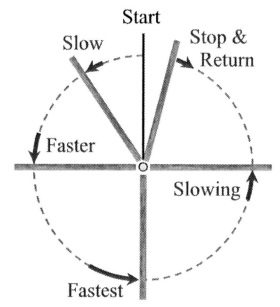

Figure 22-20. The motion of a wooden block rotating about a pivot point.

A wooden block will never be able to rotate repeatedly around the bar because the moment of inertia of the wood remains fixed at all points in the swing. The gymnast, on the other hand, is able to reduce his moment of inertia value on the "uphill" part of the swing. The figure below shows that the distance between the gymnast's toes and the bar is greater at the 9 o'clock position than at the 3 o'clock position.

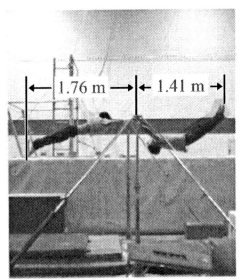

Figure 22-21. The distance between the gymnast's toes and the bar at the 9 o'clock and 3 o'clock positions on a giant swing.

By shifting his body mass closer to the axis of rotation on the "uphill" side of the swing, the gymnast reduces his resistance to angular motion. In turn, he is able to keep up enough angular velocity to "make it over" the top of the swing.

The conservation of angular momentum principle cannot be used to analyze this movement because large torques are applied to the gymnast's body as his position with respect to the bar changes. The figure below shows the gymnast's body weight force and the body's axis of rotation "pivot point". Because the body weight force is applied over a long lever arm, it will create a large torque that will tend to cause counter-clockwise rotation of the gymnast's body.

Figure 22-22. The body weight torque acting on the body during the downswing phase of a giant swing.

Note that the gymnast extends his body far from the bar during the "downhill" part of his swing to maximize the size of the body weight torque. This large torque will cause the angular momentum of the body to increase to a maximal value near the bottom of the swing. Angular momentum is clearly not conserved in this movement because the gymnast's angular velocity will be greatly reduced as he approaches the top of the swing.

It is interesting to note that even though the conservation of angular momentum principle cannot be applied to a giant swing, our understanding of moment of inertia was still very useful in the analysis of this motion. In fact, the control of the body's moment of inertia value is a crucial aspect of the performer's skill in this event. In order to accomplish the giant swing, the gymnast maximizes the torque applied to the body on the downswing portion of the swing and minimizes his moment of inertia on the upswing.

Angular Action Reaction

We have already discussed Newton's Third Law of *linear* motion in Chapter 10. This law states: "for every force that is exerted by one body on another, there is an equal and opposite force exerted by the second body on the first." This action-reaction law provided very helpful information in our analysis of ground reaction forces.

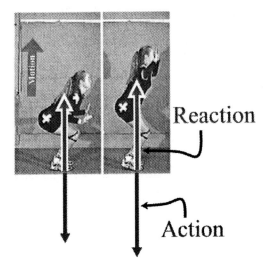

Figure 22-23. The action and reaction forces associated with a vertical jump motion.

Volleyball Serve Example

Newton's third law of *angular* motion is equally important. It states: "for every *torque* that is exerted by one body on another, there is an equal and opposite *torque* exerted by the second body on the first." For example, during a volleyball jump serve, the clockwise *action* of the arm swing will cause a counter-clockwise *reaction* on the legs.

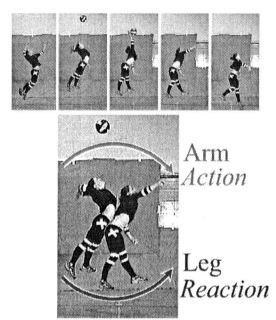

Arm *Action*

Leg *Reaction*

Figure 22-24. The angular action (of the arms) and angular reaction (of the legs) on a volleyball jump serve.

The volleyball serve example shows that the action-reaction law can be applied to the individual body segments of the human body. Thus, if a torque is applied to the player's trunk and arm segments, an equal and opposite torque will be applied to the leg segments.

The conservation of angular momentum principle confirms that a counter-clockwise reaction of the player's legs must accompany the serving arm action. Suppose that the player has jumped into the air and has zero angular momentum. Her zero angular momentum value implies that the *net* angular momentum of her body segments must be zero. When she swings her arm forward, the upper portion of her body acquires clockwise angular momentum. In order for her full body angular momentum to remain zero, her legs *must* acquire a counter-clockwise angular momentum. In effect, if part of her body has a change in angular momentum, another part of her body must experience a

compensating change in angular momentum. These changes assure that the overall angular momentum of the body will remain unchanged.

Balance Beam Example

The figure below shows a gymnast who has been pushed and is about to fall off the right side of a balance beam. In order to cause his body to stay balanced over the beam, he must move his arms in a clockwise direction. Note that his arm motion is made to the right, in the same direction as his falling motion. For this example, the *action* is the clockwise arm swing motion. The *reaction* is the desired counter-clockwise motion that keeps his body over the beam.

Action

Reaction

Figure 22-25. The angular action and reaction of a gymnast who is righting himself on a balance beam.

Kip Example

The kip in gymnastics provides another interesting example of the angular action-reaction law. The sequence of images in the upper portion of the figure below shows the complete kip movement. Note that the kip begins with the body in a pike position and makes use of a rapid swing of the legs to propel the body into an upright position.

Action

GRFy

Lever
Arm

Figure 22-27. The ground reaction force associated with a kip movement.

Reaction

Figure 22-26. The angular action and reaction associated with a kip motion performed on the floor.

The rapid extension of the gymnast's hip joint provides the action for this movement. This clockwise leg motion causes a counter-clockwise reaction torque on the gymnast's trunk. This reaction torque presses the gymnast's head and shoulder's firmly into the mat and generates a series of ground reaction forces that push upwards on the gymnast's shoulders. It is interesting to note that this movement involves a reaction torque that causes very little motion of the performer's trunk. Nevertheless, this reaction torque produces very large forces on the performer's body.

The figure below shows the peak ground reaction force that occurs during the action phase of the movement. This force propels the performer into the air and generates a clockwise torque on the body. It is this clockwise torque that allows the performer to complete the 90-degree rotation needed to attain an upright body position.

Centripetal and Centrifugal Force

We have discussed the kinematics of circular motion in Chapter 17. In this section we will consider the relationships between radial acceleration components and the forces that occur in circular motion. The figure below shows a baseball bat that is swinging with uniform angular velocity along a circular path. Note that the change in the direction of the bat end point velocity vector causes acceleration of the bat along the radial direction.

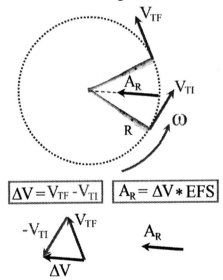

$$\Delta V = V_{TF} - V_{TI} \qquad A_R = \Delta V * EFS$$

Figure 22-28. The radial component of acceleration associated with the circular motion of a baseball batting swing.

Newton's second law of linear motion tells us that forces cause accelerations. For the circular motions shown below, *centripetal* forces are associated with the inward pulling actions that cause the bat end point to follow a curved line. In the absence of these centripetal forces, the bat end point would be expected to experience uniform motion along a *straight* line.

Centripetal forces are, by definition, always aimed in toward the center of a circular motion.

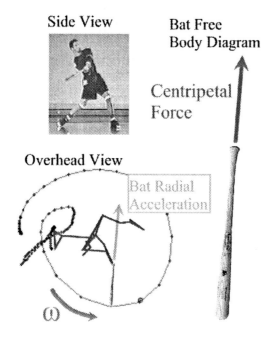

Figure 22-29. The centripetal force acting between the batter's hands and the bat.

For a baseball batting swing, centripetal forces are generated by the grip of the hands on the bat. The bat free body diagram shown below illustrates the pulling force of the batter's hands. This centripetal force acts in the direction of the bat radial acceleration vector.

Centrifugal forces are defined as those forces that pull away from the center of a circular motion. According to Newton's third law of linear motion, for every action force there is an equal and opposite reaction force. In a baseball batting swing, the centripetal force represents the action force and the centrifugal force represents the reaction force.

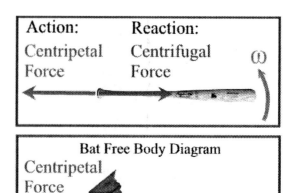

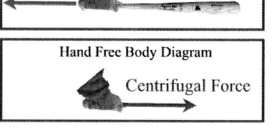

Figure 22-30. The centripetal and centrifugal forces acting between the batter's hands and the bat.

The "Action-Reaction" illustration in the upper part of the figure shows the effect of the bat pulling on the hands (the centrifugal force) and the effect of the hands pulling on the bat (the centripetal force). The middle portion of the figure shows only the forces acting on the bat free body. The lower portion of the figure shows only the forces acting on the "hand" free body diagram. We see from this illustration that centripetal and centrifugal forces always act at the same time, and the decision to study one or the other depends upon our point of view.

Centrifugal forces can place a significant constraint upon the performance of skillful human movement. For example, a sprinter running on a curve must "lean" into the curve to maximize his running speed. The body lean allows the athlete to "aim" his ground reaction force toward the center of the curve and minimize the torque acting on his body.

Figure 22-31. A performer "leans into" the curve to minimize the torque acting on the body.

Conclusions

Our review of torques, angular momentum and angular action-reaction is now complete. We have seen that a clear understanding of the concept of moment of inertia is important in the analysis of a wide variety of human movements. Further, the product of moment of inertia and angular velocity, or the angular momentum of the body, can be used to understand spinning motions that occur in the air and on ice.

Answers to Chapter Questions

Question 22-1:
At the moment when a runner reaches peak horizontal velocity, what will the horizontal component of his acceleration be?

O A. Zero.
O B. The acceleration will be a high positive value.
O C. The acceleration will be a high negative value.

The correct answer is A. Because the slope of the velocity curve is zero at the moment of peak velocity, the value of acceleration must be zero.

Question 22-2:
The following figure shows a springboard diver doing a one and one-half front somersault dive in tuck position. Figure A shows the performer at a moment close to the beginning of the airborne phase of the dive. Figure B shows the mid-portion of the dive. Figure C shows the performer near the end of the flight phase. When will the diver's angular velocity be greatest?

O A. Angular velocity will be greatest at figure A.
O B. Angular velocity will be greatest at figure B.
O C. Angular velocity will be greatest at figure C.

The correct answer is B. When the diver assumes tuck position, his body will spin more rapidly than when he is in lay out position.

Question 22-3:
The following figure shows the "High moment of inertia spin" phase of the figure skating spin motion. The time required for the skater to accomplish a single revolution is 38 video fields (or 38 * 1/60th second time intervals). What is the average angular velocity of the skater's body for this phase of the movement? Express your answer in radians per second units. (Use the Windows calculator to perform this calculation).

O A. The average angular velocity is 9.9 radians per second.
O B. The average angular velocity is 568 radians per second.
O C. The average angular velocity is 38 radians per second.

The correct answer is A. To get angular velocity in radians per second, be sure to divide angular velocity expressed in degrees per second by 57.3.

Question 22-4:
Which way is the gymnast's body rotating in the figure above?

O A. His body is rotating in a clockwise direction.
O B. His body is rotating in a counter-clockwise direction.

The correct answer is B. The gymnast has shifted his body mass closer to the bar on the "uphill" side (the 3 o'clock position) to make it easier for his body to "get over" the top of the bar.

Chapter 23: Joint Reaction Force and Joint Torque

Internal Forces

One of the most important applications of biomechanical analysis involves the computation of the internal forces and torques that cause human movement. Kinetic level analysis typically requires a combination of kinematic information (i.e., from video or film) and force measurement data (from force plates, force transducers and other electronic force measurement devices). The following sections will begin with a brief review of the ground reaction forces created during a back somersault and move on to perform a detailed analysis of the joint reaction forces and joint torques that occur during this forceful motion.

Ground Reaction Force Data

Information on the ground reaction forces generated during human movement can be calculated from video data or obtained directly from a force plate device. While video-based measures of ground reaction force are often very convenient, they are less accurate than those from force plates. However, the video-based calculation procedure for whole body ground reaction forces is nevertheless very important, because it provides the best approach to the calculation of the internal muscular forces that are generated at the body's joints.

Our work in Chapter 11 covered the calculation procedure for ground reaction force. Given center of gravity acceleration data, the net ground reaction force acting on the body can be computed for many jumping or running type movements. For example, the calculation of a ground reaction force for a back somersault take-off is shown below:

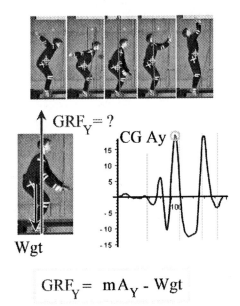

$$GRF_Y = mA_Y - Wgt$$

Figure 23-2. The vertical component of the ground reaction force at a instant during a back somersault take off motion.

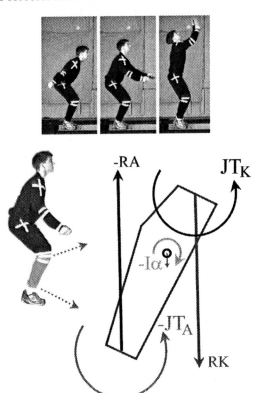

Figure 23-1. The joint reaction forces (RA and RK) and joint torques (JT_A and JT_K) acting on the shank segment during a back somersault take off motion.

Given:
Subject weight in pounds: 165
Subject mass: 74.9 kg   (where body mass in kilograms = body weight in pounds divided by 2.2)
Subject weight: -734.3 Newtons (where weight in Newtons = mass in kilograms * 9.81)
$A_X = 0.14$ mps^2 (from kinematic analysis data)
$A_Y = 19.44$ mps^2 (from kinematic analysis data)

Computation of GRF$_Y$:
$R_Y + Wgt = m\,A_Y$
$R_Y = m\,A_Y - Wgt$
$R_Y = (74.9 * 19.44) - (-734.3)$
$R_Y = 1456.1 + 734.3$
$R_Y = 2190.4$ Newtons
Force plate reading = 2142.4 Newtons

The video-based analysis of the ground reaction vertical component (2190 N) is very close to the measurement provided by the force plate system (2142 N). Note that the GRF$_Y$ value of 2142 Newtons is nearly equal to three times the participant's body weight. The body acceleration times body mass term is the primary contributor to this high level of force.

Computation of GRF$_X$:
$R_X = m\,A_X$
$R_X = (74.9 * 0.14)$
$R_X = 10.5$ Newtons
Force plate reading: -47.8 Newtons

Note that the video-based estimate of the ground reaction force X-component is not very close to the measurement provided by the force plate system. Because the values of the body's center of gravity acceleration X component data are quite small, it is difficult to accurately determine the true movement information from this portion of the video data. Thus, it is clear that a force plate system is better than video for the measurement of relatively small force components.

The above computation procedures can be repeated (ideally by a computer program) for each instant in time during the back somersault motion. The figure below shows a portion of the output of such a computer analysis. The information in the figure has been taken from the KA – JtCalc program. This program is written to display the forces between the performer and the ground as a function of time. The information in the figure shows still image, stick figure and ground reaction force vectors for the take off phase of the back

somersault. Note that this stick figure shows the vertical ground reaction force component as vectors originating at the foot and pointing upward.

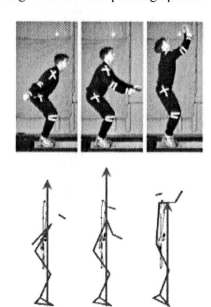

Figure 23-3. The ground reaction force vertical component at three instants in time during a back somersault take off motion.

The addition of the ground reaction force vectors within the JtCalc program allows us to visualize the *kinetic* factors that influence the movement. In the next section, we will discuss how our analysis can extend beyond the analysis of the *external* forces that are applied to the body and begin the analysis of the *internal* forces and torques that generate movement.

Analysis of Joint Reaction Force

For this back somersault example, knowledge of the center of gravity motion and the ground reaction force is only a first step in the evaluation of skill. A more detailed understanding can be determined through analysis of the joint reaction forces and the joint torques for the ankle, knee and hip. The joint reaction forces are the internal, bone on bone forces that occur between the segments of the leg. The joint torques are measures of the net turning effect generated by the muscular actions at each leg joint.

The determination of the internal forces and torques acting at a joint is a crucially important aspect of biomechanical analysis. Knowledge of the levels of force acting at a joint will certainly be important in the evaluation of injuries and/or injury prevention equipment. Similarly, data on the net muscular actions acting at a joint will be essential in the evaluation of strength training and rehabilitation programs.

A crucial restriction on the measurement of internal forces and joint torques is that *direct measurement* is rarely possible with human subjects. While it is quite practical to use force plates to provide direct measurement of ground reaction forces, it is not feasible to use similar electronic mechanisms to measure internal forces. For example, direct measurement of internal forces can only be attained if force transducers are surgically implanted into the tendons surrounding a joint. While the resulting measures would be highly accurate, the importance of the research participant's well-being far out-weighs the benefits of improved measurement accuracy.

As a result, an *indirect* mathematical approach to the measurement of internal forces is highly desirable in biomechanics research. The core logic behind this mathematical approach is a natural extension of the process described above with the calculation of ground reaction forces.

For the full human body, if we know the mass and acceleration of the body, and we know all but one of the forces acting on the body (i.e., we know the body weight force and no other forces are applied), we can compute the remaining force (the ground reaction force).

Figure 23-4. A free body diagram of a back somersault performer.

In the example shown above, we consider the full human body as a *free body* by illustrating it in a diagram with all of the applied forces shown. To do this, we figuratively "take away" the ground surface and replace it with a force vector that represents the ground reaction force acting on the foot. Newton's

second law holds for this free body, and the sum of the applied forces must be equal to the product of the body mass and the center of gravity point acceleration at any instant.

The process of defining a free body can be taken a step further by looking at *portions* of the whole body and figuratively breaking the body into its component parts. As a first step, consider the example of four cardboard boxes, stacked one upon another.

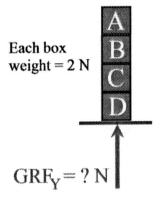

Figure 23-5. The calculation of the ground reaction force acting between a stack of four boxes and the floor.

Question 23-1:
If each box in the stack weights 2 Newtons, and the boxes are not accelerating, what will the ground reaction force be?

O A. 8 N.   O B. 2 N.   O C. 6 N.

This example is simplified by the fact that there is no acceleration of the box stack. As a result, the sum of the forces acting on the box stack free body diagram must equal zero:

$$\Sigma F_Y = m\, A_Y$$
$$W_A + W_B + W_C + W_D + GRF_Y = m\, A_Y$$
$$(-2) + (-2) + (-2) + (-2) + GRF_Y = 0$$
$$GRF_Y - 8 = 0$$
$$GRF_Y = 8\ N$$

Suppose now that our concern is not the support force needed at the floor but the "crushing" force sustained by box "D". If the maximal crushing force that can be sustained by the top surface of any box is 7 Newtons, will we be able to have a stack of 4 boxes without crushing the bottom box?

To solve this problem, we must determine the *internal* force that acts between boxes C and D. Our first step in the solution of this problem is to create a free body diagram of box D. This free body diagram will simplify our analysis because it will consider only the forces on box "D". The free body diagram must show the forces at both the bottom and top surfaces of the box. Thus, it must show the ground reaction force, the box D weight force and the force that acts on box D from above. The connecting surface between two rigid bodies is often called a "joint". Thus, the force that acts on box D from above is called a *joint reaction force*. The joint reaction force is shown as R_{CD} in the figure below.

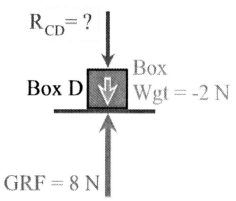

Figure 23-6. The calculation of the force between box C and box D.

The unknown *internal* force R_{CD} can be computed by solving the following equation:

$$\Sigma F_Y = m A_Y$$

This equation holds for the box D free body. As a result, the mass term represents the mass of box D and the A_Y term represents the acceleration of box D's center of gravity. For this example, the acceleration is zero and therefore the sum of the applied forces on the box (the ground reaction force, the box weight and the R_{CD} joint reaction force) must equal zero:

$$R_{CD} + Wgt_D + GRF_Y = 0$$
$$R_{CD} - 2 + 8 = 0$$
$$R_{CD} = -6$$

This R_{CD} force is simply the effect of the weight of the first three boxes upon box D. The crushing load on the upper surface of the box is less than 7 Newtons and therefore a stack of four boxes will be safe from collapse.

It is interesting to note that we can perform a separate analysis for any other individual box as well. For example, Newton's third law indicates that if Box C presses down on Box D with a force of -6 Newtons, then box D must press back up on Box C with an equal and opposite +6 Newtons. The figure below shows the equal and opposite +6 and –6 Newton forces. It is interesting to note that if these forces were *not* equal and opposite, one of the boxes would have to be accelerating away from the other.

Action - Reaction

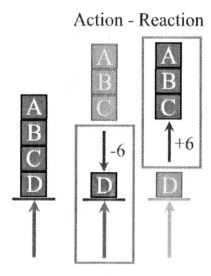

Figure 23-7. The action reaction principle applied to a stack of boxes.

The free body for box C must then show +6 Newtons acting from below and -2 Newtons acting down from the box weight. We can then compute the "unknown" joint reaction force between boxes B and C:

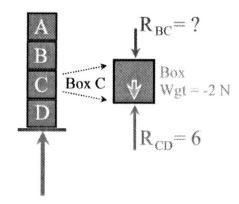

Figure 23-8. The calculation of the joint reaction force between box B and C.

For the box C free body:

$\Sigma F_Y = m\, A_Y$

Box C is not accelerating, therefore:

$A_Y = 0$
$\Sigma F_Y = 0$

The joint reaction force between box B and C can be computed as follows:

$R_{BC} + Wgt_C + R_{CD} = 0$
$R_{BC} - 2 + 6 = 0$
$R_{BC} = -4$

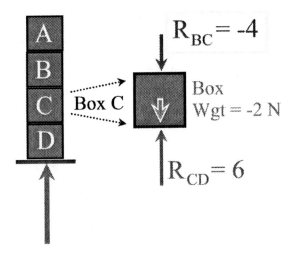

Figure 23-9. The joint reaction force acting between box B and C.

This "proximal joint" reaction force simply represents the weight of the top two boxes on box C.

Ankle Joint Reaction Force

The logic we have applied to our stack of boxes can also be applied to the segments on the human body. One important difference between an analysis of a stack of boxes and a gymnast performing a back somersault is that the gymnast is accelerating, and we will need to know the values of acceleration to solve Newton's second law:

$\Sigma F_Y = m\, A_Y$

For the box example, acceleration is zero at all times and we can simply add up the known forces to solve for the unknown force acting on any box "segment". For the gymnast, the segment accelerations are not zero, and the mA_Y terms must

be included in our calculations of any unknown joint reaction force.

Consider the full body and foot free body diagrams shown below:

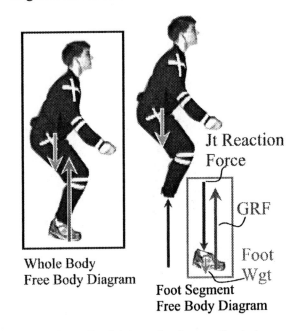

Figure 23-10. The joint reaction force acting between the shank and foot segment of a gymnast.

The left portion of the figure shows the full body free body diagram and the ground reaction force and body weight vectors. The right portion of the figure shows two free bodies, the foot and the upper portion of the body. It is very important to acknowledge that the foot can be figuratively "removed" from the whole body and studied as a separate free body. We have used the very same approach when we isolated the forth box in a stack from the upper three boxes in the stack (see figure 23-10). The joint reaction force between the foot and the upper body is labeled as the "Jt Reaction Force" vector in the figure below. This force is the only unknown vertical force acting on the foot free body. As a result, we will be able to calculate the size of the joint reaction force with the $\Sigma F_Y = mA_Y$ equation.

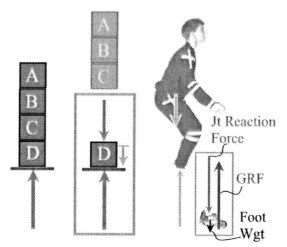

Figure 23-11. A comparison of the joint reaction forces acting between boxes and the segments of the human body.

The figure below shows the foot free body diagram with the X and Y components for all applied forces. The joint reaction force components at the ankle are labeled RA_X and RA_Y, the foot weight is labeled Wf and the ground reaction force components are labeled RG_X and RG_Y. For this free body diagram, we know all forces values except those of the ankle joint reaction force. We can solve for this internal force as detailed below.

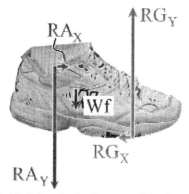

Figure 23-12. A free body diagram of the foot segment.

For the foot free body, the acceleration of the *foot* center of gravity point must be equal to the net force applied to the foot. Further, in order to solve the $\Sigma F = mA$ equation, we must know the mass and weight of the foot segment. Tables on body segment parameter information indicate that the mass and weight of the foot are 1.5% of the total body mass / weight. As a result, the foot mass and weight values are computed as follows:

Given: (from tables and kinematic analysis data)
Foot mass = body mass * 0.015
Foot mass = 74.9 * 0.015
Foot mass = 1.12 kg

Foot weight = body weight * 0.015
Foot weight = 734.3 * 0.015
Foot weight = 11.00 Newtons

The term A_Y in the $\Sigma F_Y = m\,A_Y$ equation refers to the foot segment center of gravity acceleration Y component. The digitizing process provides us with acceleration information on the toe and ankle points. Body segment parameter tables indicate that the foot's CG is located at a point 55% of the distance from the ankle to the toe. The acceleration of the foot segment center of gravity can then be approximated by the following equation:

Foot CG acceleration = 0.55 * ankle acceleration + 0.45 * toe acceleration

The video analysis provides us with the toe and ankle acceleration information:

Ankle A_X = 2.33 mps^2 Ankle A_Y = 5.73 mps^2
Toe A_X = -3.72 mps^2 Toe A_Y = 0.03 mps^2

The foot segment center of gravity acceleration components are computed as follows:

Foot CG A_X = (0.55 * 2.33) + (0.45 * (-3.72))
Foot CG A_X = -0.39 mps^2

Foot CG A_Y = (0.45 * 5.73) + (0.55 * 0.03)
Foot CG A_Y = 3.17 mps^2

We will now consider the ground reaction force that is applied to the foot. We must remember that the force plate data reflect the actions of *both* the right and left legs of the performer. For our analysis of joint reaction forces and joint torque, we will assume that each of the legs contributes equally. As a result, when we calculate the joint reaction forces for the right leg, we must assume that the ground reaction force components are half as large as the force plate readings. Thus, the force plate readings of GRF$_X$ = -47.8 and GRF$_Y$ = 2142.4 must be divided by 2 to determine the force components acting on the right foot:

Right Foot GRF$_X$ = -47.8 / 2
Right Foot GRF$_X$ = -23.9
Right Foot GRF$_Y$ = 2142.4 / 2
Right Foot GRF$_Y$ = 1071.2

We now have all of the information needed to compute the ankle joint reaction force:

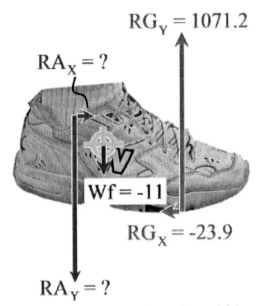

Figure 23-13. An illustration of the unknown joint reaction forces acting on the foot free body.

Computation of RA$_X$:
RA$_X$ + RG$_X$ = m A$_X$
RA$_X$ = m A$_X$ - RG$_X$
RA$_X$ = (1.12 * (-0.39)) - (-23.9)
RA$_X$ = 23.5 Newtons

Computation of RA$_Y$:
RA$_Y$ + RG$_Y$ + Wf = m A$_Y$
RA$_Y$ = m A$_Y$ - Wf - RG$_Y$
RA$_Y$ = (1.12 * 3.17) - (-11.0) – 1071.2
RA$_Y$ = -1056.7 Newtons

This procedure for computing the ankle joint reaction force can be conducted at each instant in time during the right foot support phase. Given data on the ankle joint reaction force, we can identify the times and foot positions that will be most vulnerable to injury.

The above equations involve "force terms" and the "mA" (mass times acceleration) term. The negative value of the "mA" term is often called the inertial force (force of motion) or the D'Alembert force. The figure below shows the ground reaction

force, joint reaction force, foot weight and the D'Alembert force approximately to scale.

Figure 23-14. A comparison of the foot ground reaction force and the ankle joint reaction force.

Notice that the D'Alembert force magnitude is very small (-4 Newtons) because the mass of the foot and the acceleration of the foot are very small. In the case of the whole body free body diagram, the D'Alembert term was much larger, as it contributed nearly two times the body weight to the reaction force.

The ankle joint reaction force **RA** is very nearly equal and opposite to the ground reaction force **RG**. The difference between **RG** and **RA** is a function of the -mA term (small) and the foot weight force (also small). If you have sharp eyes you will see that the foot weight force is also shown (-11 Newtons). The foot inertial force (D'Alembert force) is shown as a short arrow (-4 Newtons). By showing all applied forces and the inertial force in the figure we can visualize the segment as floating in space with all forces shown and the net effect of all forces adding up to zero:

ΣF = mA
RA + **Wf** + **RG** = mA
RA + **Wf** + **RG** – mA = 0

Where:
RA = ankle joint reaction force
Wf = foot weight force

RG = ground reaction force
m**A** = foot mass times acceleration of the foot
segment CG

The equation above substitutes the effect of motion
(m**A**) on the right side of the equation and places an
equivalent imaginary force term (-m**A**) on the left
side of the equation. If we visualize this inertial
force as the negative m**A** vector, then the net effect
of all vectors shown in the figure must add up to
zero. The ankle joint reaction represents the
"pushing down" of the shank segment and the upper
portion of the body on the foot. Similarly, the
ground reaction force is "pushing up" on the foot
segment. The sum total of the "pushing up",
"pushing down", the foot weight and the foot
D'Alembert force must equal zero.

Knee Joint Reaction Force

Our prior analysis has computed the joint reaction
force at the ankle. This force can be visualized as
the effect of the shank free body, pressing down on
the foot. The *action* of the shank pressing on the
foot must create an equal and opposite *reaction*
force pressing back up on the shank.

Force Up
on Body

Force Down
on Foot

Figure 23-15. The action reaction forces acting
between the foot segment and the shank segment.

The calculation of the knee joint reaction force
involves analysis of the shank free body diagram.
The figure below shows the forces that are applied
to the shank free body. Note that two out of the
three forces are known. The shank segment weight
can be determined from tables on anthropometric
data. The ankle joint reaction force is known from
our analysis of the foot segment. The knee joint

reaction force can therefore be solved through the
solution of the **F** = m**A** equation.

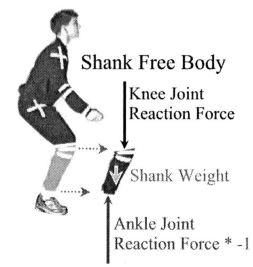

Shank Free Body

Knee Joint
Reaction Force

Shank Weight

Ankle Joint
Reaction Force * -1

Figure 23-16. The shank free body diagram.

The equation used to solve for the knee joint
reaction is shown below. Note that the mass term
represents the mass of the shank, and the
acceleration term represents the acceleration of the
shank center of gravity point.

$$\Sigma F = mA$$
$$RK + Ws - RA = mA$$
$$\mathbf{RK} = \mathbf{mA} + \mathbf{RA} - \mathbf{Ws}$$

Where:
RK = knee joint reaction force
Ws = weight of shank segment
RA = the ankle joint reaction force
m**A** = shank mass times acceleration of the shank
segment CG

The knee joint reaction force is the only unknown
term in the above equations. As a result, it can be
determined without difficulty. Once the knee joint
reaction force vector is known, we can break it
down into two components. The first component
can be set as acting along the long axis of the shank
segment (the axial compression component). The
second component can be set as acting at right
angles to the shank long axis (the sheer force
component). Analysis of these two components
during the course of the back somersault will tell us
when the performer is most at risk for knee joint
dislocation and compression fractures.

Hip Joint Reaction Force

Given the knee joint reaction force, it is apparent that we can move up one more segment and compute the hip joint reaction force. The thigh free body diagram shown below indicates that the negative knee joint reaction force vector acts at the distal end of the free body. The thigh weight, mass and center of gravity acceleration are readily available. As a result, the hip joint reaction force can be computed with the $\Sigma F = mA$ equation.

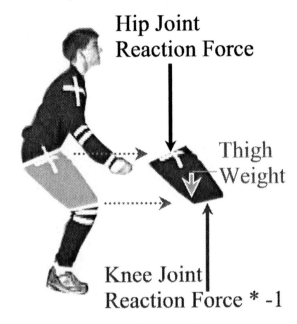

Hip Joint Reaction Force

Figure 23-17. The thigh free body diagram.

$\Sigma F = mA$
$RH + Wt - RK = mA$
RH = mA + RK - Wt

Where:
RH = hip joint reaction force
Wt = weight of thigh segment
RK = knee joint reaction force
mA = thigh mass times acceleration of the thigh segment CG

A figure showing all three right leg segment free body diagrams is shown below:

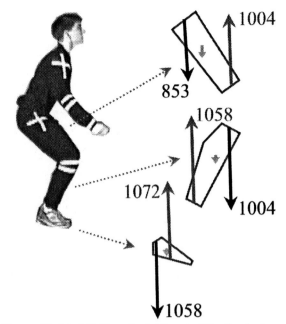

Figure 23-18. A "3 Free Body Diagram" for the foot, shank and thigh segments of the human body.

The JtCalc software "3 Free Body Diagram" shows the foot, shank and thigh free bodies on the middle portion of the screen. Each segment is displayed as a separate free body with all external and internal forces shown. The free body segments and their associated vectors change to reflect the current leg positioning as the stick figure is advanced within the JtCalc software.

Analysis of Joint Torque

Once the leg joint reaction forces are known, it is possible to compute the leg joint torque vectors and draw inferences about the net muscular actions in the leg. The figure below shows all of the forces and *torques* that act on the foot free body. The ankle joint torque (JT_A) is shown as a circular arc centered at the ankle joint. The radius of the circular arc is proportional to the joint torque magnitude. The arrowhead indicates the sign of the torque vector (clockwise = negative). The ground reaction (RG) and ankle joint reaction force (RA) vectors are also shown.

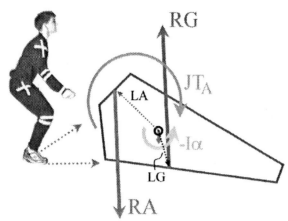

Figure 23-19. The foot free body diagram showing all forces and torques.

Joint Torque Analysis

The mathematical solution of the ankle joint torque value follows directly from Newton's second law of angular motion. This equation states that the angular acceleration of a given segment will be proportional to the net torque acting on the body segment:

$$\Sigma T = I\alpha$$

A listing of all torques acting on the foot free body is as follows:

$$JT_A + T_{RA} + T_{RG} = I\alpha$$

Where:
JT_A - the torque due to the net muscular action at the ankle
T_{RA} - the torque due to the ankle joint reaction force
T_{RG} - the torque due to the ground reaction force
I = the moment of inertia of the foot segment
α = the angular acceleration of the foot segment

The above equation is used to solve for the ankle joint torque value (JT_A). The solution to this equation can be performed mathematically (ideally by a computer) given knowledge of the following terms:

- T_{RA} - The ankle joint reaction force vector is known (from our earlier analysis) and the lever arm for this force is also available through the video data / body segment parameter literature. Note that the lever arm of this force is the perpendicular distance between the line of

action of the force and the center of gravity "pivot" point.
- T_{RG} - The ground reaction force vector is known (from our earlier analysis) and the lever arm for this force is also available through the video data / body segment parameter literature.
- $I\alpha$ – The angular acceleration of the foot is available from the video analysis data. The moment of inertia of the foot is available from the body segment parameter literature.

The results of the mathematical solution of a joint torque calculation are readily available through the JtCalc software. In addition, JtCalc shows graphical information that is designed to help us to visualize the influence of the joint torque vectors.

Joint Torque Analysis: A Graphical Analysis

The foot free body joint torque equation can be rearranged to show the D'Alembert torque (-$I\alpha$) on the left side of the equal sign:

$$JT_A + T_{RA} + T_{RG} = I\alpha$$
$$JT_A + T_{RA} + T_{RG} - I\alpha = 0$$

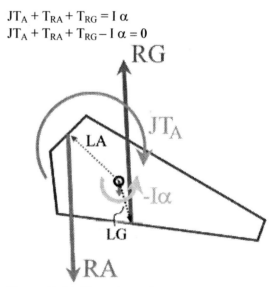

Figure 23-20. The solution for the ankle joint torque vector.

This simple rearrangement is helpful in the graphical interpretation of joint torque. In effect, we can inspect the size of all of the torques applied to the foot and assume that the free body is "balanced". Further, if three of the terms in the equation are known (T_{RA}, T_{RG}, and -$I\alpha$), the size and direction of the remaining unknown torque (JT_A) can be envisioned as of sufficient size and direction to offset the turning effect of the other three.

When visualizing the torques that act on a rigid body, it is convenient to show their effects with respect to the body segment center of gravity. Note that the small black circle near the center of the foot represents the foot center of gravity point. If we envision the foot as "pinned" at the CG point, we can easily visualize the turning effect of the forces acting on the body. For example, the torque produced by the ankle joint reaction force (RA) should be visualized as causing counter-clockwise rotation of the foot free body about the CG point. We can expect that the torque associated with the RA force will be large, because the force itself is large and the force lever arm is also large.

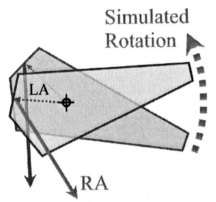

Figure 23-21. The tendency to rotate produced by the ankle joint reaction force.

Similarly, the ground reaction force (RG) will also cause counter-clockwise rotation of the free body because its line of action falls in front of the CG position. It is interesting to note that the size of the RG torque will be small, because the lever arm for this force is very short.

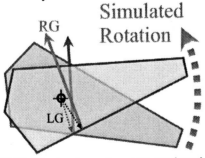

Figure 23-22. The tendency to rotate produced by the ground reaction force.

The third "known" term of the equation, -I α, may also be expected to be very small partly due to the small mass of the foot. The angular acceleration of

the foot segment is small and negative (-43 radians/sec^2). Thus the product of moment of inertia and angular acceleration must also be negative. However, the negative of the I α term will be positive, and as a result this vector is shown as small and counter-clockwise in the figure below.

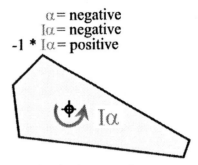

Figure 23-23. The -I α torque vector.

The net effect of the three "known" torques are as follows:

T_{RA} = Large and positive
T_{RG} = Small and positive
I α = Small and positive

Inspection of the known values indicates that their net effect must be a large and positive torque. Because the sum of all four torque terms must add up to zero, the joint torque at the ankle must be large and negative.

$JT_A + T_{RA} + T_{RG} - I \alpha = 0$
$T_{RA} + T_{RG} - I \alpha$ = Large and positive
JT_A = Large and negative

Because the ankle joint torque is negative, its vector must be shown as clockwise in the figure below.

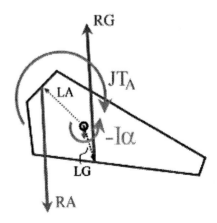

Figure 23-24. The ankle joint toque vector.

Question 23-2:
The ankle joint torque represents the net muscular action at the ankle. If the ankle joint torque is clockwise, is the performer attempting to dorsiflex or plantarflex his ankle?

O A. Dorsiflex.   O B. Plantarflex.

Knee Joint Torque Analysis

The shank free body diagram is used in the calculation of the knee joint torque. All of the forces and torques shown in the figure below are known, *except* for the knee joint torque (JT_K). As a result, the knee joint torque can be computed with the following equations:

$$JT_K - JT_A - T_{RA} + T_{RK} = I\, \alpha$$
$$JT_K - JT_A - T_{RA} + T_{RK} - I\, \alpha = 0$$

Where:

JT_K - the torque due to the net muscular action at the knee

JT_A - the torque due to the net muscular action at the ankle

T_{RA} - the torque due to the ankle joint reaction force

T_{RK} - the torque due to the knee joint reaction force

I = the moment of inertia of the shank segment

α = the angular acceleration of the shank segment

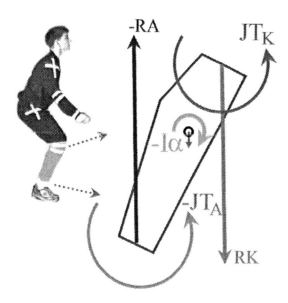

Figure 23-25. The shank free body diagram with all forces and toques shown.

Our analysis of the foot segment showed that the ankle joint torque acted in a clockwise direction. Newton's third law indicates that the distal end of

the shank must experience a torque that is equal and opposite to the ankle joint torque. As a result, the ($-JT_A$) vector is shown as acting in the counter-clockwise direction.

The visualization of the size and direction of the knee joint torque vector can be accomplished through a graphical inspection of the shank free body. The largest contributions to the knee joint torque come from the ($-RA$) and (RK) forces, and from the ($-JT_A$) torque. The ($-RA$) and (RK) force vectors create a very large tendency for clockwise rotation about the shank CG. This very large clockwise contribution is partially offset by the counter-clockwise influence of the ($-JT_A$) torque. As a result, the knee joint torque should be expected to be of moderate size and counter-clockwise.

The counter-clockwise torque acting at the knee indicates that the subject is vigorously attempting to extend his knee joint. This forceful extension of the knee joint is expected during the upward driving motion of a back somersault.

Hip Joint Torque Analysis

The hip joint torque is computed with a procedure similar to that of the knee. The peak hip joint torque value occurs at frame 101 for the back somersault file (RSFlip2S). The peak values for the ankle and knee torque values occur later, at around frame 107. The figure below shows the thigh free body diagram and the hip joint torque for frame 101.

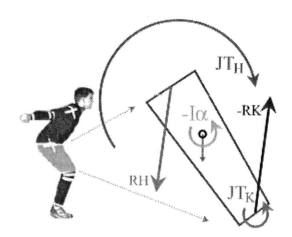

Figure 23-26. The thigh free body diagram with all forces and torques shown.

Note that the clockwise hip torque causes a tendency for hip extension. In turn, this hip extension makes a productive contribution to the upward driving motion in the back somersault.

Leg Joint Torque Timing

The timing of all three joint torque peaks is illustrated in the figure below.

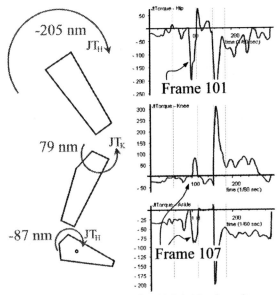

Figure 23-27. The timing of peak joint toque values during the upward driving phase of a back somersault motion.

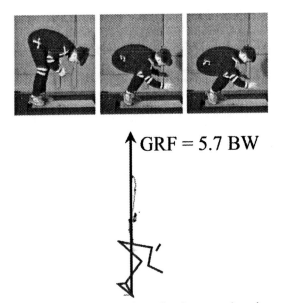

Figure 23-28. The ground reaction force produced during the landing of a back somersault motion.

The sequence in torque peaks gives us a glimpse of the coordinative process used by the skilled performer. The data show that the hip maximal torque occurs near the end of the upward driving phase and the ankle and knee act approximately in unison six frames later. The strong muscles acting at the hip are able to generate a larger peak joint torque magnitude (-205 Newton meters) than either the knee (79 Newton meters) or the ankle (-87 Newton meters).

The landing phase of the back somersault involves a peak ground reaction force that is nearly twice as large as that produced during the take off phase (4152 Newtons on landing versus 2158 Newtons on take off). As a result, the joint reaction forces and joint torques are much larger on landing than they are on take off. Further, because the performer "lands short" on this trial, he is forced to absorb a great deal of the landing force in his knee and ankle joints. The figure below shows the body motion just after the toes touch down. Note that the peak ground reaction force is equal to 5.7 times body weight.

The landing of the back somersault involves a different sequence of joint actions than we have seen in the take off phase. The ankle joint torque curve peaks first, immediately after landing, at frame 156. The hip and knee peak about 5 frames later, at frame 161.

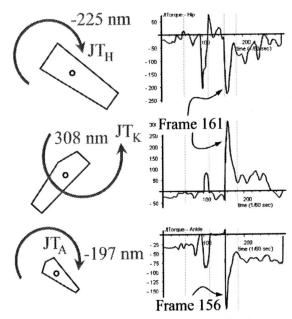

Figure 23-29. The peak joint torque timing for the landing of a back somersault motion.

It is interesting to note that the direction of the leg joint torques is the same on the landing as it was on the take off. Thus, the ankle joint produces a *tendency* to plantar flex. Similarly the knee torque produces a tendency to generate extension of the knee. However, the actual direction of motion for the ankle and knee is one of *flexion*. As a result, we see that the performer is making use of eccentric (lengthening) muscular contractions on the landing phase. These eccentric contractions are potentially more powerful than the concentric contractions that are used during much of the take off motion.

The figure below shows the peak leg joint torque values for both the landing and take off phases of the movement. The landing phase torques are larger than the take off phase torques for all joints. In particular, it appears that the knee joint is being used as the primary "shock absorber" in the landing. The organization of the leg-action movements appears to have been adapted to match the specific demands of the landing phase.

Back Somersault Joint Torque Magnitudes

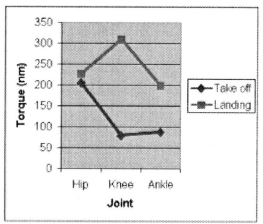

Figure 23-30. A comparison of the timing of the peak joint torques produced during the take off and landing phases of a back somersault motion.

Conclusions

Our work in the linear kinetics chapters established the relationship between the body's CG acceleration and ground reaction forces. Our work in angular kinetics has allowed us to apply Newton's second law to the analysis of individual body segments. We have seen that kinematic data is essential in the determination of joint reaction forces and joint torques. Further, we have seen that estimates of joint torque values as a function of time allows us to see "more deeply" into the underlying mechanisms that define skillful human motion.

Answers to Chapter Questions

Question 23-1:
If each box in the stack weights 2 Newtons, and the boxes are not accelerating, what will the ground reaction force be?

O A. 8 Newtons.
O B. 2 Newtons.
O C. 6 Newtons.

The correct answer is A. The sum total weight of the four boxes is 8 Newtons.

Question 23-2:
The ankle joint torque represents the net muscular action at the ankle. If the ankle joint torque is clockwise, is the performer attempting to dorsiflex or plantarflex his ankle?

O A. Dorsiflex.
O B. Plantarflex.

The correct answer is B. The performer is forcefully extending the ankle joint to add additional force to his upward jumping motion.

Part 6 – Fluid Mechanics

Chapter 24: Forces in a Fluid Medium
Chapter 25: Swimming Propulsion

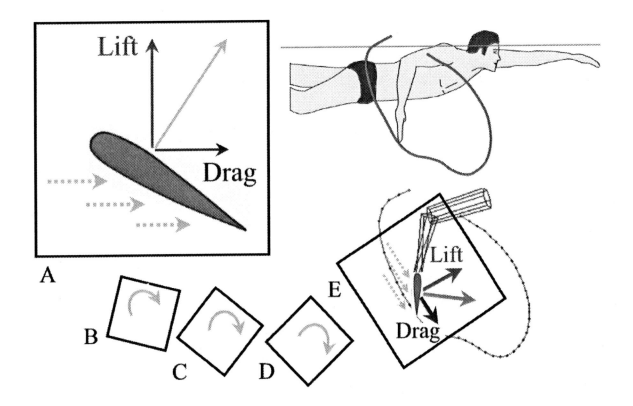

Chapter 24: Forces in a Fluid Medium

Fluid Mechanics

Fluid mechanics is a specialized area of study that helps us to understand the forces that act on objects that move in a *fluid medium*. Water is an obvious example of a fluid medium. A swimmer who pushes off the wall and glides, eventually comes to a stop as a result of the *drag* forces that are applied to his body by the water. The drag force is a result of the resistance that is created by the motion of the swimmer's body through the volume of water molecules. Similarly, *air resistance* will influence the motion of a kicked soccer ball as it moves through the air. The term "Air Resistance" simply identifies the drag force that acts between the ball and the air molecules that are disturbed by the ball's motion.

Figure 24-1. The glide phase in breaststroke.

We will see in this chapter that the principles of fluid mechanics are very general, and they can be applied equally well to the study of movement through air or water. Further, these same principles could be used to study movement through molasses or a bin of marbles. Engineers can even use the principles of fluid mechanics to design better traffic systems by envisioning each automobile as a "molecule" of fluid.

Basic Concepts

When you jog around a track, you will feel the slight forces that act on your body as a result of your motion through the air. If you try to run at the same speed in the hip deep water of a swimming pool, you will feel considerably more resistance. This difference in resistance is directly related to the high *density* of water compared to the relatively low density of air.

Density (ρ) is measured as the ratio of mass to volume for any material. Materials that are very compact, for example gold or platinum, have very high densities. Lighter materials like Styrofoam or aluminum have lower densities. The table below shows the density and weights of a variety of materials.

Table 24-1. Table of density and weight values for a variety of materials.

	1 cubic centimeter (cc)		
	Density	**Weight**	**Weight**
	g/cc	**newtons**	**pounds**
Air	0.001	0.000012	0.000003
Styrofoam	0.100	0.000981	0.000220
Water	0.998	0.009790	0.002200
Sea water	1.026	0.010065	0.002262
Aluminum	2.700	0.026487	0.005952
Mercury	13.600	0.133416	0.029981
Gold	19.300	0.189333	0.042547
Platinum	21.400	0.209934	0.047176

The density column shows how many grams of mass are associated with a single cubic centimeter (cc) of material. Thus, a cubic centimeter of water has a mass of 0.998 grams.

The second column shows the weight of a cubic centimeter of material, expressed in Newtons. The values in this column define the *specific weight* (γ) of each material. Specific weight is the ratio of the weight to the volume for a given material. The last column in the table shows the weight, expressed in pounds, for a cubic centimeter of material.

Once the density of a material is known, the remaining values in the table can be readily calculated. For example, to determine the weight at the surface of the earth (expressed in Newtons) of a given mass (expressed in *kilo*grams), multiply the mass by 9.81:

F = m A
Force (Newtons) = Mass (kg) * Acceleration
Weight (Newtons) = Mass (kg) * 9.81

Let's perform this calculation for water. Note that we must convert the mass of water (0.998 grams) to kilograms before we can use the above equation:

0.998 g = 0.000998 kg

Finally, the weight of 1 cc of water can be computed as:

Weight = 0.000998 kg * 9.81

Weight = 0.00979 Newtons

Note that the salt content of seawater causes it to be denser that normal water. As a result, 1 cc of salt water weights more than normal water.

Question 24-1:
If the weight of an object is known in Newtons, how can we convert that weight to an equivalent number of pounds?

O A. Divide the weight in Newtons by 4.45
O B. Divide the weight in Newtons by 2.2
O C. Multiply the weight in Newtons by 4.45

Question 24-2:
What will be heavier, a bucket filled with molten aluminum or a bucket filled with mercury?

O A. Mercury
O B. Aluminum

Question 24-3:
A rectangular bucket is 10 inches wide, 9 inches deep and 10 inches tall. How many cubic inches of volume are there in the bucket?

O A. 90 cubic inches
O B. 900 cubic inches
O C. 100 cubic inches

Question 24-4:
How many cubic centimeters are in a 900 cubic inch bucket? Please round your answer to the nearest 100 units. Feel free to use the Windows Calculator to help with this question.

O A. 2300 cc
O B. 900 cc
O C. 15000 cc

Question 24-5:
How much will a 15000 cc bucket of water weight? Express your answer in pounds.

O A. 3 pounds
O B. 33 pounds
O C. 330 pounds

The table below shows the weight, expressed both in Newtons and pounds, for a 15000 cc "bucket sized" volume.

Table 24-2. A table of density, mass and weight values for a variety of materials.

	1cc	1 bucket (15000 cc)		
	density	mass	weight	weight
	g/cc	grams	newtons	pounds
Air	0.001	18	0.18	0.04
Styrofoam	0.100	1500	14.72	3.31
Water	0.998	14970	146.86	33.00
Sea water	1.026	15390	150.98	33.93
Aluminum	2.700	40500	397.31	89.28
Mercury	13.600	204000	2001.24	449.72
Gold	19.300	289500	2840.00	638.20
Platinum	21.400	321000	3149.01	707.64

The weight for a "bucket full" of each material expressed in pounds is included to help you to better identify the *feel* associated with lifting materials of different densities. For example, a young child can easily lift a bucket of Styrofoam (3.31 pounds) and a teenager can lift a bucket of water (33.00 pounds). However, it would take an accomplished weight lifter to lift a bucket of gold (638.2 pounds).

It is interesting to note that the density of an object will quickly tell us if a given material will float in water. For example, the low density of Styrofoam causes it to tend to pop up to the surface if it is immersed in water. On the other hand, any material with a density greater than 0.998, will tend to "sink like a stone".

The values for density and weight in the table are expressed for typical temperature (20° C) conditions. If the temperature of a given material is increased, it will typically become less dense. As a result, if we heat the air in a hot air balloon, it will become less dense than the surrounding air and the balloon will tend to rise, or "float" in the surrounding air, just as Styrofoam tends to float in water.

Buoyant Force

Our knowledge of density will help us to understand the forces that act on human beings that are submerged in water. We can assume that if the net density of a person's body is less than 0.998, the person will float. The net density of the human body is not easily translated to a single number entry in a table. All of the materials that we have considered so far (water, aluminum, gold, etc.) are composed of uniformly distributed mass elements. The human body on the other hand, is composed of a variety of tissues, each with a different density.

The table below shows the density and *specific gravity* of water, body fat, muscle and bone.

Table 24-3. A comparison of the density and specific gravity values for body fat, muscle and bone.

Material	Density	Specific Gravity
Water	0.998	1.000
Body Fat	0.798	0.800
Muscle	0.998	1.000
Bone	1.746	1.750

Specific gravity is defined as the ratio of a given material's weight to the weight of an equal volume of water. When you are interested primarily in the forces that act under water, specific gravity provides a very clear indication of buoyant force. Materials with a specific gravity less than 1.0 will float; materials with a specific gravity greater than 1.0 will sink.

The table shows that fat is less dense than water, and therefore will tend to float. Muscle has the same density as water and therefore, will have neutral buoyancy. Finally, bone is considerably denser than water and will tend to sink.

The overall tendency to sink or float for any person will therefore depend upon their *body composition* or the percentages of their less dense (body fat) and more dense (bone and muscle) materials. Beginning swimmers discover early in their practice sessions if their body composition will be a help or a hindrance to their mastery of swimming skill. Lean, heavily muscled individuals have a tendency to sink and must work slightly harder to stay afloat. Those with above average body fat will float easily in the water.

The image sequence figure below shows the data from a biomechanical study of aqua-aerobics.

Figure 24-2. An image sequence figure of underwater jogging.

Jogging in place while submerged in water dramatically changes the ground reaction forces acting on the performer. This lightening of the "weight bearing" load will greatly reduce the tendency for injury that accompanies aerobic training activities. In addition, the dense fluid medium causes an increase in resistance to leg swinging motions and can create training loads that exceed those of land-based exercise.

Archimedes' Principle defines the forces acting on a stationary submerged body:

> *The buoyant force acting on a body equals the weight of the volume of water displaced by the body.*

If you stand at the shallow end of a swimming pool and walk down the gradual slope to the deep end, you will feel this buoyant force become larger and larger as you proceed into deeper and deeper water. As the water level rises from knee, to hip, to chest level, you will be displacing more and more water and the buoyant force will increase accordingly. The figure below shows that the buoyant force vectors become longer and longer as the person progresses into deeper water.

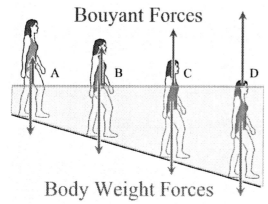

Figure 24-3. The buoyant and weight forces acting upon a partially submerged body.

When the swimmer gets to the far right side of the figure the buoyant force will be equal and opposite to the body weight force. For most people, the resulting upright floating position will occur when the top of the head is just above the water. The floating height can be changed substantially if the swimmer exhales. By emptying the lungs, the volume of displaced water becomes less and the effective body density increases. Under these circumstances, most people will sink to the bottom of the pool.

Horizontal Floating Position

The buoyant force that acts upon an upright body will typically be nearly collinear with the body weight force. As a result, the body will have no tendency to rotate. A horizontal floating position will often result in a gradual rotation of the body, where the legs sink while the head and chest remain near the water's surface.

The figure below shows a swimmer just after a push-off from the end wall of the pool. When the swimmer glides forward, the flow of water along his body and under his legs helps to keep his body in a horizontal position. As the swimmer slows down his legs will tend to sink and he will eventually come to rest in the inclined body position shown in part B of the figure. The tendency for a swimmer's legs to sink is a result of the relatively high density of the legs compared to the low density of the trunk, especially when the lungs are filled with air. The high density of the lower portion of the body causes the body's center of gravity location to be lower (closer to the feet) than the geometric center of the body. Because the weight force for the body acts through the center of gravity, its line of action will be to the left of the geometric center of the body.

The buoyant force that acts upward on the body acts at the *center of buoyancy,* or the geometric center of the volume of water that has been displaced by the body. Because the water that has been displaced by the legs has the same density as the water that is displaced by the trunk, the buoyant force must be shifted to the right relative to the body weight force. The weight and buoyant force vectors generate a force couple that causes the body to rotate counter-clockwise.

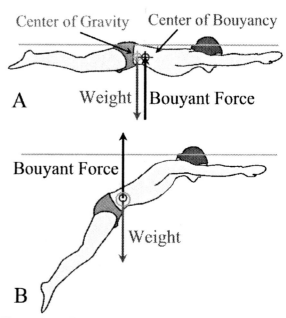

Figure 24-4. The center of gravity and center of buoyancy of the human body.

As the legs sink, the back of the head will gradually shift higher with respect to the surface of the water. This will cause the center of buoyancy to shift lower in the body. The vertical lines through the center of buoyancy and the center of gravity will eventually overlap and the torque acting on the body will fall to zero. The body will then tend to stay in this "dead man's float" position until additional forces are applied by, or to, the swimmer.

Drag Force

Our discussion of buoyant forces has focused upon the forces that act in a fluid medium in the *absence* of motion. When a body moves through a fluid medium, it is clear that the fluid tends to resist the motion of the body. This resistance force is called *drag* force.

Figure 24-5. The glide phase in the butterfly stroke.

Density and Drag Force

Let's now consider the various factors that influence the size of drag force. We have already mentioned that as the density of the fluid medium increases, so too will the drag force. (Running forward in water will produce much more resistance than running forward through air.) This relationship holds for all fluids and we can say that, if all other factors are held equal, drag force will be proportional to fluid density.

$$D \propto \rho$$

Velocity and Drag Force

The velocity of fluid flow by the body will also influence the size of drag force. To get a feel for the relationship between velocity and drag, let's conduct a "thought experiment". Imagine you are in a car and proceeding at a steady 5 miles per hour. If you extend your arm out of the window you will feel a gentle breeze on your arm, and a virtually imperceptible drag force. If the speed of the car increases 10 fold to 50 miles per hour, the force on your extended arm can be easily felt, as it will be much more than 10 times larger than the few ounces of force you felt at 5 miles per hour. Finally, imagine that you are in a passenger jet airplane moving at 500 miles per hour. Now *imagine* (do not actually do this) what would happen if you broke the window open and extended your arm outside the plane. (Hopefully you do not have a vivid imagination, because the thought of your arm being ripped out of the socket could be painful, even in a thought experiment.)

The point of our thought experiment is to show that the drag force that acts on a given body is very sensitive to the velocity of flow by the body. In fact, a 10 fold increase in body speed will result in a 100 fold increase in drag force. Mathematically:

$$D \propto V^2$$

If all other factors are held equal, the size of the drag force will be proportional to the velocity of motion *squared*.

The destructive power of a hurricane is a result of the extremely high velocity of wind that creates the funnel. When the wind speed diminishes, the hurricane becomes only a tropical storm. When the wind speed increases, entire buildings can be ripped from their foundations.

Shape and Drag Force

The shape of an object is also an important factor in the size of drag force. The streamlined shapes of jet planes and sport cars allow them to slip through the air with a minimum of resistance. The very high-speed motion of a jet plane makes the streamlined shape particularly important, because we know that the jet will produce very large drag forces ($D \propto V^2$). These drag forces translate into very high fuel costs for the jet. If the plane is streamlined as much as possible, the cost of fuel consumption over the life of the plane's service can be dramatically reduced.

Streamlining and Drag

Figure 24-6. A streamlined car shape.

There are numerous examples in sport where streamlining is used to reduce drag force and improve performance. Skiers on the long jump crouch down to minimize drag on their way down the slope. Cyclists wear helmets with streamlined trailing edges to reduce the drag on their bodies. Female swimmers wear suits with high backs to reduce the chance of pockets of water being formed along the length of the body.

A variety of shapes have been studied under laboratory conditions for the purpose of quantifying their tendency to produce drag force. The *coefficient of drag* (C_D) is an experimentally determined measure that defines the drag force producing characteristics of a given shape. The figure below shows the coefficient of drag values for typical flow conditions across a variety of shapes.

Coefficient of Drag

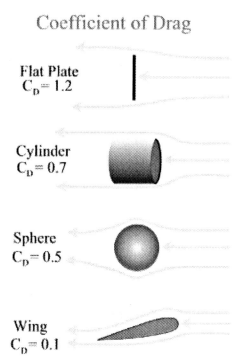

Flat Plate
$C_D = 1.2$

Cylinder
$C_D = 0.7$

Sphere
$C_D = 0.5$

Wing
$C_D = 0.1$

Figure 24-7. The coefficient of drag for a variety of shapes.

The C_D values in this figure are for typical flow conditions. If the roughness of the surfaces of the various objects changes or if the speed of flow changes, the exact value of the C_D will also change. The figure shows that the more streamlined shapes of the sphere and wing have the lowest C_D values and therefore will produce the smallest drag force for a given flow condition. The flat plate will produce the largest drag force among the various shapes in the figure.

When the C_D values for various shapes are determined in the fluid mechanics lab, a wind tunnel is typically used to facilitate the collection of drag force information. The object, for example a flat plate, is suspended in the center of the wind tunnel and then fans are used to blow air by the object. This approach is often used to determine the drag force produced by wings, entire planes and boat hulls.

It is interesting to note that the forces produced by air flowing by a fixed object are identical to those produced by a object that moves at the same rate through a stationary volume of air.

In the following question, you are asked to compare the drag force that will be produced under the following two circumstances.

1) You are in a car that is moving at 10 mph through the air on a day when there is no wind at all. You extend your hand out of the window and feel the drag force produced by the motion of the air by your hand.

2) You are sitting in a stationary car on a windy day. The wind is blowing past your car at the rate of 10 mph. You extend your hand out of the window and feel the drag force produced by the backward motion of the air by your hand.

Question 24-6:
Compare the drag force that will be produced under the following two circumstances. 1) You are in a car that is moving at 10 mph through the air on a day when there is no wind at all. You extend your hand out of the window and feel the drag force produced by the motion of the air by your hand. 2) You are sitting in a stationary car on a windy day. The wind is blowing past your car at the rate of 10 mph. You extend your hand out of the window and feel the drag force produced by the backward motion of the air by your hand.

Will there be any difference in the drag force that you feel under these two conditions?

O A. Yes.
O B. No.

In the above example, the *relative motion* of the air with respect to the hand is the same for a stationary hand in moving air or for a moving hand in stationary air. Because it is much more convenient to collect laboratory information from a stationary object, wind tunnels are used extensively in fluid mechanics research.

Question 24-7:
Can you think of a device that is commonly used in exercise physiology laboratories to simplify the collection of EMG, oxygen consumption and other measures from people as they exercise?

The figure below illustrates the pressure differences that result when air flows by a flat plate. As the air flows by the plate, a high-pressure region is produced on the leading side of the plate. Further, a partial vacuum is formed on the trailing side of the plate as the flow of air is pulled from right to left. The net effect of these pressure differences (high pressure on the right side and low pressure on the left) is represented by the drag force vector.

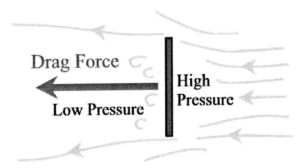

Figure 24-8. The drag force acting on a flat plate.

Figure 24-9 shows that both the leading and trailing edge of any given shape influence the size of the coefficient of drag. Rounded leading edges can reduce the high pressure area on the leading side of the object. Extended trailing edges, like that of a wing, can reduce the low pressure area on trailing edge of the object. Non-streamlined trailing edge surfaces will cause large negative pressure areas. For example, an accelerating bus creates a partial vacuum that will cause leaves to swirl and be sucked behind it due to the buses non-streamlined contour. The net effect of the leading and trailing edge pressure difference produces the resultant drag force.

Area and Drag Force

For any given object shape and speed of flow, the size of the drag force will also be influenced by the size of the object. Larger objects produce larger pressure differences and as a result, larger drag forces. The cross sectional area of the object is normally denoted by the term S. Drag force will be directly proportional to S for any given flow condition.

$$D \propto S$$

Drag Force Equation

In summary, it is clear that drag force size will be a function of four factors: density, velocity of flow, the coefficient of drag and the cross sectional area of a given object. The equation that is used to calculate drag force is given below:

$$D = \tfrac{1}{2}\, \rho\, V^2\, C_D\, S$$

Where:
D – drag force
ρ – density of the fluid
V^2 – the velocity squared of the relative motion of the fluid by the object
C_D – the coefficient of drag for the object
S – the cross sectional area of the object

In biomechanics, most of the terms in this equation are readily determined. Density is available in tables, velocity can be easily measured with video and the cross sectional area of an object is easily measured. The coefficient of drag is more difficult to determine for the various parts of the human body. Often, the value of C_D for human body parts or full body positions can only be determined through fluid lab / wind tunnel studies. We will see in the next chapter, that these types of studies have been used to improve our understanding of hand propulsion in human swimming.

Lift Force

The drag forces that act on an airplane wing are directed along a line that is opposite to the line of motion of the wing. By definition, drag forces resist the forward motion of the plane. Drag forces in no way provide support to keep the plane up in the air.

Lift force is defined as the force that acts at right angles to the flow of air (or water) past a given object. Wings are specifically designed to produce large lift forces while simultaneously producing very small drag forces. The figure below shows the lift and drag force vectors that act on an airplane wing. When you inspect this figure, visualize the air-flow as moving from right to left. Visualize the wing as being held fixed, as it would be in a wind tunnel.

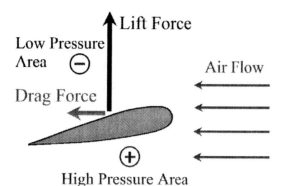

Figure 24-9. The lift and drag force acting on a typical wing.

The shape and angle of the wing cause a high pressure area to be generated underneath the wing, while a low pressure area is generated above the wing. The drag force acts in a direction opposite to the line of motion of the wing and, in effect, forces the plane to consume fuel in order to maintain a given forward air speed. The lift force acts at right angles to the line of motion of the wing (upwards) and serves to keep the plane aloft.

The pressure differences that generate lift force are difficult to visualize due to the invisible nature of the flow of air and water. The figure below shows dotted line patterns to represent the *streamlines* of air-flow past the wing.

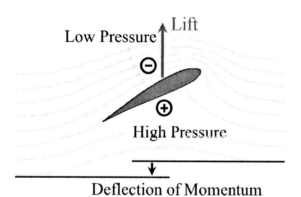

Figure 24-10. The pressure differences that create lift force.

The lightly shaded streamlines represent the direction of motion of the air molecules that flow by the wing. Notice that the downstream (left side) streamlines are all deflected downward with respect to their original positions. This *deflection of the momentum* of the air molecules represents a change in momentum of the air in the vertical direction. The impulse momentum relationship tells us that this change in momentum must be associated with an impulse of force that acts in the direction of the

change. The wing delivers an impulse of force to the air in the downward direction. In turn, the air pushes up on the wing in the upward direction and lift force results.

The mechanism for lift force production can also be explained by Bernoulli's principle:

> *Fluid pressure will increase wherever the speed of flow is forced to decrease; and*
> *fluid pressure will decrease wherever the speed of flow is forced to increase.*

The underside of the wing decelerates the free flow of air molecules that pass underneath the wing. The resulting decrease in flow velocity causes an increase in pressure on the underside of the airfoil.

The air-flow over the upper side of the wing is forced to increase as the air molecules rush to fill the partial vacuum above the wing. This increased speed of flow is associated with a decrease in the pressure above the wing.

The equation for lift force is virtually identical to the drag equation:

$$L = \frac{1}{2}\,\rho\,V^2\,C_L\,S$$

Where:
L – lift force
ρ – density of the fluid
V^2 – the velocity squared of the relative motion of the fluid by the object
C_L – the coefficient of lift for the object
S – the cross sectional area of the object

The equation indicates that the size of the lift force is very sensitive to the speed of an airplane because lift force Is proportional to velocity *squared*. The process of "take off" for a passenger airplane illustrates the relationship between velocity and lift force very well. As you begin to taxi down the runway, the speed of flow by the wing is very low and very little lift force is generated. The weight of the plane will far exceed the lift force and the net vertical force on the plane will be downward. As the plane increases speed down the runway, the lift force on the wings will increase rapidly. For every time interval where the plane speed doubles, the lift force size will increase by a factor of four. When the plane reaches take off velocity, the lift force on the wings will be greater than the gravitational force pulling the plane down and the plane will lift off.

While you are in the air, the jet engines will have ample power to maintain the forward velocity needed to create sufficient lift force to offset the pull of gravity. If you are unfortunate enough to run out of fuel while you are aloft, your air speed will diminish and the lift force produced by the wings will become less than the weight of the plane. At this point it will be a good idea to find a landing strip quickly.

Angle of Pitch and Coefficient of Lift

The pressure differences that act on an airplane wing depend upon both the shape of the wing and the wing's *angle of pitch* (α).The figure below shows a given wing with two different angles of pitch. Notice that when the angle between the wing and the approaching flow of air is increased from 6° to 25°, the lift force also increases. By increasing the angle of pitch, greater pressure differences are created between the upper and lower sides of the wing and as a result, greater lift forces are produced.

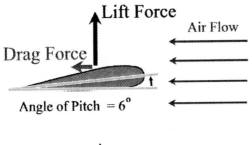

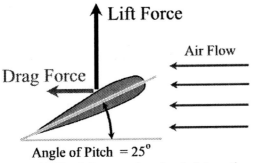

Figure 24-11. The influence of angle of pitch on the size of lift and drag forces.

Note: Because we are more interested in the motion of humans in air and water than we are in designing airplanes, we will present our coefficient of lift information for a special subset of airfoils. We will discuss *low aspect ratio* (short and stubby) airfoils in this section because we intend to apply our discussion to the study of hand propulsion in water in the next chapter. The more commonly seen high

aspect ratio wings, like those on a glider, exhibit the same general characteristics as shorter wings, however, they are rarely used at angles of pitch greater than 10°.

If the angle of pitch for a low aspect ratio wing is increased to larger values, the lift force will increase up to a point and then drop to zero as the angle of pitch reaches 90°. The figure below shows a wing for two high angles of pitch. The upper wing is positioned to generate the largest lift force possible for the low aspect ratio airfoil. The lift force generated with an angle of pitch of 40° is greater than that produced by any angle of pitch from 0° to 40°.

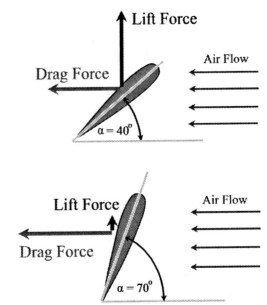

Figure 24-12. The influence of large angle of pitch measures on the size of lift and drag forces.

The lower wing in the figure shows that the lift force on the wing will drop off substantially for an angle of pitch of 70 °. If fact, all angles of pitch greater than 40° will produce less and less lift force, with a lift force of zero expected with an angle of pitch of 90°. For the given wing, the angle of pitch of 40° is known as the *critical angle of pitch*. If a pilot needs to increase altitude she can angle her plane upwards to increase the angle of pitch of the plane wings. This increase in angle of pitch will, *in general*, tend to produce more lift force. If the pilot pulls up to far, and the angle of pitch exceeds the critical angle of pitch, she will get *less* lift than expected. The plane's wings will be "stalled" and if adjustments are not made, the plane could go out of control.

Lift Force Experiment: This experiment will help you to get a feel for the relationship between the hand angle of pitch and lift force. You can conduct this experiment anytime you are out for a drive in a car and you are on a stretch of road that allows you to proceed at the speed limit for at least 30 seconds at a time.

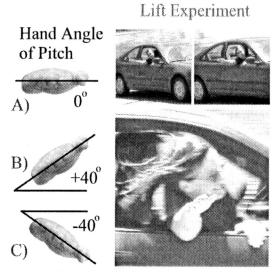

Figure 24-13. A hand "lift force" experiment.

Step 1: Stretch your arm out of the window and hold your hand at a zero degree angle of pitch (as shown in figure A above). You will feel the drag force of the air pushing your hand and arm backward, but you will feel no lift force.

Step 2: Change your hand angle of pitch to about 40° as shown in figure B above. This change in hand position will cause an increase in pressure underneath the palm of your hand and both the lift and drag force components acting on your hand will increase. You hand will be pulled back even more than before by the drag force component. The lift force component will tend to push your hand up, and you will be forced to hold your hand down to counter the effects of this lift force.

Step 3: Change your hand angle of pitch to *minus* 40° as shown in figure C above. Now the air above the back of your hand will have an increase in pressure, and the air pressure below the palm of your hand will become negative (a partial vacuum will form). In effect, the lift force acting on your hand will be aimed downward. As you make the change from a +40° angle of pitch to a -40° angle of pitch, you will feel your hand drop downward. When the hand angle of pitch is positive, you need to use your arm muscles to hold your hand down. When the angle of pitch changes to negative, you will need to change your arm forces to hold the hand up.

The Coefficient of Lift vs. Angle of Pitch

Our prior discussion of lift force production with wings has shown that the coefficient of lift for any given wing will change as a function of the angle of pitch. Thus, while there is a single coefficient of drag for a sphere under a given flow condition, there is a wide range of coefficient of lift values for a wing.

The figure below shows the lift forces associated with a wing at 5 different angles of pitch.

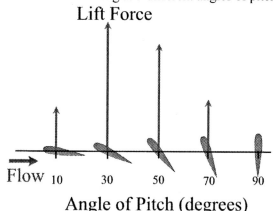

Figure 24-14. The relationship between lift force size and angle of pitch.

You should envision that the flow of air past each wing is from left to right. The figure shows the relationship between lift force size and angle of pitch for a low aspect ratio wing. A wing aspect ratio is the ratio of the wing length to the wing width. Long slender wings have high aspect ratios and have a tendency to produce maximal lift forces at angles of pitch around 5°. Low aspect ratio wings are short and stubby, much like a human hand. Low aspect ratio wings produce maximal lift forces with angles of pitch of about 35 - 40°.

The figure below shows the relationship between lift force production and angle of pitch as a continuous curve.

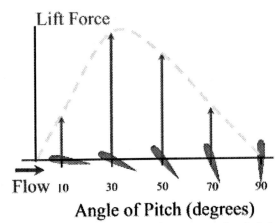

Figure 24-15. A coefficient of lift versus angle of pitch curve with wing forces shown.

The C_L curve can be used to estimate the size of the lift force at any angle of pitch for the wing as long as the velocity of flow and wing size are held constant.

$$L = \frac{1}{2}\, \rho\, V^2\, C_L\, S$$

The lift equation reminds us that the size of the lift force for any given wing's motion in air is a function of angle of pitch, wing size and velocity. As a result, the curve above provides information for only a single speed and a single wing size and shape.

The figure below shows the *coefficient of lift* versus angle of pitch curve for the low aspect wing in the prior example. Notice that the only change to the prior figure is that the vertical axis is now scaled to show coefficient of lift values.

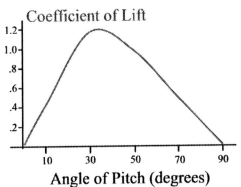

Figure 24-16. A coefficient of lift versus angle of pitch curve.

The coefficient of lift versus angle of pitch curve (C_L vs α) can be used determine the "lift force producing characteristics" for any wing with a given cross sectional shape and aspect ratio. Thus this

curve can be used to compute the lift on a model airplane wing, or a commercial jetliner for a wide range of flow conditions. The values for S (wing area) and V (velocity) can be entered into the lift equation along with the C_L value that corresponds to a given angle of pitch. The lift equation can then be used to calculate lift force.

$$L = \frac{1}{2}\, \rho\, V^2\, C_L\, S$$

Question 24-8:
What is the value for the coefficient of lift for a low aspect ratio wing when the angle of pitch is 25°? Round your answer to the nearest .2 units.

O A. 0.2
O B. 1.0
O B. 1.2

Reductionism: Lift and Drag Forces

Our discussions on lift and drag have taken advantage of reductionism to simplify the problem of visualizing and computing the forces that act on an object that moves in a fluid medium. We have identified drag as the force component that acts opposite to the line of motion of the object. Similarly, we have identified lift as the force component that acts at right angles to the line of motion of the object.

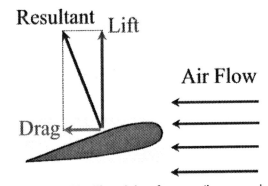

Figure 24-17. The lift and drag forces acting on a wing.

The figure below shows that the lift and drag force components can be resolved into a single resultant force vector that represents the net effect of the pressure differences that exist around the wing.

We know that in reality, there is not a single force acting on the wing. There is instead a continuous distribution of high and low pressures regions all around the wing. The figure below shows the high and low-pressure distributions that act on a wing. This relatively complex collection of force vectors, when broken down into horizontal and vertical components, will give us the lift and drag forces that we can use to understand the forces that act on the wing. It is interesting to note that by breaking down the effects of the fluid flow into logically organized categories of information (lift and drag) we are able to greatly simplify our analysis. When we study the lift force component, we know to consider the shape of the wing and the angle of pitch. This reductionistic approach allows us to define the force producing characteristics of different shapes in tables of C_L and C_D values. We will see in the next chapter that this approach will enable us to estimate the propulsive forces generated by swimmer's hands and take steps towards the objective evaluation of skill in human swimming.

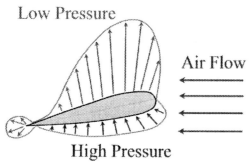

Figure 24-18. The pressure distributions acting on the surface of a wing.

Lift Forces in Water

The direction of lift, by definition, is at right angles to the line of motion of the object. For wing motions in horizontal flight, lift is aimed upward. However, there are many instances where the direction of lift is not upward.

The figure below shows the motion of a boat propeller. Note that the propeller follows a curved, helix shaped path that continually advances through the water. Each blade on the propeller has a cross sectional shape very much like that of an airfoil. Further, the blades of the propeller are angled to engage the water at an optimal angle of pitch. The propulsive force generated by the propeller is aimed straight-forwards, at right angles to the line of motion of the propeller.

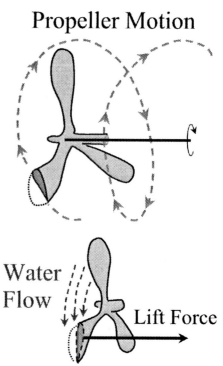

Figure 24-19. The lift force produced by propeller motions.

This propulsive force is, by definition, lift force. It is aimed at right angles to the line of motion of the blades and it is a result of pressure differences between the trailing and leading surfaces of each propeller blade.

Early in this chapter we mentioned that the principles of fluid mechanics can be applied to the analysis of motion in air or water with no modification. We see from this example, that if we understand the mechanisms for force production in a wing, we can apply this information to understand the forces generated by the motion of a propeller blade.

The figure below shows the propeller on a light commuter plane. On this plane the wings are used to generate lift upwards but the propeller is used to generate lift forces *forward* to create thrust. The motion of the airplane propeller creates a high-pressure region behind the propeller and a low-pressure region in front of the plane. The net effect of the propeller motion is lift force forward.

The lower portion of the figure shows the motion of a skilled swimmer's hand on a breaststroke arm pull. Notice that the pattern of motion of the swimmer's hand follows a nearly circular arc, much like that of a boat or plane propeller blade.

Figure 24-20. A comparison of the motions produced by a propeller driven plane and by a breaststroke swimmer.

Question 24-9:
Do you think that the breaststroke swimmer makes use of lift force as he generates forward propulsion from his arm pull?

O A. Yes. The hand appears to be creating lift force forward through the circular pattern of motion of the hand.
O B. No. The shape of the hand is not streamlined enough to allow for the generation of lift force.

Magnus Effect

The motion of various balls in sport (baseballs, tennis balls, softballs, soccer balls, basketballs, etc.), provide a fascinating source of entertainment for people all over the world. The flight of these balls through the air provides us with quite a few interesting examples that will help us to better understand the principles of fluid mechanics.

The symmetrical shape of a sphere leads us to expect that the motion of a ball through the air will not involve lift force. If we put a ball in a wind tunnel, we can expect that the pressure above and below the ball will be equal, and no lift force will be produced.

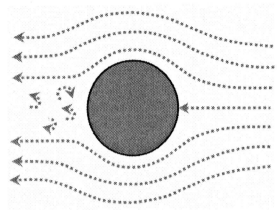

Figure 24-21. A symmetrical distribution of flow around a sphere.

Now imagine that a baseball is suspended in a wind tunnel on a horizontal rod. Further, imagine that this rod is rotated to cause the ball to spin in place as the air is blown by. The ball in the figure below is being made to spin in a counter-clockwise direction. The flow of air by the ball is proceeding from right to left.

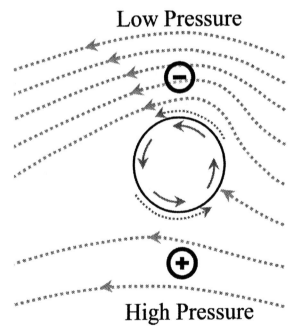

Figure 24-22. The pressure distribution around a sphere with under spin.

The spin on the ball has caused the development of an asymmetric flow around the ball as shown by the lightly shaded streamlines. As the seams on the ball circulate counter-clockwise, the air molecules in the immediate vicinity of the ball will also be pulled around in a counter-clockwise direction. There will be "air molecule collisions" on the bottom side of the ball as the counter-clockwise flow molecules close to the ball surface encounter the right to left flow of the wind tunnel air stream. These "collisions" will result in a build up of pressure on the bottom side of the ball.

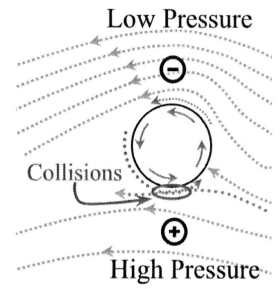

Figure 24-23. The influence of "air molecule collisions" near the surface of a spinning ball.

The counter-clockwise motion of the ball surface air molecules at the top side of the ball will be moving in the same direction as the right to left wind tunnel flow of air. Because of the ball spin, the flow of the wind tunnel air streams over the tops surface of the ball will encounter less resistance than would be the case for a ball with no spin at all. As a result, the speed of flow over the top of the ball will be faster than the flow past the bottom portion of the ball. This relatively high speed of flow over the top of the ball will be associated with a low pressure region. The "collisions" at the lower surface of the ball (see figure 24-25) will create a high pressure region.

The overall result of the pressure differences for this counter-clockwise ball spin will be a lift force acting upwards. The term *Magnus effect* is often used to describe the lift force producing conditions that are associated with spinning spheres. Figure 24-26 shows that the rotation of the ball causes a pattern of streamlines that is nearly identical to that formed around an airfoil.

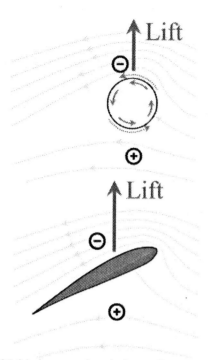

Figure 24-24. A comparison between the pressure differences around a wing and a spinning ball.

Bernoulli's principle can also be used to explain the generation of lift force by a spinning ball. Because the flow of air molecules underneath the ball is slowed down by the "collision" of air molecules, the fluid pressure under the ball must increase. Similarly, because the speed of flow of air molecules over the top of the ball is facilitated by the spin of the ball, the fluid pressure must decrease.

Our example of a ball with counter-clockwise spin in a wind tunnel is directly analogous to the motion of a fastball pitch in baseball. The figure below shows a pitcher who is releasing the ball by "rolling it off his fingertips" at the moment of release. Because the fingers apply pressure downwards against the rear portion of the ball, backspin is produced. Note that for left to right ball motion, backspin involves counter-clockwise rotation of the ball. The backspin causes high pressure to build up underneath the ball. This in turn, causes the development of a lift force upward. The net effect of this pitch is a "rising" fastball, where the lift force on the ball partially counters the pull of gravity and causes the ball to drop more slowly than normal. If a batter cannot anticipate that the incoming pitch is a fastball, he will tend to swing "under" the pitch and produce a pop-up or a strike.

Figure 24-25. A fastball throwing motion.

The Magnus effect can also be used to explain the flight of topspin ground-strokes in tennis. The figure below shows the motion of a typical forehand ground stroke. Notice that the racket pattern of motion starts low and sweeps upwards and forward during the course of the swing. This technique is designed to cause the racket to brush upwards on the back of the ball during the ball impact interval.

Figure 24-26. A tennis topspin forehand.

Note that topspin produces a clockwise spin direction for a ball that is hit from left to right. The streamlines and pressure differences produced by a topspin ball are the inverse of those produced by the backspin on a fastball pitch. Because the ball is rotating in the clockwise direction, the air molecules immediately adjacent to the ball surface are pulled up and over the top of the ball. The flow of air molecules from right to left in the figure will collide with those near the upper portion of the ball's surface. As a result, a high-pressure region will be generated above the ball.

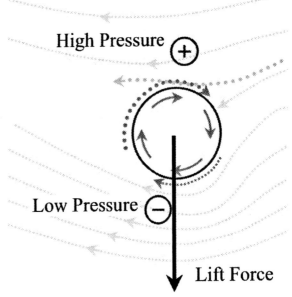

Figure 24-27. The lift force acting on a ball with topspin.

The flow of air molecules past the underside of the ball will encounter decreased resistance as a result of the clockwise ball rotation. This condition will cause the flow underneath the ball to be faster than that of a ball with no spin, and pressure will decrease. The net effect of the pressure differential is a lift force *downward*. This downward lift is consistent with the principles of fluid mechanics because it is aimed *at right angles* to the line of motion of the ball and is directed away from the high pressure region. We have seen above that propeller blades can generate lift forces forward. We see here that a topspin ball in horizontal flight will generate lift force downward.

The topspin produced by a tennis forehand allows the player to hit the ball harder and still keep the ball from sailing "long". The figure below shows the flight paths of two tennis balls. The first ball (shown by the longer dashed line curve) is hit flat (with virtually no spin). The second ball (shown by the finely dotted line) is hit with heavy topspin. Both balls have the same angle of projection and initial velocity.

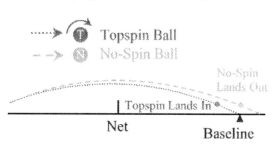

Figure 24-28. A comparison of the flight paths of a ball hit with topspin and another ball hit with no spin.

Note that the "no-spin" ball lands beyond the baseline and is "out", causing the player to lose the point. The topspin ball is hit just as hard, but falls into play short of the baseline. The figure below shows that the "no spin" ball could be made to land in-bounds if its angle of projection is lowered.

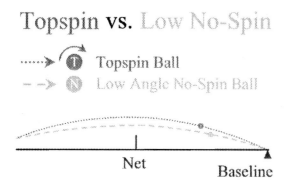

Figure 24-29. The use of topspin allows a ball to clear the net with an extra margin of error and still land in bounds.

The flat hit ball will be a difficult shot to return, as long as it clears the net. The low trajectory needed to keep the "no-spin" ball in-bounds increases the risk of a "net ball" and lost point. Most skilled tennis players today make use of topspin to increase their margin of error for clearance over the net without forcing a compromise in ball speed.

Turbulent and Laminar Flow Conditions

The motion of objects through air or water is also influenced by the energy associated with the flow conditions. *Laminar flow* is associated with smooth, continuous, uninterrupted flow around an object. Laminar flow occurs around smooth and streamlined objects such as airfoils especially at slow flow velocities. *Turbulent flow* is associated with the water/air swirls and eddies that occur when an object disrupts the continuous flow of fluid. Wings will experience regions of turbulent flow as the speed of flow by the wing increases or when slight irregularities exist on the surface of the wing. The figure below shows a wing with laminar flow conditions on the underside and turbulent flow conditions on the trailing portion of the upper-side of the wing.

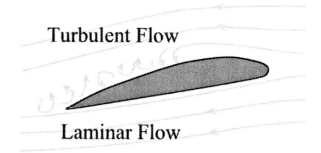

Figure 24-30. The laminar and turbulent flow conditions acting around a wing.

If a wing can be designed to support laminar flow conditions over most of its length, the drag produced by the wing will be kept at a minimum. Very slight irregularities on the surface of the wing, including the presence of sand particles in the paint, can cause a reduction in laminar flow and an increase in drag.

At high flow velocities, the laminar flow conditions around a smooth sphere cause a high value of drag because the smooth streamlines at the front portion of the sphere flow continuously to form a large "drag area" behind the trailing edge of the sphere.

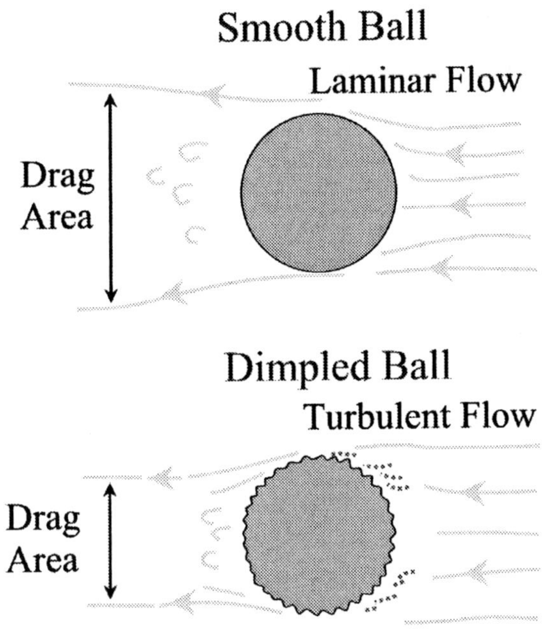

Smooth Ball
Laminar Flow

Drag Area

Dimpled Ball
Turbulent Flow

Drag Area

Figure 24-31. The influence of a ball's surface roughness on flow conditions around the ball.

Ironically, if the surface of the sphere is made rough, a turbulent, high-energy flow is created at the front edge of the sphere. This high-energy flow hugs the surface of the sphere longer and generates a smaller wake behind the sphere. This reduced "drag area" is associated with lower levels of drag force for the high speeds associated with golf drives. This phenomenon explains why golf balls with dimples can be driven further than smooth golf balls.

Conclusions

Our introduction to fluid mechanics principles is now complete. We have seen how buoyancy, lift forces and drag forces can influence the motion of objects in a fluid medium. Our discussion of forces in this chapter has been simplified through the discussion of simply shaped objects. The next chapter will focus on the propulsive forces that are generated by the human hand in swimming propulsion.

Answers to Chapter Questions

Question 24-1:
If the weight of an object is known in Newtons, how can we convert that weight to an equivalent number of pounds?

O A. Divide the weight in Newtons by 4.45

O B. Divide the weight in Newtons by 2.2
O C. Multiply the weight in Newtons by 4.45

The correct answer is A. One Newton is equal to only about one quarter pound.

Question 24-2:
What will be heavier, a bucket filled with molten aluminum or a bucket filled with mercury?

O A. Mercury
O B. Aluminum

The correct answer is A. Mercury is denser than aluminum by a factor of 5.

Question 24-3:
A rectangular bucket is 10 inches wide, 9 inches deep and 10 inches tall. How many cubic inches of volume are there in the bucket?

O A. 90 cubic inches
O B. 900 cubic inches
O C. 100 cubic inches

The correct answer is B. The volume of the bucket is equal to (10 * 9 * 10) = 900 cubic inches.

Question 24-4:
How many cubic centimeters are in a 900 cubic inch bucket? Please round your answer to the nearest 100 units. Feel free to use the Windows Calculator to help with this question.

O A. 2300 cc
O B. 900 cc
O C. 15000 cc

The correct answer is C. There are 2.54 centimeters in one linear inch. One cubic inch has (2.54^3) or 16.387 cc's. 900 cubic inches has 16.387 * 900 = 14748 cc. This answer rounds to 15000 cc.

Question 24-5:
How much will a 15000 cc bucket of water weight? Express your answer in pounds.

O A. 3 pounds
O B. 33 pounds
O C. 330 pounds

The correct answer is B. There are .0022 pounds in a cubic centimeter of water (see table). A 15000 cc bucket of water will weight (.0022 * 15000) = 33 pounds.

Question 24-6:
Compare the drag force that will be produced under the following two circumstances. 1) You are in a car that is moving at 10 mph through the air on a day when there is no wind at all. You extend your hand out of the window and feel the drag force produced by the motion of the air by your hand. 2) You are sitting in a stationary car on a windy day. The wind is blowing past your car at the rate of 10 mph. You extend your hand out of the window and feel the drag force produced by the backward motion of the air by your hand.

Will there be any difference in the drag force that you feel under these two conditions?

O A. Yes.
O B. No.

The correct answer is B. There will be no difference in the resulting drag force. The flow conditions by your hand are the same in both cases.

Question 24-7:
Can you think of a device that is commonly used in exercise physiology laboratories to simplify the collection of EMG, oxygen consumption and other measures from people as they exercise?

Answer:
The treadmill and the stationary bike greatly simplify the collection of physiological data. Imagine how difficult it would be to collect the expired gases of a runner who is performing on a regular track. You would have to load your equipment into a van and try your best to keep pace with the runner without running over pedestrians.

Question 24-8:
What is the value for the coefficient of lift for a low aspect ratio wing when the angle of pitch is 25°? Round your answer to the nearest .2 units.

O A. 0.2
O B. 1.0
O B. 1.2

The correct answer is B. A vertical line extended upward from the 25° angle will intersect the C_L curve at about the 1.0 value.

Question 24-9:
Do you think that the breaststroke swimmer makes use of lift force as he generates forward propulsion from his arm pull?

O A. Yes. The hand appears to be creating lift force forward through the circular pattern of motion of the hand.

O B. No. The shape of the hand is not streamlined enough to allow for the generation of lift force.

The correct answer is A. Skilled breaststrokers rely heavily on lift force production in their generation of propulsive force.

Chapter 25: Swimming Propulsion

In this chapter we will apply the principles of fluid mechanics to the analysis of skillful swimming performance. The movement file examples from this section will be particularly interesting, because they will show that ideal form models cannot be used to characterize optimal human performance. Further, data from Olympic swimmers will be presented to show how a biomechanical database can be used to objectively evaluate skill.

Figure 25-1. A front view of a front crawlstroke arm pull.

Mechanisms of Propulsion

Prior to 1970, the mechanism responsible for swimming propulsion was thought to be derived from a simple, action reaction – "push water backward to go forward" idea. The figure below illustrates a model "pull back" technique for human swimming and an analogous caterpillar paddlewheel form of marine navigation.

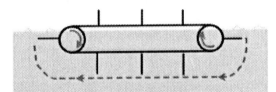

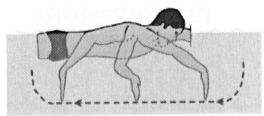

Figure 25-2. A comparison of a caterpillar paddlewheel and a straight-back arm pull in the front crawlstroke.

The caterpillar paddlewheel propulsive mechanism is particularly ineffective in producing propulsion. The first blade on a paddlewheel will initially generate propulsion as the mechanism begins to move. However, the second and third blades on the paddlewheel are not able to generate much propulsion because they are following in the wake of the first blade. Instead of pushing against "still water" the remaining blades push against water that is already moving backward. In the end, the caterpillar paddlewheel blades are limited in their ability to generate "traction" in the water. A traditional, "circular motion" propeller blade provides a far better mechanism for propulsion because each blade that better allows the blade to gain traction by continuously "finding still water".

The straight-line swimming pulling motion shown at the bottom of the figure will also involve limited force production. The figure shows the pulling pattern for a *stationary* swimmer. As the swimmer begins to achieve forward velocity, the length of the pulling pattern will become shorter and shorter. For a given time period associated with an underwater pull, this shortened pulling distance translates to lower hand velocity values. If distance is reduced and time is held fixed, velocity must decrease:

$$V = D / T$$

Further, propulsive force, in the form of lift or drag is proportional to velocity *squared*. Therefore a small reduction in velocity will produce a relatively large reduction in propulsion:

$$L \propto V^2$$
$$D \propto V^2$$

In order to generate high hand speeds with respect to the water, good swimmers purposely deviate from straight line pulling patterns. The figure below shows the similarity between the pulling patterns of skilled swimmers and that of a propeller blade.

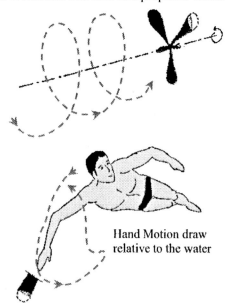

Hand Motion draw relative to the water

Figure 25-3. A comparison of a propeller motion and the curvilinear arm pull of a front crawlstroke swimmer.

The pattern of motion in the propeller shows that it moves forward through the water continuously and constantly encounters "still water" in the generation of propulsion. The swimmer in the lower portion of the figure is also using a propulsive strategy that relies upon sweeping curve line patterns of motion.

Counsilman's Theory of Propulsion

In 1971, James E. Counsilman, a professor and swimming coach at Indiana University, presented a new theory of swimming propulsion. Counsilman went on record as the first researcher to recognize the importance of lift force in human swimming. His 1971 paper: "The application of Bernoulli's principle to human propulsion in water" stressed the importance of *sculling* movements in swimming. Sculling is defined as the side-to-side and up-and-down hand motions commonly used in "treading water" and synchronized swimming movements.

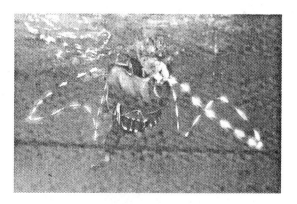

Figure 25-4. The arm pull pattern of motion for a backstroke swimmer is revealed by open shutter light trace photography.

Counsilman, an Olympic team coach, presented underwater photographic data for a wide variety of world-class swimmers. The figure above shows "light trace photography" data for an Olympic backstroker (Counsilman, 1971). The "dotted line" light pattern shows that the swimmer's hand motion follows a complex three-dimensional curve. Counsilman's data for all of the competitive strokes (front crawlstroke, butterfly, backstroke and breaststroke) showed that the hand follows a variety of elliptical pulling patterns as the swimmer generates propulsion. Counsilman concluded: "champion swimmers are not pushing directly backward, but are using a zigzag pattern of varying degrees". It is important for us to realize that Counsilman's biomechanical findings truly revolutionized the way practitioners designed and implemented training and instructional programs for swimmers. Most interesting, Counsilman's discovery was a result of a motion analysis process much like the one you are doing for this semester's video analysis project.

Swimming Movement Patterns

Front Crawlstroke Basics

The image sequence figure below shows side view video data for a skilled front crawlstroke swimmer.

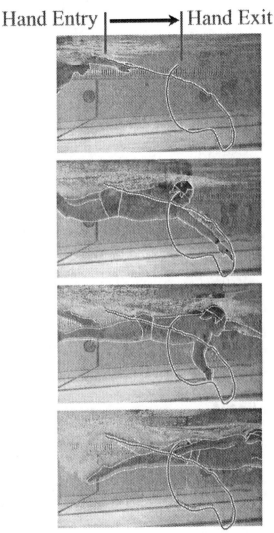

Figure 25-5. The side view pattern of motion of a skilled front crawlstroke swimmer.

Many people expect to see the swimmer's hand enter in front of him and then move backwards to accomplish the arm pull. In fact, the swimmer's hand follows a curvilinear path, and for many swimmers, the hand exits the water *in front of* the spot where it first entered the water. Because the swimmer is moving forward as he pulls his hand through the water, it is very difficult for him to generate much hand motion in the backward direction.

Note that the pattern of motion of the hand is drawn *with respect to the water*. This pattern of motion shows the propulsive actions of the hand on the water. The video images in the figure have been taken by a camera that has been held still as the swimmer swims by. If the camera were panned from side-to-side, as is often done with video that is shot for qualitative analysis, it would be more difficult to visualize the hand motions that generate propulsion.

The figure below shows a video image still frame and a wire frame body diagram (similar to a stick figure) from the Hydrodynamics Analysis Software. The vectors labeled L, D and R on the figure represent the Lift, Drag and Resultant force produced by the hand.

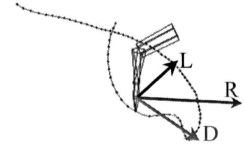

Figure 25-6. The size of the hand's propulsive force is largest near the end of the arm pull.

This side view pulling pattern shows only two dimensions from the three-dimensional swimming motion. As a result, this figure does not show the side-to-side hand movements that are into and out of the side view plane. Propeller-like hand motions can take advantage of diagonal side-to-side motions as well as diagonal up-and-down motions. As a result, we cannot truly understand swimming propulsion unless we visualize the full three-dimensional pulling motion.

Three Dimensional Movement Patterns

The figure below shows side view, front view and bottom view pattern of motion data for the front crawlstroke. These patterns show the full, three-dimensional, range of motion of the hand. Notice that the bottom view shows that the hand is sweeping side-to-side (from the body midline toward the swimmer's right hip) at the given instant in time.

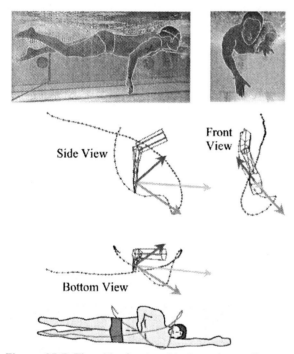

Figure 25-7. The side, front and bottom view pulling patterns of a front crawlstroke arm pull.

The side view and bottom view figures provide very important visualization information for all swimming strokes because they hold the forward dimension of motion in common. Notice that the hand propulsive force vectors in the side and bottom views indicate that the hand force is aimed mainly forward.

Question 25-1:
The front view figure shows that the resultant propulsive force vector is very short. Does this mean that the swimmer is producing very little effective force?

O Yes. The swimmer must be very weak.
O No. A force that is aimed nearly straight forward will be shown as a dot in the front view.

Diagonal Patterns of Motion

The front crawlstroke (freestyle) examples above show that good swimmers use *diagonal* pulling patterns to generate propulsive force. The figure below shows that the last portion of the pulling motion for the skilled freestyler is aimed upward and back. This diagonal line of pull is very effective in the generation of forward propulsive force.

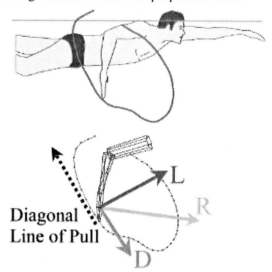

Figure 25-8. The diagonal line of pull used during the finishing portion of the front crawlstroke arm pull.

Pulling Patterns and Hand Angle

In order for a swimmer to take advantage of "propeller-like" hand motions to generate propulsion, he or she will need to use curved patterns of motion and make fine adjustments to the hand's angle of pitch to allow for the generation of lift force. The angle of pitch of the hand for the most propulsive portion of a skilled freestyler's pull is shown in the figure below.

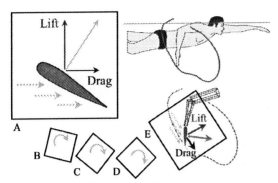

Figure 25-9. The lift and drag forces that act on an airplane wing are very similar to the lift and drag forces that act on a swimmer's hand.

The wing at the upper left corner of the figure shows the lift and drag force production for a low aspect ratio wing. This wing should be envisioned as moving from right to left on the screen, and therefore the flow of air by the wing is from left to right, as shown by the lightly shaded arrows. The pressure differences produced by the wing's motion create a lift force upward, at right angles to the line of motion of the wing. The drag force on the wing is aimed to the right, opposite to the line of motion of the wing.

The motion of the swimmer's hand through the water is shown on the right side of the figure. Note that a wing has been superimposed on top of the hand in the side view stick figure. The forces produced on the hand are very similar to those acting on the wing because both have an angle of pitch of 32°. However, because the line of motion of the hand is diagonally up and back, the lift and drag forces are rotated to accommodate this diagonal pattern. Thus, the lift force produced by the hand is at right angles to the line of motion of the hand, but it is aimed forwards and upward. The drag force acting on the hand is opposite to the line of motion of the hand, and is therefore aimed forward and down. The wing figure and hand figure are really the same, with the exception that the hand figure is rotated clockwise to match the hand's diagonal pattern.

It is interesting to note that while drag forces are "bad" for airplane wings because they increase fuel expenditure, the drag force produced by hand motions is not "bad" for swimmers. The combination of lift and drag together has produced a resultant force that is nearly straight forward for this swimmer. We will see in the remainder of this chapter that skilled swimmers manipulate their hand pitch angles in order to "aim" their propulsive forces forward.

For the example shown in figure 25-9, the hand angle of pitch is 32°. This relatively low angle of pitch implies that lift force plays an important role in the propulsion for this swimmer. In order to quantify the size of swimming propulsive forces, we will next need to review information from fluid laboratory studies on the human hand.

Hand Model Studies

While the *theory* behind lift force production in wings is relevant to the study of swimming forces, it is not appropriate to use *wing* coefficient of lift data in the calculation of *hand* forces. We can expect that the carefully crafted shape of the wing will enable it to produce larger levels of lift force than can be generated by the hand. In fact, in the 1970's some critics of Counsilman's theory claimed that, due to the hand's irregular shape, it is not capable of creating any lift force at all. To address this issue, several studies on the force producing characteristics of the human hand were conducted in the late 1970's (Schleihauf 1977, 1979, Wood, 1979).

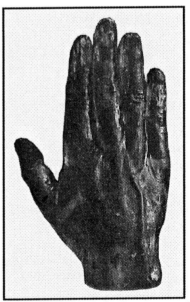

Figure 25-10. A plastic resin hand model used in Schleihauf, 1978.

The figure below shows a hand model that was used in the determination of the coefficient of lift and drag for the hand in the Schleihauf study. The plastic resin model was created from a plaster cast of a real human hand. The propulsive forces generated by the hand were measured in a fluid lab open water channel. An open water channel, like a wind tunnel, is used to study the forces that act on physical models under controlled circumstances. The forces generated between the hand model and the flow of water were recorded for a wide variety of hand positions. The resulting information was used to generate hand coefficient of lift and drag curves.

The figure below shows a comparison of the coefficient of lift data for the hand model and a low aspect ratio airfoil.

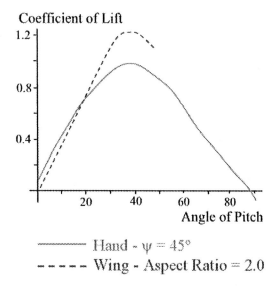

Coefficient of Lift

——— Hand - ψ = 45°
- - - - - Wing - Aspect Ratio = 2.0

Figure 25-11. A comparison of the coefficient of lift versus angle of pitch curves for a low aspect ratio wing (dotted line) and a human hand (solid line).

The wing C_L data (shown by the dashed curve) was taken from a standard NASA publication on airfoils. The C_L data for the hand (shown by the solid line curve) was taken from fluid laboratory measurements on the hand model shown in figure 25-10.

Notice that the wing is able to produce, as expected, a larger peak lift force value as indicated by the higher peak C_L value on the wing curve. The hand model produces 18% less peak lift because of the irregular surface contour of the hand. However, the basic lift force producing characteristics for the hand and the wing are very similar. The lift force capabilities of the hand start off small in the 0° - 10° range, grow to peak values in the 35° - 45° range, and then drop to zero as the angle of pitch approaches 90°. As a result, it is clear the human hand can be used to generate lift force in the same way as wings and propeller blades. This overall

finding is not particularly surprising. The hand movements of synchronized swimmers and breaststroke swimmers are very clear examples of "propeller like" movements.

Measures of Hand Sweepback

The study of hand models in the fluid lab involved problems that are not typically encountered in the study of airfoils. For example, the leading edge of an airplane wing is clearly defined, and the wing is designed to generate lift for a single line of flow by the wing. In contrast, the leading edge of a swimmer's hand will change continuously during the course of an arm pull. The figure below shows two different flow conditions by a swimmer's hand. Each of these flow conditions is associated with different leading edge portions of the hand.

During the press phase of a freestyle stroke, the flow by the hand will begin at the fingertips and flow backwards to the heel of the hand. During the inward scull phase (as the hand is swept across the midline of the body), the flow by the hand begins at the thumb side of the hand and proceeds toward the pinky finger side of the hand.

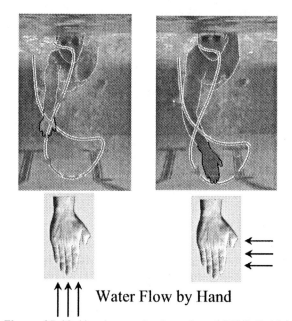

Water Flow by Hand

Figure 25-12. Hand sweepback angles of 90° (left side) and 0° (right side).

During the outward scull phase (as the hand is swept back across the midline of the body and outward toward the hip), the flow by the hand begins at the pinky finger side of the hand and proceeds toward the thumb side of the hand.

Finally, during the upward swept finishing motion the flow by the hand begins at the heel of the hand and proceeds toward the fingertips.

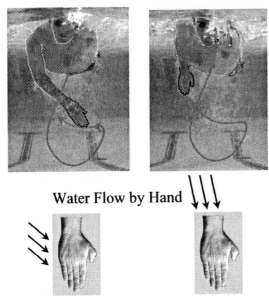

Water Flow by Hand

Figure 25-13. Hand sweepback angles of 225° (left side) and nearly 270° (right side).

As a result, we see that the flow conditions by the hand are slightly more complex than they are for a wing. In order to quantify the force production of a human hand we will need to define both the angle of pitch of the hand and the "leading edge" orientation of the hand.

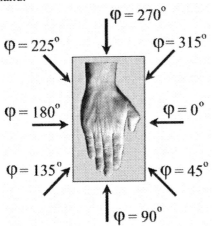

Figure 25-14. The hand sweepback angle convention (from Schleihauf, 1978).

The figure above shows the convention used to define the *sweepback angle* (ψ) of hand motions in water. The hand sweepback angle defines the leading edge of the hand for any given line of flow. For example, a sweepback angle of 0° is associated with flow that is directed from the thumb side of the hand towards the pinky side.

For any given angle of pitch, it is possible to have an infinite variety of sweepback angles. For example, the figure below shows two examples of a hand position with a 30° angle of pitch. The upper portion of the figure shows a 30° pitch angle with a sweepback angle of 0°. The lower portion of the figure shows a 30° pitch angle with a sweepback angle of 90°. The angle between the plane of the hand and the line of motion of the hand is same for each. However, the sweepback angle is quite different. The next example will help you to evaluate the influence of sweepback angle on force production.

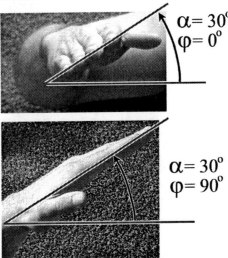

Figure 25-15. Two examples of hand positions with an angle of pitch of 30°. The upper portion of the figure shows a sweepback angle of 0°; the lower portion of the figure shows a sweepback angle of 90°.

Imagine that you are at the airport awaiting a flight and you are told that two planes are ready for boarding. Further, you are told that both planes are identical with the exception that plane A has its wings extending out in the tradional 90° orientation. Plane B, on the other hand has the same size wing and employs the same angle of pitch. However, this plane has its wing placed sideways along the length of the plane (see figure below).

Question 25-2:

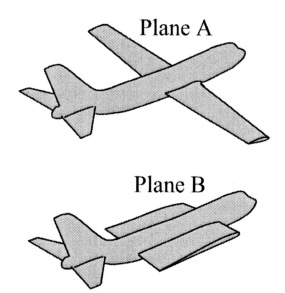

Plane A

Plane B

Figure 25-16. A comparison of two planes with identical wing areas but different sweepback angles.

Which of these 2 planes will you choose to board?

O Plane A, because it does not look like plane B will fly.
O Plane B, because it looks like this plane will provide for a more adventurous traveling experience.

Our plane wing example makes it clear that force production in wings will certainly be influenced by both the angle of pitch and the angle of sweepback for a wing. This will also be the case for human hands. As a result, in order to define the force producing characteristics of the human hand, we need to have information on the coefficient of lift and drag values for the hand expressed with respect to a variety of sweepback angles.

Hand Coefficient of Lift Values

The figure below shows the coefficient of lift versus angle of pitch curves for four different hand sweepback angles (Schleihauf, 1979). Each curve represents data for a different "leading edge" orientation of the hand.

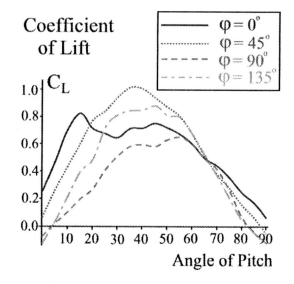

Coefficient of Lift

Figure 25-17. The hand coefficient of lift curve for sweepback angles of 0°, 45°, 90° and 135°.

Note that the solid line coefficient of lift curve (sweepback = 0°) shows that the peak hand lift force will occur at an angle of pitch of only 15°. We will see later in this chapter that skilled breaststroke swimmers use this particular hand orientation to generate lift-dominated propulsion. A similar trend in hand lift force production is shown for the sweepback angles 180° - 315°.

The coefficient of lift curves show that, depending upon the angle of sweepback, the human hand will generate peak lift forces at angles of pitch ranging between 15° and 55°. However, the overall trend in the data is the same for all of the various coefficient of lift curves. The coefficient of lift values are small for small angles of pitch. They increase to maximal values for "middle size" angles of pitch. Finally, the C_L values drop to near zero for angles of pitch near 90°.

Hand Coefficient of Drag Values

A typical graph of the coefficient of drag for the hand is shown below (Schleihauf, 1978).

Coefficient of Drag $\varphi = 0°$

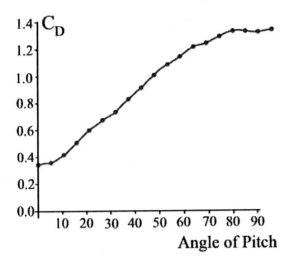

Figure 25-18. The hand coefficient of drag curve for a sweepback angle of 0°.

The graph shows that the drag produced by a hand increases from 0.34 at 0° to 1.36 at 90°. As expected, drag will be smallest when the hand "knifes" through the water with a 0° angle of pitch. When the hand is turned to a 90° position, large pressure differences between the palm and back of the hand cause maximal values of drag force.

Coefficient of Drag

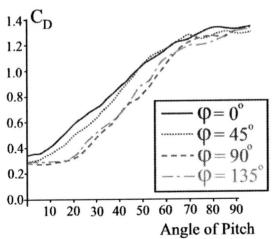

Figure 25-19. The hand coefficient of drag curves for sweepback angles of 0° - 315° (with 45° increments).

The figure above shows the coefficient of drag curves for four different sweepback angles for the hand. The small differences in coefficient of drag

between the various curves are primarily related to the cross sectional area that is presented to the water flow. For example, the narrow hand cross section associated with a 90° sweepback angle has slightly lower coefficient of drag values than the broad cross section presented by a hand held at a 0° sweepback angle.

Calculation of Hand Propulsive Force

Lift Force Calculation

Given our fluid lab information on hand coefficient of lift and drag values, we are now in position to calculate hand force estimates for any swimming motion. The figure below shows the hand force generated on the finishing sweep portion of a freestyle arm pull.

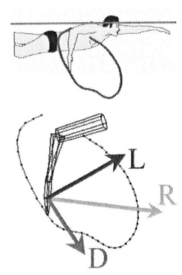

Figure 25-20. The lift and drag forces generated during the finishing sweep portion of a front crawlstroke arm pull.

An analysis of the video data, coupled with information we have discussed above can provide us with all of the information necessary to solve the lift force equation:

$$L = \frac{1}{2} \rho \, V^2 \, C_L \, S$$

To solve the equation we need to determine the values for each of the terms to the right of the equal sign. Our final value for lift will be expressed in Newtons. As a result, we must express density in terms of kilograms / cubic meter, velocity in meters per second and hand area in square meters. The coefficient of lift term can be read from $C_L - \alpha$ tables, as soon as the values for hand angle of pitch and sweepback are specified.

The values for each term in the lift equation are as follows:

$\rho = 998$ Kg / cubic meter (from tables on water density)
V = 3.88 mps (from a 3D video analysis of the movement)
S = .0176 square meters (taken from a hand tracing of the swimmer)

Finally, the C_L value can be determined if the hand angle of pitch and sweepback can be measured from the video data. The calculation of these angular measures can be readily computed through an analysis of the three dimensional data on the hand points (Schleihauf et al., 1983). For this particular frame, the angle of pitch is 32° degrees and the angle of sweepback is 225°. The figure below shows the hand coefficient of lift curve for a sweepback angle of 225°.

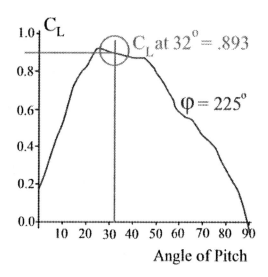

Figure 25-21. The coefficient of lift for a hand with a pitch angle of 32° and a sweepback angle of 225° is 0.893.

$C_L = 0.893$ (from table)

Given this information, we can solve for the size of the lift force:

$$L = \tfrac{1}{2} \rho V^2 C_L S$$

$\rho = 998$ Kg / cubic meter; V = 3.88 mps ; S = .0176 square meters; $C_L = .893$

$$L = .5 * (998) * (3.88)^2 * (0.893) * (0.0176)$$

$$L = 118 \text{ Newtons}$$

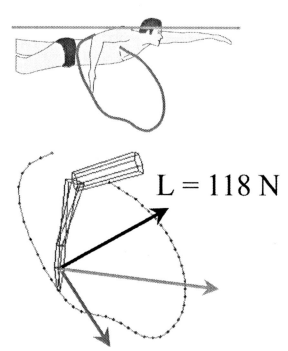

$$L = 118 \, N$$

Figure 25-22. The lift force component at an instant during the finishing portion of a front crawlstroke arm pull.

Drag Force Calculation

The drag force equation is shown below.

$$D = \tfrac{1}{2} \rho V^2 C_D S$$

All of the terms in this equation are identical to those used above with the exception of the C_D value.

For the instant in time shown in the above figure, the angle of pitch is 32° degrees and the angle of sweepback is 225°. The figure below shows the hand coefficient of drag curve for a sweepback angle of 225°.

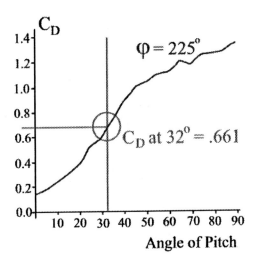

Figure 25-23. The coefficient of drag for a hand with angle of pitch of 32° and a sweepback angle of 225° is 0.661.

$C_D = .661$ (from table)

$D = \frac{1}{2} \rho V^2 C_D S$

$\rho = 998$ Kg / cubic meter; $V = 3.88$ mps; $S = .0176$ square meters; $C_D = .661$

$D = .5 * (998) * (3.88)^2 * (0.661) * (0.0176)$

$D = 87$ Newtons

The figure below shows that the drag force line of action is opposite to the line of motion of the hand.

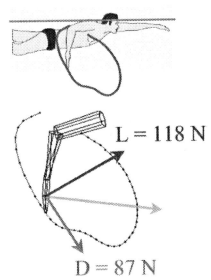

Figure 25-24. The solution to the hand drag force calculation.

Hand Resultant Force

The net effect of the lift and drag force vectors is given by the hand resultant force vector.

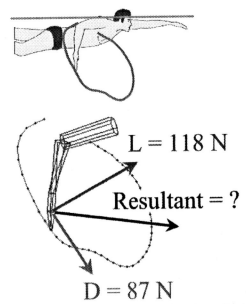

Figure 25-25. The calculation of the hand resultant force given information on the lift and drag force magnitudes.

Question 25-3:
What is the size of the resultant force for the figure above? (Use the Window's calculator to compute your answer.)

O 147 Newtons
O 205 Newtons

The resultant hand force is very effective in generating forward propulsion for the swimmer because it is "aimed" nearly straightforward. Skill in swimming is a byproduct of a number of interrelated factors. For most swimmers, the last one third of the underwater pull is the most forceful. To generate maximal force, the swimmer must coordinate his arm and trunk motion to produce a high speed upward swept hand motion. His wrist angle must be modified to produce "just the right size" angle of pitch. The ideal angle of pitch will produce an optimal combination of lift and drag force that will in turn generate a resultant force that is nearly straight forward.

Thus, skill in swimming is much more than brute force – straight back pulling motions. The skilled swimmer uses his hand as an "instrument of propulsion". Just as a concert violinist finds the optimal way to manipulate the bow, so too, the skilled swimmer continually adjusts his or her hand position to generate optimal propulsion.

Swimming Force Distributions

The Hydrodynamic Analysis (HA) software calculates the propulsive hand force for every frame of motion during the course of an underwater pull. Analysis of hand forces as a function of time provides us with information on the movement *process* associated with skilled swimming.

The figure below shows a cropped down program screen shot from HA.

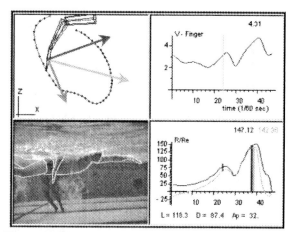

Figure 25-26. An illustration of data from the Hydrodynamic Analysis (HA) software program.

The upper left quadrant of the figure shows the hand and arm wire frame diagram for a moment near the end of the pull. The video image at the lower left shows the video frame for the selected instant in time. The upper right side quadrant shows the fingertip velocity curve. The highlight bar in the velocity curve shows the velocity value for the given instant in time. The lower right hand corner shows the "R/Re" hand propulsive force curves. Note that two force curves are shown for the hand propulsion. The upper, dark colored curve shows the full size (magnitude) of the resultant (R) hand force vector. The lower, light colored curve shows the *effective hand force component* (Re). The effective hand force is the component of the total force that is aimed in the forward direction. The light and dark bars in the figure indicate the size of the hand force measures for the given instant in time. At the moment shown, a large percentage of the total hand force is aimed forward, and as a

result, the light and dark bars are nearly the same height.

The R/Re curves can be used to estimate the efficiency of a given swimmer. In general, a swimmer that produces effective resultant forces (Re) that are nearly as large as the total resultant (R) can be assumed to be very efficient.

It is interesting to note that early in the pull, it is nearly impossible for the swimmer to generate effective propulsion. The figure below shows frame 15 of the 47 frame pulling motion.

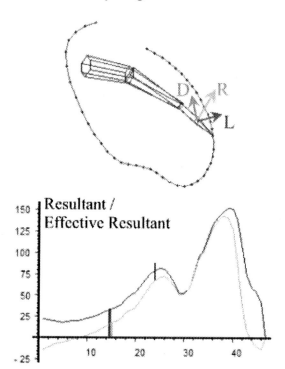

Figure 25-27. The hand force generated during the early portion of the arm pull is shown.

At this point in the pull, the swimmer's hand is moving downward and forward. As a result of the net forward motion of the hand, the drag force component actually creates *resistance* to forward motion (it tends to slow the swimmer down). Note that the drag force horizontal component (Dx) is aimed *backward* in the figure below.

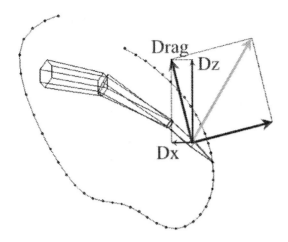

Figure 25-28. The hand drag force vertical and horizontal components are shown.

The figure shows that the drag force vector can be broken into two components. The horizontal Dx component is aimed backward and will tend to slow the swimmer down. The upward component (Dz) will tend to elevate the swimmer to a higher than normal body position.

The figure below shows the vertical and horizontal components of the lift force vector. The horizontal component (Lx) is aimed forward and makes a positive contribution to forward propulsion. The vertical component (Lz) tends to elevate the swimmer's body position.

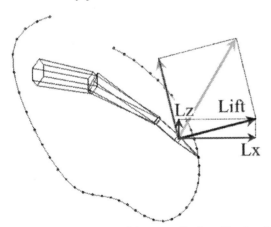

Figure 25-29. The hand lift force vertical and horizontal components are shown.

The hand resultant force components are shown in the figure below. The letter R is used to identify the total resultant force. Note that the "R" force is shown by the darkly shaded line in the hand force versus time curve at the bottom of the figure. The effective resultant (Re) is equal to the X component (Rx) of the R vector. Note that the "Re" force is

shown by the lightly shaded line in the hand force curve at the bottom of the figure.

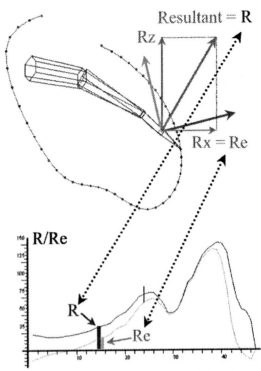

Figure 25-30. The hand resultant force (R) and effective resultant force (Re) are shown.

The R/Re curve shows the changes in hand propulsion that occur from instant to instant in the arm pull. For this skilled swimmer, the largest hand forces are generated during the last third of the underwater pull (see figure 25-31). The earlier portions of the pull involve relatively small propulsive forces that gradually build up in size as the swimmer becomes able to take advantage of diagonal pulling motions.

The timing of the large force pulse at the end of the pull reveals important information about swimming skill. The swimmer is "telling us" that some portions of the pull are far more important than others. We have seen in prior chapters that skilled tennis players and dancers often choose to maximize their movement speed and / or force production at a particular moment in time. Being able to identify the *critical range of motion* for a given movement is enormously important because it allows teachers of movement skills to prioritize their instructional strategies.

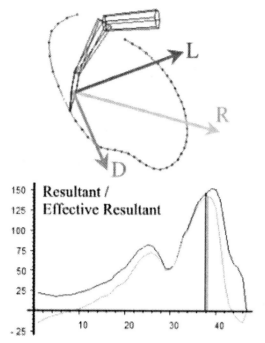

Figure 25-31. An instant in time with maximal hand force production for a performer in the front crawlstroke.

Swimming coaches can use the hand speed, pattern of motion, wrist angle and force production information shown in the figure above in the design of instructional programs. The swimmer in the figure has "designed" his stroke around this critical range of motion. A diagonal pattern of motion is used to allow for a near optimal combination of lift and drag force. Further, the strong muscle groups of the trunk are being used in combination with the arm movements to maximize force production.

Errors in Swimming Propulsion

The understanding of skillful motion is sometimes improved through the study of *poor* technique. We can expect that an aquatic motor genius will find very efficient ways to swim. But what about "normal" people? Can we expect that anyone who trains long enough to develop consistent movement patterns will have found "the right" movement for themselves?

The following discussion will give us an opportunity to compare the techniques of two swimmers. One is an Olympic gold medalist and world record holder. The other is a hard working, college age competitive swimmer with fatally flawed stroke technique. Your challenge in the next question will be to decide which swimmer is more skilled from the HA data alone. In this example, the

photo information is withheld to "protect the innocent".

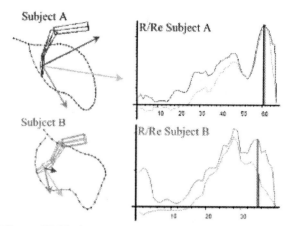

Figure 25-32. A comparison of a highly skilled and flawed stroke technique.

Notice that the units on the R/Re curves have been purposely removed. The challenge in this exercise is not to find the most forceful swimmer. The challenge is to find the swimmer who gets the most out of the forces that are generated. As we mentioned in Chapter 2, brute strength and skill are not the same. Good technique in swimming is a result of a skillful, well coordinated, hand and arm movement. If we were to compare a nationally ranked 12 year old to the college swimmer we would not expect the 12 year old to produce more force. However, we *would* expect to see the 12 year old exhibit many of the same "skillful" techniques that are seen in Olympic swimmers.

The stick figure and force curves for swimmer A are shown in the upper two quadrants of the figure. The stick figure and force curves for swimmer B are shown in the bottom two quadrants of the figure. Carefully inspect the hand force vectors and the R/Re curve information for both swimmers before you answer the next question.

Question 25-4:
Which swimmer is more skilled?

O A. Swimmer A (shown in the upper portion of the figure) is more skilled.
O B. Swimmer B (shown in the lower portion of the figure) is more skilled.

In effect, swimmer B is "throwing water at the ceiling" on the end of his pull. This pulling motion will tend to cause the swimmer's hips and legs to be pulled further underwater. Because the Re component of swimmer B's hand force is very small, his efforts on the finishing sweep will have little effect on his forward propulsion.

Question 25-5:
Which of the following suggestions for change in technique will be most helpful for swimmer B?

O A. Pull the hand harder and faster during the last one third of the pull to increase the size of the hand resultant force.
O B. Extend the wrist to cause a reduction in the hand angle of pitch.
O C. Shorten the length of the pull by sliding the hand out of the water at the level of the waist.

The error in swimmer B's technique is sometimes called "a stiff wrist finish". Because the swimmer is not making changes to his wrist joint angle, he is not able to make adjustments to his hand angle of pitch. His angle of pitch is 58° during the last part of the pull. This high angle of pitch will result in low lift force and high drag force. The figure below shows that most of swimmer B's hand force is aimed downward at the end of the pull.

The hand R/Re curve shows that only a small percentage of the hand resultant force is aimed forward. The marked separation between the darkly shaded (R) and the lightly shaded (Re) curves during this critical range of motion is a clear indication of an error in technique.

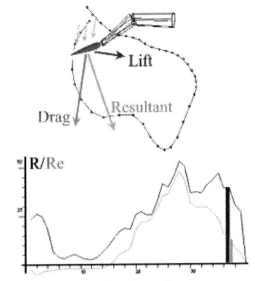

Figure 25-33. An error in wrist angle causes a reduction in effective propulsive force.

Skill Self Evaluation

The preceding example provides clear evidence that skill involves much more than brute strength. We see that there is no guarantee that a given individual's ability to generate force will be used productively. As you read these words, a number of competitive swimmers are swimming laps and making the very same error shown in the figure below. These swimmers feel force on their hands and make the assumption that their movements are productive. Ironically, highly skilled swimmers feel large forces on their hands as well. So what is the difference between an aquatic motor genius and a hard working but ineffective swimmer?

This example indicates that highly skilled swimmers do *two* things to evaluate their own efficiency. First, they feel large forces acting on their hands during the critical range of motion in the stroke. Second, they feel their body's forward velocity increase as a result of their hand's motion. This second step, the ability of an individual to sense the effect of their movements, is the crucial part of the aquatic motor genius "natural adjustment" process. Swimmers of moderate skill level may never fully make the connection between the forces they feel on their hands and the acceleration that is transmitted to their bodies. However, this situation does not imply that only a motor genius will ever master a given skill. Skilled teachers of human movement can structure the learning environment to facilitate the learner's connection between the movement process and the movement effect. For example, a swimming instructor can use single arm – glide stroke drills to help swimmers to improve their techniques. In this drill the swimmer is asked to pull with one arm only and glide for 3 seconds after each finishing motion. The figure below shows a skilled swimmer performing this drill. Swimmers with "stiff wrist finish" problems will pull hard but will have very little body glide forward after each stroke. Swimmers with extended wrist positions will experience long glides after each arm pull. This instructional strategy allows swimmers to become aware of technical flaws in their movements. Given the proper follow up instruction, swimmers can make changes to their wrist angles and be made aware of the relationship between their hand forces and their body accelerations. When this step is accomplished, the teacher will have educated the pupil so well that her technique could well become indistinguishable from that of a motor genius.

Figure 25-34. An image sequence figure of a single arm pull drill.

Our discussion of the "stiff wrist finish" problem in swimming has implications for many other instructional situations. Given the information from the biomechanical analysis of a movement, we can determine those factors that are most closely associated with proficient performance. We can then design instructional programs that focus the learner's attention on the most critical aspects of the movement.

Biomechanical Database Information

The data from our previous examples have provided clear examples of effective and ineffective swimming techniques. However, the evaluation of "marginal" techniques will involve more difficult decisions. As mentioned in Chapter 2, a *biomechanical database* can be used to identify the range of effective movement solutions for any closed skill. Further, if that closed skill is a maximal force output skill (like swimming), we may expect to find clear-cut guidelines that could be used in the design of instructional programs.

The figure below illustrates the range of effective movement solutions for the front crawlstroke. Swimmers that fall within the central oval boundaries in the graphic are identified as skilled. Swimmers that fall between the central ovals and the outermost circular line have "flaws" in technique, and the severity of the flaw increases for cases that fall furthest from the central oval areas.

Freestyle Swimming

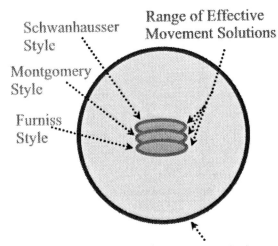

Figure 25-35. The range of effective movement solutions for front crawl stroke swimmers.

The figure shows that the range of effective movement solutions is not centered upon a single ideal form model. Instead, model techniques from three different swimming styles are shown. This figure reminds us that "one size *does not* fit all" and we can expect that people with different morphological characteristics and natural tendencies should aspire to different model techniques.

Competitive swimming provides very clear evidence of the shortcomings of ideal form models. Some world record holders, like Matt Biondi, are well over 6 feet tall and swim with very long and powerful strokes. Other world record holders, like Cynthia Woodhead, are less than 5'2'' and make use of very efficient high rate of turnover (with many strokes per lap) swimming styles. The fact that the movements of many champion swimmers *look* different does not mean that one is "right" and

another is "wrong". It simply means that each has adapted their techniques to match their own unique strengths and capabilities.

Thus, our biomechanical database should not be thought of as a vehicle that provides a simple ideal form template for skill evaluation. Instead, the biomechanical database must be flexible enough to recognize proficient swimmers with different styles as skillful, and at the same time provide specific information that can be used to identify inefficient techniques.

Studies on Olympic swimmers (Schleihauf, 1987) have identified three measures that are of value in the evaluation of swimming proficiency:

1) Diagonality Index
2) Lift - Drag Index
3) Force Distribution Index

We will discuss each of these index measures in the following sections.

Diagonality Index

The diagonality index (DI) provides a measure of the role of sculling motions in a swimming underwater pull. The diagonality index is calculated as the angle between the negative line of motion vector for the hand and the forward direction, taken at the moment of largest effective hand force production. The figure below shows diagonality index data for a skilled freestyler.

The negative line of motion vector for the hand is aimed along the same line as the drag force. The dark colored vector indicates the forward direction. The angle between these two vectors is 63° for the swimmer in the figure. Note that this angle is measured at the moment when the largest hand effective resultant force is produced.

The purpose of the diagonality index is to clarify the role of sculling motions in swimming propulsion. A swimmer who employs a diagonality index of 90° is using "pure sculling" hand motions, where lift force is the only important component of propulsion. A swimmer who employs a diagonality index of 0° is using a "pure straight back" pulling motion where drag force is the only important component of propulsion.

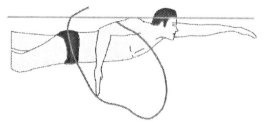

Diagonality Index

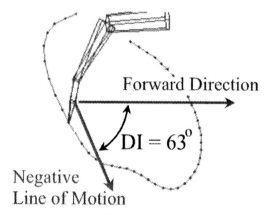

Forward Direction

DI = 63°

Negative
Line of Motion

Figure 25-36. The diagonality index for a sampling of skilled performers on the front crawlstroke arm pull.

Diagonality index measures were collected for the US Olympic swimming team. The average DI for the freestyle portion of the sample is shown below:

Freestyle Diagonality Index = 59° +/- 13°

This finding indicates that highly skilled swimmers, as a group, use diagonal hand motions that are a full 59° away from straight back pulling motions. The standard deviation for this measure is relatively small. The +1 to -1 standard deviation range for this measure is 46° - 72° (59° – 15° = 46°; 59° + 13° = 72°). Thus, 68% of the Olympic team sample employs pulling motions with DI measures between 46° - 72°. Counsilman's original observation that swimmers "are using a zigzag pattern of varying degrees" is well supported by this finding.

Lift - Drag Index

The Lift-Drag index (LDI) is a measure of the lift – drag ratio at the moment of largest effective hand force production in the pull. The figure below shows the calculation of the LDI measure.

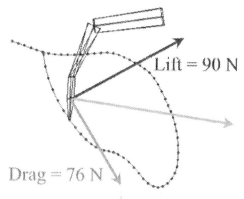

Lift = 90 N

Drag = 76 N

Lift - Drag Index = 90 / 76
Lift - Drag Index = 1.18

Figure 25-37. The lift – drag index for a sampling of skilled front crawlstroke swimmers.

The lift - drag index for the freestyle portion of the Olympic team is provided below:

Lift – Drag Index = 1.04 +/- 0.28

This finding indicates that lift and drag forces are equally important in the force production of highly skilled swimmers. The standard deviation for this measure indicates that 68% of the Olympic team population employ a LDI within the 0.72 – 1.32 range. This shows that some swimmers (those with LDI measures under 1.0) adapt their hand pitch to generate slightly more drag than lift. Other swimmers (those with LDI measures greater than 1.0) employ more lift than drag. We can presume that these differences in lift drag ratio reflect subtle hand adjustments that allow the swimmers to effectively aim their forces in the forward direction.

Force Distribution Index

A review of the propulsive force curves produced by skilled swimmers indicates that a large "pulse" of force is typically delivered during the critical range of motion of the pull. The force distribution index (FDI) identifies the "location" of the largest force pulse produced in the pull. The FDI measure is expressed as the following percentage:

FDI = (Time to peak Re force) / (Time duration of underwater pull)

Where: the time intervals can be expressed as frame counts.

The figure below shows the calculation of an FDI measure for a skilled freestyler.

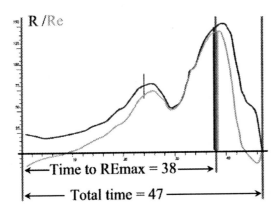

Force Distribution Index = 38 / 47
Force Distribution Index = 0.81

Figure 25-38. The force distribution index for a sampling of skilled front crawlstroke swimmers.

We see that this swimmer generates his largest effective hand force late in the arm pull. The Force Distribution index for the freestyle portion of the 1984 Olympic team is provided below:

Force Distribution Index = 0.82 +/- 0.07

This finding indicates that greatest hand forces for skilled swimmers occur about 82% of the way into the underwater pull. The standard deviation for this measure is low, indicating that there is not much variability among skilled swimmers on this measure. The range of scores from minus one to plus one standard deviation represents 68% of the Olympic team sampling. As a result, 68% of skilled swimmers exert their largest forces between 75% and 89% of the way into the pull.

Variations in Cross-Over Measures

The biomechanical database measures from the last section define movement characteristics that are held in common across a sampling of highly skilled competitors. During the search for "commonalities" across skilled competitors, we sometimes encounter interesting surprises. For example, during the analysis of the Olympic team data, we expected that the hand *crossover* used by skilled competitors would provide valuable information for the biomechanical database. The hand crossover in the freestyle arm pull is a measure of the side-to-side distance between the fingertip and the midline of the body at the moment when the hand moves furthest across the body.

The figure below shows a crossover measurement for a skilled swimmer.

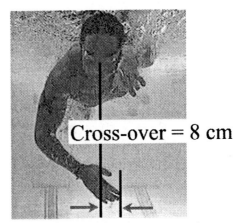

Figure 25-39. An example of a measure of cross-over in the front crawlstroke.

The figure shows that, for this swimmer, the fingertip crosses 8 cm beyond the midline of the body at the moment of "maximal crossover". Because we thought that this measure could be useful in the design of instructional programs, we computed the mean and standard deviation information for the Olympic team freestylers:

Cross-Over Measurement = 2.5 +/- 11.25

Notice that the standard deviation score for this measure is very large. The range of cross-over measures for +/-1 standard deviation is between – 8.75 and +13.75 cm. Thus, some Olympic swimmers use "wide" pulls with negative cross-over where the hand never sweeps past the midline of the body and other skilled swimmers sweep their hands well past the midline to generate positive cross-over (see figure 25-40).

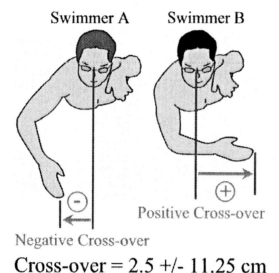

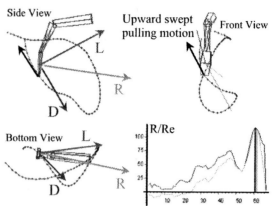

Figure 25-40. The range in effective movement
solutions for the cross-over measure.

Figure 25-41. The Biondi style stroke in the front
crawlstroke.

The Olympic swimmer crossover data provides us
with very important information. It shows that some
movement characteristics are *not* held in common
across skillful performers. Crossover is a *stylistic
variable* in movement technique that is not closely
associated with proficiency.

As a result, we see that the information from a
biomechanical database can be used in two ways.
Measures that are held in common across skilled
performers can be used to define instructional
guidelines. Measures that are *not* held in common
across skilled performers, like the crossover
variable, should be left free to vary within broad
limits. The next example will show that setting strict
guidelines on stylistic variables could in fact cause
harm to our students.

A Comparison of Styles

The figure below illustrates the "classic" sprint
freestyle characteristics of world record holder Matt
Biondi. This style of swimming involves a low
stroke turnover rate, where the swimmer takes very
few strokes per lap. As a result of an extremely
forceful finishing portion of the pull, the swimmer is
able to glide forward briefly after each pull before
beginning the next.

Question 25-6:
The bottom view figure shows the hand force lift (L)
and drag (D) force components. Lift and drag forces
act at right angles to one another. Why does the
bottom view figure show the angle between the L and
D vectors as less than 90°?

O A. There must be an error in the bottom view
graphic.
O B. The bottom view illustration is correct.

Our question points out that the plane formed by the
lift and drag vectors is shown in "edge view" in the
bottom view figure. As a result, the bottom view
does not provide a clear representation of the hand
motion in 3D space. The side view provides a better
illustration of the most forceful portion of the pull
for Biondi, because his hand motions are directed
primarily backward and upward. As a result, the
critical range of motion for the Biondi style exhibits
an "upward swept pulling motion" as shown in the
figure. This style of swimming involves force
distribution, lift-drag and diagonality index data
well within the recommended range of the
biomechanical database.

The Woodhead style of front crawlstroke
technique is shown below. This style of swimming
involves a high stroke turnover rate, where the
swimmer's arms "spin" around smoothly and
continuously. The smooth transition from arm pull
to arm pull makes this stroking style extremely
efficient.

Woodhead Style Stroke

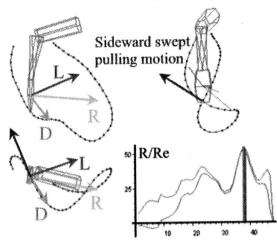

Figure 25-42. The Woodhead style stroke in the front crawlstroke.

The most forceful portion of the pull is best seen from the bottom view, because it is directed mainly toward the side and backward. As a result, the critical range of motion for the Woodhead style exhibits an "sideward swept pulling motion" as shown in the figure. This style of swimming involves force distribution, lift-drag and diagonality index data well within the recommended range of the biomechanical database.

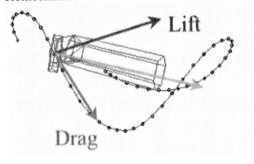

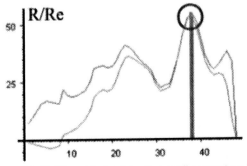

Figure 25-43. The side to side diagonally swept motion is best seen in the bottom view of the Woodhead style stroke.

The key to Woodhead's style is the sideways motion of the hand near the end of the pull. As the hand sweeps from the body midline towards the right hip, the drag force is aimed forward and to the swimmer's left. The lift force vector is aimed forward and toward the swimmer's right. The resultant force is aimed nearly straight forwards, as indicated by the close match between the R and Re curves.

Woodhead's style shows that efficient swimming motions can be achieved through a variety of pulling techniques. While Biondi makes use of an upward and back pulling motion, Woodhead achieves an equivalent result with a side-to-side pulling motion.

When we first studied Woodhead's technique, we thought that she may be "losing" potential force production on the last 20% of the pull. The figure below shows that Woodhead purposefully reduces her hand forces at the same place in the arm pull where Biondi achieves maximal propulsion.

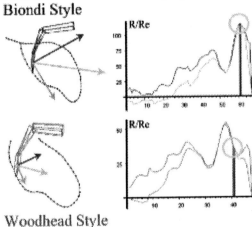

Figure 25-44. A comparison of the Biondi and Woodhead styles.

Woodhead's purposeful reduction in hand force near the end of the pull is entirely consistent with her overall movement strategy. Because her stroke relies upon a high rate of turnover pulling style, it is important for her to have a smooth transition between the end of one underwater pull and the beginning of the over-water recovery for the next pull. By slowing her arm pull and softening her force production, Woodhead is able to make a very smooth transition from stroke to stroke, and the force output from her many "smaller" strokes is equivalent to the summation of a lesser number of more forceful strokes.

Question 25-7:
Two twin sisters are pedaling up a gradual slope on 10 speed bikes. Sister A is in the lowest gear and is pedaling at 80 revolutions per minute. Sister B is in 5th gear and is pedaling at 40 revolutions per minute. Both are moving up the slope at exactly the same speed. Is sister A working harder than sister B?

O A. Yes. Because she is moving her legs faster, she must be working harder.
O B. No. Sister A will exert about the same amount of work as sister B to get up the slope.

The bicycle example helps us to understand that the number of strokes does not necessarily indicate the speed of the swimmer. Woodhead's stroke is "in a lower gear" than Biondi's, but that does not mean that her "high-rev engine" is less efficient.

The most important lesson to be learned from this discussion is that ideal form models are not appropriate for use in the instruction of movements like swimming. All swimmers are *not* alike, and intelligence is required in evaluation and modification of any person's technique. If a coach were to blindly apply the Biondi model to the instruction of a swimmer like Woodhead, he would cause much more harm than good.

It is interesting to note that the biomechanical database measures mentioned above (FDI, DI, LDI) can all be used to evaluate swimming proficiency without reference to any ideal form model. Instead, the measures from a biomechanical database define the movement *principles* that are associated with skill.

Breaststroke and Butterfly

Our analysis of freestyle technique has provided clear examples of the movements associated with skillful technique. We have seen that different people can make use of slightly different styles of swimming and still attain biomechanically sound results. In this section, we will see that the rules governing breaststroke and butterfly swimming cause swimmers to find solutions to movement problems that are considerably different from those we have seen for freestyle.

Breaststroke

The rules for breaststroke specify that both arms must be moved simultaneously and that the recovery motion must be performed underwater. The figure below shows the hand motions of a skilled breaststroker. Note that the near circular pattern followed by the hand is similar to that of a propeller blade.

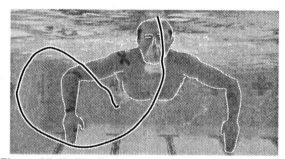

Figure 25-45. The breaststroke front view pattern of motion.

The rulebook's requirements effectively force the swimmer to solve a movement problem that is very different from that of freestyle. As a result of these requirements, the length of the breaststroke pull is much shorter than that of the other competitive strokes. Good breaststrokers rarely pull their hands beyond the level of the chest. This shortened pulling length, coupled with the body's forward motion through the water, makes it virtually impossible for breaststrokers to have an extended backward component in their pulling motions. The figure below shows the breaststroke motion from the side view.

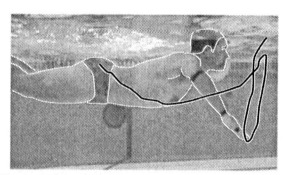

Figure 25-46. The breaststroke side view pattern of motion.

During the early part of the pulling motion, the hands are gliding forward as the swimmer takes advantage of the propulsion generated by the legs kicking motion. The largest hand propulsive forces occur later in the movement, during the inward swept phase of the pull.

The figure below shows HA generated wire frame diagrams at a moment when large propulsive forces are generated for most skilled breaststrokers.

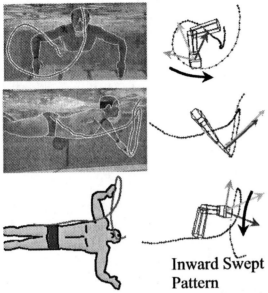

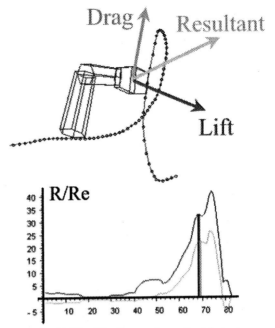

Figure 25-47. Breaststroke front view, side view and bottom view patterns of motion for a skillful swimmer.

The front view shows the hand inward swept pattern of motion very well, but it cannot show the forward component of the hand propulsive force vectors. The side view shows that the hand forces are aimed forward and up, but this view cannot show the inward swept pulling motion. The bottom view provides the best view of the pulling motion and the propulsive force vectors. The drag force vector is shown acting toward the swimmer's right and slightly forward. The lift force is shown acting in the forward direction and slightly toward the swimmer's left. The resultant force vector is aimed mainly forward.

The inward swept pulling motion cannot be effective unless the swimmer can generate very large lift forces. At the moment in question, the swimmer is using a hand angle of pitch of 17° and a hand sweepback angle of nearly 0°. This hand orientation is associated with nearly the largest lift forces possible and nearly the smallest drag forces. As a result, the swimmer has generated a very high lift drag ratio of 1.42. The lift-dominated propulsion helps the swimmer to aim his force mainly forward.

Figure 25-48. The lift, drag and resultant forces generated on the inward sweep phase of a breaststroke arm pull.

Biomechanical database information from the Olympic team study shows that breaststroke swimmers make unique adaptations to the breaststroke movement problem. The diagonality index for breaststroke is 81° +/- 9°. This measure is much larger than what we have seen above for freestyle (59°) and very close to the pure sculling score of 90°. The lift drag index for breaststroke is 1.25 +/- 0.21. This measure is consistent with the example swimmer data shown above. Breaststroke is clearly a stroke where proficiency is a by-product of skillful manipulation of the hand's angle of pitch.

It is interesting to note that on most college and high school swimming teams, breaststrokers are often not very good at freestyle and freestylers are likewise not good at breaststroke. The fact that these swimmers are all well conditioned and have "strong arms" is not sufficient to guarantee their success in all strokes. It seems that the mastery of skill for sculling in breaststroke is independent of skill mastery for freestyle hand motions. It appears that a given swimmer's "feel" for the water can be good for sweepback angles of 0° (as needed in breaststroke), but not good for sweepback angles of 225° - 270° (as needed for freestyle) and vice versa. This reinforces our position that skill involves far more than brute force and conditioning.

Butterfly

Our discussion of the relationships between the principles of fluid mechanics and skillful swimming will not be complete until we look at one more movement example. We will see in this section that the butterfly stroke presents swimmers with a movement problem that is different from both freestyle and breaststroke.

The butterfly stroke involves simultaneous pulling motions for both arms, followed by an over-water recovery motion. Because the head and shoulders are lifted above the surface of the water for each breath, this stroke requires considerable strength and flexiblility. The figure below shows the front view of a skilled butterflyer.

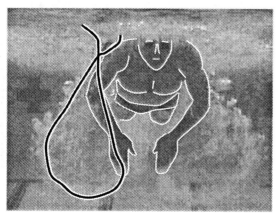

Figure 25-49. The butterfly stroke front view pulling pattern.

Notice that the side-to-side movement of the hand is restricted by the nature of this stroke. If the swimmer attempts to sweep his hand across the body midline, the two hands will collide with one another and disrupt his pulling motion. As a result, butterflyers are limited in their ability to take advantage of side-to-side sculling motions.
The side view of the butterfly motion is shown in the figure below.

Figure 25-50. The butterfly stroke side view pulling pattern.

This view appears similar to that of the freestyle stroke, although it also involves movement restrictions. In freestyle, the swimmer is able to roll his shoulders to increase the range of motion of the last part of his pull and add strength to this upward swept finishing motion. In butterfly, a shoulder roll is not possible because both arms must be recovered over the water simultaneously. As a result, the up-and-down sculling actions we have seen in freestyle are slightly inhibited in the butterfly stroke.

The figure below shows the moment of maximal effective force production for a skilled butterflyer.

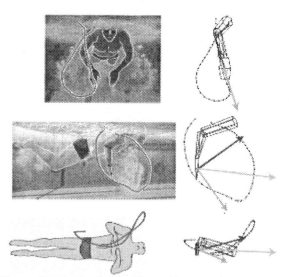

Figure 25-51. The front, side and bottom view patterns of motion for a skilled butterfly swimmer.

The bottom and front view patterns of motion show that the hand's side-to-side motion is limited for this swimmer. As a result, the side view plane provides a virtually undistorted view of the hand's propulsive movement.

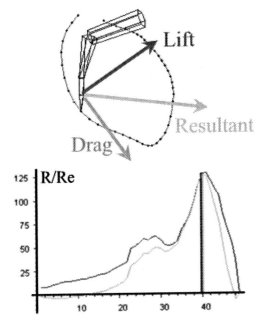

Figure 25-52. The lift, drag and resultant forces used in the finishing portion of a butterfly arm pull.

The illustration below shows that the finishing sweep motion for butterfly is very similar to that of freestyle. The swimmer has utilized a diagonal line of pull, coupled with a small angle of pitch to generate a combination of lift and drag force that results in nearly straight forward propulsion.

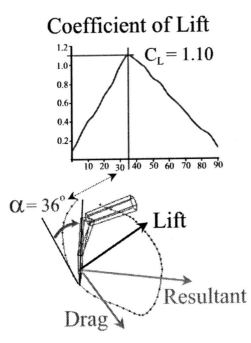

Figure 25-53. The hand angle of pitch from the finishing portion of the arm pull of a skillful swimmer.

The swimmer for this example has optimized the lift force component of his propulsion by selecting the hand angle of pitch associated with the highest possible C_L value. The figure above shows the coefficient of lift values for a hand with a sweepback angle of 270°. The peak value for C_L occurs at the hand angle of pitch (α) of 35°. The swimmer in our example is using a near perfect hand angle of pitch of 36°.

The biomechanical database information for butterfly is as follows:

Diagonality Index = 44° +/- 21°
Lift – Drag Index = 0.95 +/- 0.39
Force Distribution Index = 0.81 +/- 0.06

The limited side-to-side and up-and-down range of motion for butterfly is responsible for keeping the diagonality index measure (44°) well below that found for freestyle (59°). The lift – drag index is also lower for butterfly (0.95) than for freestyle (1.04). This finding is consistent with the diagonality index finding. Pulls that involve less "pure sculling" can be expected to have a slightly reduced reliance on lift force. The force distribution index (0.81) is very similar to freestyle (0.82), indicating that butterflyers focus their largest force production in the last part of the pull.

The biomechanical database measures focus upon only the most forceful moment during the course of the arm pull. Some of the other, sub-maximal forces generated in butterfly are also very interesting. For example, the middle portion of the pull often involves very large force production in skilled butterflyers.

The figure below shows hand force and body motion data for a skilled butterflyer. At the moment shown, the swimmer's shoulders are underwater. Two tenths of a second after this instant in time, the pull will be complete and the swimmer must attain a body position that is high enough to allow him to lift his arms above the surface of the water. (In butterfly, when the underwater arm pull is complete, the swimmer must swing both arms over the water during the recovery motion). As a result, the swimmer must generate sufficient upward force with his arm pull to allow for this body motion in the forward and upward direction. The resultant hand force shown above has been aimed forward and upward to accomplish this task.

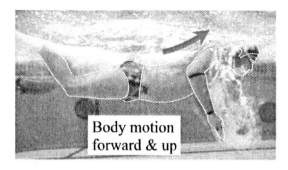

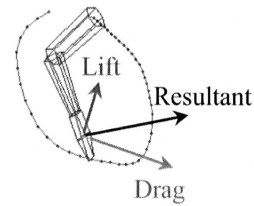

Figure 25-54. The hand resultant force from the middle portion of the butterfly arm pull.

This particular example is very interesting because it shows a solution to the "swimming movement problem" that we have not seen before. For this portion of the butterfly pull, the drag force is used primarily for propulsion, the lift force is only for support, and the lift – drag ratio is purposely kept low. (This is the opposite of the breaststroke movement solution, where the lift force component is crucial to propulsion, drag in primarily "lost" to the side and the lift – drag ratio is purposely kept high.)

We may be tempted to criticize the swimmer's use of a low lift – drag ratio at the moment shown (0.68), because the lift – drag index for butterfly is considerably higher at 0.95. However, this criticism would be unwarranted on three counts.

First, a greater production of lift force at mid-stroke in butterfly may, in fact, result in wasted energy expenditure. The swimmer needs to elevate the shoulders just above the water's surface. Climbing still further above the water will be unnecessary.

Second, the lift – drag index measure is computed for the most forceful portion of the pull only. We should not try to apply this measure to all parts of the pull.

Third, the standard deviation for the butterfly lift – drag index is quite large:

Lift – Drag Index = 0.95 +/- 0.39

Many skilled swimmers in butterfly use lift – drag ratios as low as 0.56 (one standard deviation below the mean). Thus, even on the most forceful portion of the pull, butterflyers will often use lift and drag forces like those shown above to provide both propulsion and support for upward body motions.

A Theoretical Advantage of Lift Force

The above discussion for butterfly shows that for some swimmers, low lift - drag ratios can be used to produce very effective propulsion. It should be noted, however, that our prior discussions showed that freestylers and breaststrokers use high lift - drag ratios. Presumably, the higher lift - drag ratios seen in freestyle and breaststroke are in part due to the freedom for side-to-side and up-and-down movements that is present in these strokes. The remaining portion of this section will help us to understand why skilled freestylers and breaststrokers gravitate toward lift-dominated propulsion.

Schenau (1981) has made the important observation that swimming performance is limited by three factors:

1) The net propulsive force produced (as discussed above).
2) The active drag or the resistance created by the swimmer's body as he/she progresses through the water.
3) The propulsive efficiency created by the combination of the swimmer's muscular effort and the mechanics of his motion.

The third point above is frequently overlooked in the literature. While a swimmer's performance may seem to be a simple interaction between propulsion and active drag, it is also important to note that a given net propulsive force output may be produced with a variety of physiological efficiencies.

To evaluate the physiological efficiency of swimming motions we will need to understand the relation between the *muscular contraction speeds* used in the generation of an arm pulling motion and the resultant hand speed that is generated with respect to the water. The following example will show that faster muscular contractions will not always produce proportionally faster hand movements in the water.

Straight Back Pulling Motions

The figure below shows a swimmer performing a straight back freestyle arm pull under two conditions. In both of the conditions, the swimmer is contracting his muscle with sufficient speed to cause his hand motion backward with respect to (wrt) his body to be exactly 5 mps.

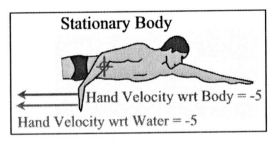

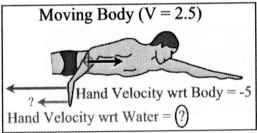

Figure 25-55. The effects of body motion on the hand velocity generated with respect to the water in a straight back arm pull.

The upper part of the figure shows the pull of the swimmer when he is held in a fixed position in the water. You can imagine that he is tied to the wall with a rope and his body is not permitted to move forward as a result of his pull. Because his body is stationary, the speed of his hand, as measured with respect to the water is -5 mps.

Now consider the lower portion of the figure. In this figure the swimmer is contracting his muscles at exactly the same speed as before. As a result, the hand speed as measured with respect to his body is -5 mps. However, in this condition, the swimmer's body is moving forward at a speed of 2.5 mps. You can imagine that the swimmer is swimming forward at this speed in a normal swimming pool. You could also imagine that the swimmer is swimming upstream in a river.

Question 25-8:
Will the swimmer's hand speed, as measured with respect to the water, be the same for both the upper (body velocity = 0 mps) and lower figures (body velocity = 2.5 mps) conditions?

O A. Yes.
O B. No.

The faster the body moves forward with respect to still water, the less hand speed will be "translated" to the water. Mathematically, the hand velocity with respect to the water is computed as the vector sum of the "Hand Velocity wrt Body" vector and the body velocity vector:

$$VHX_W = VHX_B + VBX_W$$

Where:
VHX_W = the X component of the velocity of the hand with respect to the water
VHX_B = the X component of the velocity of the hand with respect to the body
VBX_W = the X component of the velocity of the body with respect to the water

This equation states, in effect, that the hand velocity with respect to the water vector equals the hand velocity with respect to the body vector plus the body velocity vector.

$$VHX_W = VHX_B + VBX_W$$
$$VHX_W = -5 + 2.5$$
$$VHX_W = -2.5$$

If the body were to be pulled forward at a rate of 5 mps, the hand motion with respect to the water would fall to zero. The situation is similar to "swimming upstream" in a river.

Diagonal Pulling Motions

Now let's consider the case of a swimmer who is using a diagonal pulling motion. The figure below shows diagonal pull data for both a stationary and moving body. Note: in this and the remaining figures, the numerical velocity magnitude values are shown, and the positive and negative components are considered later within separate calculations.

Stationary Body

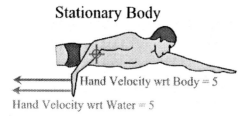

Hand Velocity wrt Body = 5

Hand Velocity wrt Water = 5

Moving Body (V = 2.5)

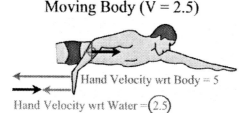

Hand Velocity wrt Body = 5

Hand Velocity wrt Water = 2.5

Figure 25-56. The hand speed with respect to the water for a diagonal line of pull.

The angle between the diagonal vector and the negative X-axis is 60°. As a result, the hand has a backward velocity component of –2.5 mps with respect to the body. The magnitude of the VHX_W component can be computed with the vector component formula (trigonometry):

$$|VHX_W| = VH_W * Cos(60°)$$
$$|VHX_W| = 5 * .5$$
$$|VHX_W| = 2.5$$

Where:
VH_W = the hand velocity vector expressed with respect to the water.

The trigonometric calculation gives us the length of the triangle leg. Because the 2.5 mps component is aimed in the X direction, $VHX_W = -2.5$ mps. The vertical component of the hand velocity with respect to the water is 4.33 mps:

$$|VHZ_W| = VH_W * Sin(60°)$$
$$|VHZ_W| = 5 * .866$$
$$|VHZ_W| = 4.33$$

Where:
$|VHZ_W|$ = the vertical component of the hand velocity with respect to the water

The backward component of the diagonal vector is equal to the vector sum of the forward body velocity and the net backward motion of the hand:

$$VHX_W = VHX_B + VBX_W$$
$$VHX_W = -2.5 + 2.5$$
$$VHX_W = 0$$

The net *backward* motion of the hand, expressed with respect to the water is therefore zero. However, the vertical component of the VH_W vector is not influenced at all by the body motion forward. As a result, the diagonal pull "translates" 4.33 mps of vertical hand speed to the water.

It is very important to remember that the straight back pull and the diagonal pull examples both involved exactly the same muscular contraction speeds. In both cases, the arm muscles contracted quickly enough to generate at 5 mps hand motion with respect to the body. However the effects of the muscular contractions are not equal when we compare the hand speed that is generated with respect to the water. The backward hand motion generates 2.5 mps of hand speed. The diagonal hand motion generates 4.33 mps of hand speed.

In order for the swimmer to generate equal hand speeds in the water, he will have to contract his muscles faster for the straight back pull. The figure below shows that a hand speed with respect to the body of 6.83 mps can produce a hand speed of 4.33 mps with respect to the water.

Moving Body / Straight Pull (V = 2.5)

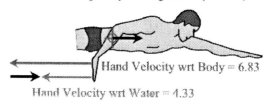

Hand Velocity wrt Body = 6.83

Hand Velocity wrt Water = 4.33

Moving Body / Diagonal Pull (V = 2.5)

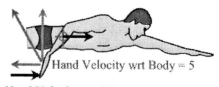

Hand Velocity wrt Body = 5

Hand Velocity wrt Water = 4.33

Figure 25-57. A comparison of two arm pulls that produce a hand motion of 4.33 mps with respect to the water.

There are two important differences between the two conditions. First, the straight back pull generates a hand velocity vector that is also straight back, while the diagonal pull generates a VH_W that is straight up. Second, the contraction speed needed to create the two equal speed hand motions is higher for the pull back motion.

The preceding examples have used rounded numbers to simplify the mathematics associated with calculating hand speeds with respect to the water. The figure below shows the hand speed data for the more typical hand and body speeds that are used by skilled swimmers. In each of the illustrated motions, the hand speed with respect to the water (and therefore, the approximate force potential) is identical ($VH_W = 3.05$ mps). However, the movement speeds relative to the swimmer's body are not the same. In the straight pull motion, 4.71 mps relative to the body is required to produce 3.05 mps relative to the water. In the diagonal pulling motion, only 4.15 mps relative to the body is required to produce a 3.05 mps hand speed. This information implies that sculling motions translate hand movement speeds to the water more efficiently than push back motions.

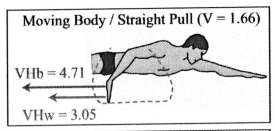

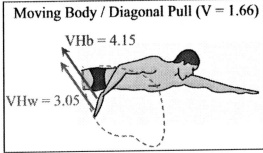

Figure 25-58. A comparison of two arm pulls that produce a hand motion of 3.05 mps with respect to the water.

Hill's Equation

Hill's equation defines the relationship between the maximal muscle force and the speed of contraction for a given muscle.

Muscle Force v.s. Contraction Speed

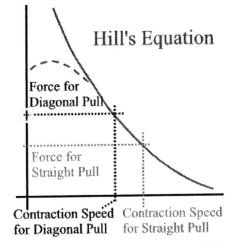

Figure 25-59. A comparison of the potential force levels available for a diagonal and a straight-back pull.

The solid curved line in the figure represents Hill's equation. It shows that as contraction speeds increase, the maximal available muscle force decreases. The dotted line extension to the main Hill's equation curve shows Perrine and Edgerton's (1978) in-vivo force velocity relationship for human muscle. The maximal force possible at a given speed of contraction is represented by the height of the illustrated curve. Note that the maximal potential force of a slower contraction speed is higher than that of a fast contraction speed. Thus, the slower movement speed (4.15 mps) associated with the diagonal swimming motion discussed above involves a higher potential force production than the push back 4.71 mps motion. As a result, we see that diagonal sculling motions have a greater muscular force potential than push back motions.

Further, the figure below of a breaststroke pulling motion shows how a large lift force component can take maximal advantage of the muscle's force velocity characteristics. In the figure, a large shoulder joint torque component is required to balance the hand lift force. It is interesting to note that while this shoulder joint torque seemingly attempts to create a rotary motion about the long axis of the upper arm, there is actually minimal motion of the arm in this direction – the breaststroke inward scull action is primarily inwards. As a result, the shoulder joint torque is created with very slow muscular contraction speeds. Again, the muscle force velocity relationship indicates that the force potential of these near isometric contractions is much higher than that associated with straight back pulling motions. As a general rule, the slow contraction speed advantage such as that shown in the figure below will occur whenever high lift – drag ratios are used in the pulling motion.

Breaststroke Pull
Pattern drawn relative to the body

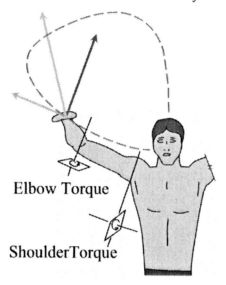

Elbow Torque

ShoulderTorque

Figure 25-60. The elbow and shoulder joint torques associated with a breaststroke pulling motion.

It should also be noted that in freestyle, curvilinear sculling motions tend to be combined with shoulder roll actions. The combination of body roll along with the upward swept finish of a freestyle stroke, allows the strength of the large muscle groups of the trunk to be effectively transferred to the hand.

Elbow Motion

Shoulder Motion

Shoulder Roll

Figure 25-61. The influence of shoulder roll in front crawlstroke arm pull.

The figure above shows that sculling finishing motions combine the strengths of the trunk muscles along with the shoulder and elbow joint muscle groups. In contrast, a straight back pulling motion - with no forceful upward swept movement component - cannot take full advantage of the shoulder roll or the potentially powerful shoulder joint rotations.

A Historical Lesson

Now that we have completed our discussion of swimming propulsion, it will be instructive to look back at how Counsilman's theory of swimming propulsion influenced students and practitioners in kinesiology. Prior to the publication of Counsilman's theory of swimming propulsion, many swimming coaches based their instructional strategies upon the "feelings" of their own swimming motions and upon the "naked-eye" observations of the swimming motions of others. It is often said that very good performers often make poor teachers, because these performers have difficulty translating their feelings for good technique to their less skillful pupils. Further, most swimmers have the impression that a freestyle arm pull begins 2 feet in front of their head and ends back by their hip. The resulting overall impression is that the hand moves backward about 5 feet *with respect to the swimmer's body.*

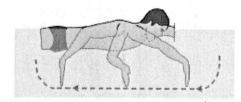

Figure 25-62. A straight-back arm pull.

As a result, prior to 1970, almost all coaches and coaching publications stated that, for optimal swimming performance, swimmers should pull backwards against the water to obtain propulsion. This approach to swimming propulsion emphasized the use of hand angles of pitch of 90° and discouraged the use of side-to-side "feathering" motions of the hand. Newton's third law (Action – Reaction) was used to establish the scientific foundation of the push back theory.

Further, at the time of Counsilman's paper, most programs in Physical Education offered only a course in Anatomical Kinesiology for students, and little time was available for the study of biomechanical concepts. While it is appropriate for a course in Anatomical Kinesiology to focus on describing human motion with respect to an anatomical reference frame, it is not appropriate to limit our biomechanical analysis of human movement to this anatomical reference. Swimming hand motions, drawn with respect to still water, coupled with up to date propulsive theory are essential in the analysis of swimming motions.

Diagonal Pull = Forward Propulsion

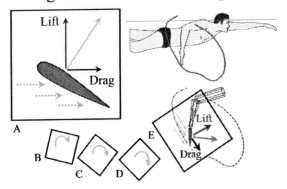

Figure 25-63. The value of diagonal lines of pull and lift force producing hand motions is shown.

This example of swimming theory and its influence on the design of instructional programs carries two very important lessons for students of kinesiology everywhere:

Lesson #1: Do not accept the opinions of even experienced practitioners unless these opinions are backed up by measurements of actual human movements. The idea that the hand could follow a 5 foot long backward line of motion could not have withstood the scrutiny of any student in biomechanics with the where-with-all to place a camera underwater. Further, no student of biomechanics would attempt to make measurements from a camera that panned to follow the motions of a swimmer so as to express those movements with respect to the body. This entire course is filled with video images taken from fixed position camera setups. Imagine the confusion that would be created if we attempted to compute ground reaction forces for a volleyball jump with a camera that moved upwards to keep the jumper's head in the center of the picture. The body's center of gravity position and acceleration from such a moving camera setup would not be expressed with respect to an inertial reference frame, and none of our measurements would be correct.

Lesson#2: Do not use textbook theories to guide instruction without supporting information from a biomechanical database. The use of Newton's third law to justify the use of straight back pulling motions sounds reasonable until you actually study the motions of skilled swimmers. If one skilled swimmer does not observe the action reaction idea, he can be dismissed as an oddball. If the data from

the entire Olympic team does not support the action reaction approach, it is time to look for a new theory. Ironically we do not have to look far to find the appropriate mechanical principles – in this book, we musk skip ahead from Part 3 – Linear Kinetics to Part 6 – Fluid Mechanics. In hindsight, it is a little surprising that in the 1960's, those interested in designing instructional swimming programs did not take a harder look at the principles of fluid mechanics.

One of the most unsettling observations of the "push back" propulsion misunderstanding is revealed by Counsilman's anecdotal observations. During the 1970's Counsilman visited many coaches of Olympic swimmers and often encountered those who felt that backward pulling motions were ideal and the new theory was incorrect. Counsilman would then often take underwater films of the coach's Olympic contender and play the movies back for the coach and swimmer. The films would show that the swimmer was not pulling straight back, as his coach had told him to do, but was instead using curved pulling motions. Often the swimmer would deny that the films were of him, clearly indicating the many skilled swimmers rely upon subconscious impressions in the regulation of their movements. The swimmer's coach would often express surprise that the swimmer had failed to follow his instructions, indicating that he had never really checked the swimmer's underwater pulling technique before.

This story shows that the aquatic motor geniuses that qualify to swim on the Olympic team can often be expected to find the optimal way to swim by themselves. In fact, these swimmers are so talented that they will ignore the incorrect instructions they receive from coaches, at least on a subconscious level. On the other hand, the remaining 99.9% (non-genius) portion of the sampling of competitive swimmers may *not* be expected to find optimal movement patterns without specific guidance. These swimmers may be expected to actually follow the instructions of their coaches, and, if these instructions are incorrect, perform more poorly as a result.

These not so distant stories from the past provide a wake up call for any student who intends to observe human movement and make recommendations for changes in movement technique. We should study the movements we intend to teach carefully and perform critical reviews of the latest scientific publications on the movement. Hopefully, your work in this semester's term project will help you to accomplish this goal and prepare you for even more advanced analysis in the future.

Conclusions

Our discussion of swimming propulsion is now complete. The wide variety of movement examples presented in this chapter have hopefully given you a better appreciation of the flexible relationship between mechanical principles and skillful human movement. We have seen that the skillful performer makes subtle adjustments in hand pitch, pulling pattern orientation and in the force distribution of the underwater pull for each of the various competitive strokes. Our search for "answers" to the various swimming movement "problems" has shown us that multiple model techniques should be used to represent skill in swimming. These multiple model techniques, coupled with the information from a biomechanical database can be expected to provide the information necessary for the design of effective instructional and training programs.

References

Counsilman, J.E. The application of Bernoulli's principle to human propulsion in water. Swimming I, Lewillie and Clarys (eds.), pp. 59-71, 1971.

Perrine, J.J. and Edgerton, R. (1978). Muscle force velocity and power velocity relationships under isokinetic loading. Medirine and Science in Sports, 10:159-166, 1978.

Schenau, G., A Power Balance Applied to Speed Skating. Academish Proefschrift, Vrlje Universitite de Amsterdam, 1981.

Schleihauf, R.E., Higgins, J.R., Hinrichs R.N., Luedtke, D.L., Maglischo, C.W., Maglischo, E.W., Thayer, A.L. (1987). Propulsive Techniques: Front Crawlstroke, Butterfly, Backstroke and Breaststroke. In B. Ungerechts (Ed.), Biomechanics and Medicine in Swimming, Champaign, IL: Human Kinetics Publishers.

Schleihauf, R., Gray, L., DeRose, J. Three-dimensional analysis of hand propulsion in the sprint front crawlstroke. Biomechanirs and Medicine in Swimming, Hollander, Huijing, and de Groot (eds.) Human Kinetics Publishers, Inc., Champaign, Illinois, 1983.

Schleihauf, R.E. A hydrodynamic analysis of swimming propulsion. Swimming I11, Terauds and Bedingfield (Eds.). University Park Press, Baltimore, pp. 70-109, 1979.

Schleihauf, R.E. Swimming propulsion: a hydrodynamic analysis. 1977 A.S.C.A. Convenfion Clinic Yearbook, R. Ousley (Ed.), A.S.C.A. Fort Lauderdale, 1977.

Wood, T.C. A fluid dynamics analysis of the propulsive potential of the hand and forearm in swimming. Swimming III, Terauds and Bedingfield (Eds.), University Park Press, Baltimore, pp. 62-69, 1979.

Answers to Chapter Questions

Question 25-1:
The front view figure shows that the resultant propulsive force vector is very short. Does this mean that the swimmer is producing very little effective force?

O Yes. The swimmer must be very weak.
O No. A force that is aimed nearly straight forward will be shown as a dot in the front view.

The correct answer is B. The front view shows motions in the side-to-side and up and down dimensions. However, it does not show movement or hand force information along the forward-back dimension at all. Because the illustrated hand force is nearly straight forward it is barely seen in the front view.

Question 25-2:
Imagine that you are at the airport awaiting a flight and you are told that two planes are ready for boarding. Further, you are told that both planes are identical with the exception that plane A has its wings extending out in the tradional 90º orientation. Plane B, on the other hand has the same size wing and employs the same angle of pitch. However, this plane has its wing placed sideways along the length of the plane (see following figure).

Which of these 2 planes will you choose to board?

O Plane A, because it does not look like plane B will fly.
O Plane B, because it looks like this plane will provide for a more adventurous traveling experience.

The correct answer is A. We can expect that the 0º sweepback angle of plane A will provide more lift force than the 90º sweepback angle of plane B.

Question 25-3:
What is the size of the resultant force for the figure above? (Use the Window's calculator to compute your answer.)

O 147 Newtons   O 205 Newtons

The correct answer is A. Because the lift and drag force components act at 90° to each other, we can use the vector magnitude formula to compute the resultant force. $R = sqr(L^2 + D^2)$; $R = sqr(13924 + 7569)$; $R = sqr(21493)$; $R = 147$

Question 25-4:
The stick figure and force curves for swimmer A are shown in the upper two quadrants of the figure. The stick figure and force curves for swimmer B are shown in a light shade in the bottom two quadrants of the figure. Inspect the data for the two swimmers and carefully.

Which swimmer is more skilled?

O A. Swimmer A (shown in a dark shade) is more skilled.
O B. Swimmer B (shown in a light shade) is more skilled.

The correct answer is A. The hand forces for swimmer A are aimed nearly straight forward during the last one third of the pull. These forward propulsive forces will cause the swimmer to swim faster.

Question 25-5:
Which of the following suggestions for change in technique will be most helpful for swimmer B?

O A. Pull the hand harder and faster during the last one third of the pull to increase the size of the hand resultant force.
O B. Extend the wrist to cause a reduction in the hand angle of pitch.
O C. Shorten the length of the pull by sliding the hand out of the water at the level of the waist.

The correct answer is B. A smaller hand angle of pitch will cause the size of the lift force to increase and it will also cause the size of the drag force to decrease. The resultant hand force will then be aimed more straight forward.

Question 25-6:
The bottom view figure shows the hand force lift (L) and drag (D) force components. Lift and drag forces act at right angles to one another. Why does the bottom view figure show the angle between the L and D vectors as less than 90°?

O A. There must be an error in the bottom view graphic.
O B. The bottom view illustration is correct.

The correct answer is B. The L and D vectors are at right angles to one another in *3D space*. The bottom view does not show the plane of the L and D vectors and therefore it cannot be used to measure the true angle between the 3D vectors.

Question 25-7:
Two twin sisters are pedaling up a gradual slope on 10 speed bikes. Sister A is in the lowest gear and is pedaling at 80 revolutions per minute. Sister B is in 5th gear and is pedaling at 40 revolutions per minute. Both are moving up the slope at exactly the same speed. Is sister A working harder than sister B?

O A. Yes. Because she is moving her legs faster, she must be working harder.
O B. No. Sister A will exert about the same amount of work as sister B to get up the slope.

The correct answer is B. The gear system on the bicycles will allow sister A to work less hard on each revolution and she will exert about the same amount of work as sister B to get up the slope.

Question 25-8:
Will the swimmer's hand speed, as measured with respect to the water, be the same for both the upper (body velocity = 0 mps) and lower figures (body velocity = 2.5 mps) conditions?

O A. Yes. O B. No.

The correct answer is B. The swimmer will generate only 2.5 mps hand speed with respect to the water.

Appendix

Biomechanics of Human Movement
Software Guide

Robert E. Schleihauf - San Francisco State University

Introduction

This guide introduces the software programs in the Biomechanics of Human Movement courseware suite. The BHMViewer and KAPro software programs are almost always made available to students through their college departments. If your college department has not purchased the BHM / KAPro software, see the KAVideo web site (at www.kavideo.sfsu.edu) for details on how to purchase individual copies of the software.

Your course this semester will include both an interactive textbook and a collection of biomechanical data analysis programs. The course textbook viewer (BHMViewer) will "bring to life" the material from traditional printed textbooks by showing an abundance of color graphic images, movement videos and interactive questions. The textbook theories will be further clarified through the display of research data on dozens of "real life" movement examples. You will be able to visualize virtually every important concept in the course through inspection of both video and biomechanics data in our Kinematical Analysis (KA) software examples.

If you do not own a home PC yet, do not be concerned. The print version of our course textbook contains all of the information (less the video clips and software links) from the BHMViewer software. You will still be able to experience the multimedia aspects of the software based textbook by scheduling time to play the viewer software in your department's teaching laboratory. When your department purchased this courseware suite, it acquired the right to place the course software on all college computers and student home PCs.

BHMViewer Software

A good textbook is a very important part of any effective college course. The BHMViewer software makes a full length textbook available on your PC's hard drive. The viewer software CD-Rom holds the complete 390 page textbook and more than 950 color graphic images. A screen shot from the viewer software is shown below:

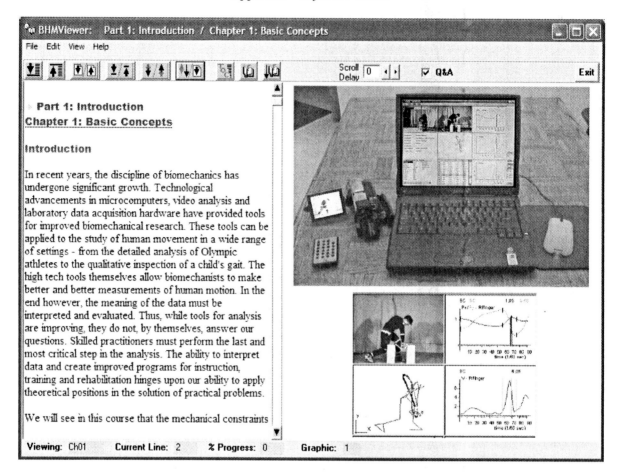

Once you have installed the viewer software, you will be able to open any chapter for review. The program window shows the text for each chapter in the left hand pane. The right side graphics pane shows images that are tied to the text discussion topics. The program toolbar contains buttons that allow you to easily scroll to any "page" in the chapter.

It is important to note that the viewer software is designed to do more than just scroll text. In fact, this viewer is really designed to behave like a PowerPoint presentation with expanded text content. When you sit in a lecture hall and listen to a presentation, you get to hear the text content and see the graphic images associated with the text at appropriate instances in time. When the speaker gets to a given point in the lecture, she clicks the mouse to show you the image or critical text on the next slide. The viewer software is designed to show critical graphics and animations at specific times within the text content. However, because *you* control the pace of the presentation, you are provided with the tools to trigger the display of graphics, animations and questions.

To learn more about the BHMViewer program, install the software on your PC (as described below). Once the software is installed, the "Viewer Software Basics" chapter will be set to be run the first time you start the software. This introductory chapter will explain everything you need to know about using the BHMViewer software.

BHMViewer Software Installation

The viewer software is designed to run on all mainstream versions of Windows: Windows 9x, Windows ME and Windows XP. The software will not run on Windows 3.x, Windows NT or Windows 2000.

To install the software, do the following steps:

1) Place the BHMViewer / KAPro CD-Rom into your CD-Rom or DVD drive.
2) Use Windows Explorer to display the contents of the CD-Rom root folder.
3) Double click on the BHMSetup.exe program.
4) Close the Windows Explorer window.
5) Follow the prompts to install the viewer software.

The BHMViewer installation software will copy only 6 Mb of program and core data files onto your hard drive. The viewer CD-Rom also has about 200 Mb of graphics files (color still images and video animation files). When you run the software for the first time, you will be prompted to select a storage location for the viewer's graphic files.

If you have at least 500 Mb of space free on your hard drive, accept the default option to have the graphic files copied to your hard drive. This option has two advantages: 1) the viewer graphic files will load and playback more quickly; and 2) you will not need to keep the BHMViewer CD-Rom disk in your CD-Rom drive when you run the software to read the various chapters in the book.

If you hard disk space is limited, you can opt to have the viewer software read the graphic files from the CD-Rom disk whenever the software is run. If you elect to install the software with the CD-Rom based graphics option and later decide that you want to place the graphics files on your hard drive, simply uninstall and then re-install the software.

If you experience difficulties with the BHM Software installation, please see the BHM Software Troubleshooting section at the end of this document.

Kinematical Analysis Software

The Kinematical Analysis (KA) software is a suite of biomechanical analysis programs that can be run on any Windows 95/98/Me/XP based PC. We will use the software for three purposes this semester:

1) Many of the examples from the Biomechanics of Human Movement textbook have been drawn from KA research projects. These examples will provide clear illustrations that will help you to visualize the most important theories and biomechanical concepts from this course.

2) KA homework exercises are included at the end of many of the textbook chapters. These exercises will allow you to use KA to examine how mechanical principles influence "real life" movement examples.

3) Your instructor may elect to use KA to perform a number of pilot study research projects this semester. In many instances, you, and other members of your class, will be able to propose a movement for analysis. You will then collect video data on that movement and capture the video onto your school lab PC. The KA software can then be used to perform a detailed biomechanical analysis of the movement.

The KA suite of programs consists of three main parts: KAVideo, KA2D and KA3D. These programs are described in Chapter 3 of this textbook.

KAPro Software Installation

The KAPro CD-Rom holds the KAPro program files and about 120 MB of example image set files that will be used for homework assignments. When the program and data files are expanded, they will take about 600 MB of space on drive C of your PC. If you do not have at least 1.5 Gb of free space on your drive, you should install the main program and tutorial image files only. To minimize storage space requirements, you can install the other example image sets one by one as they are needed for homeworks, and then remove them from the hard drive to regain space. However, if you have sufficient hard drive storage space, it will be simpler to install all of the example files along with the KAPro programs.

The instructions below detail the installation procedure:

1) If a prior version of KA is installed on your PC, use Add/Remove Programs to uninstall the existing version of KA. (When prompted, select "No to All" to leave shared programs on the hard drive.)

2) Put the BHMViewer / KAPro CD-Rom disk into your CD-Rom or DVD drive. Run the Windows Explorer program. Right click on the drive C: icon in the left side "Folders" column. Select "Properties" from the context menu. The free space on hard drive C: will be shown:

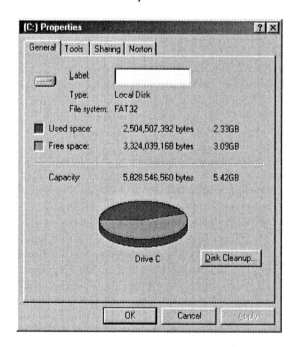

If you have less than 1.5 GB (1,500 MB) free on Drive C:, you will not have space to copy the KA example image sets to your drive.

To install the KAPro program, do the following:

a) Use Windows Explorer to show the contents of your CD-Rom drive.
b) Double click on the KAPro.exe file.
c) Close the Explorer window (and any other open application windows).
d) Click "Yes" to continue with the installation

e) Accept the defaults to install KAPro.
f) At the end of the installation procedure, check the "Launch Application" check box.
g) Create the Tutor files when prompted.

If you have sufficient space on your hard drive, you will be prompted to install the KA Example data files. Note that this part of the installation process will typically take about 15 minutes for all of the image set files to be expanded.

Manual Installation of Selected KA Example File Image Sets

If your hard drive is low on space you can install and remove any KA Example image set on your PC one by one as needed. For example, Chapter 5 includes a KA exercise that makes use of the AKTenF1S image set (a tennis serve video clip and stick figure file). The filename for the exercise image set is shown at the end of the chapter in the KA Exercise section:

KA Exercises

Click the red circle marker below to perform an analysis of the velocity data for a tennis serve:

⊙ Ch05-1-Velocity / AKTenF1S / KA2D

Click the red circle marker below to perform an analysis of the acceleration data for a soccer volley.

⊙ Ch05-2-Acceleration / ZPVolley1S / KA2D

Before you run the first exercise (Ch05-1-Velocity) you must install the AKEenF1S image set files. To perform this single image set install operation, do the following:

1) Put the KAPro CD-Rom disk in your CD drive.
2) Copy the AKTenF1SSml.zip file from the \KV\XDat folder on the CD drive to the C:\KV\XDat folder on your PC.
3) Run the KAVideo program and select the Process, Zip/UnZip option.
4) Click the Un-Zip Image Sets option button at the upper portion of the screen.
5) Select the AKTenF1SSml file and click the Expand Zip File(s) button.

The tennis image set and stick figure files will be installed and you will be able to perform the KA Exercise.

Once you have completed the exercise you can optionally remove the AKTenF1S image files from your hard drive to regain free disk space:

1) Use Windows Explorer to show the contents of your C:\KV\XDat folder. Select and delete the AKTenF1S folder, the AKTenF.kap file, and the AKTenF1SSml.zip files.

Repeat the above procedures for any KA Example files you would like to use.

Setup Troubleshooting Guide

Problems with Windows XP and Limited User Accounts

The BHMViewer and KAPro software must be run by a user who is logged on through an account that has Administrator privileges. If you are unable to move from chapter to chapter and save bookmark settings, change your account settings in XP to include Administrator privileges.

Technical Details

The file C:\Program Files\BHMViewer\BHMViewer.cfg can be edited with Notepad to manipulate the setup of the software. An example of the content of this BHMViewer.cfg file is as follows:

Line 1:   3
Line 2:   \BHMViewer\
Line 3:   C:\Program Files\BHMViewer\Graphics\
Line 4:   Ch00
Line 5:   2
Line 6:   0

Note: The Line numbers are added for our convenience in this document. The text "Line 1: " etc. is not included in the actual file.

Line 1: The number on this line indicates the screen resolution of your PC. The number 2 represents 800x600 resolution. The number 3 represents 1024x768. Other values are not used.

Line 2: This text indicates the name of the program folder (the text "C:\Program Files" is automatically added to the text on this line to specify where the BHMViewer.exe file is located).

Line 3: This text indicates the full path to the base graphics folder. The Ch00, Ch01, etc. folders and their graphic files must be stored directly under this base graphics folder. You can change this line to any other existing location (i.e., "D:\BHMGraphics\") to reset the location to another drive and/or folder. Of course, you must copy the graphics chapter folders to this location to allow the viewer software to function properly.

Line 4: This line indicates the current chapter.

Line 5: This line indicates the current line in the current chapter.

Line 6: This line indicates the current scroll delay factor setting.

Index

Printed in the United States
22982LVS00001B/5-12